Governing Higher Educat

International growth in higher education, the introduction of new providers and increased public and state interest in university structures, levels of fees and funding models have made governance in higher education a vital and sometimes controversial topic.

Governing Higher Education Today provides challenging perspectives on the longer-term dynamics and policy trends in a world market for higher education. Through international perspectives and case studies, it considers:

- The emerging national responses, which are likely to shape institutional governance in the next decade.
- An analysis of the trends and strategic directions in governance and policy in higher education.
- Insights from practising thought leaders on the future of higher education governance and policy.
- Traditions and values within higher education governance.
- Lessons and trends in the interaction of institutions and government.

Whether you sit on a governing body, work in a university leadership role or in a governance or policy team, teach or study higher education, *Governing Higher Education Today* provides a thoughtful yet practical guide to the future of university governance with international applicability.

Tony Strike is University Secretary at the University of Sheffield, UK and a member of the executive boards of the European Higher Education Society (EAIR) and the UK Higher Education Strategic Planners Association (HESPA).

Jonathan Nicholls is University Secretary at the Open University and was successively the Registrar of the University of Warwick, the University of Birmingham and the Registrary of the University of Cambridge. He was Chair of the UK's Association of Heads of University Administration (AHUA).

John Rushforth is Executive Secretary of the Committee for University Chairs (CUC) and until 2014 was Deputy Vice-Chancellor and Clerk to the Board of Governors at the University of the West of England.

Governing Higher Education Today

International Perspectives

Edited by Tony Strike, Jonathan Nicholls and John Rushforth

Routledge
Taylor & Francis Group

LONDON AND NEW YORK

First published 2019
by Routledge
2 Park Square, Milton Park, Abingdon, Oxon, OX14 4RN

and by Routledge
52 Vanderbilt Avenue, New York, NY 10017

Routledge is an imprint of the Taylor & Francis Group, an informa business

British Library Cataloguing-in-Publication Data
A catalogue record for this book is available from the British Library

Library of Congress Cataloging-in-Publication Data
Names: Strike, Tony, editor. | Nicholls, Jonathan (Jonathan W.), editor. Rushforth, John, editor.
Title: Governing higher education today : international perspectives / edited by Tony Strike, Jonathan Nicholls and John Rushforth.
Description: Abingdon, Oxon ; New York : Routledge, 2020. | Includes bibliographical references and index.
Identifiers: LCCN 2019002237|
Subjects: LCSH: Universities and colleges—Administration—Cross-cultural studies. | Higher education and state—Cross-cultural studies.
Classification: LCC LB2341 .G664 2020 | DDC 378.1/01—dc23
LC record available at https://lccn.loc.gov/2019002237

ISBN: 978-1-138-36698-5 (hbk)
ISBN: 978-1-138-36699-2 (pbk)
ISBN: 978-0-429-42997-2 (ebk)

Typeset in Galliard
by Swales & Willis Ltd, Exeter, Devon, UK

MIX
Paper from responsible sources
FSC
www.fsc.org   FSC™ C013985

Printed in the United Kingdom
by Henry Ling Limited

Contents

Notes on editors   viii
List of contributors   ix
Acknowledgements   xi
Abbreviations   xii

Introduction: located voices   1
TONY STRIKE

PART I
Different voices   7

1 The role and perspective of a UK Chair of the
   governing body   9
   CHRIS SAYERS

2 The University Secretary: at the heart of governance   25
   TONY STRIKE

3 Higher education governance and policy on trial   47
   JONATHAN NICHOLLS

PART II
Global perspectives   59

4 Changing governance models in North American
   higher education   61
   ROBERT A. SCOTT

5 Shaping European universities: a perspective from
   the Netherlands   81
   STEPHAN VAN GALEN

 6 Diverging governance models in a devolved system:
    case studies from Scotland and Wales   100
    GERALD WEBBER AND REBECCA DAVIES

 7 Changing university governance in South Africa   113
    DAVID J. HORNSBY AND RUKSANA OSMAN

 8 Changing governance models in
    Australian universities   125
    GIOCONDA DI LORENZO AND JULIE WELLS

 9 Can there be a universal framework of good
    governance?   140
    NINA ATWAL, MARK BUTLER, DIVIA MATTOO AND MICHAEL WOOD

PART III
The English experiment   151

10 How current trends in UK corporate governance
    might influence future higher education governance
    and policy   153
    LORRAINE YOUNG

11 The legal framework for university governance
    in England: how to understand, comply and
    build on it   173
    SMITA JAMDAR

12 The development and purpose of corporate
    governance codes   191
    JOHN RUSHFORTH

13 Regulating higher education markets: the English
    policy experiment as a case study   202
    DAVID PALFREYMAN

PART IV
Elements of governance   217

14 Public good(s), public benefit and the public interest:
    a critical examination of three public purposes of
    English universities   219
    ADAM DAWKINS

15 Effectiveness and effectiveness reviews   239
    ANDY SHENSTONE

16 Assurance of academic standards and quality by
    and beyond the academy   252
    JOHN RUSHFORTH

17 Performance and risk: the light and shade of trust
    and accountability   268
    TONY STRIKE

    Index   278

Editors

Tony Strike is University Secretary at the University of Sheffield. He was successively Director of Human Resources in an NHS Trust, then at the University of Southampton, before becoming Director of Strategy, Planning and Governance at Southampton and then at Sheffield. He is an elected board member of the European Higher Education Society (EAIR) and the Higher Education Strategic Planners Association (HESPA). He was chair of Russell Group Directors of Strategic Planning until 2018. Tony edited *Higher Education Strategy and Planning: A Professional Guide* published by Routledge in 2018.

Jonathan Nicholls is University Secretary at the Open University. He was successively the Registrar of the University of Warwick, the University of Birmingham and the Registrary of the University of Cambridge. He was Chair of the UK's Association of Heads of University Administration (AHUA), and has been a governor of schools, an NHS Trust, and served as a director on various companies and boards. Formerly a consultant at Shakespeare Martineau, he is an independent member of the Council of the University of Sheffield.

John Rushforth is Executive Secretary of the Committee of University Chairs and was Pro-Vice Chancellor of UWE Bristol. He was responsible for the UK HE Code of Governance and for national guidance on Remuneration Committees, and Academic Governance. He held a range of posts within the Higher Education Funding Council for England.

Contributors

Nina Atwal, Consultant, the Good Governance Institute

Mark Butler, Director of Development, the Good Governance Institute

Rebecca Davies, Pro Vice-Chancellor and Chief Operating Officer, Aberystwyth University

Adam Dawkins, Head of Governance and Secretary, University of Northumbria at Newcastle

Stephan van Galen, Secretary-General, University of Groningen

David J. Hornsby, Associate Vice-President (Teaching and Learning), Carleton University

Smita Jamdar, Partner and Head of Education, Shakespeare Martineau LLP

Gioconda Di Lorenzo, University Secretary, University of Melbourne

Divia Mattoo, Public Senior Consultant, Deloitte

Jonathan Nicholls, University Secretary, Open University

Ruksana Osman, Dean of Humanities, University of the Witwatersrand

David Palfreyman, Fellow, New College, University of Oxford

John Rushforth, Executive Secretary, Committee of University Chairs

Chris Sayers, Chair, Committee of University Chairs, UK and Chair and Pro Chancellor of Northumbria University

Robert A. Scott, President Emeritus, Adelphi University

Andy Shenstone, Director of Business Development and Delivery, Advance HE

Tony Strike, University Secretary, the University of Sheffield

Gerald Webber, formerly University Secretary, Edinburgh Napier University, now writes in a personal capacity

Julie Wells, Vice Principal and Projects, University of Melbourne

Michael Wood, Partner, the Good Governance Institute

Lorraine Young, Past President, ICSA, the Governance Institute

Acknowledgements

Bruce Roberts at Taylor & Francis invited the proposal for this book, to follow *Higher Education Strategy and Planning: A Professional Guide*, published in 2018, and neither book would exist without his encouragement.

The idea to look at higher education governance was Tony's, and in discussion with Jonathan and John over an afternoon tea in Manchester the concept, purpose and shape of the book were resolved into a shared proposal and a plan. From there the project was a team effort and a pleasure to pursue.

The contributing chapter authors each agreed to share their perspectives and in doing so have given this book the power to make the familiar exotic by offering readers different voices from which to critically reflect on their own contexts.

We would like to thank Angela Davison for her skill and patience in handling the contact lists, files, version control, formatting and administration involved in seeing this project to its successful conclusion.

Abbreviations

AAUP	American Association of University Professors
AAUS	Association of Australian University Secretaries
ACE	American Council on Education
ADEA	Association for the Development of Education in Africa
AGB	Association of Governing Boards
AGM	Annual General Meeting
AHUA	Association of Heads of University Administration
AICTE	All India Council for Technical Education
AIM	Alternative Investment Market
APR	Annual Provider Review
ASA	Advertising Standards Agency
BAME	Black, Asian and Minority Ethnic
BBC	British Broadcasting Corporation
CA	Consumers Association
CA2006	Companies Act 2006
CEO	Chief Executive Officer
CIMA	Chartered Institute for Management Accountants
CIRCLE	Centre for Information and Research on Civic Learning and Engagement
CMA	Competition and Markets Authority
COO	Chief Operating Officer
CRA15	Consumer Rights Act 2015
CUC	Committee for University Chairs
CVCP	Committee of Vice Chancellors and Principals
DfENI	Department for the Economy in Northern Ireland
ENQA	European Association for Quality Assurance in Higher Education
EQAR	Quality Assurance Register for Higher Education
ERA	Education Reform Act 1988
ESRC	Economic and Social Research Council
EU	European Union
FoIA	Freedom of Information Act
FRC	Financial Reporting Council

FSSG	Financial Sustainability Strategy Group
FTE	Full Time Equivalent
FTSE	Financial Times Stock Exchange
GPA	Grade Point Average
GPE	Global Partnership for Education
HE	Higher Education
HEC	Higher Education Corporation
HEFCE	Higher Education Funding Council for England
HEFCW	Higher Education Funding Council for Wales
HEI	Higher Education Institution
HELP	Higher Education Loan Programme
HEP	Higher Education Provider
HEP-S	Higher Education Provider-Student
HEQSF	Higher Education Qualifications Sub-Framework
HERA17	Higher Education and Research Act 2017
HOAK	Higher Education: Autonomy and Quality
ICSA	Institute of Chartered Secretaries and Administrators
IGOPP	Institute for Governance of Private and Public Organisations
KPI	Key Performance Indicator
KRI	Key Risk Indicator
LEO	Longitudinal Education Outcomes
LFHE	Leadership Foundation for Higher Education
LTIP	Long Term Incentive Plan
MOCW	Ministry of Education, Culture and Science of the Netherlands
MP	Member of Parliament
MSP	Member of the Scottish Parliament
MUB	Modernisering Universitaire Bestuursorganisatie
NAAC	National Assessment and Accreditation Council
NAO	National Audit Office
NBA	National Board of Accreditation
NCHE	National Commission on Higher Education
NED	Non-Executive Director
NHS	National Health Service
NI	Northern Ireland
NMITE	New Model Institute of Technology and Engineering
NPM	New Public Management
NRC	NRC Handelsblad
NSS	National Student Survey
NUS	National Union of Students
NVAO	Accreditation Organisation of the Netherlands and Flanders
OECD	The Organisation for Economic Co-operation and Development
OFFA	Office for Fair Access
OfS	Office for Students
OFT	Office for Fair Trading

OIA	Office of the Independent Adjudicator
OISE	Ontario Institute for Studies in Education
QAA	Quality Assurance Agency
QMUL	Queen Mary, University of London
REF	Research Excellence Framework
RMIT	Royal Melbourne Institute of Technology
SFC	Scottish Funding Council
SLC	Student Loans Company
SMT	Senior Management Team
SNP	Scottish National Party
SPP	Student Protection Plan
STEM	Science, Technology, Engineering and Mathematics
TE	Tertiary Education
TEF	Teaching Excellence Framework
TEQSA	Tertiary Education Quality and Standards Agency
TU	Trades Union
UCL	University College London
UFC	University Funding Council
UGC	University Grants Committee
UK	United Kingdom
UKRI	United Kingdom Research and Innovation
UNAM	National Autonomous University of Mexico
UNESCO	The United Nations Educational, Scientific and Cultural Organization
US	United States
UUK	Universities UK
VC	Vice-Chancellor
VfM	Value for Money
VSNU	Association of Universities in the Netherlands
WBFGA	The Well-being of Future Generations (Wales) Act
WGSB	Welsh Government Sponsored Bodies
WHW	Higher Education and Research Act
WUB	The University Government Reorganisation Act

Introduction

Located voices

Tony Strike

Introduction

This book opens by introducing in Part I the idea of 'different voices' – a Chair of a governing body (Chapter 1), a University Secretary (Chapter 2) – and an argument that 'whose voice' it is matters (Chapter 3).

The book then looks in Part II at the contemporary governance challenges facing universities from a series of 'global perspectives', and it does so consciously through a series of differently located voices that seek to amplify by comparison and to respect the differences on each continent.

While some commonalities can be found across the chapters the purpose was not to search for them, so a common template has not been imposed on those chapters. By reading through Part II, a world tour is conducted that illuminates the issues in one place by comparison with others and it is the diversity, dipping into other worlds, that we hope produces a richness of understanding.

The North American, European, African and Australian perspectives are very obviously highly contextualised.

What becomes clear is that the world is a living laboratory, and different systems are each evolving in ways that will evoke a readerly response.

Part III contains chapters that focus on England, partly because it is the editors' home country, but also because an unusual and radical experiment in marketisation, competition and consumerism is being conducted. This political experiment deserves critical attention from those who can be neutral international observers of the consequences of it for the government, higher education providers and students in relation to cost, quality and societal impact. The comparative chapters also drive the editors to remind themselves that alternative forms can and do exist and so not to be uncritically captured by the rhetoric of the domestic politics of time and place. Other people hear our voices differently than we do. Other readers may also find the intellectual displacement of being put in other systems or perspectives helpful in considering their own countries and institutions governance systems.

Part IV, 'Elements of governance', presents topical governance issues: the public good or benefits of universities (Chapter 14); effectiveness and effectiveness reviews (Chapter 15); academic quality assurance (Chapter 16); and performance and risk management (Chapter 17).

If there are any common threads that we can see running through these different accounts, it is that those involved in governance are increasingly in the political and public spotlight, that the demands on them continue to grow and vary, that those involved need to be able to learn from the past and each other (including hearing voices from outside the sector) to deal with a changing and complex present.

Scope

This book is about the governance challenges facing higher education institutions around the world today and the new directions being taken. It is not a 'how to' guide and nor does it attempt to stand as a code. Those who are engaged in the practices of higher education governance were asked to thoughtfully address the challenges faced by them, their institutions and countries and how these policy initiatives are being responded to. In some cases a particular window on higher education governance – legal, constitutional or occupational – is taken.

The book does not attempt to present the challenges facing higher education systems and institutions in each place as similar, although there are similarities, as well as important differences. The book addresses responses to the different challenges found each in their own context and discusses the future without falling under the spell of a search for a common narrative or a universal sense of what represents 'good' governance.

Definition

Governance is a value-laden term, which requires a great deal of care. Governance as a topic is concerned with individual and collective responsibility, given authorities, freedom to act and accountability for the proper ethical exercise of power that establishes and maintains trust and legitimacy. That is with:

- the sources of any given authority;
- decision-making and the holding to account of decision-makers;
- the roles and identities of individual, institutional or national personalities and how they relate to, bind, empower or influence each other;
- the structures, processes and values which exist, or which should exist to facilitate or restrict the exercise of a given power.

Governance operates at transnational, national, regional, institutional and individual levels, without assuming these to be in a hierarchy. Individuals can hold power and lend that authority to voluntary collective bodies, whether delegated up or down, to act on their behalf in pursuit of what they perceive as their common good.

For example, an institution using bottom-up processes can appoint academics as peers, and those academics (who control their curriculum) can agree to elect heads of discipline, and to meet as a Senate and give that Senate authority over their individual discretion.

Higher bodies can also delegate power to subsidiary ones. For example, the government can make a law giving universities a statutory form and powers, which the university governing body then acquires and delegates to internal subsidiary bodies. Hybrids are common, where statutory power lies with institutional governing bodies who then delegate to groups who are enabled to elect members to the governing body.

This cascade and escalation of authority can distribute power whether centrally, locally, on principals of subsidiarity or efficiency. These many variables produce a diversity of outcome, which should not be surprising. Institutions can behave in different ways cyclically through time with a changing context – so a governing body dealing with a retrenchment or financial crisis will operate very differently to one with a large surplus or expansion plans.

The public, government, students or companies can have trust in and respect for their civic institutions or they can mistrust perceived elitism and demand greater transparency and accountability. When a governance failing becomes a public scandal, the differences between a stakeholder's expectations and institutional behaviours are starkly exposed.

This does require governance principles, standards, processes and procedures to be set out and, ideally, to be understood and accepted by those who exercise power, by those affected and by interested others.

'Good' governance

If someone says 'good' governance is about how well committees work, they refer to only one possible set of processes for decision-making. If they say good governance is about fairness or justice, they only refer to some possible values to guide decisions. If 'good' governance is about well-formed proposals, papers and minutes then this refers to some of the possible processes by which decisions are taken. But all this requires care as individuals can make decisions as well as committees, privacy is a value as much as transparency and decisions do not require bureaucracy. Legitimate alternatives are possible and likely.

The found variety in different forms of governance raises a question, what is 'good' governance? To say whether power was exercised, or decisions were made, well or badly, in good or bad structures, using good or bad processes requires that someone must apply a normative test or criteria, which takes a particular framework for reference in making a judgement. This is complicated as Western democracies will likely choose a frame that differs from those which might be selected by others; and equally the European liberal and conservative traditions will judge by different values, and institutional types will have different traditions and habits. This book presents located voices, without laying over them any normative judgements about what is good.

Institutions are diverse, we have no agreed model (nor should we) of what constitutes a 'good' university. The worst offenders in this case are the university league tables compilers, who impose a set of measures suitable only for international research universities on all universities without consensus or consent, and create single hierarchies or ranks of those institutions of different types, which lead others to judge them unfairly and regardless of their actual mission. The chapters that follow show that relevance, strength and resilience come from proactively responding to contemporary and diverse national contexts.

Conforming to the perceived current norms or being tested by the norms of another system is not a guarantor of 'good' governance. Some homogenisation of the view of what represents 'good' governance between nation states and institutions and over time may be possible but care is required not to impose the values and processes from one tradition on another system, a neo-colonialist behaviour. Particularly when we ask the question from a point of view – different stakeholders will have different perspectives – so what represents 'good' will vary between academics, students, governments, the banks and the media.

Diversity of social and cultural contexts

The imposition of values can be seen as a managerial tool or as an irritant. For example, in some countries presidents or vice-chancellors are democratically elected and in some they are appointed, who elects and who appoints also differs. Which is 'good'? In some countries, the university is an autonomous legal body and in other cases an organ of the state. Which is 'good'? In some countries the reform of universities to provide them with greater autonomy from the state is viewed negatively by some in those systems, for its abrogation of public responsibility. In others cases the threats to institutional autonomy from the state are what are feared. The role of a governing body may be important in repelling externally imposed 'values' and reinforcing 'desired' values, which can be positive in defending academic freedom, or supporting social inclusion, where these are threatened. The public dispute between the Central European University (CEU) and the Hungarian government that ultimately led CEU to relocate its US accredited degree programmes to Vienna from September 2019 is perhaps an extreme example of a university governing body having to act defend its core values.

The heterogeneity found in this book legitimately results from context, culture, identity and history. It is possible to examine any governance system by analysing the sought outcomes, regardless of the differences, and infer something about effectiveness. Such analysis may help optimise a system without imposing normative types. National and international comparisons and competition can make any national or institutional system seem exotic, subject to analysis or expose its strengths and weaknesses. For example, the constitution of governing bodies, the Board size, composition, appointment process, status, authority and so on are parameters but not necessarily causal parameters for effectiveness. Copying between institutions or countries is not likely to be an improvement, even if it were possible to move instruments between institutional and national cultures without creating new unintended divergences. Surface level comparisons from an external point of view of a particular system can give an impression of similarity or difference, which can be exposed as naïveté through hearing the internal discourse or viewing behaviours.

The question remains whether anything in university governance can be fixed as an internationally recognised good? Is 'institutional autonomy', for example, good or is it as legitimate as a 'well managed national system'?

Searching for universality

Not everything has to be viewed as contingent or ideologically inspired. If this analysis evades a universal model or an international 'code' that does not mean everything must be contingent on place and time. All reasonably minded people might agree that corruption has no place in university governance, although perceptions of what represents corrupt behaviour may shift. Some may feel the same about nepotism. But some, successful, private providers are in fact family businesses, where people are on the board because they are family. Some might defend academics' freedom to put forwards unpopular or controversial opinions within the law without fear. All might agree a university curriculum should not be constrained by a single ruling ideology that puts any journey of discovery in the pursuit of knowledge out of bounds. But as Nicholls reminds us in Chapter 3 early forms of the *studia generalia* were under papal jurisdiction and what was taught was prescribed and limited. More controversially, all might agree that learning and discovery are a human good (even a human right), whatever the more instrumental outcomes sought by way of social capital, employment, earnings and tax returns to the state. A utopian or impractical vision? A sector with a long tradition of self-governance, treating students as members of a learned society of scholars, may rile against the rise of imposed regulation, consumerism and the marketisation of higher education. Some think universities create (or reinforce) an elite educated class of society, reinforcing power imbalances between groups and enabling structural inequality to continue while others believe universities are engines of social change and mobility (see Chapter 7).

These and similar propositional statements expose the ethical underpinnings of universities as institutions. The academic freedom to discover and to teach new knowledge might be a shared identity, based in a belief about universities. The rejection of some governing principles at the same time reject what it is to be a university or to be 'this' university. What a university is, what values it espouses, what it stands for, needs presenting again to inform how they are governed, to explain their purpose to contemporary audiences and to (re-)establish trust and legitimacy in the public realm.

The OECD, the World Bank or EU as transnational bodies may properly report on the university governance structures they observe but need to take care in forming any value judgment. Supra-national standards can be found which attempt to have or are given some universal applicability. The Magna Charta

Universitatum Observatory intends to issue a Living Values toolkit, purporting to offer universal guidelines. The King IV Report on Corporate Governance (Institute of Directors of Southern Africa, 2016) and the Nolan Principles of Public Life (Committee on Standards in Public Life, 1995) also offer strong possibilities.

This search for universality may be a mistake, because what is defined as evidenced best practice or even as the best processes to reach chosen values can be a cloak for what is necessary, popular or fashionable in time or place. There is no universally agreed canon of governance values in higher education and expectations can shift through time.

The character of 'good' governance lies in something other than its form and content; to norms, values and cases. The answer to the question 'what is good' seems to lie in the active endorsement of relevant stakeholders to what is intended, acting in ways which are entirely consistent with those intentions, and the ability of the governing system to anticipate or respond to changing standards and expectations. Because societal expectations can quickly change, and are located in time and place, those governing higher education today face the challenge of discerning the right choices in complex circumstances and steering the institution in ways that demonstrably and sustainably achieve its core aims. 'Good' governance might lead to clearer decisions, higher performance, control that is more effective, improved accountability, greater trust and public legitimacy. It is clear that those charged with governance responsibilities, particularly in this age of transparency and accountability, give a great service to the world's universities by bringing experience, expertise, insights and integrity to bear. Whether you sit on a governing body, work in a university leadership role or in a governance or policy team, teach or study higher education, we hope this book provides a thoughtful yet practical guide to the future of university governance with international applicability.

References

Committee on Standards in Public Life (1995), 'The 7 Principles of Public Life'. [Accessed at www.gov.uk/government/publications/the-7-principles-of-public-life]

Institute of Directors of Southern Africa (2016), 'The King IV Report on Corporate Governance for South Africa'. [Accessed at www.adamsadams.com/wp-content/uploads/2016/11/King-IV-Report.pdf]

Part I

Different voices

The role and perspective of a UK Chair of the governing body

Chris Sayers

'A bend in the road is not the end of the road . . . unless you fail to make the turn'. This well-known quote is widely attributed to Helen Keller,[1] someone who knew and overcame challenges that most of us would find hard to imagine. Despite being left both blind and deaf at the age of 19 months after contracting scarlet fever, she became the first deaf-blind person to earn a Bachelor of Arts degree. This was an even more remarkable achievement as she graduated in 1904 when women in general were not even admitted to university. She then went on to become a highly regarded author, political activist and lecturer, and campaigned for women's suffrage, labour rights, socialism, antimilitarism and other causes. Hardly a straightforward journey through life, but she navigated her way through some daunting challenges to achieve much more than many people of her day would have thought possible.

The difference between a bend in the road being the end of the journey or it being merely a change of direction lies in the ability to do a number of seemingly simple things. First, we have to see that the bend is coming up; second, we need to decide where and when we are going to turn and, last, we have to make sure that we do it. This is as true in business as it is anywhere, where the difference between those organisations that are successful and sustainable is their ability to navigate and successfully adapt to change. In the world of higher education (HE), our road is becoming increasingly twisty, and this chapter reflects on what governing bodies need to do to ensure that their institutions spot the bends and make the appropriate turns.

Universities occupy a vital position in the UK and, as in the fabric of any developed economy; they contribute to society in many ways. At the economic level, they play a significant role locally, nationally and globally. Universities are huge employers, with 3 per cent of all jobs in the UK linked to the HE sector, and in 2017/18 they put nearly £100bn into the UK economy. Perhaps even more importantly, the generation of new ideas is the oxygen of innovation and progress, and universities are an essential contributor to the ongoing development of civilised society. Nothing has more impact on the culture and progress of any society than education and, as university governors, we are entrusted with the governance of the highest of all educations.

Of course, universities do not run themselves. Running a university is a team sport and the players are the members of the university staff, led by the Vice-Chancellor (VC) and the executive team. The governing body, however, often occupies the role of team coach; agreeing the game plan, encouraging and motivating, observing from the side-lines and looking for ways to improve performance. And, like a team coach, when things are going well, governance is almost invisible but, as soon as anything does go wrong, the first question generally asked is, 'What were the governors doing?'. This neatly shines a light on the joint purpose of governance: it must ensure the conditions that will support others to get on with their jobs and succeed, whilst at the same time looking out for potential problems that could trip us up, which could come from any quarter and, increasingly, from unexpected directions.

In UK universities, governance has an added complexity because we are always striving to find the appropriate balance between the differing agendas driving our institutions. We must react to the influence of market forces whilst being constrained to some extent by state control and all the while operating according to our charitable objects and remaining true to our individual institution's mission. The impact of these different factors can vary to a substantial degree in different parts of the UK and across different parts of the sector, and they can change over time.

Good governance as well as good management underpins the success of any institution, but it is not a given, and organisations can fail because of problems at the governance level. Ineffective governance compromises the ability of the management to succeed, whilst effective governance is an important component of the overall leadership, strategy setting and assurance that all institutions need.

The key role of the governing body is to ensure the sustainability and long-term reputation of the institution – and it does that by making significant and strategic decisions, establishing policies, and overseeing the institution's activity. In practice, this means overseeing management, the finances, the academic quality and organisational culture, setting the strategic direction, building community relationships, establishing ethical standards, values and culture, and appointing the head of the institution and monitoring his or her progress.

Out of all of these, I believe that the two most important tasks that governing bodies have to perform are: (1) to select and develop the right leadership; and (2) to establish the direction and culture (in terms of values and acceptable behaviours) of their organisation. While these fundamental priorities remain constant, any governing body must also be ready to respond to new and different pressures, in order to remain up to date and effective.

Up until relatively recently, governance was mainly concerned with the integrity of the day-to-day running and reputation of an institution, which reflected a time when there was less financial uncertainty due to an assured number of undergraduate students and a relatively stable undergraduate and government grant income.

However, there was a quiet earthquake in the world of UK academia in 2011/12, when the government announced that not only would the full fee for undergraduate teaching become attached to the student, but that the control of the number of students going to individual institutions would also be removed, thereby allowing universities to attract as many students as they could or wanted.

This fundamentally altered the nature of the HE sector because, at a stroke, the undergraduate HE system went from being a primarily state-managed system, with limited competition based around the desire to attract the best qualified students, to being a competitive, open market.

Since then, several additional factors have intensified this competitive pressure:

- the decision to leave the European Union in 2016;
- the demographic decline in the number of 18-year-olds leaving school each year;
- fee levels not being increased by inflation, and the potential for a further funding review;
- a government policy of making it more difficult for many institutions to recruit international students coming to the UK; and
- the Higher Education and Research Act (2017) (HERA17) that has opened up even wider competition through alternative providers and an increasing range of options for 18-year-olds that include not going to university.

The net result is that there are fewer 18-year-olds in the system and that they have more options. In order to protect their income, universities now need to fight for market share and have had learn to compete more for students. To do this, they have had to become more business-like, more accountable and they are now expected to deliver much more than ever before.

As a result, many governing bodies today are facing a raft of new challenges, which require a different response, necessitating a different focus and a different working relationship with their executive teams. My observation over the last six years is that decisions taken today are often more far-reaching than they were in the past, chiefly because of the climate of greater financial uncertainty that we are currently operating in. There is a real need to make sure that our governance is, and remains, up to the task in hand.

In truth, the governance practices in some universities have not significantly changed for decades and, given the level of change the sector has been through and continues to face, it would be surprising if they are all now still fit for purpose. I believe that if a governing body is to keep abreast of the new changes facing the sector and hopes to manage them effectively, then there has to be some change both in the focus for governing bodies and in how they operate.

It is clear that many universities are changing quite dramatically, and the role of governance in those institutions is going to have to keep pace with those changes. As a discussion in the *Guardian* (Swain, 2016) higher education network in May 2016 explained:

When universities were first created in medieval times, they were mainly communities of ecclesiastical scholars. Now, they are multi-million-pound businesses with complex leadership teams, human resources departments, mission statements, international strategies, communications executives and directors of enterprise.

Like it or not, universities will need to operate in an increasingly commercially focused way; with many becoming more global in their operation and overall, carrying greater risks, and with less protection from the state.

The risks are high – HERA17 makes provision for the possibility of a university failing, and the new regulator, the Office for Students (OfS), has confirmed that its role is not to protect institutions but to protect the interests of the students (Adams, 2018). Since the Act was passed, there have been various stories in the media (Perkins, 2018; Vaughan, 2018) speculating that some universities are on the verge of bankruptcy.

An open, efficient competitive market can be a very good thing – it makes providers think about what people really want and need and can drive improvements in quality and value – but the flip side of any market economy is that a provider who can't compete will not get the custom, and therefore neither will they get the income. Although it would be a mistake to start thinking of students as consumers or customers, the general principle is still true, and students are increasingly choosing to attend universities based on perceived quality, reputation and value for money and what it will do for their employment prospects. Universities now have to do more to convince potential students of the benefits that they offer.

We are already seeing market dynamics playing out in our sector, with some universities growing while others shrink. Some universities have realised the opportunity that competition brings to expand and grow, whilst others are now grappling with the unprecedented level of financial uncertainty and top line revenue volatility. As risks have increased (both of failure and missed opportunity) and government has been articulating ever more requirements on governing bodies, governors' requirements of their institutions have also changed. They are wanting more engagement, are becoming more challenging and are looking for more assurance.

Some governing bodies are now using a whole new lexicon in the boardroom. Discussions have shifted from relatively straightforward reports on the state of finances, student applications, research success and property to also talking about student satisfaction, corporate plans, marketing plans, financial dashboards, scenario planning, cash flow management, competitive strategy, customer segmentation and buying decisions, the differentiation of educational offering, culture and the student experience and how all of this impacts the academic portfolio. Some universities were very quick to adapt, others not, but from the evidence of discussions with other Chairs at Committee for University Chairs (CUC) Plenaries, it seems that most are now thinking like this.

We are also seeing a very different approach to marketing with almost every university seemingly claiming to be top ten or number one at something or other, accompanied by an expansion in digital marketing activities and the recognition at some institutions that professional marketing is now a fundamental part of a university's business. The National Audit Office (NAO) report on 'The Higher Education Market' says that:

> Most providers we (NAO) spoke to were focusing increasingly on marketing and advertising since student number caps were removed. For example, one provider had tripled the size of its marketing team, while another was planning a £400,000 summer advertising campaign in the run-up to A-level results. Our interviewees were aware of some providers offering gifts such as football season tickets or iPads to entice students, though none did so themselves. Similarly, providers are increasingly willing to make unconditional offers, particularly to high-achieving students, to discourage them from looking elsewhere.
>
> (NAO, 2017, p.30)

Meanwhile, the marketplace for key skills, recognised as being critical for an institution's success, has resulted in some universities now paying their top people salaries that are attracting attention, and governing bodies need to consider carefully their remuneration strategies.

The net result is that we who are responsible for these complex institutions, at a time of such disruptive change, must make sure that our governing bodies are equipped to able to make strategic decisions and to find the right balance between competitive confidentiality and the increasing requirement for public accountability and transparency. Governing bodies will need to be better informed, benefit from a greater skills mix, have a stronger partnership relationship with the Executive and be even more actively involved in setting the leadership tone.

To achieve this, all governing bodies must have the right expertise around the table to deal with the critical issues of the time. Of course, as the CUC (2017) Illustrative Practice Note 7 states, it is:

> important that post-holders can question intelligently, debate constructively, challenge rigorously, decide dispassionately, appreciate the difference between governance and management and be sensitive to the views of others, both inside and outside governing body meetings.
>
> (CUC, 2017, p.3)

But they also need to bring a sufficient breadth of personal experience and understanding to the debate. Today's governing bodies clearly need governors with commercial and business backgrounds, but we also need IT, digital, marketing and fundraising skills, to name but a few, to supplement the traditional mix.

In addition, there must be sufficient quality boardroom time to talk about the key subject areas, such as the well-being and experience of students, staff, money (costs and income), competition, an institution's competitive offering and its reputation management. There can be a challenge in how to use board time well so that we do not have interminable meetings where concentration flags, but still manage to allow time for in depth consideration of important issues and for determining the direction of travel for the institution. At Northumbria University, we have addressed this by reversing the agenda – all the strategic discussion items are tabled first while all routine, update and constitutional items are handled at the end of the meeting. This ensures that we discuss the most important matters first and make our strategic decisions when we have both time and maximum energy in the room.

Thus far, I have been discussing how the sector has been responding to the known changes and challenges it faces, but governing bodies also have a responsibility to ensure the long-term sustainability of their institution. Change is a constant process and we need to continually adapt our governance models to meet not just today's challenges and opportunities but also those that we anticipate in the future.

Therefore, I believe that it is important for governing bodies to speculate on the likely changes that could have impact on HE in the future, such as:

- the degree of regulation in England and its likely impact on the current level of autonomy;
- the degree of future market pressure and the nature of that competition;
- the future needs of society and how HE can meet them;
- domestic and global demographic trends;
- wider environmental changes (technology, geopolitics, societal) that will raise questions about how universities can best serve the needs of people in the future;
- the global market for the best (human) resources – we need to recruit and retain the best global talent if we are going to sustain a world class system;
- future financial pressures (such as pensions); and
- technological advances.

Some key questions that these should raise for our governance in the near future are:

- How do we to ensure governance delivers the requirements of a truly regulated sector?
- How do we operate in an environment where governing bodies are more accountable, visible and externally challenged?
- How do we to keep governance aligned with the needs of universities as the sector continues to change and the HE market becomes increasingly global in nature?

From an autonomy and governance perspective, there are now growing differences between universities in the devolved administrations and in England – differences in the degree of state control or influence, which certainly manifests itself in terms of differences in funding and the size of universities, but also in governance terms.

In England, we are moving from a system where the Higher Education Funding Council for England (HEFCE) operated as a buffer body between government and the institutions and where the sector was managed predominantly through funding incentives, conditions and penalties, to one where the importance of government funding is diminished and regulation operates through the mechanisms of a register and licence to operate.

The regulatory tools available to the OfS are the Teaching Excellence Framework (TEF), the Research Excellence Framework (REF) and the potential introduction of a Knowledge Exchange Framework (KEF).[2] In addition, we have a new research funding body. To be fair, the OfS has reiterated its commitment to institutional autonomy but, in discussions with Chairs, there is clearly a degree of anxiety that these changes will see the sector being driven more in line with the desired political outcomes of the day. As Boyd makes clear:

> This means that a government minister has the power to give directions, demand advice and require reports from the regulator. The new agency has already been clear that it doesn't intend to get involved with policy, leaving a much more centralised system under direct government control.
>
> (Boyd, 2018)

In Scotland, universities already operate with a greater degree of direct state control – controlling funding certainly but also with changes to university governance through the Higher Education Governance Act of 2016. Scottish universities are now working to implement the Act's provisions, which most notably include requirements to add certain categories of governing body member, including nominees of trade unions, and for students and staff to elect the Chair of the governing body when a vacancy arises.

Wales continues with its own funding arrangements, reporting to the Higher Education Funding Council for Wales, and in Northern Ireland the state control over financing has resulted in significant underfunding of undergraduate education compared to England (to the tune of £2,500 per student). This has meant that in 2018 there were 2,260 fewer undergraduate places available to Northern Ireland school leavers than compared to five years before. As a result, 36 per cent of NI students studied outside NI and only one-third of those return. In comparison, the Republic of Ireland exports only 3.1 per cent of its school leavers.

This gives an indication as to why differences in the level of autonomy are important. Looking at HE systems around the globe, a paper produced by the European Commission (2010) shows that there is strong correlation between performance achieved (and value for money) and the degree of institutional autonomy, which is not surprising. Institutions driven by what they see as being best for their students and staff will always be looking to innovate in order to differentiate and keep themselves relevant, especially in a market environment. The worst thing that any organisation that needs to compete in an open market can do is to stay the same – eventually it will be overtaken, and it will go out of business. Of course, innovation carries risk but it is more about taking the risk of success. In contrast, in an excessively state-controlled system, organisations are not always incentivised to innovate and change because failure can carry more risk than the benefits of success. Institutions can, and do, thrive in different political environments around the globe, but in broad terms I think that market forces combined with institutional autonomy will generally result in more positive change, while state control generally makes organisations more risk-averse. I think that's likely to be as true in HE as anywhere else.

English universities currently sit somewhere in the middle of the spectrum as the last few years have shown a further move towards being market driven, while the devolved administrations lean more towards state control. Are these differences important and what would be the significance of a potential change in the degree of institutional autonomy? As we see many other countries, especially in the East, rapidly expand their HE capacity and capability, it is crucial that UK institutions are able to continue to compete with the best in the world. Changes in the degree of state control may have a significant impact on that ability and government bodies need to think through the potential risks and opportunities in this. On one hand, if there was an increase in state control of governance and funding, it might well reduce an institution's appetite for ambition and some may decide to play safe. On the other hand, it could also be argued that a reduction in funding might be just the burning platform required to drive innovative new ways of delivering HE at a lower cost and better value. It will be interesting to see which way the UK governments decide to lean, but how an individual institution responds to any future change will largely depend on the response of its governing body.

We haven't yet had time to see what the establishment of the OfS will ultimately mean – but we hope that it is not more 'red tape' as overloading a board with signing off statutory returns and reports is a sure-fire way of crowding out the time to talk about the really important issues. Organisations can fail spectacularly when their governing bodies take their eye off the ball and stop talking about the things that really matter

The OfS does say that the new regulatory framework will result in a reduction in the level of statutory returns and a greater freedom to determine, at an individual institutional level, how best to comply with the expected standards. That is to be welcomed, but the OfS states that it is not there to support institutions; instead it is there to ensure that the student interest is protected. I would argue that it is absolutely in the student interest to have a highly effective governing body. Therefore, all governing bodies should be aware that this is not about making things easier, it is about the OfS demanding that governing bodies pay even more attention to the student experience and that we will be held accountable if that is perceived to be falling short. If an institution is judged to be failing the student interest, then we should expect the OfS directly to intervene and question the role of that institution's governance.

Based on my experience of other regulated sectors in the UK, my view is that the OfS will choose to impose greater responsibilities on governing bodies over time and hold them ever more to account to ensure an institution's performance, financial sustainability, student protection, quality of experience and the value for money delivered.

It is inevitable, then, that if governing bodies are held to be more and more accountable, they are going to have to be more transparent about decisions that they make, especially when those decisions are deemed to be in the public interest; such as how governing bodies set senior pay, oversee academic standards and support free speech.

We should continue to expect there to be further pressure on universities to respond to the changing political and social expectations at home. We need to be able to have answers to the real concerns about social inequity, the deplorable lack of social mobility today in the UK and questions about what value for money for students really means.

But regulation and competition can also have wider impacts on governing bodies. The combination of a more regulated and competitive environment is likely to drive universities to think even more carefully about:

- their cost base – not just about cost saving and doing more with the same resources, but also looking at selective outsourcing and collaboration with other organisations and exploring different delivery models;
- quality – in any market where there is no real price differential then perceived quality becomes the competitive advantage; and
- where they can aggressively move into non-regulated areas of HE, such as Trans-National Education, international operations, commercial ventures and enterprise income.

Unless there is a radical change of political direction, market pressure is only going to intensify, and over the next few years I think that the focus of governing bodies is likely to shift from being mainly preoccupied with the domestic market to considering their institutional performance much more in the context of the global market. This will be due partly to Brexit, but more to the fact that US and UK dominance will be continue to be challenged (and potentially overtaken) by India and China (McRae, 2018). Over the next decade, most forecasts predict an increasing shift of geopolitical power towards China and the East. Coupled with an increase in global urbanisation and a massive rise of global middle classes this will inevitably result in even larger numbers going to university, mostly in East Asia. This could eventually result in a shift in the centre of gravity of the knowledge economy from West to East. The writing is on the wall. According to the Ministry of Education of the People's Republic of China (2017), over eight million students will graduate from China this year alone, which is ten times the number that graduated in 1997 and already twice the number of US graduates this year. China and India will account for 40 per cent of all young people with a tertiary education in G20 and OECD countries by the year 2020, while the United States and all European Union countries combined will account for just over 25 per cent. By 2025, 50 per cent of graduates worldwide are likely to be from China and India. So ask yourself, where will the world's best universities, researchers and students be in ten or 20 years' time? What will happen to UK institutions if and when China and India have a better capacity and capability to educate than the United Kingdom and United States? What would happen to our international student market? Considering that today there are already 200,000 foreign students that are electing to study in China, a number that grows year on year, is it conceivable that the flow of international students might one day reverse and start going from Europe to the East? How would we respond? What would this mean to UK universities?

Governing bodies ignoring the changes in the global market will be doing so at their peril, and the right skills will be needed both to understand and navigate this particular challenge.

Next, we need to be realistic that we will see some serious changes in the way that HE works in the near future. The way that undergraduate education is delivered hasn't fundamentally changed in a very long time, but there are wider environmental changes and technology advances that signal a real disruption to our sector.

Business disruption happens when the right number of factors converge at the same time (whether technological, societal, political or demographic), the combination of which allows a competitor to develop a disruptive commercial model that makes a traditional model obsolete very quickly. History is full of them:

- Kodak – who invented digital photography but whose board dismissed it as an irrelevance. In 2000, Kodak had their best ever year for profits, in 2012 they filed for bankruptcy.
- Uber – a technology-enabled new commercial model which now has more taxi business in the United States than all other taxi services combined.
- Airbnb – another great example of commercial disruption – using simple technology to bring a brokerage service to the market.

So, what's this got to do with HE? Part of what we have to do in our governing bodies is to look for the signs of the big changes on the horizon – the disruptors – that eventually impact every industry, including ours.

Let me digress. If you visit Japan, one of things that you notice anywhere near to the coast is that you always see a sign saying how high you are above sea level and what route that you need to take to go to the highest land as quickly as possible. The Japanese authorities do not know when a tsunami will happen but they do know that it *will* happen one day, and they have already thought through the scenarios and what should happen when disaster occurs. This is a nice metaphor for our governance challenge, as organisations often get into trouble when their governing bodies stop thinking about what might swamp them in the longer term. We have seen recent examples of this in the construction, financial and health sectors which are classic board failures – failure to look after the cash, failure to look after the people you are serving and more generally, failure to look in the right direction when disaster struck.

Personally, I think that one of the key roles of any board (in HE or otherwise) is to create space to discuss future business scenarios, to assess the changing (global) environment, and to continually examine possible scenarios so that the organisation has thought through future challenges before they become disruptors.

Much of this change will come from developments in technology, or at least it will be enabled by it. I'm not talking about the false dawn of the rise of Massive Open Online Courses (MOOCs), or other extensions to distance learning. I think the real change will come from developments in Artificial Intelligence (AI) and human/computer interfaces which are making huge advances – it is expected that AI will be able to teach to 'A' level standard by the early 2020s.

When you factor in the developments of Virtual Reality, Virtual Learning Environments, immersive experience technologies, robotics, and the much more seamless connectivity now enabled by super high speed networking, then it seems obvious that in the next ten, and certainly, 20 years, we are going to see HE providers offering a totally different approach to undergraduate education and research that will make what we currently deliver look like something out of the ark. Young people already access information in ways that are different to the majority of HE staff (Bloom, 2015). We need to start thinking now about what we will do when a competitor starts offering an AI-supported, location independent, world-class teaching programme at a tiny fraction of our current cost structure. What would that mean to the future of UK HE? Would our mainstream institutions be able to compete? And then there is the consideration of when to choose to adapt a business model in the light of disruptive change? These are all very important questions which are impossible to answer without some really good horizon scanning and serious scenario planning, which are not, I suspect, the normal agenda items of today's governing bodies. The tragic part of the Kodak story is that it was they that invented the technology that led to their own business model being overtaken. The irony for us is that the ideas that will ultimately challenge how universities deliver in the future are likely to come from within universities themselves – the question is going to be whether or not our governance will recognise the opportunity when it arises.

Although financial scrutiny will always be a core element of governance, there are some new factors that could lead to more time being spent on this area of responsibility, in particular the unfolding impact of changes to pension funding and benefits, which will have a raft of consequences for universities to deal with for many years. Furthermore, as undergraduate funding appears to be becoming more of a political issue, future government policies will inevitably result in there being less direct money in the system to fund university teaching, and managing that consequence will clearly continue to be a priority for governing bodies.

All the above factors have an impact on each other, so overall it makes for a complicated landscape and it is very difficult to predict the future accurately. However, governing bodies clearly need to do their best to think about the likely scenarios in five, ten, 15 and 20 years' time, because if there is one thing that we can be sure about, it's that the global landscape will not stay static. Universities that do not look to the future, that don't adapt or continue to compete and seize new opportunities as they arise, will inevitably decline, possibly to the point of becoming unsustainable.

So, the question posed was 'How is governance likely to evolve in the light of these potential changes?' Presupposing that future governance is designed for the future, and not just how we have always done it, then I think that we will see some key changes in the next few years.

First, as we respond to the challenges of greater global competition, we will need to see much more strategic capability being recruited at the board level, in order to help to develop strategies where universities are delivering a more diverse student offering (and not just at a subject level) across the sector in order to secure competitive advantage.

Skill sets in general are likely to change, with governors selected for new skills to supplement the traditional ones (e.g. finance, legal, HR), including:

- greater strategic capability;
- modern IT and digital skills;
- having the ability to imagine future delivery scenarios;
- skills in scenario planning for immediate and long-term challenges;
- digital marketing;
- fundraising and philanthropy;
- business innovation; and
- international HE understanding.

As this skill set changes, we will probably also start to get younger and more diverse governing bodies on average and greater diversity. The make-up of boards is beginning to change, and the appointment of women governors has significantly increased over the last two years (with over 45 per cent of new appointments being women in all categories (external, staff and student)). However, wider diversity indicators for age and ethnicity still show that most boards are far from being balanced. A key part of the solution to increasing the skill mix could be a greater use of co-opted members onto committees, bringing in specific and niche skills to raise the level of expertise and objectivity in certain sub-committees, and I would expect that to become more prevalent.

I am also sure that we see a response to both social and political pressure that will call for a more integrated governance model. We will see governing bodies recognising that it is time to start thinking of new models of governance that involve and engage the community and the staff more, and deeper consideration being given to how we measure success, broadening this out from employment outcomes to measuring more meaningful social value (BUFDG, 2016).

A recent example is the change shepherded in by the CUC remuneration code (CUC, 2018) asking for greater openness and transparency, which will change the way that governing bodies report about senior pay decisions. I suspect that this is likely to be start of an increasing trend for more public information about the decisions that universities make and why. Governing bodies will need to become more accustomed to dealing with external scrutiny. The pay debate has, to some extent, let this particular genie out of the bottle, and it will not be going back in. We are already seeing a small but significant number of universities appointing students and staff onto their remuneration and finance committees, and it is likely that this will gradually become the norm.

As governing bodies will be required to give even greater scrutiny to financial matters, they are likely to demand an increasing use of analytics, with more detailed financial reporting, more emphasis on benefits realisation and return on investment and this in turn will compound the need for new skills on some governing bodies. In addition, it will not just be skills in financial analytics that are needed, as institutions increasingly make use of education and marketing analytics.

What about the trend of remunerating chairs and governors? Is this inevitable if we want the best candidates to put themselves forward, who are expected to shoulder greater responsibility and spend more time dealing with new, complex challenges that institutions are now facing?

Traditionally, independent governors have almost universally been volunteers, but a few universities have started to go down the route of remunerating their Chair or committee chairs, in the same way that chairs of private sector governing bodies, NHS trusts and sector bodies are already widely remunerated. If we want to continue to attract from the most experienced resource pool available, then I think that it is likely that we will see this trend increasing. And there are benefits – not only does it secure a person's commitment in a more tangible way as they are much more likely to prioritise their university commitment when there is a pull on their time, but also it opens up the door for a meaningful discussion about performance. Chairs and governors must be held to account if their performance is important to the success of the institution, and their performance needs to be reviewed regularly and assessed against the needs and performance of the university.

Regardless of how experienced and skilled our individual governors may be, there is still a question about how we get the most out of the limited time that they have available, and ensure they are genuinely being used effectively so that they are adding value, as board time becomes increasingly prioritised to monitor strategic direction.

Lastly, we need to be much better at promoting what universities do and the value that they deliver. This includes the need to explain how university governance operates and to clearly demonstrate the value that it brings. We are hampered at the moment as university governance is neither well understood by the public at large (including students, staff, politicians and policy makers) nor does it enjoy a very good reputation; in fact there is a general lack of confidence and trust in how universities are managed.

This may be rather unfair, and almost universally unfounded, but that is still the perception that has been stoked up by a rather one-sided public narrative recently on senior remuneration, expenses, remuneration committees and an accusation of cosy governance, and the reality is that we have lost a measure of the trust that universities enjoyed in the past. We have to earn that trust back. So not only do we have to rise to the challenges, but we also do need to win back public confidence before the reputation of the sector becomes further tarnished.

To recap, although many universities are already adapting their governance structures and practices, the sector-wide trends that we are likely to observe will be a result of how institutions find answers to the following questions:

-   What do we actively need to do to keep governance aligned with the needs of our universities as the sector and society continues to change (with greater competition, more risk, global competition etc.)?
-   How do we ensure that governance delivers the requirements of a truly regulated sector? A key consideration will be how university governance remains relevant in a regulated environment. As seen in utilities, schools and the NHS, government regulators have a history of going way beyond policy-setting, at times encroaching well into both institutional governance and institutional management. The more that happens, the less impact the board has to effect real change. How do we recognise that risk, and ensure that an effective area of responsibility is preserved for university governing bodies?
-   What do we need to change in our operating environment as governing bodies become more accountable and have to deal with increased external scrutiny and challenge?
-   How is our governance designed for the future, rather than the past? How do we ensure that governing bodies are structured in an appropriate way, operate professionally and are populated with the right skills, against a backdrop of increasing personal responsibility and liability?
-   Are governing bodies staying awake to the threats and opportunities of disruptive change? Governing bodies need to find the time and space to think long and think big! They need to ensure that the big challenges and their implications for the university are really well understood, and make sure that they have a strategy that gives them the best possible chance of succeeding.

From my experience as Chair of the CUC, I have observed that the standard of governance across the sector is already high, but the changing environment will demand that we look to raise our game even further. There is going to be even more onus on governing bodies to be truly transparent about what they are doing, as well as an increased scrutiny on; how money is spent, why we are setting priorities in the way that we are and what value we are delivering. Therefore, we must be able to justify the decisions that we make and make them public. We need to be able to explain these complex issues in a way that all our stakeholders understand, and I think that this will mean that all governing bodies should challenge themselves about how they can be even more effective and better promoters and ambassadors for the sector.

Governing bodies have never had as much responsibility as they have now, facing challenges that governing bodies in the past didn't have to think about. We are navigating a level of change that is unprecedented, and this is just the start – we have to deal with the now, and still find the bandwidth to look to the future, or the risk is that we will suddenly find that we are still trying to sell film in a world of digital photography.

Notes

1 Quotes from Helen Keller. Retrieved from www.goodreads.com/author/quotes/7275. Helen_Keller
2 These are data-driven frameworks, introduced by the government to communicate levels of perceived excellence in teaching, research and knowledge exchange activity.

References

Adams, R. (2018) 'We won't bail out failing universities, says higher education regulator'. *Guardian*. Retrieved from www.theguardian.com/education/2018/nov/06/failing-universities-bailouts-michael-barber-office-for-students

Bloom, A. (2015) 'Read a book? Teenagers prefer YouTube, survey finds'. TES. Retrieved from www.tes.com/news/read-book-teenagers-prefer-youtube-survey-finds

Boyd, C. (2018) 'A beginner's guide to the Office for Students'. Wonkhe. Retrieved from https://wonkhe.com/blogs/a-beginners-guide-to-the-office-for-students/

BUFDG (2016) 'Integrated reporting in HE: helping universities tell their stories better'. Efficiency Exchange. Retrieved from www.efficiencyexchange.ac.uk/wp-content/uploads/Integrated-Reporting-IR-in-HE-Web-v3-5.pdf

CUC (2017) 'The role of the nominations committee'. Illustrative Practice Note 7, Committee of University Chairs. Retrieved from www.universitychairs.ac.uk/wp-content/uploads/2017/11/IPN7-Nominations-Committee.pdf

CUC (2018) 'The higher education senior staff remuneration code'. Committee of University Chairs. Retrieved from www.universitychairs.ac.uk/wp-content/uploads/2018/06/HE-Remuneration-Code.pdf

European Commission (2010) 'Efficiency and effectiveness of public expenditure on tertiary education in the EU'. Retrieved from http://ec.europa.eu/economy_finance/publications/occasional_paper/2010/pdf/ocp70_en.pdf

Higher Education and Research Act (2017) HMSO. Retrieved from www.legislation.gov.uk/ukpga/2017/29/contents

McRae, H. (2018) 'By 2030, economies like China and India will hold dominance over the West – and influence our decisions'. *Independent*. Retrieved from www.independent.co.uk/voices/hsbc-economies-china-india-emerging-west-east-technology-a8556346.html

Ministry of Education of the People's Republic of China (2017) 'Educational statistics in 2017'. Retrieved from http://en.moe.gov.cn/Resources/Statistics/edu_stat2017/national/201808/t20180808_344698.html

National Audit Office (2017) 'The higher education market'. Retrieved from www.nao.org.uk/report/the-higher-education-market/

Perkins, A. (2018) 'A bankrupt university was inevitable'. *Guardian*. Retrieved from www.theguardian.com/commentisfree/2018/nov/02/university-bankrupt-inevitable-market-forces

Swain, H. (2016) 'The business of running a university'. *Guardian* higher education network. Retrieved from www.theguardian.com/higher-education-network/2016/may/14/the-business-of-running-a-university

Vaughan, R. (2018) 'Three UK universities on the brink of bankruptcy and more reliant on short-term loans to survive'. Retrieved from https://inews.co.uk/news/education/university-bankruptcy-reliant-on-loans/

Chapter 2

The University Secretary
At the heart of governance

Tony Strike

Introduction

This chapter will focus on the role of the University Secretary. Working on behalf of the Chair of the governing body and the governors this is the person who embodies the institutional governance/legislative function of a higher education institution. The Chair and other members of the governing body rely on the Secretary to ensure they have the information and time needed in order to function effectively. Whatever the particular job title used, the object of attention here is the senior person or role responsible for providing secretaryship, advice, support and services to the main governing body of a higher education institution.

University administrations at their most senior levels will have either a single chief professional officer at an apex or they will divide the accountabilities perhaps between two, three or four separate roles in a flatter structure with governance, financial and executive management responsibilities. It is quite usual to find a Secretary, a Bursar (or Chief Financial Officer) and commonly now a Chief Operating Officer (or Pro Vice-Chancellor – Services/Operations) reporting directly to the President or Vice-Chancellor.

The term Secretary is traditionally utilised to describe the most senior role occupied by the person with governance responsibilities, although other titles are now in use, such as board administrator, clerk or Director of Governance. David Holmes, Registrar and Secretary, University of Birmingham, said of this person when writing about them more than twenty years ago:

> although we have seen the relative demise of the generalist administrator . . . there is still a vital role for the professional administrator as the steward of the constitutional and business rules and procedures; the co-ordinator of the flow of business, in terms of both timing and content; the recorder of discussions/decisions and the transmission of them through the, hopefully, minimalist committee structure; and as the provider of information and papers on items of business (including the picking up of external signals and changes) with now an increased emphasis on the independent role of the clerk to the Governing Body's role in corporate governance matters. Nobody should underestimate this function.
>
> (Holmes, 1998, p. 112)

The role Holmes described then still exists, in a changed context, within which with variations, national and regional governments have stepped back from direct control of higher education institutions, and those institutions find greater autonomy. This means higher education institutions need more effective governing or legislative bodies which can take on new legal, strategic or executive powers and personalities. But sound governance is also a necessary condition for that greater autonomy, or as David Fletcher (2007) put it, 'better governance = more trust = less regulation' (p. 103). This increase in institutional autonomy and related governing competence can be observed in international trends observed differently in each country but variously including the:

- provision to higher education institutions of a separate legal personality, rather than treating them as agencies of the state;
- dominance of legislative over executive power, expressed through participative institutional decision-making structures;
- introduction of governing bodies and their greater localised authority;
- move to block or per-student budgets in place of 'line by line' funding, including staff salaries;
- academic loss of civil service employment status, in favour of employment by the institution itself;
- strengthening of the executive role of the President/Vice-Chancellor, through the centralisation of authority inside institutions;
- weakening or elimination of Senates or of collegial academic decision-making in the Professoriate in favour of hierarchical governance.

While it might be possible to claim these changes are being imposed by the European Union, OECD (OECD et al., 2010), UNESCO or the World Bank (Fielden, 2008) to promote a Western neo-liberal agenda on to global higher education, the reports of those bodies are retrospective, descriptive and summative rather than causal. It is more likely that nation states have responded to common or local pressures on their national systems, or as Shattock (2014) put it:

> Nevertheless all these systems – the Humboldtian, the Napoleonic, the Japanese, the Anglo-Saxon and the American – have been subject to change driven by state recognition of the importance of universities to the knowledge economy, by austerity and by government pressures to compete in international markets.
>
> (p. 3)

The international trend to increase the autonomy of higher education institutions by making them more independent, or even self-governing organisations, whatever the reason, means the institution itself becomes an accountable corporate actor and needs to know its own powers and exercise them responsibly. Each institution also needs to protect its autonomy while responding to legitimate governmental and public interest. These trends have put a spotlight on the strength of institutional governance structures inside institutions and on those who support them, linking local governance and administration. For these reasons governance technicality and the expert control of its instruments has received even greater emphasis (Magalhães and Amaral, 2010). For all its history and tradition, the Secretary (and its equivalents) thus remains an influential senior role in the modern management structures of higher education institutions.

By turning the spotlight on the contribution of the Secretary and investigating governance from this perspective it is possible to move from structure to social interaction and from institution to individual, to more fully understand the institutional governance environment (Llewellyn, 2009) and to locate its beating heart.

World nomenclature

There is no standard international codification of internal governance structures, roles or processes in higher education as a sector or of its institutions nor is there a shared vocabulary. This section attempts to provide a shared language to enable the discussion of the particular role of the Secretary in context.

Governance

The term 'corporate governance' appeared during the 1980s and the first book titled 'Corporate Governance' was published in 1984 (Tricker, 1984) and explained that if management was about running the business, governance was about seeing that it was run properly. The first UK code of governance (from Adrian Cadbury) was not published until 1992 (Committee on the Financial Aspects of Corporate Governance, 1992).

Lazzeretti and Tavoletti (2006) provide a working description:

> We can say that university governance refers to all processes and institutions that rule the division and managing of power inside universities and national university systems. Here, power means making decisions that are binding for others.
>
> (p. 21)

The mechanics of governance concern the:

- granting or reservation of rights or powers by the state or other third-party actors or provision of the ex-ante freedom to act;
- delegation of that right or authority to corporate bodies or persons inside the institution;
- processes those authorised must use to exercise rights, powers, or to take decisions or actions;

- ex-post reporting or assurance owed to any internal or external legal or supervising authority;
- recording and communication of rights or powers exercised, decisions made or actions taken.

Ethical principles of governance, or proper conduct, are set out in national and sector codes and often include, for example, selflessness, integrity, objectivity, accountability, openness, honesty, leadership (Committee on Standards in Public Life, 1995).

This description should not leave a Weberian impression that following correct procedures and due processes trumps achievement of results. This description does not represent a rejection of leadership. Good governance empowers, supports and encourages decision-takers, simplifies and improves decision-making processes and demonstrates trust and competence to others.

Governance must add value to the achievement of the institutions stated objectives and strategy. Sound governance also legitimates actions taken while maintaining trust and providing external assurance. In O'Neill's landmark Reith lectures from 2002 (O'Neill, 2002) she warns against conceptions of accountability which superimpose managerial targets and bureaucratic processes, burdening those who have to comply. Governance should demonstrate trustworthiness to others through valid ethical principles, genuine accountability and transparency.

Governing body

The term 'governing body' is used here for the main or most senior governing or supervisory body located within the higher education institution, which may be called the Council, Court, Congregation, Board of Governors (Hochschulräte), Board of Trustees or Regents, Board of Directors, Supervisory Board (Raad van Toezicht) and equivalent. Respecting that, the membership of this body varies by country in the means of appointment (election or selection by the institution or by government) and by characteristic (internal or external members, administrative or academic). It is nevertheless the senior responsible supervisory body. The persons who serve on that governing body are called members here in preference to, for example, (charitable) trustees, non-executive directors, governors or lay members.

President

The head of the higher education institution meaning the President, Vice-Chancellor, Principal, Rector, Rector Magnificus or equivalent; who is here referred to as the 'President'. This position, depending on the country, can be appointed by the governing body, appointed by the government or be elected by the academic staff. They can chair the Senate (see below), and their powers can vary from being *primus inter pares*, first among equals, with relatively weak decision-making powers, or the position can have great influence as the chief academic and executive officer.

Chair

Where the President is elected they tend also to chair the main governing body. In countries where the President is appointed by and does not chair the governing body, and the position is taken by one of the external members, the chair of that governing body is referred to here as the 'Chair'.

Senate

The senior or supreme academic body is here called the 'Senate'; in preference to academic board, academic affairs committee, board of deans, education and research council, Collegium or Vakgroep, being the institution's academic organ with the power to decide on matters relating to academic standards, educational programmes, research, publication activities and the students' experience. In countries where collegial self-governance is the traditional mode, the Senate can be the highest decision-making body within the institution (for example in Germany). In these cases, the Senate can appoint the Council/Board. In others it can be equal to the governing Council/Board (in so-called bicameral structures) and in some jurisdictions it is subordinate to the governing body (such as in the UK).

Executive board

The senior academic and administrative officers who manage and run the institution, accountable to the President, as chief executive, are here called the executive or 'executive board' in preference to administrative board, administrative council, president's cabinet or central executive board (College van Bestuur). Executive management is often, after the governing body and Senate, the highest decision-making group in the institution.

While the history and constitutional forms of individual higher education institutions may differ and so the nomenclature, duties, powers and responsibilities will vary by jurisdiction, the basic structure should be familiar. Collegial, executive, academic or managerial cultures or individual personalities may change the power dynamics between these roles, however named, as much as the country-specific constitutional position. These different bodies have a separation of powers but a shared responsibility to ensure the success of the institution and the achievement of its goals. As Shattock (2003) put it:

> [S]uccessful universities try to ensure that governance is kept in balance between an active lay contribution, strong corporate leadership, an effective central steering core and an involved and participative senate/academic board. Where any element is weak the institution is disadvantaged.

(p. 97)

The University Secretary occupies this world as a guarantor, co-ordinator, helper and guide.

The Secretary

The role of the Secretary (and Registrar) varies significantly according to the peculiarities of each higher education institution, the national characteristics of the law and by the institutions own governing instruments. In some cases, the Secretary is narrowly defined as clerk to the governing body, with no further responsibility, whereas in other contexts they are more broadly responsible for ensuring good governance throughout the institution, as a secretary-general. In others they may be responsible for ensuring the governing body meets all its external regulatory and legal responsibilities. Shattock (2006) put this corporate responsibility thus:

> The registrar may not personally 'service' a faculty board but will be as concerned about the proper conduct of business there as at the senate and council where he/she might expect to take a personal responsibility for the discharge of business. Such a position acts as a guarantee for the way the institution as a whole reaches corporate decisions.
>
> (p. 22)

In some cases, therefore, the role is combined with being clerk to the Executive Board (or responsibility for that person if not performed personally) and for being clerk to the Senate or Academic Board.

A second differentiator might be whether the role is defined by its administrative duties only or seen as an adviser and source of good counsel to the Chair, President, governing body and Senate. Scott (2018) highlighted the role of the Secretary as a source of independent advice and information, as follows:

> Board administrators must be not only meeting planners and minutes scribes, but also the link between the president and the board. As such, they can be put in a position of mixed loyalties, wanting and needing to be a member of the institution team, but also finding that they are in a position to hear negative comments about the president or asked probing questions about the administration.
>
> (p. 95)

Hampshire-Cowan (2016) describes this advisory role more positively and deliberately:

> The board professional, when empowered to do so, can act as an adviser and resource to the president, the board chair, and the entire board. When deployed and empowered by the president and/or board chair to act beyond the traditional functional role, the board professional becomes a trusted

strategic adviser to the president, board chair, board members, and the president's cabinet. Each entity plays an important role in the pursuit of a high-performing board. While board professionals have a limited span of authority, their spheres of influence can be immeasurable.

To some extent, and perhaps increasingly, elements of the role of the Secretary have become codified. The English CUC Code (2014, revised 2018) makes seven references to the Secretary, the Irish Code (HEA, 2012) has six, as compared to the Committee of the Chairs of Scottish Higher Education Institutions (2017) which references the Secretary on thirty-two occasions.

Separating governance and management

The professional and support services in higher education institutions continue to evolve. As the institution itself becomes an actor with authority, with a legal personality of its own or self-determining powers, it is possible to see developing a deliberative governance structure (Council, Senate), separated from the executive structure (President and Vice-Presidents), and separated again from the administrative structure (Director of Administration, Chief Operating Officer and other administrative directors). Many readers will be familiar with the academic and administrative descriptors for different estates in universities, despite the near-universal trend towards 'professional services' as the term. Individuals may occupy different parts of this internal leadership and management structure 'wearing different hats,' for example, a Faculty Dean will head a faculty, may also be a member of the executive board, of the Senate and then be appointed to the governing body.

In 'dual' systems, the Vice-Presidents/Pro Vice-Chancellors can report to the Vice-Chancellor and the administrative directors can report to a Director of Administration. In a 'functional' system, the administrative reporting can be divided between various senior academic and administrative roles. Increasingly administrative directors work in a matrix structure, with reporting to both a senior academic and senior administrative role.

The introduction of Deputy and Pro Vice-Chancellors, of Chief Operating Officers or Directors of Administration has changed and arguably diminished the more traditional senior administrative role of Secretary (and Registrar). The role of Secretary can be combined with these other senior roles in the university, such as the Chief Operating Officer, General Legal Counsel and others, for example, or it can stand alone. This dynamic variety is a consequence of the Secretary being a connector between the network of individuals, roles, groups and structures that lead, manage and govern a higher education institution.

In the United Kingdom, for example, in pre-1992 universities, created as private chartered corporations, the clerk to the governing body also typically had some managerial responsibilities. In the newer Higher Education Corporations, established by the Education Reform Act 1988 as designated statutory bodies, they did not. Increasingly as higher education expands, higher education institutions grow in size and specialisation increases so the secretarial, managerial and advisory elements are increasingly likely to be separately recognised. For example, the UK Association of Heads of University Administration (AHUA), which is the representative body for senior university managers, now says of its members:

> Each institutional member can nominate up to two individuals as its representatives. They must be senior university managers, responsible for their institution's professional services and/or the administration of the governing body, and report to the Vice-Chancellor or Chair of Council or equivalent. Job titles include Registrar, Chief Operating Officer, Head of Administration, University Secretary.[1]

This clear recognition of the separation of executive and governance functions is also found in the Association of Australian University Secretaries (AAUS), formed in September 2011. The purpose of the Association is:

> to ensure that good corporate governance frameworks, systems, processes and practices exist within Higher Education Providers and that the officers responsible for the provision or oversight of such governance responsibilities can offer their Governing Bodies, Chancellors and Vice-Chancellors a broad range of advice on issues, contemporary practices and benchmarking comparisons around corporate governance practices within the sector.[2]

Membership is open to officers of Higher Education Providers in Australia who:

> occupy the role of or undertake the duties of a University Secretary, Head of a University Secretariat, Head of a Governance Office or like roles or such other persons approved as a member by the Executive Committee.

In Ireland the Code titled 'Governance of Irish Universities' (HEA, 2012) makes detailed provisions for the Secretary, as follows:

> 2.1.2 The role of university Secretary shall include the duty to keep governing authority members briefed in respect of all relevant developments in governance and accountability.

> (p. 30)

And:

> 3.1.1.5 All members of the governing authority should have independent access to the advice and services of the Secretary of the university who must ensure that governing authority members are fully aware of the appropriate rules, regulations and procedures.

3.1.1.6 In the normal course outside legal or other advice required will be obtained by the Secretary on behalf of the governing authority in accordance with the collective nature of its responsibilities. Notwithstanding the foregoing, a governing authority should consider making provision for the seeking in exceptional circumstances of independent legal or other professional advice by an individual member or group of members at the reasonable expense of the university; the Secretary shall deal with the matter in accordance with procedures to be laid down by the governing authority.

(p. 42)

An OECD *et al.* (2010) report on governance in higher education summarised the position as follows:

Administrative positions, and especially those in direct contact with the governing board and the chief executive, are recognised as major power players whose influence far exceeds administrative duties. The Irish, United Kingdom and Scottish guidelines identify the secretary as an important and independent official who provides full information to the governing board and the CEO, including legal advice.

(p. 55)

Outside of higher education, the governance role described in this chapter most closely correlates to the company secretary. In higher education even when the role of Secretary is combined with others it is more often than not named separately, e.g. Registrar and Secretary. For the purposes of this chapter, the term Secretary, therefore, is preferred given the focus here is on higher education governance and not on the management of professional administrative services. Regardless of the variances, what each person with the title will have in common is that they will be a chief administrative officer of a higher education institution, in charge of a secretariat, supporting the main governing body.

Where the role of Secretary is combined

The question for those institutions where the role of Secretary is combined is whether any individual occupant can at the same time remain independent and objective. Leaving aside the assessment of workload in any wider remit, the primary consideration must be whether conflicts of interest will arise between the separate roles, which impede the independent exercise of the role of the Secretary. The Chair, Vice-Chancellor, the main governing body or executive board will look for independent advice and if any joint role impedes independence, or the appearance of independence, then it may become problematic. Back in 1979 Geoff Lockwood, the Registrar and Secretary at the University of Sussex, expressed this perception problem as follows:

It is often difficult to believe that a Registrar can advise a Vice-Chancellor on one line of action but be neutral in the Senate debate on it and then record and implement the Senate's amendments or rejections – faithfully and thoroughly.

(Lockwood, 1979, p. 309)

Lockwood's same perception problem can also arise when the main governing body want advice on, seek to reject or amend proposals from the Vice-Chancellor or the executive more broadly, or want to amend their reserved and delegated powers.

For example, a Chief Operating Officer or Director of Administration is likely to be closely involved with the running of the university and may be the Vice-Chancellor's aide in that task. The Secretary will be ensuring good governance, adherence to the governing instruments, and oversight by the governing body – advising the Chair. Although in most circumstances both roles will be possible (where combined) through a careful balancing of advice, in any period of friction or issue of trust between the governing body and the executive board the performance of both roles may become problematic. There will be occasions when everyone needs to understand that the Secretary is appointed by, reports to, is instructed by the governing body, and is independent of the executive management of the institution. In the event of dispute between the Vice-Chancellor and the Chair, or the governing body and the executive, the Secretary has to form an independent and impartial view on the powers and procedures, apply good governance principles, and advise each as to what is correct and in the best interests of the institution.

The Secretary should, from time to time, undertake a (re-)consideration of their role and how they are functioning within it, to ensure they are able to be and are seen to be objective, independent and dispassionate.

Constitutional status

The national law on higher education may make provisions for how a higher education institution is internally constituted and run. National law can dictate not only the necessary roles or bodies an institution must have but also their competences, membership, selection processes, size and decision-making processes.

In the listed company environment, the UK Corporate Governance Code, issued by the Financial Reporting Council (FRC) early in 2018, retained a provision for the appointment and removal of the company secretary as a matter for the board as a whole, which acts as an important precondition of their independence.

The English Committee for University Chairs Higher Education Code of Governance (CUC, 2014) similarly states:

The Secretary (or Clerk) is responsible to the governing body for the provision of operational and legal advice in relation to compliance with governing instruments, including standing orders. He/she is also responsible for ensuring information provided to the governing body is timely, appropriate and enables an informed discussion so that it may effectively discharge its responsibilities.

(p. 26)

Further that:

> All members of the governing body must have access to the services of the Clerk. Arrangements for the appointment or removal of the Secretary/Clerk may be defined by governing instruments; where they are not, it must be a decision for the governing body as a whole.

(p. 26)

The Scottish Code similarly gives this protection, as follows:

> The Secretary to the governing body must ensure compliance with all procedures and ensure that the governing body is appropriately supported such that it is able to discharge its duties. All members must have access to the advice and services of the Secretary to the governing body, and the appointment and removal of the Secretary must be a decision of the governing body as a whole.
> (Committee of the Chairs of Scottish Higher Education
> Institutions, 2017, p. 19)

This provision gives the role of Secretary a constitutional status. In some cases, in the UK, the role of Secretary in a higher education setting is protected in the governing instruments of the institution, so they are appointed by and can only be removed by the governing body. For example, the Statute of the University of Leeds contains the powers of Council, in which is included the power:

> To elect – and where appropriate remove from office – the Secretary to the University for such periods and under such conditions as may be determined by the Council after consultation, as appropriate with the Senate.
> (www.leeds.ac.uk/secretariat/statutes.html)

Where that specific provision, or similar, is not already present the CUC Higher Education Code of Governance (or its Scottish equivalent) provides it.

Characteristics of the role of Secretary

While defining the role of Secretary in constitutional or structural terms may be problematic given the different national contexts, it is perhaps easier to set out the characteristics required of the role or person to perform the role successfully, however constituted. Hampshire-Cowan (2016) set out what she called the 4 C's:

there are four essential characteristics necessary for the board professional as a helpmate in the advancement of a strong and effective president-board chair relationship. The board professional must garner the trust of both the president and the board chair and demonstrate the first three Cs: competence, character, and courage. These three characteristics are preconditions to the fourth C, credibility, the basis upon which the board professional engenders the respect and trust of the president and the board chair.

While not as 'catchy' perhaps, and not to negate Hampshire-Cowan's list, seven characteristics are described below: competence, credibility, impartiality, empathy, trust, courage and influence.

Competence

The Secretary should know or have independent access to advice on the applicable national higher education law, have a working understanding of the institutional governing instruments, procedures and protocols that apply in their sphere of operation. They need knowledge of what good governance is and how it can be achieved, including the application of any national or institutional Governance Code or best practice guidance. They need to understand what external reporting or assurances are required to be given to third parties, supervisory, funder or regulatory bodies. They should understand the institutional strategy and the wider policy context. The Secretary should be a recognised institutional expert and trusted source of advice; making available a reservoir of knowledge to the Chair, President, governing body and Executive Board. The administration of the functional roles and responsibilities of the secretariat should be done effectively and efficiently. An effective secretariat does not guarantee good governance but good governance is impossible to achieve without being served by competent administration.

Credibility

Some mistake the term secretary in its modern common usage as denoting a junior administrative role. The term originally had had something to do with keeping secrets, or confidences. The Secret-ary. The Medieval Latin '*secretarius*' meant a clerk and confidant, a title applied to those whose duties pertained to private matters, linked to the Latin '*secretarium*', a Council chamber, conclave or consistory. The King's Secretary dealt with the monarch's correspondence. Those involved with the correspondence, and activities of the powerful, assumed the title of Secretary. This did not of course mean the Secretary was powerful, influential perhaps, but they could be characterised as a literate and faithful servant.

In the UK government, senior politicians still have the title Secretary of State, and the most senior civil servants are titled Permanent Secretary or Private Secretary. However, the closest correlate within modern government, where derived from the Westminster system, is the Cabinet Secretary, responsible for policy advice and administrative support to the Prime Minister and to the Cabinet. They prepare the agenda of cabinet meetings, administer the Ministerial Code, govern the conduct of ministers, and have responsibility for day-to-day procedural matters of the Cabinet and Cabinet committees.

In a higher education context, this responsibility was put (overly) simply in the Halpin Review (2018):

> It is the job of the Chair of Council to run the Council and the job of the Vice-Chancellor (the most senior employed officer of the university) to run the university. The Council as a collective and through the Chair does not manage the university but holds the Vice-Chancellor to account for its successful running and for achieving the Strategy as determined from time to time by Council. The Secretary ensures regulatory compliance and facilitates good governance. The three officers: Chair, Vice-Chancellor and Secretary have a crucial role in working collaboratively to ensure effective governance.
>
> (p. 10)

In this 'Chair, Vice-Chancellor and Secretary' triadic relationship, the Secretary should be visibly independent, confident in speaking without fear and acting objectively in the best interests of the institution within the law. This involves credibility and integrity but also professional knowledge and understanding of the regulatory framework within which the institution operates.

Impartiality

The UK Committee for University Chairs (CUC, 2014) Higher Education Code of Governance states:

> Good governance requires a set of strong relationships based on mutual respect, trust and honesty to be maintained between the governing body, the Clerk to the Board, the Vice-Chancellor and the senior management team.
>
> (p. 5)

Maintaining healthy working relationships with both the Chair and the President, based on trust and competence, requires impartiality towards both. The Secretary must be trusted to hold of the confidences of each. While the Chair can say, for example, 'my Council', and the President can say 'my Executive Board' the Secretary cannot say either but they can say 'my institution' alongside the other two. Equally, the Chief Operating Officer and Chief Financial Officer will have operational responsibilities for delivery of the running of the institution, or have some share of the distributed authority within the institution, which the Secretary (often) does not share. As both the Chair and President will change, as will the members of the governing body and Executive Board, it is important not to over personalise the loyalty owed to the Chair, President, to the governing body or to Executive members. The Secretary must rather, instead, maintain an appropriate emotional distance and transcend any person, personality or faction and guard the constitution. They must maintain their stance as a trusted and impartial advisor on all matters within their remit, with those involved knowing that the advice given is itself given in confidence. From time to time specific issues will arise where the Chair (and the governing body) and the Vice-Chancellor (and the Executive) will need to work closely together, but each from their own proper perspective, with the Secretary as a trusted conduit in order to ensure effective governance where each other's needs and concerns are properly understood.

Empathy

Impartiality should not though be mistaken for lack of empathy or perhaps as the need for any isolationism of governance activities from the daily pressures and politics, which run through the institutions committee rooms. As efficient as governing bureaucracies need to be they are not cold or uncaring. Good governance facilitates the institution to be true to itself, to be successful, transparently to live out its core values, to achieve its (founding) aims and goals. Secretaries should care deeply about the history, culture, values and goals of the institution they serve and for the people who work with and for it. Secretaries are often part of the contested decision-making processes; ensuring the decisions needed are well-framed, considered in the right place, by the right people, that those involved are well-informed, that the decisions needed are transparently made, the outcome recorded, retained and communicated. The Secretary is often present as decisions are being made and is aware of the alternatives, the risks, the possible negative outcomes, aware of who was in favour and who not and why. Empathy does not compromise independence; the Secretary faces the same dilemmas as their senior colleagues but with a particular perspective.

Trust

The Secretary should be readily available to advise the Chair. Sitting next to the Chair at governing body, for example, means advice can be given as required and it signals the accountability of the role to the governing body. It holds that members of the governing body should have access to the advice of the Secretary, who is responsible for advising the whole of the governing body on all governance matters. Where members want to exercise their rights to access independent advice the Secretary can and should facilitate it. The Secretary, by maintaining an independent stance allows the members of the governing body to be properly independent. The Secretary stands as a trusted advisor on governance matters to all members, and should always do whatever is necessary within the law to ensure that the independent status of governing body members is protected so they can effectively provide constructive challenge and hold the executive, including the

Vice-Chancellor, to account. To maintain trust and accountability, this requires that advice given by the Secretary is accurate, well founded, evidenced, factual and defensible.

Courage

Good governance and a healthy corporate culture can and occasionally must be challenging, to avoid failures. It is the job of the Secretary to alert the President, governing body or the Executive when a proposed action would exceed its powers, or be contrary to a legislative requirement or a regulatory condition. Where the governing body or Executive Board have set out schemes of delegation to other groups or individuals, who are given authority to act, the Secretary can remind those people or groups of their powers and the limits of that delegation. For this, the role therefore requires the seniority, independence, impartiality and judgement, needed to work effectively in line with the principles of good governance.

When a recommendation is not accepted or a decision taken but not as expected, often the Secretary has diplomatically to communicate this, but also enforce the will of the governing body. Clarity is often needed on when a matter is being reported for note, because the decision has already been validly taken as compared to when a recommendation is made for consideration and decision because authority has not been delegated. Similarly, to be clear when a matter relates to the provision of information sufficient to provide assurance without transferring accountability back to the senior body which is being assured. A clear-headed focus on powers, their allocation and the terms of delegation is required to maintain the required transparency and discipline in decision-making and reporting that makes for effective governance. Where courage is most needed is where there is personal risk. For example, where the triadic relationship between the Chair, President and Secretary breaks down. Or in instances when the Secretary has to act out the role of the steward of the long-term interests of the university by challenging behaviour or ultra vires acts or the misuse of executive or governing power. The Secretary advises the Chair where potential or actual conflict exists between the governing body and the President and/or his/her Executive Board.

Influence (but not power)

Lockwood (1979) wrote about a perception problem he perceived he had in the role he then held, as follows:

> Some groups see the Registrar as a sinister influence, hiding behind an image of servile neutrality but performing an obstructive political role in defence of the status quo; a manipulator of both events and the interpretations of them. Other groups see the Registrar as the wise steward using his [sic] duties and permanency to protect the institution against radical whims.
>
> (p. 308)

A problem that he amplifies as follows:

> the better the Registrar's advice, the more likely it is to be regularly accepted and presented to committees by senior officers. Therefore, members begin to assume that the Registrar has too much power. It is also easy to sympathise with suspicions that a Registrar cannot with-stand the temptation to use his [sic] control over agendas, papers, minutes and implementation to minimise or unduly control decision-taking by committees. However, recognising those perceptions as genuine does not mean that they are accurate since they overlook the key role of Vice-Chancellors, deans or committee chairmen [sic].
>
> (pp. 309–310)

What is being wrestled with here is Robert Berdahl's distinction (1999) between procedural autonomy (deciding or advising on 'how' to do something in university governance) and substantive autonomy (advising on 'what' to do). Many are comfortable to see the Secretary advising on procedure but, of course, he/she will also be called to give independent advice on the matters themselves, to communicate decisions once made, to assert the outcome on behalf of the relevant authority and to report on implementation. None of this behaviour transfers the proper locus of authority from the deciding authority to the secretary who supports its effective functioning. It does mean that well-timed advice, given with good intention, has influence on the proper exercise of power.

Possible elements of the Secretary role

The Secretary must act on the instructions of the governing body itself. The role of the Secretary is to ensure sound governance. That is, ensuring that the main governing body and the Senate operate in accordance with the highest standards of governance as set out, for example, in any institutional, national or international Higher Education Code of Governance. National guidance defining good university governance now exists in several countries including Australia, Denmark, the United Kingdom, the United States and Ireland. The activities, which together ensure sound governance, may vary and any list, as below, can only be indicative.

Clerk to the governing body, Senate/Academic Board and Executive Board

This aim may be practically achieved by the Secretary serving as the clerk to the governing body, and often its sub-committees, advising the Chair, setting the agenda, providing guidance to the governing body about its responsibilities, scope of powers and discretion, as set out in the institutions governing instruments, e.g. Charter (founding law), Statutes (semi-permanent primary law) and

Regulations (secondary adjustable law). In some cases, this may extend to also being clerk to the Senate and Executive Board or managing the people who perform these roles. Whether or not this is the case, there may be a role to ensure there is an appropriate interface between the governing body and the Senate/Academic Board and to the executive.

Effectiveness reviews and governor development

Regular reviews of the effectiveness of the institution's governance arrangements help ensure continuous improvement and development and to identify issues that need remedy. Often this work also facilitates the appraisal of members of governing bodies and enables them to express their development needs.

Maintaining and amending regulations

Where there is discretion to do so the Secretary may have to ensure the institution has in place adequate and effective governance arrangements, for example, by maintaining and updating regulations (the Calendar) of the governing body and the Senate or Academic Board. This may include details of the membership and terms of reference of key committees (the Almanac) and a scheme of delegation to designated persons or committees.

Agenda setting

In preparing an annual schedule of business and a particular agenda for each meeting, the Secretary ensures the matters brought to the governing body and to the Senate are appropriate to their scope and powers. The Secretary is expected to ensure that papers are supplied to members in a timely manner, are concise and appropriate in content, and to advise on the matters if required. They may also ensure compliance with and make necessary amendments to the governing body and Senate's schemes of delegation. Here the Secretary is at the service of the governing body and cannot amend schemes of delegation or set the agenda, both are collaborative or subordinate ultimately to the Chair and the governing body itself.

Providing protocols

The Secretary may be turned to for advice or a ruling on the conduct of meetings and in those circumstances may want to ensure the existence of procedures or protocols for the conduct of business. This could include, for example, when Chair's action can be taken, the calling of special meetings, the establishment of task and finish groups, how agenda items are proposed, how attendance at meetings is decided, the rules for debate, protocols for dealing with urgent business, format of minutes, closed items, late papers, voting and quoracy.

Succession planning, recruitment and induction

The Secretary may have a responsibility for ensuring succession planning in the case of memberships of the bodies they serve. Supporting where they exist the Nominations Committees in the appointment of members to those bodies and their associated committees, including maintaining a skills and experience matrix, and a recruitment strategy for appointed Council and Senate members. The Secretary also may be responsible for the induction of new governing body and Senate/Academic Board members.

Managing conflicts of interest

The Secretary will ensure the members of the governing body and members of the executive (those with senior management responsibilities) are fit and proper persons, that a Register of Interest is maintained and any conflicts of interest, gifts and hospitality are declared and managed appropriately. This may extend to wider ethical matters in the institution, including, for example, effective operation of a framework for decision making on ethical matters or responsibility for a Code of Ethics. Where positions are elected the Secretary may be the Returning Officer for those elections.

Maintaining records

As the Secretary maintains a record of decision-making – who made what decision, when and with what information – this often extends to the management of corporate records including the organisation and retention (whether on paper or electronically) of the institutional record; controlling the creation, version control, distribution, filing, retention, storage and disposal of corporate records. For example, keeping minute books which are retained and stored in an institutional archive. When a controversy breaks, often, the first matter to determine is who knew what, when, what was done and what the record shows. If a reliable record is not (made) available problems can be compounded by what is then seen as a lack of transparency or in the worst cases as an alleged attempt to cover-up.

Providing constitutional and legal advice

The Secretary must ensure compliance with all relevant procedures. It is the responsibility of the Secretary to alert the governing body that any proposed action would exceed the governing body's powers, be contrary to legislation, to any national code or local institutional constitutional rules. The Secretary will often have responsibility for providing or obtaining legal advice for the governing body or other senior officers. In-house legal advisors may be part of the governance and compliance team (the Secretariat) and/or the institution may maintain a panel of legal firms whose advice is retained under contract.

Providing assurance

The Secretary may directly provide assurance to internal or external bodies or where appropriate obtain on behalf of governing body and Senate/Academic Board necessary reports, from the responsible persons internally, which seeks to assure them. Governance assurance schedules or 'maps' can identify individuals who have responsibility for reporting on various matters, e.g. Health and Safety, Anti-Bribery, Anti-Money Laundering, Fraud Policy and Procedures, Data Protection, etc. and when these will or should come to the governing body. This may include, importantly, managing the interface between governing body and Senate/Academic Board with regard to the institutions academic governance and provision of assurance about academic standards.

Performance and risk

Where the governing body adopts a strategic plan, aims and goals they will then want to receive information about or approve key strategies and plans to execute the intentions in the Strategic Plan. This can include approval of key performance indicators, which are then monitored by the governing body. It may assess all aspects of the institutions performance, in the broadest sense, using a range of mechanisms. In these instances, the governing body must be satisfied they have processes in place to monitor and evaluate the performance and effectiveness of the institution against those plans and key performance indicators. The Secretary may have a role in ensuring that performance data are presented to the governing body in a format agreed by them and which allows the discharge of responsibility for institutional performance measurement. Equally, the institution may operate risk management and control arrangements, monitoring risk through a corporate risk register. A significant trend is towards the creation of Governance and Compliance Offices in the light of regulatory requirements. Some of these now have responsibility for internal audit. In the corporate world compliance offices or teams are common, and again because of the growth of regulatory requirements.

Transparency and accountability

National or regional governments, regulators, funders and professional bodies – indeed any number of external third parties including individuals – may claim rights or place obligations to receive information and assurances or demand certain institutional actions. The Secretary may have a role to determine their legitimacy in the first place. Where these are legitimate legal, regulatory or public interest demands on the institution the Secretary will want to ensure the governing body is able to meet the obligations. This can extend to publishing the agenda, minutes or decisions of internal bodies or responding to requests for information. In some instances, the Secretary may advise the governing body that a particular obligation or intrusion is unwarranted and the request declined.

In the service of transparency and accountability, the governing body may have important sub-committees where the independence of the Secretary is required, such as an Audit Committee or a Senior Remuneration Committee.

The above duties are examples that cannot be other than illustrative and not intended to be comprehensive or defining.

Conclusion

In this chapter, the Secretary has been viewed as being at the heart of good governance. The secretarial role has been used as a device to personify the values, characteristics and functions of institutional governance. It has been argued that good governance is both a consequence of and a necessary precondition for devolution or decentralisation of autonomy and independence at the institutional level and that this has (re-)emphasised governance, alongside management and leadership. The presence of the Secretary as a steward provides a constitutional guarantor for external and internal stakeholders that delegated statutory and regulatory rights and powers have been legitimately exercised within the leadership and management of the higher education institution. The Secretary facilitates the exercise of collective and individual rights and powers in pursuance of institutional goals. With the focus on corporate governance, accountability and regulation of increasingly autonomous institutions, the role of the Secretary has grown in importance. In many ways, the Secretary is the guardian of the university's proper compliance with the law, its own governing instruments, any imposed regulatory conditions and best practice as expressed in national codes.

Notes

1 https://ahua.ac.uk/membership/
2 www.jcu.edu.au/association-of-australian-university-secretaries

References

Berdahl, R. (1999) 'Universities and Governments in the 21st Century: The US Experience', in D. Braun and F.X. Merrien (eds) *Towards a New Model of Governance for Universities? A Comparative View*, Higher Education Policy Series, Jessica Kingsley Publishers Ltd., London/Philadelphia, pp. 59–77.

Committee of the Chairs of Scottish Higher Education Institutions (2017) 'Scottish Code of Good Higher Education Governance' [Retrieved 31 December 2018 from www.scottishuniversitygovernance.ac.uk/wp-content/uploads/2016/08/Scot-Code-Good-HE-Governance-A4.pdf]

Committee on the Financial Aspects of Corporate Governance (1992) 'Report of the Committee on the Financial Aspects of Corporate Governance 1 December 1992', Gee and Co Ltd. [Retrieved 31 July 2018 from www.icaew.com/-/media/corporate/files/library/subjects/corporate-governance/financial-aspects-of-corporate-governance.ashx?la=en]

Committee on Standards in Public Life (1995) 'The 7 Principles of Public Life'. [Retrieved 31 July 2018 from www.gov.uk/government/publications/the-7-principles-of-public-life/the-7-principles-of-public-life--2]

CUC (2014) 'The Higher Education Code of Governance', Committee of University Chairs. [Retrieved 28 July 2018 from www.universitychairs.ac.uk/wp-content/uploads/2015/02/Code-Final.pdf]

Fielden, J. (2008) 'Global Trends in University Governance'. Education working paper series no. 9, World Bank, Washington, DC. [Retrieved 31 July 2018 from http://documents.worldbank.org/curated/en/588801468140667685/Global-trends-in-university-governance]

Fletcher, D.E. (2007) 'Recent Developments in Governance in the UK Higher Education Sector', in IAUGB (ed.) 1st Meeting of International Association of University Governing Bodies – Society Meets University (Granada 23–24 October 2007), International Association of University Governing Bodies, Madrid, pp. 103–108.

Halpin Review, The (2018) 'A Review of Council Effectiveness at the University of Bath', Halpin Partnership Ltd, London. [Retrieved 30 July 2018 from www.bath.ac.uk/publications/the-halpin-review/attachments/halpin-review.pdf]

Hampshire-Cowan, A. (2016) 'The Four Cs of Board Leadership', *Trusteeship Magazine*, September/October edition. Association of Governing Boards of Universities and Colleges. [Retrieved 31 July 2018 from www.agb.org/trusteeship/2016/septemberoctober/the-four-cs-of-board-leadership]

HEA (2012) 'Governance of Irish Universities', Higher Education Authority. [Retrieved 29 July 2018 from http://hea.ie/assets/uploads/2017/05/Governance-of-Irish-Universities-2012.pdf]

Holmes, D.R. (1998) 'Some Personal Reflections on the Role of Administrators and Managers in British Universities', *Perspectives*, Vol. 2, No. 4. pp. 110–117.

Lazzeretti, L. and Tavoletti, E. (2006) 'Governance Shifts in Higher Education: A Cross-National Comparison', *European Educational Research Journal*, Vol. 5, No. 1, pp. 18–26.

Llewellyn, D. (2009) 'The Role and Influence of the Secretary in UK Higher Education Governing Bodies', Leadership Foundation for Higher Education. [Retrieved 30 July 2018 from www.guildhe.ac.uk/wp-content/uploads/2013/05/role_of_secretary.pdf]

Lockwood, G. (1979) 'The Role of the Registrar in Today's University', *Higher Education*, Vol. 8, pp. 299–320.

Magalhães, A. and Amaral, A. (2010) 'Mapping Out Discourses on Higher Education Governance', in J. Huisman (ed.) *International Perspectives on the Governance of Higher Education: Alternative Frameworks for Coordination*, Routledge, London, pp. 182–197.

OECD, Hénard, F. and Mitterle, A. (2010) 'Governance and Quality Guidelines in Higher Education: A Review of Governance Arrangements and Quality Assurance Guidelines', OECD, Paris. [Retrieved 30 July 2018 from www.oecd.org/education/imhe/46064461.pdf]

O'Neill, O. (2002) *A Question of Trust: The BBC Reith Lectures 2002*, Cambridge University Press, Cambridge.

Scott, R.A. (2018) *How University Boards Work: A Guide for Trustees, Officers, and Leaders in Higher Education*, Johns Hopkins University Press, Baltimore.

Shattock, M. (2003) *Managing Successful Universities*, The Society for Research into Higher Education and the Open University Press, Maidenhead.

Shattock, M. (2006) *Managing Good Governance in Higher Education*, Open University Press, Maidenhead.

Shattock, M. (ed.) (2014) *International Trends in University Governance: Autonomy, Self-Government and the Distribution of Authority*, Routledge, London.

Tricker, R.I. (1984) *Corporate Governance: Practices, Procedures and Powers in British Companies and their Boards of Directors*, Gower Publishing, Aldershot.

Chapter 3

Higher education governance and policy on trial

Jonathan Nicholls

In Charles Dickens' *Our Mutual Friend*, the illiterate Boffins (from whom we derive the familiar nickname for a person engaged on arcane research) come into a great fortune and decide to adopt an orphan. They are recommended to Betty Higden, an old woman, who herself fosters orphaned children. One of her wards is Sloppy who can read:

> 'For I aint, you must know,' said Betty, 'much of a hand at reading writing-hand, though I can read my Bible and most print. And I do love a newspaper. You mightn't think it, but Sloppy is a beautiful reader of a newspaper. He do the Police in different voices.'
>
> (Dickens, 1865, Book the First, Chapter Sixteen)

In other words, in the accounts of criminal trials that were a stock-in-trade of newspapers of the time, Sloppy animates his readings by giving character to the police called to the witness stand.

This chapter is necessarily focused on England, but the book of which it forms a part ranges across the United Kingdom and internationally. It will seem that, particularly perhaps, in England, because of the events narrated here, but more generally too, policies that are shaping internal models of governance and those models themselves are on trial and under scrutiny such as we have not experienced in England since perhaps the 1980s. And there have indeed been different voices of those appointed to uphold standards and to regulate. Why we have reached the current point with new regulatory powers imposed on institutions, and the more direct policing of standards and quality, and what consequences may follow, are the subject of this chapter.

It is doubtful whether universities have ever enjoyed complete freedom from external authority and the exercise of power by governments. Early forms of the studia generalia (the formal status in the medieval period for what we would call universities) were under papal jurisdiction. What was taught and studied was prescribed and limited. Discoveries were made, and new ideas were generated but if these were heterodox then secular and religious punishment could follow. Favouritism might lead to the suppression of rival centres of learning and the promotion of others. Oxford and Cambridge flourished as a duopoly in England for so long, not because they asserted their independence from worldly or religious authority, but because their status was guaranteed by regal proclamation that forbad the founding of other universities and because the universities themselves required an oath on their masters (their staff) that they would not lecture outside the two cities. These protectionist policies led quickly to the suppression of infant universities in the thirteenth century such as those in Northampton and Stamford. It is indeed arguable that the longevity of the idea of a university and especially the particular examples that celebrate foundations of 500 years or longer is because they have been of value to the state and/or the church and fulfilled their needs even during periods of institutional moribundity, such as the eighteenth century in England. The institutions have accommodated themselves to those needs, even at times of great civil stress and disruption.

As most recently David Willetts points out in *A University Education* (Willetts, 2017, p. 14), within this framework of external authority and power, the term 'university' means something like an independent community or entity; it does not mean a place 'where all the arts and faculties are studied' (a rare solecism in Dr Johnson's Dictionary). Other medieval uses of the Latin word 'universitas' make this point clear (see for example the entry in *The Dictionary of Medieval Latin from British Sources* [Ashdowne *et al.*, 2013]). As Willetts points out, as those other uses (for example of a town community) became obsolete, the singular use for a university stuck. This idea of an independent and self-governing community is enshrined in the legal identity of the Universities of Oxford and Cambridge: 'Chancellor, Masters, and Scholars', the formula by which all their business is transacted, both academic and corporate. The power of the idea has shaped the governance models of those two universities, with their large 'governing bodies' of the Congregation (Oxford) and Regent House (Cambridge) under whose deliberative, electoral and legislative powers the subsidiary executive organs of governance operate. Yet those universities of today have been shaped, not so much by internal governance reform (which has taken place incrementally), but by the exercise of successive external reform imposed on them during the course of the nineteenth century and the early part of the twentieth century by various Acts and statutory reform (the principal Universities of Oxford and Cambridge Acts referred to in this period became law in 1859, 1877 and 1923). The legal status, and principles and values of self-governance may have survived but the state has never been unwilling to intervene to impose its view of what it and the society it represents required of those two institutions.

A wider view of how the state has shaped higher education and how it has been governed during the last hundred years or so is admirably dealt with by Professor Michael Shattock in a synoptic working paper published in 2017 (Shattock, 2017). Shattock draws on a lifetime's experience as a senior leader in higher education and from his knowledge as a leading scholar of educational governance and management. He makes the point that critics of current trends in university governance tend to look back to a utopian traditional model but that the evidence suggests that the internal balances between for example academic bodies and the governing body (often a Senate and a Council) were always to a considerable extent contingent on external conditions and fluctuated accordingly. He ascribes less direct influence by the state through imposed constitutional change (other than in the case of the Higher Education Corporations as the model for the incorporation of the former Polytechnics in 1988) but by the pressure for change to which institutions reacted – and sometimes over-reacted. The legislative evidence would support this view regarding constitutional change. But I would depart from Shattock in arguing that it is too easy to underestimate the power of other legislation, the agency of government departments, individual ministers, and various non-legislative acts and policies that have determined the future of universities, tested their purposes, and shaped the form and practice of their governance.

The history of the Universities Grant Committee (the UGC, subsequently the Universities Funding Council and, in England, the Higher Education Funding Council for England [HEFCE]) is also explored by Shattock and other commentators in separate publications (Shattock and Burdahl, 1984; Shattock, 1994). Its loss under the Higher Education and Research Act of 2017 is still lamented by many. No doubt, as its defenders would argue, the UGC, while originally advising the government about the funding of universities, over time came to fulfil a vital role as an interpreter between universities and government to deflect, improve or propose alternatives to ministerial whim or initiative. Yet, in less than thirty years since its establishment, it had also been given new powers by ministers that extended its original role in significant ways. Between 1919 and 1946, for example, the original terms of reference of the UGC, as established by government, were expanded from 'To enquire into the financial needs of the University education of the United Kingdom and to advise the Government as to the application of any grants that may be made by Parliament to meet the', by, in 1943, the addition of 'To collect, examine, and make available, information relating to university education throughout the United Kingdom', and by this, in 1946:

> to assist, in consultation with the universities and the other bodies concerned, the preparation and execution of such plans for the development of the universities as may from time to time be required in order to ensure that they are fully adequate to national needs.
>
> (Shattock and Burdahl, 1984, p. 473)

Here plainly, immediately post-war, was the explicit development of a body that originally was to enquire and advise to one that was to assist in a planning role to meet national needs.

Shortly after the article was published from which this history is taken, the UGC became the body through which the assessment of research was first initiated in the United Kingdom in 1986 and later, in the early 1990s, the assessment of teaching through the Teaching Quality Assessment programme.

It became a regulator. A regulator which remained a hand's breadth from government (no longer fully arm's-length), had powers of funding and took a stewardship role over a definable sector of institutions. But a regulator nonetheless. It just did the police in different voices. Consider, for example, its role on behalf of the Charity Commission to regulate universities-as-charities, to check compliance with Prevent Duty legislation, to take a direct interest in the development and performance of governance and audit, to require financial information, and maintain a risk register of institutions in peril. All these – and there are many other examples that could be cited – have the voice of external authority and regulation. Much of this was done on behalf of, and at the behest of, government. There was no corner of the growing range of university activities, and the growing number of registered providers of higher education, in which the HEFCE did not shine a light or provide advice or expect co-operation. Yet it did also speak for institutions in the shadowy game of negotiation with government departments, it could facilitate resolutions to crises, and it was a powerful voice when it came to settlements about fees and funding. Why therefore have its regulatory roles transferred to the Office for Students (OfS) and UK Research and Innovation (UKRI)? And what, in this new settlement for students and universities, are the future prospects for the exercise and management of governance arrangements in higher education?

There is a gap in the scholarly literature for a detailed history of the last decade or so of the relationship between universities and government. That is not the purpose of this chapter. Nonetheless, the answer to my questions would be part of such a history. This has been a time of the greatest change in higher education in the United Kingdom since the Robbins Report of 1963 and the accompanying expansion of universities and student numbers in the 1960s. In terms of central planning and intervention it is unmatched since the 1980s. The arguments about the funding of universities, how a market might operate more fairly for new providers and for students, and for whose benefit universities exist, has been conducted under intense scrutiny about social justice, quality and standards, and pay and performance. The backdrop to this drama is a political and social landscape that has been altered beyond recognition by the consequences of the financial crisis of 2008, the rise of populism and threats to long-standing international arrangements that date back to the post-war settlements. The phenomenon of social media has connected more people than ever before. It has encouraged and facilitated alternative views of events that refreshingly may correct self-serving elitist narratives. But it can also dismayingly propagate falsehood and mistrust. In a vacuum of truth, trust and reliability, regulation and micro-accountability often flourish as the reflex of the need for control. We have needed the intellectual rigour, enquiry and disinterested examination of universities more than ever to help us understand the contemporary world in the flux briefly described here. Universities have been more adept in this space than they have in responding intelligently to the consequences of student fees and the determination of the government to redress the perceived imbalance whereby the interests of the paying student are seemingly subordinate to strongly vested interests in retaining the status quo of power and authority.

It would be easy to overlook in surveying this history, the principal recommendations of Lord Browne of Madingley's *Independent Review of Higher Education Funding and Student Finance*, which was established in November 2009, reported in October 2010, and on which the coalition government's proposals to introduce the capped £9,000 fee regime was based. That would be a mistake. A member of the Review was Sir Michael Barber, now Chair of the OfS. Another member was Sir David Eastwood, then the immediate former Chief Executive of the HEFCE. A number of features of the Review are worth noting. The student interest was prominent. The proposals 'put students at the heart of the system' (the significance of this comment in relation to the White Paper of 2011 with the same title is profound). The inadequacy of advice and guidance for students was highlighted. Competition for students between institutions was one of the perceived benefits. A Higher Education Council – independent of institutions and government – would be created and have the primary aim of protecting students' interests; of investing in high value courses; of safeguarding value for money; of setting and enforcing minimum quality levels; of overseeing measurable progress of access of students from disadvantaged backgrounds; of ensuring students received the benefit of more competition; of regulating the admission of new providers to the system; of looking after students' interests when an institution was at risk; of being the final resolver of disputes between students and institutions; and of providing an annual report to Parliament explaining how it was investing taxpayers' money and safeguarding students' investment. Those proposed functions were the product of arguments to reinforce measures to promote a market (with students as consumers; Competition and Markets Authority, 2015) and to invest further powers in a reformed funding body.

The Browne Report's recommendations on fees and funding were not adopted – prominently a capping mechanism for fees was introduced rather than letting the market determine the rate of fees to be charged by each institution. Many of the functions which were to be given to the proposed but never formed Higher Education Council (which would have combined the roles of the HEFCE, the Office for Fair Access [OFFA], the Quality Assurance Agency [QAA], and the Office of the Independent Adjudicator [OIA]) are however now secured through the Higher Education and Research Act 2017 (HERA) and the establishment under it of the OfS. The OfS includes within it the former role of OFFA as a quasi-independent function, and it determines which organisation shall be its designated quality body and designated data body. Currently these tenders have been won by the QAA and the Higher Education Statistical Agency but neither have a guarantee of continuing to be designated in the future. Only the OIA remains fully independent.

It is also worth reflection that the proposed Higher Education Council would have had no role in relation to research. The Review was not established to consider the funding of research but this absence under a body whose title suggested a holistic brief for the purposes of higher education providers, is telling and prophetic. The separation of research and its governance and funding from the governance and funding of education is possibly the most profound outcome of HERA. For the first time, these two purposes come under different government departments, although a single minister currently has responsibility for both students and science. It may encourage disintegration of governance systems within universities as well as accelerating the trend towards the establishment of major research institutes outside universities where place and regional economic need may have greater influence than quality in their location. There are practical consequences too for certain types of students, not least those undertaking research, who while as much a student as an undergraduate will be subject to two systems whose ability to collaborate meaningfully on such matters and on other key questions such as institutional financial sustainability is yet to be tested.

If HEFCE and institutions did not fully interpret the pitch and meaning of the Browne Review, it had a second chance with the White Paper, *Students at the Heart of the System*, published in 2011 and whose title, as we have seen, was drawn from a prominent phrase coined by Browne. It fumbled that chance too.

The White Paper introduced the new funding arrangements for the capped fee regime; measures to improve the student experience through 'a more responsive system'; a more diverse sector by removing regulatory barriers for alternative providers; arrangements to promote student advice and information; to improve student mobility; and to reform the regulatory environment. It also proposed a new role for the HEFCE as 'student champion'. The chapter in the White Paper on a new fit-for-purpose regulatory framework envisaged a new role for the HEFCE:

> there will be a major change of emphasis as the reforms take hold, requiring different powers and appropriate remodelling as it [the HEFCE] evolves from being primarily a funding council to also being the lead regulator for one of our most important sectors. This will include a new, explicit remit to promote the interests of students, including as consumers, with a duty to take competition implications into account when making decisions on funding. This will complement the work of the OIA in relation to individual complaints and we will legislate for reserve powers for HEFCE to intervene if evidence is found of widespread poor treatment of students.
>
> (*Higher Education: Students at the Heart of the System*, 2011, section 6.10)

The authors' regulatory framework wished to preserve the separate functions of the HEFCE, OFFA, QAA and OIA (unlike Browne who wanted to bundle them all together as noted earlier, without due regard to the conflicts of interest this might create). Work on the regulatory framework became bogged down with the Higher Education Better Regulation Group under the aegis of Universities UK picking up some of the burden; and work was underway in government departments and sector bodies to consider the best way of implementing change in the absence of new legislation. But other forces were also at work. In 2013, the former Office for Fair Trading launched a *Call for Information on the Undergraduate Higher Education Sector in England*. It conducted interviews and invited evidence. It published a report in 2014 and handed over some further lines of enquiry to the newly created Competition and Markets Authority, including for recommending proposals to improve the regulatory arrangements for higher education and to test how universities complied with consumer protection law in their dealings with students. Both enquiries led to reports, the former of which pointed out ways in which the regulatory framework no longer suited a system based on competition and choice where the student was, in effect, a consumer; and the latter which has led to the requirement for registration with the OfS for a self-assessment of how the provider complies with consumer law in this respect.

This is a simplified and highly compressed account of events and publications leading up to the ground-breaking White Paper *Success as a Knowledge Economy: Teaching Excellence, Social Mobility, & Student Choice* published in 2016. In retrospect, the conclusions of that White Paper and the urge to legislate to cut through the fog and delays, was predictable. For those working in the sector and with active involvement in national representative bodies, with civil servants, and with politicians, it became all too clear that the perceived inability of the HEFCE to champion students as expected of it, the prevarication of the universities to demonstrate better self-regulation in tune with government policy, especially with regard to what was seen as protectionist attitudes to new providers, created a frustration to ministerial ambition that was not to be thwarted. A new kind of regulator was the result.

As this chapter is being written, the process for the first registration of providers in England under the Office for Students (OfS) is underway and not yet complete. The long-term impact on governance models in the sector is uncertain. In law, through the HERA, both the OfS and the Secretary of State must have regard to the protection of institutional autonomy in the discharge of the Office's functions, and in the guidance that the Secretary of State may give to the OfS. Academic freedom is also protected in law. 'Institutional autonomy' is defined in HERA as follows:

(a) the freedom of English higher education providers within the law to conduct their day to day management in an effective and competent way,
(b) the freedom of English higher education providers—
(i) to determine the content of particular courses and the manner in which they are taught, supervised and assessed,
(ii) to determine the criteria for the selection, appointment and dismissal of academic staff and apply those criteria in particular cases, and
(iii) to determine the criteria for the admission of students and apply those criteria in particular cases.

(HERA Part 1, 2 General Duties, [8])

This does not specify the freedom to choose a particular governance model or principles. The Act permits the OfS to set a non-mandatory registration condition which it refers to as the public interest governance principle. This has become a list of required conditions for registration (varied to some degree between the class of registration that is sought) imposed by the OfS. The public interest governance principle has therefore in effect become mandatory. The OfS has addressed this in a different voice from the Act but it has the force of law. The list of required conditions is not stable. It may be changed at any time by the OfS – after consultation with the sector. The OfS has therefore decided to set a framework of principles for governance which have, by and large, the same status as the mandatory registration conditions in HERA of transparency, the fee limit, and an access and participation plan. But it has allowed itself to vary or add to them under the pressure of events or presumably political expediency. With regard to research, HERA gives the power, to the Secretary of State, subject to regard to the Haldane Principle and the balanced funding principle (HERA, 2017, section 103, which defines both principles) to give UKRI directions about the allocation or expenditure by UKRI of grants received from him or her.

This chapter has inevitably given more attention to the OfS than to the UKRI but the arrangements for determining research funding and priorities under UKRI and its subsidiary research councils and other bodies are of similar significance to the shaping of the sector by the OfS. Those arrangements will have a similar impact in the response from institutions in terms of their mission and strategy and the governance models they adopt.

When considering the regulatory framework set by the OfS, and its impact on individual providers, the four objectives that the Office has set itself are a vital point of reference.

> All students, from all backgrounds, and with the ability and desire to undertake higher education:
> Are supported to access, succeed in, and progress from, higher education.
> Receive a high quality academic experience, and their interests are protected while they study or in the event of provider, campus or course closure.
> Are able to progress into employment or further study, and their qualifications hold their value over time.
> Receive value for money.
>
> (Office for Students, 2018a, p. 14)

As the leaders of the OfS make plain at conferences and in conversation, the Office has no remit for the sector, per se. It is entirely focused on the interests of students and how these objectives are met by each provider. Never before has the collective of providers seem less represented. Universities UK does not include in its membership all providers – because its current tests for membership exclude many new providers, some of whom do bear the title of university – and the mission groups are self-regulating clubs, with many other providers uninterested or disenfranchised from inclusion. Who in the future will speak for the collective sector? Whether ultimately this state of affairs is in the best interests of students is doubtful. Student Protection Plans (designed to protect students in accordance with the second objective adopted by the OfS and policed by it) are one thing. Who will lead and negotiate the best outcome for students to continue their courses or to retain a qualification of value in the event of institutional failure is uncertain. What is certain is that imposing regulation and assuring compliance with it, to the satisfaction of a regulator, is no guarantee against failure. The history of regulators is that they tend to react to failure rather than prevent it.

Institutional autonomy is protected under law, but that protection does not include full self-determination when it comes to governance arrangements, which have now been constrained by the OfS through its conditions for registration. There is another effect of these new arrangements which must also be noted. Shattock's 2017 working paper, previously cited, illustrates nicely the ebb and flow of influence over several decades that can be charted between the two governance poles of the Senate and the Council in the older part of the sector. The OfS insists under Registration Condition E3 that 'The governing body of a provider must accept responsibility for the interactions between the provider and the OfS and its designated bodies [and] ensure the provider's compliance with all of its conditions of registration and with the OfS's accounts direction' (Office for Students, 2018a, p. 112). This could be read as transferring absolute responsibility for many academic functions to the governing body such as the maintenance of quality and standards. Prior to the establishment of the OfS, a governing body had to provide assurance of academic quality. The public interest governance conditions set by the OfS clarify that it too is requiring *assurance* from the governing body in this respect. But the change of verb from 'assure' to 'ensure' in E3 is troubling and could lead to inappropriate and improper interference by a governing body in the academic governance of a provider, in effect arrogating powers to itself which had been vested in the academic authority of that provider. This does not mean that I am calling into question a governing body's status as the ultimate authority of a provider. I do however believe that a governing body works best when in concert with the academic community who are best placed to propose, arrange and deliver the academic programme and to set the arrangements for testing its quality and standards through established peer review and student input. The governing body needs to test the systems through which these things are done and to require the evidence that would enable it to give assurance that the systems are working effectively. It cannot undertake the academic mission of the provider on behalf of the academic community.

In one respect, however, the new arrangements provide more latitude for thinking differently about governance models than the comply-or-explain regime of the Committee of University Chair's (CUC) Guide to HE Governance, adopted by the HEFCE as the benchmark for the sector it funded and registered. In recognition that a provider should be able to adopt any code or none to shape and test its governance arrangements (Office for Students,

2018a, p. 111 [paragraphs 431 and 432]), the OfS has liberated providers from the monopoly of the CUC Guide as long as the public interest governance principles are met. This is a constraint on innovation but not a straitjacket. There are some very interesting governance models emerging in the newest part of the sector – as well as some different thinking in the older part. After all, governance must add value and enhance the principles and mission of a provider rather than being a necessary but deadweight instrument of compliance that enhances bureaucracy but nothing more. For all the frustrations and faults of the governance models of Oxford and Cambridge, they are designed to preserve the founding principles of self-governing academic communities and the values that they uphold and cherish, especially those concerning academic freedom, freedom of speech, transparency and an inclusive democracy. To contribute to the pursuit of these aims, their executive governing bodies (the Councils) do not have a majority of independent members as proposed by the CUC Guide in order that more places are representative of the wider internal community. The attempt to introduce a model based on an external majority at Oxford, over a decade ago, led to revolt and retreat. Independent advice and judgement is vital but it does not, in their cases, need to be delivered through a majority of such members. It is to be welcomed that the OfS's principle regarding governing bodies is that their size and composition should be appropriate for the scale and complexity of the provider.

In Hereford, the New Model Institute of Technology and Engineering (NMITE) has adopted a governance model that embraces the essential principles of the partnership model well-known through John Lewis. Profit-sharing would of course be inappropriate in what is also a charity, but the equation that Knowledge + Influence = Reward is a founding concept for the engagement of all employees and their formal voice and influence through an Advisory Council that appoints members to the Board and can hold the President directly to account. The NMITE model is novel and will be worth longitudinal study as that institution takes full shape. The model has already been watched carefully by other new providers who have considerable interest in what is in effect a variant of employee ownership or a co-operative by other means. In the older part of the sector, recent disputes about pay and pensions have exposed how distant governing bodies can seem from the wider community of the university. This distance may be exaggerated by the requirements of the OfS which has much to say about student engagement but whose governance prescriptions do not consider wider engagement, so important to the health of communities built on trust and distributed models of power and authority. Within the latitude permitted by the OfS, it is an urgent task for universities to rediscover the balance between the authority of a governing body and its role to uphold the institutional character, mission and values by re-engaging purposefully with the wider academic and support staff community and their representative bodies. If this project fails, the defence of current governance models from more external interference and imposed standards will be severely weakened. Universities and other providers have to gain the confidence to advocate their models of governance as integral to the pursuit of their strategies and mission. That advocacy needs to come from the collective voice of the community.

The risk of further interference is real. It can be illustrated by the Accounts Direction set by the OfS with regard to reporting on senior pay (Office for Students 2018b, pp. 12ff.). This was seemingly added to its Framework during its drafting under political pressure concerning the high pay of certain Vice-Chancellors and the arrangements by which their remuneration had been agreed. The original proposals were significantly altered after consultation but neither institutions or the OfS emerge with much credit. Institutions because some poor practice about the membership and procedures of remuneration committees gave ammunition to their detractors, and the OfS because its readiness to regulate on this one aspect does not provide confidence about how quickly it may react to the next crisis or campaign about some matter or other in the sector. Institutions had lost touch with their internal and external communities and how they explained the setting of senior leaders' salaries. The swift response of a new regulator is a comminatory act that is different in kind from what may have been expected from HEFCE and is a warning for the future.

In the early versions of *The Wasteland*, T.S. Eliot called his emerging poem *He Do the Police in Different Voices*. *The Wasteland* is a poem of many different voices and is a work given to performance like Sloppy's reading of the newspapers. Perhaps too, the title expressed to Eliot the oppression and depression that he felt post-First World War where there was more than one voice crying in the wilderness of a Europe in turmoil and flux with weakened political and cultural authority. I do not wish to suggest that higher education is in an exactly similar position. We are not post-war but the external environment is very definitely unsettled as I have suggested in this chapter. We have entered a new era of a different regulatory voice with a fragmented response from a sector that has been used to a different relationship with government in which it has been a respected partner. Where this will lead is uncertain. The conditions for further change are set. If institutional autonomy is truly to be protected and its importance justified, there is much work to be done in demonstrating that co-regulation works and that the values and principles of a university model that dates back centuries still has relevance in the twenty-first century.

References

Ashdowne, R., Howlett, D. and Latham R. (2013) *Dictionary of Medieval Latin from British Sources*. Oxford University Press, Oxford.

Competition and Markets Authority (2015) *UK Higher Education Providers: Advice on Consumer Protection Law*. CMA33. Crown Copyright. [Retrieved from https://assets.publishing.service.gov.uk/government/uploads/system/uploads/attachment_data/file/428549/HE_providers_advice_on_consumer_protection_law.pdf]

Dickens, C. (1865) *Our Mutual Friend*. Chapman and Hall, London.

Eliot, T.S. (1922) *The Waste Land*. Horace Liveright, USA.

Higher Education: Students at the Heart of the System (2011) White Paper. Cm 8122. Crown Copyright. [Retrieved from https://assets.publishing.service.gov.uk/government/uploads/system/uploads/attachment_data/file/31384/11-944-higher-education-students-at-heart-of-system.pdf]

Higher Education and Research Act 2017. [Retrieved from www.legislation.gov.uk/ukpga/2017/29/introduction/enacted]

Office for Fair Trading (2014) *Higher Education in England: An OFT Call for Information*. [Retrieved from https://webarchive.nationalarchives.gov.uk/20140402194821/http://www.oft.gov.uk/shared_oft/markets-work/OFT1529.pdf]

Office for Students (2018a) *Securing Student Success: Regulatory Framework for Higher Education in England*. [Retrieved from www.officeforstudents.org.uk/media/1406/ofs2018_01.pdf]

Office for Students (2018b) *Regulatory Advice 9: Accounts Direction*. [Retrieved from www.officeforstudents.org.uk/media/b846fd9c-211a-43ec-8e60-d14bb0ea31b1/ofs2018_26_amended.pdf]

Securing a Sustainable Future for Higher Education: An Independent Review of Higher Education Funding and Student Finance [The Browne Report] (2010) [Retrieved from https://assets.publishing.service.gov.uk/government/uploads/system/uploads/attachment_data/file/422565/bis-10-1208-securing-sustainable-higher-education-browne-report.pdf]

Shattock, M.L. (1994) *UGC and the Management of British Universities*. The Society for Research into Higher Education and the Open University Press, Maidenhead.

Shattock, M.L. (2017) 'University Governance in Flux. The Impact of External and Internal Pressures on the Distribution of Authority within British Universities: A Synoptic View'. Working Paper No. 13. Global Centre for Higher Education. [Retrieved from www.researchcghe.org/perch/resources/publications/wp13.pdf]

Shattock, M.L. and Burdahl, R.O. (1984) 'The British University Grants Committee 1919–83: Changing Relationships with Government and Universities'. *Higher Education*, Vol. 13, No. 5, pp. 471–499.

Success as a Knowledge Economy: Teaching Excellence, Social Mobility, and Student Choice (2016) White Paper. Cm 9258. Crown Copyright. [Retrieved from https://assets.publishing.service.gov.uk/government/uploads/system/uploads/attachment_data/file/523546/bis-16-265-success-as-a-knowledge-economy-web.pdf]

Willetts, D. (2017) *A University Education*. Oxford University Press, Oxford.

Part II

Global perspectives

Chapter 4

Changing governance models in North American higher education

Robert A. Scott

Introduction

It is important when comparing systems to indicate areas of similarity between and among them as well as to highlight areas of difference. The role of governing systems is generally the same and universities everywhere face similar forces for change due to demographics, economics, societal issues, student behaviour and technology. This is true even when the composition, structure and sources of authority of the boards differ. Governing boards in Canada, Mexico and the United States are citizen organisations charged with preserving the mission and autonomy of the institution as well as with protecting its future.

The term 'governance' covers the structures, strategies and priorities that make up the actions designed to fulfil the institution's mission and purpose. Forces for change include emerging economic and employment dynamics, union negotiations, legal and regulatory requirements, new forms of credentialing for continuous and life-long learning, new models for charging fees for programmes and services, new instructional delivery systems for students in distant and under-served locations, and establishing campuses and centres in new locations in the country or in other countries.

A significant difference in these systems is found in the fact Canada and Mexico have Ministries of Education that have more extensive authority over education than that of the Department of Education in the United States. A second difference is that university governance in Canada and Mexico is bicameral, i.e. in two parts, while university governance in the United States is tripartite, with three parts. A third difference is that governing boards in Canada and Mexico include experts in higher education as a matter of design, not as a matter of choice as in the United States.

Still another difference is found in the ways these three countries provide 'consumer' protection to university students, with Canada and Mexico adding provisions and the United States weakening existing protections for students. This is especially true relative to the growth of for-profit universities in each country.

The bicameral system includes a university council as a mostly external governing board and an academic board that is mostly internal. The tripartite system in the United States encompasses an external governing board, the faculty of the institution and the university president. Both systems are described further in the following pages.

While there are differences in how governing boards are composed and members selected, and in the role of the president or chief administrator in these systems, the authority for institutional mission and the responsibility for academic freedom and institutional autonomy are similar.

Scale and scope

In Canada, with a population of 37 million people, there are 96 public and 35 private universities. The public universities enrol about 1.7 million students in a $35 billion dollar Canadian enterprise. The private universities enrol about 170,000 students. All data are for 2016. The oldest university is Laval in Quebec City, founded in 1663.

In Mexico, with a population of 127.5 million people, there are some 1,250 institutions of higher education in six subsystems of institutions. Traditionally, the public universities have had a great deal of legal autonomy while other public institutions were guided either by the federal Ministry of Education or by state governments. The public universities enrol more than 71 per cent of the 3.6 million students, with the growing independent sector enrolling the remainder. The first universities were established in 1551, long before the nation's independence in 1821 (Paoli-Bolio, n.d.; Clark and Monroy, 2013).

In the United States, with a population of 327 million, there are 6,643 colleges and universities, 2,902 of which are four-year or more, 1,932 are two-year, and 1,808 are less than two-year. In 2017–2018, these institutions enrolled 26.7 million individual students, of which 22.9 million were undergraduates and 3.8 million were graduate students (US Department of Education, 2017). It is generally agreed that Harvard is the oldest institution, founded in 1636.

International student enrolment is important in each country. To support student and faculty exchanges between and among the three countries of North America, the US Department of Education sponsors an Institutional Cooperation and Student Mobility in Higher Education programme. In addition, many institutions in each country have exchange agreements with partner institutions or groups of institutions in another country. There also is the Canada–Mexico Partnership promoting collaboration in higher education and research partnerships (Canadian Bureau of International Education, n.d.; Helms and Griffin, 2017; Koprowski, 2016).

'Good' governance

The mission defines the purpose of an institution. By definition, it establishes priorities. Governing boards fulfil their duties and accomplish their goals by acting in accord with the mission when approving and monitoring plans; approving the sources of revenue and the allocation of resources; selecting, nurturing and evaluating executive leadership; and abiding by the duties of care, obedience and loyalty. The late sociologist David Riesman is reported to have said that the trustee governing board is responsible for saving the university of the future from the actions of the present day.

University trustees need to be trained in the complexities of higher education governance, financing, quality controls, government regulations and legal requirements, financial aid policies, and other issues if they are to be effective in their roles. Universities are different from other social institutions in that students are not 'customers' engaging in a transaction. Instead, they willingly engage in an act of transformation with a tutor or professor. They are not a customer or client or patient; they are a student, i.e. 'one who studies'. For these reasons, trustees should be provided with an ongoing orientation to their responsibilities.

This is as it should be, as the university's role is three-fold: creator, curator and critic. In fulfilment of its mission of teaching, research and service, the university serves as a creator of new knowledge and understanding. It is a curator of what is known, serving as a repository of the past. Finally, it teaches independent thinking, encouraging students to be responsible critics of the status quo.

While as a universal principle the governing board is responsible for guiding the fulfilment of the mission of its institution, the activities of a board are determined by the powers, duties and responsibilities delegated to it or conferred on it by an authority outside of itself. In the United States, that authority is either the state government, the state constitution or, in a few locations, *state-wide elections*. Boards, whether public or private, are responsible for fulfilling statutory law. In Canada and Mexico, the authority lies with the federal or the state or provincial government.

University governance in the United States

In the United States, governing boards of private non-profit institutions are generally self-perpetuating, electing their own members and setting the terms of office. Members are often graduates of the college or university they govern and have an emotional attachment to their alma mater. Public institutions generally have trustee members appointed by the state governor, the state legislature or some combination of the two. Federally sponsored military institutions have governing boards appointed by a federal process.

For-profit colleges and universities are governed by a corporate board of investors and the institutions operate as private businesses, even when they are owned by shareholders who possess publicly traded stock certificates. However, as more for-profits seek tax-exempt status, the nature of their governance will necessarily change.

One of the ironies of university governance in the United States, especially when compared to corporate boards in business, is the trustees' lack of knowledge about higher education. One cannot imagine a successful business including as directors persons with little or no expertise in the purpose, technology, market and competition of the enterprise. Yet this happens in both private and public higher education institutions. Less than 10 per cent of American college and university trustees have professional experience in academe. Most are from business and finance because of higher education's priority for fundraising (Scott, 2018). This is not the case in Canada and Mexico.

The best board practices can be found in many institutions, whether small liberal arts colleges, community colleges, major research universities or state-wide systems of public institutions. Each board and member must fulfil the duties of care, loyalty and obedience, no matter what the size or the mandate of the institution. The board sets the standards for institutional deliberations. It can support a culture of respect and transparency, or one of secretiveness. Transparency is necessary for trust, and both are essential for good governance.

The composition of governing boards in the United States

Over time, the composition of governing boards in the United States has evolved in response to external pressures, whether economic at private institutions or political at public ones. The earliest institutions, the Colonial colleges, borrowed from the 'Oxbridge' model of 'resident' boards consisting largely of faculty members and the president. In response to external imperatives, this model gave way to a 'non-resident' board made up largely of members who were not academics. The president then became an administrator of the college and represented the board, serving ex officio (Kirkwood, 1925).

Nevertheless, the tradition of faculty involvement in governance continued and became codified in law and in protocols. Hence, in the United States, we think of a tripartite governance system linking trustees, the administration and the faculty.

One of the challenges to this tripartite system of governance in the United States is the number of different board types. The simplest model is a single governing board for a single campus and its various activities. However, when a public college or university is part of a multi-campus system governed by an overarching governing board, or when the single campus also has a local advisory board, governance can become complicated.

Some state higher education institutions are governed by boards of regents that have authority over all institutions. The case of New York State is particularly significant in that the Board of Regents has authority over the charters of all tax-exempt organisations, including both public and private colleges and universities.

In addition, many state governments have so-called 'coordinating' boards or commissions that have authority over state-wide academic planning, academic programme approvals and capital expansion projects for public institutions. In some cases, these commissions also cover private institutions in their planning criteria, programme approvals authority and state budget recommendations.

At many public institutions, there also are limited purpose or private foundation boards devoted to fundraising and community engagement or oversight of auxiliary enterprises such as residence halls and food services. While not governing bodies per se, they must operate in coordination with the governing board. The recent development of the public benefit corporation model brings with it another model of governance.

The role of the governing board in the United States

With proper continuing orientation, the board should be able to avoid conflicts of interest and controversy. The board's role is to consider decisions in terms of institutional mission, strategy, priorities, risk and ethical concerns. Missteps in reaching a decision can have unintended consequences both on- and off-campus because procedures and protocols are viewed as essential obligations.

It is often said that the most important job of the board is the selection of a person to serve as the chief administrative officer or president. In the United States, terms of office may vary, with an initial appointment of three to five years and no fixed limit to the number of terms. Nevertheless, the average length of presidential service is close to five years.

The board is responsible for oversight of a strategic plan. Strategic plans are required by accrediting bodies and bond rating agencies, and are necessary for routine governance, leadership and management. Such plans address the topics of accessibility, affordability and accountability, including accreditation and other forms of external quality review (Scott, 2018).

Some of the important topics that can arise in strategic planning include changing the mission to become more research-focused, succession planning for administrative officers and the board, and moving to a higher-level athletic league, the latter being a uniquely American phenomenon.

There are strategic questions that lie within the province of the board's role even when particular questions about academic or scholarly accomplishment and teaching effectiveness are not. The board's role is to ask questions about how recommendations relate to goals. This is why it helps to have those with professional experience in higher education on the board, in addition to those who can help in fundraising.

The historical forces for change in US university governance

As higher education in the United States has evolved over time, so has institutional governance. The challenges facing Colonial-era colleges dedicated to preparing ministers and teachers were quite different from later years after the development of many more academic programmes and formal academic departments, and when faculty members held advanced professional degrees. The evolution from seminaries to teaching colleges, to research-focused institutions, to complex organisations required more complicated governance structures over time. Financial challenges were different too. As a consequence, governance evolved from 'resident' trustees, i.e. the president and faculty, to 'non-resident' trustees consisting of leading members of the broader community (Kirkwood, 1925).

The Colonial period ended with the Revolutionary War, which disrupted college enrolments and funding. The Federal period followed, from 1780 to 1830, and saw many innovations that influenced college governance and programming. It was a period that witnessed the development of many private institutions with local roots first and a broader reach later. During this period, the US Constitution was ratified, the Northwest Ordinance was enacted, and the two federal Land Grant Acts were approved.

This was a period when the state was weak, the economy strong and churches were divided. The federal government sold land to raise money (Labaree, 2017). The Land Grant Acts prompted small private liberal arts colleges to assume new missions in engineering and agriculture and to expand in enrolment. The late nineteenth century also saw not only the Civil War but also the establishment of colleges for women, African-Americans, and those with special assistance needs in learning.

The first half of the twentieth century was witness to dynamic developments in US society in general and higher education in particular. A college degree became a source of status for students and the establishment of a college became a source of pride for states and localities. Societal disruptions included two world wars, the Great Depression and the development of computers.

In higher education, the century included the development of community colleges; Carnegie initiatives in philanthropy; the standard credit unit; the Flexner Report on medical education (Flexner, 1910); the development of aptitude tests; the formation of a teacher retirement plan that still exists; the GI Bill (Veterans Readjustment Act); and the Truman Commission report that helped spur a doubling of college enrolments ('History Timeline', n.d.).

Federal and state initiatives around the GI Bill prompted changes in both private and public colleges. Those that had been single-sex for decades became co-educational and all were encouraged to increase in size to accommodate the returning veterans.

Changes in US society and universities in the second half of the twentieth century were no less dramatic. In the aftermath of the Second World War and Korean conflict there were federal and state 'loyalty oaths' challenging academic freedom. The Sputnik programme of the Soviet Union prompted massive federal investments in science and technology, and in areas of the social sciences and humanities focused on languages, linguistics, anthropology and geographic regional studies.

This period also saw major advances in the civil rights and equal opportunity for minorities, women and those with learning and physical disabilities. Affirmative action in admissions and diversity in the classroom became priorities. The period also saw significant disruptions on campus and off due to protests against the Vietnam War.

Other challenges to the common order were developments in information technology; the formation of large for-profit universities; federal reports on the status of education; federally sponsored student loans; the federal Higher Education Act and the formation of state higher education coordinating boards; protests against fossil fuels, Apartheid in South Africa and limitations on free speech; and both challenges to affirmative action and advancements in the rights of gay and transgender people, including students.

There is more, of course, including the growth of faculty and staff unions on campuses, but the point here is to indicate the number and variety of challenges to governance and leadership. Incidents in the community like police shootings became the focus of campus rallies and sexual assaults on- and off-campus produced new tests of campus leadership. University trustees and leaders had to respond to disruptions in the status quo regarding these issues and the following: who could be admitted, who could teach and be granted tenure, how was student behaviour to be regulated, where could institutional funds be invested, and how should the administration relate to the surrounding community.

As a consequence, governance became much more complicated compared to the periods when most students were Caucasian men studying for the ministry and teaching, and campuses were mostly residential in nature. The greater diversity of students and institutional types; the higher level of professional expectations of faculty, especially for research; the accelerated emphasis on government grants and private gifts to support university operations; the increase in students who study part-time and live off-campus; and increased legal and regulatory rules all affected the evolution of governance.

In response to these and other challenges, as well as external recommendations for change, boards adjusted admissions, hiring, student discipline and investment practices. Student support staff members were added, including some expert in federal and state regulations. Boards also became more sensitive about their membership. They added more lawyers and became cognisant of the diversity of membership in terms of gender, ethnicity and race as well as age and profession. The demands for these kinds of changes continue.

Boards also considered how best to include philanthropy as a criterion for membership. While some boards had and still have a set level of giving per trustee, others employ different criteria. These variations can be described as 'Work, Wealth, and Wisdom' or 'Time, Talent, and Treasure', with every member obligated to fulfil two of the three.

Current forces for change in university governance in the United States

If we look again at the variables of population, politics and public policy that seem to have shaped university growth in the United States and elsewhere, what might these variables suggest about forces for change in the future?

The United States still faces issues of population, although the concern is no longer about the movement of people to frontier territories. Today, there are potential students of all ages who live in so-called higher education 'deserts', rural areas and urban centres that lack access to post-secondary opportunities. Another change in population dynamics is represented by the increase in non-traditionally aged students, who are now the majority in higher education. The 18–24-year-old cohort is the minority. Forty per cent of all students attend community colleges; only 14 per cent live on campus (US Department of Education, 2017).

The majority of university students have been out of secondary school for years, have jobs and families, and often have difficulty managing class schedules. They also are more demographically diverse, often coming from underserved communities and often are the first in their families to attempt college. On many campuses, there are more female than male students. Trustees have to be aware of how their institutions are organised to serve these non-traditional, non-residential students with non-traditional policies and practices.

Another force with which to contend is the rising 'populism' in public policy debates and the consequent change in priorities for public funding. This is occurring even when studies indicate the need to increase the percentage of the population with a college education. With prisons and pensions squeezing state budgets, and politicians expressing criticism of 'liberal arts' education, colleges and universities must find more effective ways to advocate for the societal as well as the individual benefits of higher education.

Still other challenges are related to what are called 'culture wars' concerning the goal of a university education, contested histories and the legacies of earlier oppression or discrimination of minority groups, freedom of speech, the use of race in admissions decisions, and priorities in humanities curricula.

Boards and presidents also need to find ways to change their institutional cost structures, including more collaborative arrangements for sharing expenses. An effort at restructuring costs must be taken in order to reduce the discounting of tuition as a way of providing financial assistance and merit scholarship aid. On many campuses, the discount rate exceeds 50 per cent. In addition, campuses must find new sources of revenue beyond that which students themselves can bring without diminishing institutional commitments to purpose and mission.

One problematic approach is to charge differential tuition according to the subject matter, thus making it more expensive to study certain disciplines. Another is to hold tuition constant, or even reduce it, a policy that ignores the potential effects of declines in enrolment and increases in the inflation rate.

Other shifts shaping the future of higher education in the United States include the declining number of high school graduates in many sections of the country; the absence of a sensible and fair system of immigration; whether students will study full-time, part-time or online; and employment prospects for recent graduates. Forecasters have proposed varying models of institutional development for the future. All of these are among the topics for governing board deliberations.

Forces for change also include heightened political tensions as well as initiatives for 'free' tuition at public colleges. While it is true that many public colleges were tuition-free in years past, there are differences between those policies and the ones proposed now. Today, the proposals for free tuition include criteria that favour more affluent families and discriminate against lower income students who have the most to gain but must study part-time due to work and family obligations. The consequences of tuition subsidies at public institutions in terms of their original mission and the subsequent admissions competitiveness due to the influence of socio-economic status on student preparedness are often ignored. In New York State, for example, the socio-economic status of families in the state university system is greater than in the independent institutions.

Finally, major forces for change are found in the technological breakthroughs we have witnessed. One of the top drivers of costs in higher education, after tuition discounting, compensation and health care premiums, is the investment made in technology. The computing and information technologies that facilitate university teaching and learning and help improve administrative efficiencies are also being used to create new providers of postsecondary education. These new entrants challenge the traditional ways of organising college curricula and providing instruction, and offer new as well as traditional credentials. Lessons can be learned from them in both how to achieve goals and what pitfalls to avoid, especially with regard to aggressive recruiting and revenue diversity.

These various forces are prompting new thinking in the United States about what a university is and how universities and colleges should be governed. A university or college receives a public charter and is dedicated to the search for evidence-based truths and to the preparation of students as professionals and citizens. The goals of higher education in the United States have been to widen access, especially at the undergraduate level, for students of all ages and backgrounds, whether enrolled full-time or part-time, and to promote excellence in teaching and research for the common good.

The 'business' or economic model of higher education in the United States

Complaints about the 'business' model of colleges and universities are common. Politicians and pundits rail against increases in the price of tuition, the slow pace in adopting technology to reduce personnel costs, and the construction of country club-like amenities.

In response, defenders of higher education complain about the imposition of corporate or managerial models of governance and evaluation methods on academic institutions, and point to the damaging effects of reductions in state funding, often as a consequence of tax cuts. These cuts in state funding are cited as a leading cause of reduced graduation rates and increases in tuition. Defenders also refer to the increased focus of public policy on job training as opposed to general and liberal education as preparation for the professions and citizenship. They decry the use of rare examples of excess to make broad-brush claims.

A frequently cited sign of corporatisation, and a consequence of reductions in funding, is the increasing reliance on part-time and contingent faculty. Some colleges teach nearly 70 per cent of course sections with part-time faculty because they cost less. This is not to deny the value of employing some part-time faculty whose expertise would be too expensive on a full-time basis. Nor is this to say that universities must ignore the financial bottom line. But part-time faculty members are not as available as full-time faculty for advising students, sponsoring student clubs, developing curricula, managing internships, nurturing younger faculty, and serving on faculty and university-wide committees.

In addition, the growing competition for students who can pay tuition and stay to graduation makes university admissions more and more a marketing enterprise. This can lead to distortions in the priorities for funding, especially for facilities and sports intended to attract students. As tuition is the most significant source of funding for private colleges, and increasingly essential source for public institutions, the use of tuition discounting to create student financial aid is a growing problem. The failure to achieve adequate net tuition revenue can lead to discussions of faculty lay-offs and even of merger or closure.

The evolution of governance in US universities

In the United States, an important source of checks and balances to governing boards and campus or system presidents is the faculty. A 1966 Statement on Governance published by the American Council on Education national association of presidents, the American Association of University Professors, a professional association of professors, and the Association of Governing Boards, the national association for trustees of colleges and universities, outlined the respective responsibilities of the three parties (AAUP-ACE-AGB, 1966).

This 1966 statement of principles was built upon a long history of efforts to define the roles of trustees in overall fiduciary responsibility for a campus or system; the president's role as the executive responsible for fulfilling the mission in a legally, ethically and financially sound manner; and the faculty's role in setting academic standards and admission requirements, establishing the curricula, hiring and nurturing faculty, institutional and programmatic accreditation, and participating in strategic planning, setting priorities and searches for senior administrators.

These efforts included the 1819 Supreme Court case of *Dartmouth* v. *New Hampshire* in which the Court affirmed the sanctity and autonomy of independent college and university charters (Dartmouth College Case, n.d.).

Nearly a century later, in 1915, the American Association of University Professors (AAUP) published a 'Declaration of Principles on Academic Freedom and Academic Tenure', a statement on the freedom of the teacher to teach and the student to learn (AAUP, 1940). In 1920, the AAUP published its 'Statement on Government of Colleges and Universities', which emphasised the critical role of faculty in the selection of administrators, other personnel decisions and determining educational policies ('Governance in Higher Education', n.d.).

In 1957, the State of New Hampshire attempted to curtail Professor Paul Sweezy's teachings and speeches by claiming him to be subversive. The United States Supreme Court decision in the case concluded that the faculty as a collective are responsible for the four 'essential freedoms' of a university, who may teach, what may be taught, how it shall be taught, and who may be admitted to study (*Sweezy* v. *NH*, n.d.).

These statements and judgments are among the foundations of the tripartite system of shared governance in the United States involving trustees, faculty and the administration.

Shared governance as a concept in US higher education

Support for shared or participatory models of governance has declined for several reasons. First is the pace of change, especially in revenue shortfalls and the onset of fiscal austerity, whether caused by a decline in state support or enrollment shortfalls. Boards and presidents want fast action to balance the budget and faculty senates are not always willing to do more than sanction across the board cuts. Senates also are generally not in session between academic semesters. When one adds the public pressures from pundits and politicians for universities to act more like businesses and make faster decisions, the wait for faculty action can seem long. It is often these outside forces that complain about the business model in higher education being 'broken'.

The increasing size of many colleges and universities and the existence of systems of multiple campuses can make it difficult for trustees and presidents to know their own institutions, much less individual faculty and students. With size and complexity can come more layers of management that filter information from the leaders and add time to decision-making. It should be no surprise that many of the worst scandals in recent years have been at giant universities with distant boards and presidents who seem remote from the faculty.

Some argue that institutional governance would be improved if faculty and students served on boards of trustees. In some cases they do serve, but this is the exception, not the rule (Ehrenberg *et al.*, 2013).

One of the major impediments to having campus faculty serve on a campus or system board is that most public universities and many private ones have faculty unions. Since a Collective Bargaining Agreement is the result of negotiations approved by the governing board, it would be a conflict of interest to have faculty on a board that decides on the contract.

Some states have legislation providing for students to serve on boards as voting members, but not in executive sessions devoted to personnel and fiscal matters. In other cases, the student representative serves ex officio without a vote. Boards also include students on selected board committees and invite students to attend board meals and receptions in order to foster communication.

The public's confidence in US higher education

If university governance is to be effective in terms of guidance for the institution, and held in confidence by campus stakeholders, politicians and the public, there must be trust. There must be trust that governing boards are paying attention to academic priorities and are not permitting excessive support for other priorities such as competitive athletics. There must be confidence that boards do not turn a blind eye to misbehaviour in the fraternity system. The same is true for sexual assault and related scandals. Too often, it seems, university leaders have been more interested in 'protecting the campus reputation' than in seeking the truth about an incident and acting on it.

The public should have confidence that universities are committed to recruiting well-prepared students, or have programmes of support for those who need it, no matter what their economic circumstances. Antipathy by the local public can lead to requirements that the tax-exempt university pay a PILOT (a payment in lieu of taxes). These can be significant amounts, totalling millions of dollars (Scott, 2018).

Boards should be seen as responsible parties, not just as cheerleaders for alma mater. They should serve as active partners in achieving the institutional mission through governance and philanthropy, and be organised to be effective.

University governance in Canada

University governing boards are chartered by provincial governments in Canada. In the beginning, Canadian universities were Colonial colleges and their governance systems were composed of members of the Colonial legislature. By the nineteenth century, institutions moved from a Colonial model to an independent institution governance model grounded in the structure of sponsoring religious denominations. During this period, the bicameral system, or two-houses system, of a University Council, largely external, and an Academic Board, largely internal, became institutionalised. In this way, the faculty voice became embedded (Jones, 2012).

Today, Canadian universities are authorised by provincial government legislation as private non-profit corporations, thus giving them significant autonomy from direct government control (Schwartz, 2014a). In some cases the president is appointed by the governing board; in other cases, the president is appointed by the Ministry (Jones, 2012).

The average governing board size in Canada is about 27 members, similar to boards in the United States. A major difference is that in Canada about one-third of the members are internal, with two-thirds, the 'lay' members, appointed by the government or by the board. Some 17 per cent are faculty members and

9 per cent are students. In addition, the university president is a voting member of the governing board.

This board is the external governing body, even with the internal members. In addition, there is an internal governing body, the Senate. In some cases, it is called the Academic Board. These boards include faculty, about 44 per cent; students, about 18 per cent; other internal representatives plus alumni, members of affiliated colleges, a government appointment or two in recognition of government support, and the Chancellor as a member in 41 per cent of cases. The size of a Canadian university senate ranges in size from about 20 to over 190 (Jones, 2012). Over time, the governance system has become more inclusive, complicated and local (Jones, 2012). The federal government plays a minimal role (Peacock *et al.*, 2015).

The internal Academic Board or Senate consists of the president and academic leadership such as department heads and deans. This body consists of faculty, students and university administrators, with senior administrators holding 25 per cent of the seats. Only rarely are faculty members qua faculty included. As a consequence, what is called 'shared governance' in the United States, with representative faculty who are not also academic administrators included, is not evident (Clark, 2013; McGuinness, 2016).

One of the recommendations of an External Governance Review Committee, commissioned at Concordia University in Canada following a 'crisis in governance', concerned faculty involvement in government. The eight principles enunciated included: (1) bicameralism (two bodies) and shared governance; (2) clear roles and responsibilities; (3) transparency; (4) strong academic administration accountable to an effective governance system; (5) managing conflicts of interest; (6) board and senate renewal; (7) the necessary distinction between collective bargaining and university governance; and (8) mutual respect. These principles are (arguably) universal, not limited to Concordia or Canada (Schwartz, 2014b).

The forces for change in Canadian higher education governance

In 1867, Canada adopted the British North America Act, which was renamed the Constitution Act in 1982. The Act assigned constitutional authority for higher education with each of the ten provinces of the country. The universities are autonomous, non-profit corporations. The Canadian federal government has a limited role in higher education similar to that in the United States. Funding is basically a provincial concern. The federal role is limited to the military academy and institutions for indigenous peoples (Schwartz, 2014a).

Nevertheless, reductions in funding have caused an increasing reliance on part-time faculty and greater pressure on faculty to find external funding for research and scholarly activities (Bouchard St-Amant, n.d.).

The rise of unionised faculty in the 1970s interfered with shared governance because of the tendency for the role of unions in negotiating terms and conditions of employment to become conflated with the broader role of the faculty on the Academic Board and in curriculum development and the quality of education (Findlay, 2011; Center for Higher Education Policy Studies, 2012).

Canadian universities have had to contend with student protests, union strikes, cheating and sexual assault scandals, complaints of anti-Semitism, and other contentious issues. Canadian governing boards and university administrators have met these and other challenges, sometimes successfully but not always quickly. Some graduate student strikes over the adequacy of stipends have lasted weeks and required both increases in undergraduate enrolment for revenue and changes in organisational structure to save money (Ratcliffe, 2015).

University governance in Mexico

Mexico, officially the United States of Mexico, is the second largest country in Latin America. The country is a Republic with 32 federal units or states and one federal district that includes the capital, Mexico City. One consequence of this organisation is that there are 33 educational systems at all educational levels, including higher education (Center for Higher Education Policy Studies, 2012).

The federal Constitution includes the provisions for free public education, the governance of schools by lay officials, the 'autonomy' of public universities, and the 'freedom to teach'. At the federal level, higher education is under the responsibility of the Secretariat of Public Education and the National Council for Science and Technology (Center for Higher Education Policy Studies, 2012).

The General Law on the Coordination of Higher Education of 1978 was created to generate diversity in the types of higher education institutions, govern the use of the title 'university', and foster better coordination between and among the federal and state institutions. This authority was revised in the year 2000 in order to take into account the growth of for-profit institutions operating as universities.

The model for higher education in Mexico is the National Autonomous University of Mexico (UNAM), whose origins trace to 1551. One of the largest universities in the world, it is chartered by the Secretariat of Education and has a major campus in Mexico City, with satellite centres in each state and in other countries.

In addition, there is a system of technological institutions encompassed by the National Polytechnic Institute with at least one campus in each state. This system is controlled and regulated by the Sub-secretary of Technical Education in coordination with the government of each state. Private higher education institutions are governed by their own statutes under authority of the government.

The Organic, or fundamental, Law of the National Autonomous University of Mexico defines the institution as a public corporation decentralised from the state with full legal capacity and enumerates its mission for teaching, research and service. It also specifies the principle of academic freedom and research and the authority to set admission standards.

Furthermore, the Law specifies the roles and authority of the Government Board; the University Council; the Board; and the Directors of the Faculties, Schools, and Institutes. Of particular note, the Government Board has authority to appoint and remove the Rector, or president, with at least ten of the 15 members approving. It is urged, when prudent, to explore the opinion of university students. The Government Board also has the authority to appoint the other officers.

The University Council consists of the Rector; the directors of faculties, schools and institutes; representatives of the faculty and students of each unit; a professor representative of the extension centers; a representative of the employees of the university; and the Secretary-general of the university. The role of the University Council is to oversee the technical, educational and administrative operations of the university.

The Rector is the Head of the university and president of the University Council. He or she will be in office for four years and may be re-elected once. If the Rector vetoes an action of the University Council, the issue in question must be resolved by the Government Board.

In the UNAM, teachers and researchers belong to the same union as administrative workers. Other public universities have a union for the academic sector and another for administrative workers. Collective bargaining contracts are made between the university authorities and union members.

There is a national evaluation system for quality control based on institutional self-studies and external evaluators. The system is managed by the Council for the Accreditation of Higher Education.

In Mexico, the multi-annual National Plan sets forth goals for coverage (or access), equity, quality, social relevance and funding, thus providing a federal framework in which institutions operate individually (Paoli-Bolio, n.d.).

The forces for change in Mexican higher education governance

Forces for change and reform in university governance include the need to ensure and coordinate quality assurance measures, a transparent degree credit system, and the recognition of foreign credentials, among others (Center for Higher Education Policy Studies, 2012).

While the demand for university enrolment is encouraged, it is not adequately supported and lags neighboring countries in the region (Clark and Monroy, 2013; Lloyd, 2010). Interest in advanced study in the United States is strong, but discouraged by current policies regarding visas for students (Magaziner, 2016). In part because of the increasing desire and encouragement for university education, and the lack of spaces in the public sector due to inadequate funding, the private sector has grown, even though many are considered to be of low quality (Clark, 2013).

Many of these for-profit institutions have been accused of fraudulent practices, as has happened in the United States. For-profit colleges have corporate owners, not the form of governance found at non-profit and government-sponsored universities. Unlike the United States, there is only minimal state support for students attending for-profit institutions (Hicks, n.d.).

The challenges to the educational system result from the need to balance quickly growing enrolment and the quality of educational results, and the varied customs in the different states, making it difficult to achieve effective coordination of national, state, and institutional policies. Challenges also include the lack of resources, the need to increase and diversity the curricula, and a growing for-profit sector (Paoli-Bolio, n.d.).

In addition, massive student protests against institutional and government policies have challenged the leadership and governance on individual institutions. These protests have occurred in the past and will no doubt challenge both state and local officials in the future if the fundamental societal issues are not addressed (Knowland, 2018).

In Canada and Mexico, significant historical forces also were related to the Catholic Church, the recognition of the needs of indigenous peoples and the establishment of external assessments of institutional quality (Henard and Mitterle, 2003; Marmolejo, 2016; Schwartz, 2014b).

Conclusion: changing governance models in North American higher education

The forces affecting policies on student access, institutional affordability and external forms of accountability exist in all countries, including Canada, Mexico and the United States. So do the scandals and ethical challenges that distract institutional governing boards and leaders from focusing on their primary purposes on instruction, research and service.

A university has a form of covenant with the society that grants its licence. Can the purpose be pure, 'knowledge for knowledge's sake', when the market economy of the sponsoring society dominates thinking about purpose? How does a university balance its obligations to student learning, knowledge creation, economic development and community improvement?

How can campus leaders keep their focus on institutional mission and purpose when the external pressures on funding are so strong? How can leaders avoid the temptation of 'mission creep' because of the allure of prestige associated with research priorities?

These are parts of the continuing challenge to university governance. Does higher education serve a public purpose, or does it exist for the private gain of those who enter? What are the arguments for public funding if the purpose is believed to be private gain? Public perceptions about quality and value, about the connection between education and employment, are important to consider and counter. Governing boards are advocates as well as governors.

These questions have existed for decades, perhaps centuries, and will continue to bedevil university governance. Governing boards are civic bodies intended to protect a public trust. How, then, do they balance the accountability to external constituencies with accountability to internal stakeholders?

Going forward, will the involvement of faculty and students in governance continue to grow, or will it diminish as the proportion of faculty and students who are part-time continues to increase? Will the role of faculty unionisation at institutions of higher education wane as it has in other areas of society? Of what effect will this be?

Will the trends in thinking about students as consumers or customers, and universities as 'providers' or vendors, continue? Will such trends lead to new definitions of the 'contract' between a student and his or her university? What will be the legal obligations of boards for quality control? Will boards and presidents be required to certify academic results as they do financial statements? Will new forms of information be made available so that prospective students and families will be better able to compare the effectiveness of different universities? Will institutional autonomy and academic freedom of inquiry be protected or weakened?

The professoriate is one of the only professions that do not require a supervised residency and licensure. Compare this to physicians, dentists, engineers, architects, etc. Will changes in laws and regulations lead to a diminution of judicial deference to 'academic judgement'?

The major forces for change in governance are concerns about institutional costs and the fees for students, learning outcomes, and pressures for universities to be active instruments of state economic development (Clark, 2013). Other forces include revising the academic calendar from one or two starting points to one of many start dates to increase responsiveness to societal needs, expanding the use of Artificial Intelligence and other technological developments, and fostering new forms of partnerships, even engaging in mergers and acquisitions for delivering programmes and services. These forces, and the competition from new entrants into the higher education space, all require attention from governing boards and administrators.

If the role of the faculty is diminished because of the proportion that are part-time, who will be responsible for the curriculum, the development of new programmes, the validation of new certifications, and other academic duties?

Institutions of higher education in North America have taken responsibility for expanding opportunities for indigenous peoples and others who were historically disadvantaged. Will the roll back of the priority for affirmative action for African-Americans and other groups in the United States be matched by similar actions in Canada and Mexico?

These and related challenges to systems of governance are equally true in Canada, Mexico and the United States.

Acknowledgements

I am grateful to several people for exceptional assistance in preparing this chapter. First, Michele Mendelssohn of Oxford and McGill Universities introduced me to colleagues in Canada. Through her, I was introduced to Glen Jones of OISE, Pier-Andre Bouchard St-Amant of L'Ecole Nationale d'Administration Publique in Montral, Bram Freedman of Concordia University and Donat Taddeo of Loyal High School in Montreal. I learned a great deal from each of them. I owe special thanks to Stephen Blank, a friend, professor and consultant, who is a commentator on Canada and North American economic integration.

I also am deeply indebted to Professor Francisco Paoli-Bolio of Universidad Nacional Autonoma de Mexico who provided extensive information in response to my questions. Maya Faison translated the Spanish for me.

I would be remiss if I did not acknowledge the excellent assistance of Melanie Locay, Research Study Librarian at the New York Public Library, where I have been a Frederick Lewis Allen Room Scholar.

Finally, I thank my friend and colleague Aims McGuinness of the National Center of Higher Education Management Systems, one of the most knowledgeable students of higher education governance in the United States.

References

AAUP (1940) 'Appendix I: 1915 Declaration of Principles on Academic Freedom and Academic Tenure'. American Association of University Professors. [Accessed at www.aaup.org/report/1940-statement-principles-academic-freedom-and-tenure]

AAUP-ACE-AGB (1966) 'Statement of Principles'. [Accessed at www.aaup.org/report/statement-government-colleges-and-universities]

Bouchard St-Amant, Pier-Andre (n.d.) Personal correspondence.

Canadian Bureau of International Education (n.d.) [Accessed at https://cbie.ca/media/facts-and-figures/]

Center for Higher Education Policy Studies (2012) 'Final Report: Comparative Study between the EU and Mexico'. European Centre for Strategic Management of Universities, 30 September.

Clark, I. (2013) 'University Governance in Canada: Challenges and Opportunities'. School of Public Policy & Governance, University of Toronto, 13 June.

Clark, N. and Monroy, C. (2013) 'Education in Mexico'. [Accessed at https://wenr.wes.org/2013/05/wenr-may-2013-an-overview-of-education-in-mexico]

Dartmouth College Case (n.d.) [Accessed at https://en.wikipedia.org/wiki/Dartmouth_College_v._Woodward]

Ehrenberg, R.G., Patterson, R.W. and Kay, A.V. (2013) 'Faculty Members on Boards of Trustees'. *Academe*, Vol. 99, No. 3, pp. 13–18.

Findlay, S. (2011) 'What Happened to Tenure?' Macleans. [Accessed at www.macleans.ca/education/uniandcollege/whatever-happened-to-tenure-2/]

Flexner, A. (1910) 'Medical Education in the United States and Canada'. A Report to the Carnegie Foundation for the Advancement of Teaching. New York.

'Governance in Higher Education' (n.d.) [Accessed at https://en.wikipedia.org/wiki/Governance_in_higher_education]

Helms, R.M. and Griffin, J. (2017) 'U.S.-Mexico Higher Education Engagement: Current Activities, Future Directions'. American Council on Education-Center for Internationalization and Global Engagement. Washington, DC.

Henard, F. and Mitterle, A. (2003) 'Governance and Quality Guidelines in Higher Education: A Review of Governance Arrangements and Quality Assurance Guidelines'. OECD, Paris. [Accessed at www.oecd.org/education/skills-beyond-school/35747684.pdf]

Hicks, Jimmy (n.d.) 'Privatization in Mexican Higher Education'. [Accessed at www.indiana.edu/~spaiu/journal/editions/2017/8%20Privatization%20in%20Mexican%20Higher%20Education.pdf]

'History Timeline' (n.d.) [Accessed at www.eds-resources.com/educationhistory timeline.html]

Jones, G. (2012) 'Trends in Academic Governance in Canada'. Academic Governance 3.0, Confederation of University Faculty Associations of BC.

Kirkwood, J. (1925) *The Rise of Non-Resident Government in Harvard University and How Harvard is Governed*. G. Wehr, Ann Arbor.

Knowland, D. (2018) 'Massive Student Protests Hit Mexico City Universities'. World Socialist Web Site. [Accessed at www.wsws.org/en/articles/2018/09/11/unam-s11. html on 11 September 2018]

Koprowski, E. (2016) 'Canada-Mexico Agreement to Boost Student Mobility'. [Accessed at www.bachelorstudies.it/news/Canada-Mexico-Agreement-to-Boost-Student-Mobility-640/]

Labaree, D.F. (2017) *A Perfect Mess: The Unlikely Ascendancy of American Higher Education*. University of Chicago Press, Chicago.

Lloyd, M. (2010) 'Mexico's Universities Struggle to Respond to Demand for Degrees'. *The Chronicle of Higher Education*, July, 5. [Accessed at www.chronicle.com/article/Mexicos-Universities-Struggle/66143]

Magaziner, J. (2016) 'Education in Mexico'. WENR. [Accessed at https://wenr.wes.org/2016/08/education-in-mexico]

Marmolejo, F. (2016) 'What Matters Most for Tertiary Education: A Framework Paper'. SABER Working Paper, No. 11. World Bank, Washington, DC. [Accessed at https://openknowledge.worldbank.org/handle/10986/26516]

McGuinness, A. (2016) 'State Policy Leadership for the Future: History of State Coordination and Governance and Alternatives for the Future'. NCHEMS, Boulder. Draft, 7 January.

Paoli-Bolio, Francisco (n.d.) Personal correspondence.

Peacock, L., Jones, G.A. Leclerc, J.M. and Li, S.X. (2015) 'Assessing the Role and Structure of Academic Senates in Canadian Universities'. *Higher Education*, Vol. 70, pp. 503–518.

Ratcliffe, R. (2015) 'University Protests around the World: A Fight against Commercialization'. [Accessed at www.theguardian.com/higher-education-network/2015/mar/25/university-protests-around-the-world-a-fight-against-commercialisation]

Schwartz, P. (2014a) 'A Short Overview of University Governance in Canada'. *Onepagepolicy*. [Accessed at https://saulschwartz.com/2014/01/03/a-short-over view-of-university-governance-in-canada/]

Schwartz, P. (2014b) 'The 2010–2012 Governance Crisis at Concordia'. *Onepagepolicy*, 16 February.

Scott, R. (2018) *How University Boards Work*. Johns Hopkins University Press, Baltimore.

Sweezy v. *NH* (n.d.) [Accessed at https://supreme.justia.com/cases/federal/us/354/234/]

US Department of Education (2017) 'Postsecondary Institutions and Cost of Attendance in 2017–18; Degrees and Other Awards Conferred, 2016–17; and 12-Momth Enrollment, 2016–17'. First Look (Preliminary Data). US Department of Education, NCES2018-060.

Chapter 5

Shaping European universities
A perspective from the Netherlands

Stephan van Galen

Introduction

The governance of Dutch universities has undergone several significant changes over the past half-century, most of which find their parallels in other continental European countries. Major changes in governance structures have been implemented by successive Dutch governments seeking to deal with issues such as the sharp increase in numbers of students and staff from the mid-1960s, reform of university curricula in the 1970s, and the balance between academic freedom and accountability in the 1980s. The growth of Dutch universities between the 1960s and 1980s was a major impetus for change, as it was across the rest of Europe. This tumultuous period was followed by a period of relative stability and consolidation coupled with an only marginal increase or even slow decline in student numbers between 1990 and 2000; during this period, critical reforms of university governance have made Dutch universities more autonomous, flexible and innovative. In continental Europe, comparable reforms have taken place with the aim of strengthening the executive capacity of universities and to deal with the effects of mass higher education (Ritzen, 2010, p. 162). The reform agendas had a number of items in common, including the enhancement of institutional autonomy, the professionalisation of institutional leadership and administration, and the introduction of more competitive, performance-oriented funding models (Gornitzka *et al.*, 2017, p. 274; Hicks, 2012; Westerheijden, 2018).

The sustained growth of universities from 2010 onwards, and the market-driven and network-based mode of governance of the twenty-first century present challenges to Dutch and European universities, as their many stakeholders have divergent policy goals and expectations concerning university strategy and policy. This is of course one of the results of the success of universities, as Noorda (2018) has observed, 'they are seen as essential engines of development, fertile grounds for new generations of professionals, and indispensable providers of smart solutions to future questions' (p. 25). Governments have developed policies to improve the contribution of universities to the Knowledge Society, but, as we will see, these policies have met with only partial success (Van Vught, 2008, pp. 151, pp. 164–172).

In this chapter, I describe and analyse the development of university governance in the Netherlands from circa 1960 until the present, and argue that in the current multi-actor network-based mode of governance, a stronger role for the European Union in university governance as a supra-national agency could serve to further focus and strengthen the quality and impact of education, research and innovation of European universities. Universities operate in an international context, and the governance of universities should therefore also be reconsidered from this perspective.

The Bologna process, which aimed to introduce the bachelor-master system across Europe and to promote mobility within Europe, still lacks a European statute for universities and a single European Accreditation Agency. Bologna is potentially a boost to the competitiveness of European universities. However, the implementation seems too nation-specific, so that the transparency of European universities has not increased as much as could be possible. Transparency is important as the higher education market has some major imperfections. To correct these imperfections, credible and independent information is needed for students and society, so that they are able to judge the quality of education and research (Van Vught, 2008, p. 167). The current system of governance has rightly been characterised by De Boer *et al.* (2007) as:

> a complex jumble, more and more a hybrid combination of multiple coordination forms. It is a blend in which hierarchies, markets, networks and communities are conveyed without clear dominance of any one of them. Within these realities the university as an organization has come to the fore . . . as a corporate actor.
>
> (p. 30)

I conclude in the sections below that this corporate actor has been severely tied up in a bewildering web of contradictory government regulation, as governments increasingly realise the importance of universities to the development of society and the economy. The present system of governance of Dutch universities has as a result become increasingly incoherent and problematic. Universities, in short, run the risk of becoming unmanageable. I will argue that the 'Macron initiative' to create European universities could offer a way out of the jungle of recent policy reforms, as a first step to a new governance paradigm that takes into consideration the international character of universities.

Universities between autonomy and control

Dutch higher education has a binary system, which means that a distinction is made between research-oriented education and higher professional education. This difference in orientation has continued to exist after the introduction of the bachelor-master degree structure in 2002. Research-oriented education takes place primarily at research universities, *universiteiten*, and higher professional education at universities of applied sciences, *hogescholen*. As well as the different objectives, each of the two types of education has its own admission requirements, programme duration and governance structures. The Dutch research universities are the only institutions of higher education in the Netherlands allowed to award PhD degrees. This chapter limits itself to the governance of government-funded research universities.

Independence

The post-war growth of universities resulted in 1960 in a significant change in the governance structure of Dutch universities. In 1960 universities got the status of an independent legal entity formally disconnected from the state as a result of the new law on Scientific Education, *Wet op het Wetenschappelijk Onderwijs.*

This autonomy was nowhere more clearly manifest, or concrete, than in the transfer of legal ownership of university buildings from the state to the university. Although the state remained financially responsible for the upkeep and maintenance of the buildings until 1995, those buildings were from 1961 formally owned by the university. Buying and selling, building new laboratories, lecture theatres or office space now became the prerogative of the university. Although it is clear from, for example, the archives of the University of Groningen that it took a while before civil servants from central and local governments really got to grips with the new reality (University of Groningen, 1961). Departments of planning and real estate were created at each university to assist and advise management on the complexities of real estate planning and development. In fact, universities had grown so fast that it had become unfeasible for central government to deal with the demands of university real estate on a central basis. The continuous and unprecedented growth of student numbers during the 1960s and the associated increase in the numbers of staff would however also end this new-found but rather short-lived autonomy. The state soon felt pressured to intervene in university policy, and a new order, characterised by an increase in state intervention, dawned at the end of the 1960s.

Table 5.1 Students enrolled at Dutch universities

Year	Students
1945	22,000
1950	25,000
1960	50,000
1970	100,000
1980	150,000
1990	190,000
2000	170,000
2010	240,000
2017	275,000

Source: CBS (2018).

Democracy

Universities in the Netherlands were until the 1970s governed by a *duplex ordo* consisting of a mainly honorific board of regents, *curatoren*, who oversaw the administrative side of the university; its tasks were de facto executed by the Secretary-General, *secretaris*, of the university, who was the head of the administrative staff, and on the other hand, the Senate, composed of full professors, who were in charge of education and research, chaired by the *rector magnificus*. According to Ritzen (2010), the Dutch university system 'very much resembled the Humboldt system of academic oligarchy' (p. 161).

The University Government Reorganisation Act of 1970 (*WUB*) fundamentally changed the nineteenth-century order at Dutch universities. The Act can be seen as a response to the May 1969 revolts at the campuses of Dutch universities, but from an international perspective neither student ideologies nor student tactics were really original. Students derived their ideas from the United States, Paris and Germany. Student agitation was, according to Daalder (1982), therefore far from original or persistent. The main driver behind the 1970 Act must be found in universities themselves. The increase in student numbers had led to a large increase in university staff. The Senate became unmanageable and younger staff members were generally excluded from the Senate. This led to cries for the professionalisation of the university on the one hand and the demands for more democracy on the other hand from junior staff (Daalder, 1982, pp. 178–180)

The 1970 Act introduced a condominium of two bodies, an executive board, *College van Bestuur*, and a university council, *Universiteitsraad*. The council was elected by and from three different constituencies, and one-sixth of its members were appointed by the crown on the nomination of the elected members from society at large. The executive board was a mixture of appointed and elected members. The law did not introduce 'direct democracy' nor did it present the university community with some sort of 'parliamentary' university government, but it had some far-reaching consequences. The Act, in short, navigated between introducing 'democracy' and 'management'.

The relation between the executive board and the university council was one of the most controversial issues in the implementation of the 1970 Act. Members of Parliament (MPs) demanded that the university council be the sole sovereign body in matters of university government and that the executive board should have no independent powers. They demanded a parliamentary democracy model. The executive board, however, got powers of its own and a guaranteed tenure for a fixed period. The board was to inform the council, but was not only responsible to the council, but also first and foremost to the Minister for the proper exercise of its powers (Daalder, 1982, pp. 173–175).

The relation between the university council and the executive board has changed significantly since 1970, but it has remained rather complex. From 1970 the powers of the executive board have increased step by step, as successive governments addressed the university as an independent entity. Steering university policy required a single addressee for central government, and the university council embodied the anarchistic, devolved institution, which had proved immune to government interference. Interestingly, recent amendments to the current law have increased the influence of the university council again in an apparent attempt to curb institutional autonomy. The question remains for how long this trend can continue; by increasing the powers of the devolved institution central government automatically diminishes its own ability to steer university policy. A clear example is given by De Boer *et al.* (2007):

> In December 1990, the minister and the chief executive boards of the universities reached an official gentlemen's agreement after lengthy negotiations with respect to the main policy objectives (the so-called Hoofdlijnenakkoorden 1990–1993). However, this agreement could hardly be described as effective since a number of university councils, having the formal authority to do so, rejected the agreement. The then existing governing model of 'mixed leadership' of Dutch universities, in which both the executive and the elected councils had decision-making powers, created a situation in which the relevant minister could not make a credible agreement. In other words, the government's attempt to steer this sector were frustrated by not having an addressee.
>
> (p. 31)

The 1970 Act did not stop at defining the governance of the university at the central level, it also prescribed the internal organisation of faculties, with elected faculty councils and even further down the line so-called *vakgroepen* or academic disciplines organised in departments, which were to be governed by all academic and non-academic staff in a certain discipline in a *vakgroep* board. This complex structure was only fully implemented in 1982, after years of experimenting and drafting new rules and regulations on all levels. Faculty regulations required approval at the university level, and university rules needed approval from the ministry. Organisational autonomy, or the ability for institutions to decide on their own internal governance structures as well as to develop their own procedures to select their institutional leadership, is still limited across Europe in general. In many European countries, the organisational autonomy is restricted by national legislation, regulations and guidelines. In the other words, the state frames the organisational structure of European institutions to a large extent. Only a few countries in continental Europe have implemented reforms that have seriously transferred to the universities the power to decide on their internal governance structure (Daalder, 1982, pp. 176–177; De Boer, 2018).

The fiction that central government could command and control university policy through the issuing of detailed regulations of course fitted the general opinion at the time that society was manageable, but nowhere was this idea more thoroughly embedded in legislation than in higher education. The expanding detail of interference by central government oversaw these changes by means of an expanding range of laws, decrees, procedures, regulations and administrative supervision.

At the same time, academic matters were almost exclusively the domain of the professionals. In fact, academic self-governance (regarding academic matters) and state regulation (regarding non-academic matters) went hand in hand (De Boer *et al.*, 2007, p. 29). The introduction of elected councils at all levels across the institution meant of course that university decision-making came to a virtual standstill during the 1970s and early 1980s. The system created by the 1970 Act was inspired by the concept of 'worker self-determination' as practised in communist Eastern Europe at the time. Almost all members of staff were automatically members of the departmental board. As a result, board meetings of disciplines, institutes or laboratories were often conducted in an auditorium. Everything had to be agreed upon by everyone, and as a result little was achieved. Willem Frederik Hermans, a lecturer in physical geography at the University of Groningen, as a literary author famous for his venomous pen, described university life in a bitter and satirical manner in an interview with the newspaper *NRC* in 1973 just before he left the Netherlands for his self-chosen 'exile' in Paris:

> Ever since the introduction of 'democracy' we are obliged to spend our time babbling in endless meetings. Imagine you need rubber bands. A day's meeting will not be enough . . . Any idea about the costs? A professor spending his days chattering? But anyway, meetings are not the only thing. After the meeting forms need to be filled-in, letters need to be written . . . all in all a waste of time and money.
>
> (Hermans, 1973)

The vision underlying the democratisation of university governance structures across Europe assumed that the performance of the university would be improved by reducing the influence of professors, and enhancing the involvement of non-professorial academic staff, administrative staff and students in university governance. The result was that after the 1970s, decision-making power was concentrated in democratically elected, representative councils. This implied that all major decisions, for example, in the budget and personnel areas, of the university leadership had to be approved by one or more democratic councils (Gornitzka *et al.*, 2017, p. 278).

Daalder (1982) concludes that more democracy within the university did not lead to more autonomy from central government; the new governance was the result of intervention from government in the first place. Central government engaged on the contrary in more detailed intervention in response to the challenge of increasing student numbers. The reforms that followed the 1970 Act did not make the universities more open to change, whether prompted from within or from the outside, and all the new regulatory powers did not provide government with more control, but they did have a paralysing effect on the universities (Daalder, 1982, pp. 208, 225).

Government introduced regulations in the early 1980s aimed to increase graduation rates, change the structure and content of curricula, push for competitive research funding, and rationalise the overall cost of the system. Furthermore, a conditional research funding system was introduced, but this system met with little success. These policies are defined as remedial or corrective, and they represented a clear attempt to shift towards New Public Management (NPM) according to Westerheijden *et al.* (2009). The 1970s reforms did not provide an answer to the general dissatisfaction with higher education, and higher education became a hot political issue during the 1970s and early 1980s (Capano, 2018).

Autonomy

The second half of the 1980s shows quite another governmental approach. Instead of structural intervention, the emphasis was on the government stepping back and an increase in autonomy of higher education institutions. This indicates a fundamental change in the governmental attitude towards universities. It shows the loss of confidence in the government's capacity to centrally plan and control the higher education system and a willingness to take self-regulating capacities of Higher Education Institutions (HEIs) seriously (Van Vught, 1991, pp. 114–115, 126–127).

In 1985, a policy paper was published by the Ministry of Education, Culture and Science of the Netherlands (MOCW, 1985), the *Higher Education: Autonomy and Quality* (in Dutch: HOAK) document, setting out guidelines for a new reform strategy. Roel in 't Veld, the main author of this paper, applied new insights from NPM to higher education governance (McDaniel, 1997). This moment was a watershed not only in Dutch policy development but also in the evolution of higher education in continental Europe. This document was the first governmental declaration that the traditional strategy of command and control, which had characterised higher education for the previous century, had to be abandoned in favour of a steering-at-a-distance strategy. Autonomy and quality assessment were ideas/policy tools launched by that document and formalised by law in 1992 (Goedegebuure and Westerheijden, 1991).

In the HOAK document, a new steering philosophy as presented by the minister was deemed necessary because, according to the government, 'many in and around the higher education system are of the opinion that the present administrative and legislative higher education mechanism can no longer be considered optimal to meet the future demands which have to be placed on the system' (MOCW, 1985). The central concept of the philosophy presented is a substantial increase in the autonomy of the institutions through abolishing regulations, combined with the introduction of a system of retrospective quality control (Goedegebuure and Westerheijden, 1991, p. 500).

Since the mid-1980s, a number of important powers regarding financial policy were transferred to the universities. First of all, government subsidies were transferred as lump-sum subsidies, granting universities financial discretion. Central university management is allowed to cross-subsidise teaching and research and to make their own distributions across their faculties and institutes. Regulations that had limited the use of income from sources other than the government were abandoned. On average, about 25 per cent of a university's budget stems from contract activities; at some universities, this percentage is more than 30 per cent. Moreover, a priori ministerial approval of university budgets was dropped, and universities were granted independent borrowing powers. Since 1987, the universities have the power to appoint the professoriate without interference from the central government. Working conditions and labour relations are negotiated through the Association of Universities in the Netherlands (VSNU) on behalf of the universities. Academics are no longer civil servants but employees of a university. Since 1992, universities also bear full costs of any severance pay. Another step in this development of university-controlled resources has been the abolition of government involvement in the planning and funding of new buildings and building maintenance. Universities have owned their buildings since 1961, but they bear full costs only since 1995 (De Boer *et al.*, 2007, p. 37).

The first half of the 1990s also saw the introduction of University Holdings, in which universities are the sole shareholders. The Holdings were a response to the growing importance of market-oriented activities. University Holdings are usually composed of several businesses or companies ('subsidiaries') that 'valorise' scientific knowledge. Through this 'privatisation' of activities that are linked to the university, Dutch universities react to the new task of 'valorisation' that the government allotted to them (De Boer *et al.*, 2007, p. 37).

Universities, however, never received self-accrediting powers, also part of the HOAK philosophy, and consequently always needed government consent when starting new programmes.

The law *Modernisering Universitaire Bestuursorganisatie* (MUB) modernised university governance. The law was proposed by the then Minister of Education Ritzen in 1997, it was a further step towards more flexibility and autonomy for universities. Professional boards were introduced at both the central and faculty level, and management was no longer regarded as a part-time job. The role of 'councils' in decision-making was reduced from co-deciders to advisers with a strong influence. The law created full accountability for the administration towards society. The administration was placed in the hands of an executive board of three members, to be selected by a supervisory board of five members appointed by the minister (Ritzen, 2010, pp. 169–171).

Greater accountability also means that higher education institutions have to redefine the ways in which they inform their stakeholders about their performances. The introduction of accreditation and the development of performance agreements should therefore be seen as a natural result of the development of a more independent university at the start of the twenty-first century. In the next two sections, the introduction and effects of accreditation and performance agreements as new tools for government steering through networks of stakeholders will be described.

Accreditation

The biggest change in the higher education system in recent years was the introduction of the bachelor-master system in 2002 in order to increase students' international mobility (MOCW, 2018). In 2002, accreditation was introduced simultaneously to assure the quality of the new degree programmes. From 2003, the Accreditation Organisation of the Netherlands and Flanders (NVAO) has been responsible for the validation of all degrees in the Netherlands and Flemish-speaking Belgium.

In Europe in general, a similar evolution of governance systems took place at the same time, involving actors from various levels outside central government. Authorities and powers in higher education systems have consequently been redistributed across these levels (De Boer, 2018). In many countries, coordination has changed from a classical form of regulation dominated by a single actor, the state, to forms in which various actors at various system levels govern the system, like in the Netherlands and Flanders, for instance, the NVAO. Thus, in the Netherlands and in Europe, enhanced institutional autonomy has taken place together with higher levels of accountability, and more stringent and detailed procedures for quality assurance have been introduced.

In 2011, the Netherlands introduced a so-called institutional audit as part of a new two-tier accreditation system. This system aims to focus quality assurance and accreditation in higher education more exclusively on the content of the programme and learning outcomes and is intended to reduce the administrative burdens of internal and external quality assurance processes (Jongbloed et al., 2018a, p. 672).

The aim of the institutional audit is to determine whether or not the executive board of an institution, on the basis of its vision regarding the quality of the education it provides, has in place an effective system of quality assurance that can guarantee the quality of the programmes. The central question is whether the executive board is 'in control', and as such the introduction of the institutional audit perfectly fits the steering-at-a-distance philosophy introduced by the HOAK paper and the MUB. This revision of the accreditation system should also have increased academic ownership of quality assurance systems within higher education institutions and have introduced a 'light touch approach' based on 'high trust' earned during 25 years of external quality assurance procedures introduced after the HOAK paper in 1986 (Van Galen et al., 2013, pp. 1–25). In these 25 years, the system has undergone a profound shift from quality enhancement to accountability. The new two-tier accreditation system was intended to steer back to a more quality enhancement-led approach (Van Galen et al., 2009, pp. 1–5).

The initiative for the revision of the accreditation system in the Netherlands came during the summer of 2007 from the Dutch Minister for Education Plasterk. The need for a revision of the system was broadly felt in the Netherlands. From the perspective of HEIs, accreditation focused too much on procedures and processes not directly relevant to education, was not cost-effective, and was felt to be too bureaucratic. HEIs felt that the system had become geared too much towards accountability and had almost lost the important enhancement function. From the government perspective, as well as from the perspective of politics, accreditation was not flexible enough to be able to react quickly to public concerns about quality issues in higher education. Students felt that accreditation was helpful in eliminating programmes that did not meet standards, but were also concerned that accreditation was focusing too much on the procedural end of quality assurance. Prior to 2007, this uneasiness with the accreditation system had initiated a debate, led by the Dutch Association of Universities (VSNU), advocating the adoption of institutional accreditation, leaving the assessment of individual programmes to the internal quality systems of HEIs. These proposals were not accepted by politicians and students (Van Galen et al., 2009).

After having conducted a thorough study of the development of accreditation processes on the institutional and programme level in several other continental European countries and having identified the strong and weak points of these systems, the first step taken by NVAO was to involve its European partners in the development of the basic set up of the system. In the discussion with the international partners, it became rapidly clear that many quality assurance systems in Europe are moving towards a mix of institutional review and programme assessment and seem to be converging towards a combined approach where institutional review and programme assessment complement each other (Van Galen et al., 2009). In Europe today, there is a general consensus about the design of external and internal quality assurance systems. The 2015 *Standards and Guidelines for Quality Assurance in the European Higher Education Area* (ESG) from the European Association for Quality Assurance in Higher Education (ENQA, 2015) reflect this consensus. A single European accreditation agency under EU law would be a significant step forward in the Bologna process as it can substantially increase transparency on the quality of provision and will certainly stimulate and facilitate mobility of staff and students within the EU (Jongbloed et al., 2018b, pp. 445–447). The proposed agency can build upon the work of ENQA and the European Quality Assurance Register for Higher Education (EQAR).

Performance agreements

The introduction of performance agreements in 2012 is, like the introduction of accreditation, another example of the emergence of networked governance. This development was described by Jongbloed et al. (2018b, p. 444) as the result of the diversity of needs and approaches, combining state supervision with increased autonomy for institutions with a new focus on local networks of students, stakeholders and government authorities. Networked governance relies more on negotiations, collaborations and partnerships, it widens perspectives from NPM's focus on efficiency and effectiveness to include public values such as social equity, societal impact and value from knowledge (Jongbloed et al., 2018b, pp. 441–444), and as such can also be seen as the next step in the development of NPM.

It should be noted that, of course, a substantial part of a university's block grant has always in some way or another been tied to performance, as student numbers and numbers of degrees granted have for a long time already been part of the nation-wide funding mechanisms.

The new performance contracts tie a small part of the funding of universities to targets agreed beforehand with government. In the Netherlands, universities made agreements on increasing diversity in terms of degree programmes, student success rates, teaching qualifications for research staff, and, for example, the percentage of students participating in honours classes (Jongbloed *et al.*, 2018a, pp. 677–678).

The introduction of targets is the new element in the performance-based approach. For the period 2012–2016, 7 per cent of the core grant for education, or about €130 million in total, was included in the agreements. An independent review committee was installed by the Minister of Education to oversee the performance agreements. The committee concluded in 2016 that many universities had achieved substantial success in meeting their targets. Completion rates had risen on average from 60 to 74 per cent, and dropout rates declined. The second objective, to stimulate diversity of provision, met with less success (Jongbloed *et al.*, 2018a, pp. 678–684). This should not come as a surprise as in the complex environment of university governance it is much harder for executive boards to force academics to introduce new study programmes and open up new avenues for research in areas desired by central government. The fact that the state has by law attributed responsibility for the quality of education directly to deans of faculties and also granted elected faculty councils co-decision rights on this subject makes central intervention in this area of course difficult. The law governing higher education is also, on the one hand, centred around the concept of a degree programme, and accreditation still takes place at the programme level. This can be viewed as to be in conflict with the settlement of many powers, on the other hand, at the top level. As De Boer (2018) already concluded, 'in Europe in general one can witness a growing recognition that relationships in higher education are extremely complex and dynamic, involving actors from various levels outside central government. Authorities and powers in higher education systems have consequently been redistributed across these levels' (pp. 2–3). This recognition has however not been met with a new and coherent approach by government in the design of new policy initiatives such as the performance agreements, and as such they can develop into a major barricade obstructing effective government steering (Van Vught, 2008).

Although Jongbloed *et al.* (2018a, p. 684) conclude that the performance agreements have met with a general approval by the public, the reception in parliament, by students and the universities, has been mixed. The focus of the agreements of indicators and targets has received much criticism and was one of the reasons that sparked the most serious riots since the 1960s at the University of Amsterdam (Gornitzka *et al.*, 2017, pp. 274, 280). The next round of performance agreements will as a result be rebranded as Quality Agreements, stressing the fact that the agreements should enhance the quality of provision for students. The Review Committee will be superseded by NVAO, de facto creating a higher education authority. It can be questioned if the rebranding of the agreements will fundamentally change their character, and it is also questionable how the effectiveness of central steering by the executive board will be increased. A new measure to increase this effectiveness is the requirement to include the university council in the drafting of the agreements. How effective this will be has to be seen. The fact that the composition of the university council changes every year leaves a large question mark in this respect. Apart from this, the university council bears no executive responsibility and is not accountable to government.

University management

The governance structure of universities in the Netherlands, including the formal appointment procedure of the members of the universities' supervisory board and executive board, have been laid down in the Higher Education and Research Act (WHW). There are three governing bodies at the central level: a supervisory board, *Raad van Toezicht*, consisting of a maximum of five external members, an executive board, *College van Bestuur*, consisting of a maximum of three members (including the rector), and the university council, *Universiteitsraad*, an elected representative body for staff and students. Universities can determine themselves whether or not to split the university council into two separate councils for staff and students. In essence, this is a clear example of the Rhineland-model of a two-tier board, with a representative council of elected students and staff for co-decision making. A Dutch speciality is the collegial board, where board members have an equal vote; the President's vote only decides when no majority can be found otherwise. The supervisory board and the executive board both operate on the basis of these principles. The principle of the collegial board means that board members work and operate on a more or less equal footing. It also means that sometimes the *Rector Magnificus* is the de facto chair of the board, although this position is normally reserved for the president of the board. Some universities have experimented with a system in which the role of president and *Rector Magnificus* are combined in one person, keeping the total number of board members at three.

Supervisory board

Supervisory boards were created after 1995. The five members of this council cannot be active politicians or (senior) civil servants from central government, and are generally CEOs of (large) multinationals or hospitals, senior judges, or directors of cultural institutions. The supervisory board of a public university is appointed by the Minister of Education, Culture, and Research. The appointment of a member of the supervisory board has to be made on the basis of a job description and profile that has to be submitted for advice to the university council.

In practice, the appointments of members of the supervisory board are made more or less on the basis of co-optation. Civil servants at the ministry do not intervene in the process, and the selection of candidates is left to the supervisory board itself, although the possibility exists for ministers to intervene in the process, and some ministers have indeed done so, some appointing 'political friends'. The university council has the right to nominate a member of the supervisory board. This nomination should consist of more than one candidate. The member nominated by the university council has the so-called 'special confidence' of the university council.

The supervisory board's main role is to oversee the work of the executive board and to advise the board. The supervisory board appoints and dismisses the members of the executive board, designates the chairperson, and determines the amount of the remuneration of the executive board within the limits of the law. It approves university statutes and bylaws, the budget, the accounts, the annual report, and the strategic plan. From 2010 the board is also responsible for the internal system of quality assurance (WHW art. 9.8). If and when the supervisory board neglects its duties, the Minister can force the board to act and issue them a directive (WHW art. 9.9 and 9.9a).

Appointment procedure: executive board

The supervisory board has to consult the university council in a variety of ways before it appoints one of the three executives. The law is however quite unclear on the precise involvement of the university council in the procedure as frequent changes of the WHW since 1997 have resulted in a legal structure that is sometimes contradictory and outdated. It is, for example, unclear how many times and at which moment the university council should be involved in the appointment procedure, and what their rights precisely are (WHW art. 9.3-3, 9.33a-3, 9.40).

The appointment of a member of the executive board has to be made on the basis of a job description and profile that has to be submitted for advice to the university council. The supervisory board subsequently appoints a selection committee. The university council has the right to nominate two members of this committee, one nominee representing the students and one representing the staff. The number of committee members taking part in the selection process is not prescribed and is left to the discretion of the supervisory board. The selection committee advises the supervisory board on the appointment of a candidate, but the supervisory board decides in the end whom to appoint, but not before the supervisory board has again consulted the university council on the proposed appointment. Ministerial consent or approval is not required for the appointment of members of the executive board. More detailed procedures about the nomination and appointment of executives can be laid down in university bylaws. The WHW explicitly indicates that, for example, the supervisory board can consult the deans before taking a decision on the appointment of the rector. The law thus provides an opening for the involvement of deans in the process, but at the same time it is not clear how this special involvement of the deans is to be reconciled with the formal procedure described above. In sum, the appointment procedure for members of the executive board has become almost unmanageable and leads to confusion of the roles of the different stakeholders. The university council has gradually been granted more influence in the process, but earlier and overlapping and conflicting rights of this elected council have not been removed from the law when new features were added, leading to a cumbersome procedure in an already delicate process.

Executive board

The executive board is charged with the management and administration of the university as a whole. The president of the executive board is the legal representative of the university. The board appoints the deans, who have full authority in faculties. The board also appoints the director(s) of the administration and services who in turn control those departments. The executive board was in full control of the budget until 2015, but recent changes to the WHW have re-introduced co-decision powers for the university council. The council has now the right to approve the outline of the budget. However, the law does not specify what has to be considered an 'outline' and what not. The second round of performance agreements, or 'quality agreements', have to be made with the Department of Education by the executive board in joint agreement with the university council. This has partly reintroduced the situation of the 1970s in which university decision-making can be brought to a standstill if there is no agreement between the university council and the executive board. As a result, central government will also lose the ability to steer the university from a distance as it is not clear who is actually in charge, and, as mentioned earlier, frequent changes in the composition of the university council will also affect the commitment of the council to agreements made by predecessors.

University council

The members of the university council represent the academic community. They constitute the highest democratically elected body within the governance of the university. Delegates are elected by the students from their midst. Staff elect an equal number of representatives from among them every other year. The members jointly appoint a chairperson – either or not from their midst (University of Groningen, 2018). Universities can choose to replace the university council with separate councils for staff and students, in which case there is an obligation to convene delegates from those councils in a joint meeting when discussing university strategy, or for example the budget. This then results in three councils instead of one (Radboud University, 2018).

The university council consults with the executive board regarding university-wide policy on teaching, research, finances and human resources. The council provides the board with solicited and unsolicited advice and has the right of consent on university strategy, quality assurance, university bylaws and statutes, labour conditions and several other topics. The council also has the right to advice on a variety of other issues (WHW 9.33 and 9.33a).

A governance jungle

Capano (2018) showed that between 1988 and 2015 'the Dutch government has clearly and repeatedly stated the goals of its design' (p. 687). These goals consist of an increase in the graduation rate, the internationalisation of the system, and profiling and institutional differentiation. The emphasis may have changed over time; however, the same basic goals have been pursued and effectively communicated to universities. As noted above, in the last few years government policy in the field of university governance has however become unclear and contradictory (Westerheijden et al., 2009). It seems, thus, that there is no such clear vision on the direction of governance in higher education that relates to the wider policy objectives of the government in the development of the knowledge economy. On the contrary, increased autonomy and consumer sovereignty or the relative privatisation of higher education have failed to consider the importance of reputation and the race to the top. According to Van Vught (2008), the dynamics of higher education are first and foremost a result of the competition for reputation. Reputation brings in resources, and this leads to an increase in mimicking behaviour amongst HEIs (pp. 166–172).

Apart from the examples given in the previous sections, there are several more occasions in which government policies enacted in recent years will lead to indecisiveness at the university level. One major example is that, instead of introducing institutional accreditation, which should have been the logical consequence of the introduction of the institutional audit, and which would have been the jewel in the crown of the Ritzen reforms of 1997, Minister Bussemaker, in carrying out the student-loan policies of her liberal predecessor Zijlstra, re-introduced co-decision rights on 'the main items' of the university budget for the university council, without describing what is meant with 'the main items'. This is perfectly in line with the theory of a networked governance, but a serious impediment to an effective executive. Another example is a recent law providing co-decision powers to the representative programme boards that overlap with the powers of the elected faculty council. A situation has been created in which two representative councils composed of staff and students can hold each other hostage if they do not agree on certain rules and regulations over which they have co-decision authority. Ironically, the 2016 law was christened the 'Law on Enhanced Governance'. Admittedly, amendments to the law, like the one discussed immediately above, were not a result of a conscious government policy, but rather the result of spontaneous interruptions of activist MPs, but government caved in to the demands of parliament, and in doing so it has created all the circumstances that make it possible for a university to spiral out of control.

This return of overregulation and micromanagement can seriously hinder the successes of higher education. I believe that more autonomy within higher education will improve the performance of our institutions and, as the result of that, of the higher education system overall. The rationale for this belief rests on the autonomous higher education institution being able to control and steer its outcomes and performance. The reforms of the past few years are a serious obstacle in this respect. Noorda (2018, pp. 25–26) observed that autonomy is the *conditio sine qua non* of universities; how could they otherwise have the capacity and freedom to inquire, to teach, and to criticise or approve? But Noorda also, and rightly so, states that universities should 'realise that they are partners in a social contract'. Governments and society at large have realised that universities are too important to be left alone. This should be seen as the main reason behind increased government regulation in the last decade. Therefore, it should be noted that university autonomy is not carved in stone forever. Universities are bound and steered by the dynamics of economic realities, political preferences, business priorities, and social diversity (Noorda, 2018, pp. 25–26). In general, this means that we need to find a new trade-off between autonomy and accountability in the design of the governance of higher education. The big question is whether or not this new solution can be found at the national level, or should be constructed in the context of the international arena in which universities operate today.

European universities

The European Universities initiative, as first outlined by the former Dutch Minister of Education Jo Ritzen in 2010 in his book *A Chance for European Universities* and, perhaps unconsciously, embraced by the French President Emanuel Macron in a speech at the Sorbonne in 2017, presents a way of strengthening and deepening existing successful university collaborations. It is also an opportunity to form new partnerships across Europe (Ritzen, 2010). The idea of the European university is a significant opportunity to bring the governance of European universities more in line with their increasing European character and enhance and bolster their effectiveness and role in European society as promoters of European citizenship and producers of high-skilled graduates. Although the Macron version of the idea of a European university is perhaps the result of a 'quintessential' French solution to tackle institutional change in higher education; to add a new category of institutions to affect institutional change on a larger scale.

The European Universities initiative could be the basis of a new contract between Europe and its universities. It can build on the role of universities as engines for innovation and policy impact, and improve the quality of education and research by pooling resources. These communities of universities can further reinforce the interchange between research, teaching and innovation, and strengthen the institutional excellence through the exchange of people, knowledge and ideas in a trusted space. Establishing deeper collaboration will also provide a great opportunity to foster European identities and contribute to the education of a more internationally minded and flexible workforce.

The European Universities initiative will enable universities to jointly develop new and transformative strategies for becoming truly European, through networks that each have their unique selling points and a mission to act as models for the university sector. To enable this transition, universities need a European statute with a single principal: the European Commission, and a European-wide accreditation and quality control system. Ritzen (2010) has suggested that a special statute for European universities can contribute to a solution; the university would be accountable to a single agency related to the European Commission. Such a European university then should retain its block grants originally allocated by national government, but have them transferred to the independent European agency. It also should be able to compete for research grants in all European countries (Ritzen, 2010, pp. 128–129).

Conclusion

For Dutch universities to be effective, they need autonomy, a clear strategic focus, and a strong commitment to deliver on their objectives in a continuous dialogue with their stakeholders. The introduction of a European statute with European quality control and accreditation can maximise the impact of universities in a European context. The professionalisation of the Dutch university sector over the last 50 years has made these universities world-class providers of education and research. The current trend in Dutch politics to reintroduce elements of the 'workers' paradise doctrine' of the 1970s will seriously harm the quality of provision in the Netherlands and undermine the leading position of Dutch universities, as it can cause a standstill in decision-making processes. The EU initiative to create European universities can offer a way forward for institutions that have already become truly international. It is crucial that universities participating in the European Universities project share a joint vision for the future, and that the underlying objectives of organisational integration and of creating educational quality are defined from the beginning. The networks must be governed with maximum effectiveness and minimum extra bureaucracy. The governance of the network could at the start be based on regular meetings by the university leaderships, which would take ownership of the network's success. To distinguish themselves from traditional types of university partnerships, networks of European universities should commit to the creation of a common pool of physical, virtual, intellectual and administrative resources to be used by their communities.

In order to be successful, the initiative must be bold and ambitious and build on a concerted action from universities, governments and EU institutions. The support should not only cover the provision of long-term funding but also a commitment to achieve mutual recognition of degrees and resolve barriers to mobility as well as differences in quality assurance that exist between many European countries. The governments and national agencies should enable enough flexibility for the piloting of solutions leading to the interoperability of regulatory environments. In sum, the European Universities initiative should reflect the fact that universities have become truly international institutions, in search of a new 'social contract'.

References

Capano, G. (2018). Policy design spaces in reforming governance in higher education: The dynamics in Italy and the Netherlands. *Higher Education*, 75, 675–694. doi:10.1007/s10734-017-0158-5

CBS (Central Statistics Office of the Netherlands) (2018) *Jaarboek onderwijs in cijfers* [*Annual report: Education in figures*]. The Hague: Author.

Daalder, H. (1982) The Netherlands: University between the 'new democracy' and the 'new management'. In H. Daalder and E. Shils (eds), *Universities, politicians & bureaucrats: Europe & the United States* (pp. 173–231). Cambridge: Cambridge University Press.

De Boer, H.F. (2018, February) *The governance of higher education systems and institutions in Europe*. Working paper for the international workshop 'A comparative study of university governance, institutional leaders and leadership in East Asia', Hiroshima, Japan.

De Boer, H.F., Enders, J. and Leisyte, L. (2007) Public sector reform in Dutch higher education: The organizational transformation of the university. *Public Administration*, 85, 27–46. doi:10.1111/j.1467-9299.2007.00632.x

European Association for Quality Assurance in Higher Education (ENQA) (2015) *Standards and guidelines for quality assurance in the European higher education area*. Retrieved from http://enqa.eu/index.php/home/esg/

Goedegebuure, L.C.J. and Westerheijden, D.F. (1991) Changing balances in Dutch higher education. *Higher Education*, 21, 495–520. doi:10.1007/BF00134986

Gornitzka, Å., Maassen, P. and De Boer, H. (2017) Change in university governance structures in continental Europe. *Higher Education Quarterly*, 71, 274–289. doi:10.1111/hequ.12127

Hermans, W.F. (1973, 27 July) [Interview]. *NRC*. Retrieved from https://andereti jden.nl/aflevering/507/Onder-professoren

Hicks, D. (2012) Performance-based university research funding systems. *Research Policy*, 41, 251–261. doi:10.1016/j.respol.2011.09.007

Jongbloed, B., Kaiser, F., Van Vught, F. and Westerheijden, D.F. (2018a) Performance agreements in higher education: A new approach to higher education funding. In A. Curaj, L. Deca and R. Pricopie (eds), *European higher education area: The impact of past and future policies* (pp. 671–687). Dordrecht: Springer.

Jongbloed, B., Vossensteyn, H., Van Vught, F. and Westerheijden, D.F. (2018b) Transparency in higher education: The emergence of a new perspective on higher education governance. In A. Curaj, L. Deca and R. Pricopie (eds), *European higher education area: The impact of past and future policies* (pp. 441–454). Dordrecht: Springer.

McDaniel, O.C. (1997) *The effects of government policies on higher education: In search of alternative steering methods*. The Hague: VUGA.

Ministry of Education, Culture and Science of the Netherlands (MOCW) (1985) *Nota Hoger Onderwijs: Autonomie en Kwaliteit HOAK* [*White paper higher education: Autonomy and quality*]. The Hague: Author.

Ministry of Education, Culture and Science of the Netherlands (MOCW) (2018) *Higher education*. Retrieved from www.government.nl/topics/secondary-vocational-education-mbo-and-higher-education/higher-education

Noorda, S. (2018) Autonomy: A practice serving a purpose. In A. Heijnen and R. van der Vaart (eds), *Places of engagement: Reflections on higher education in 2040 – a global approach* (pp. 23–29). Amsterdam: Amsterdam University Press.

Radboud University (2018) *The works council*. Retrieved from www.ru.nl/english/about-us/organisation/works-council/

Ritzen, J. (2010) *A chance for European universities: Or, avoiding the looming university crisis in Europe*. Amsterdam: Amsterdam University Press.

University of Groningen (1961) Bestuursarchief Rijksuniversiteit Groningen 1960–1995 [Archive of the Board of the University of Groningen 1960–1995] (Inv. nr. 900). University of Groningen, Groningen.

University of Groningen (2018) *The university council*. Retrieved from www.rug.nl/about-us/organization/administrative/participation/uraad/?lang=en

Van Galen, S.E.A., Dittrich, K. and Frederiks, M. (2013) Das Neue Niederländische Akkreditierungssytem [The new Dutch accreditation system]. In W. Benz, J. Kohler and K. Landfried (eds), *Handbuch Qualität in Studium, Lehre und Forschung* (F8.9, pp. 1–25). Berlin: Raabe Verlag.

Van Galen, S.E.A., Woutersen, M., Martens, T. and De Jonge, H.L. (2009, November) *Balancing quality enhancement and accountability: Reforming the Dutch and Flemish accreditation system*. Paper presented at the European Quality Assurance Forum EQAF, Copenhagen.

Van Vught, F. (1991) The Netherlands: From corrective to facilitative governmental policies. In G. Neave and F. van Vught (eds), *Prometheus bound: The changing relationship between government and higher education in Western Europe* (pp. 109–127). New York: Pergamon Press.

Van Vught, F.A. (2008) Mission diversity and reputation in higher education. *Higher Education Policy, 21*, 151–174. doi:10.1057/hep.2008.5

Westerheijden, D.F. (2018) University governance in the United Kingdom, the Netherlands and Japan: Autonomy and shared governance after new public management reforms. *Nagoya Journal of Higher Education, 18*, 199–220.

Westerheijden, D.F., De Boer, H. and Enders, J. (2009) Netherlands: An 'Echternach' procession in different directions: Oscillating steps towards reform. In C. Paradeise, E. Reale, I. Bleiklie and E. Ferlie (eds), *University governance: Western European comparative perspectives* (pp. 103–125). Dordrecht: Springer.

WHW – Higher Education and Research Act, the Netherlands.

Chapter 6

Diverging governance models in a devolved system
Case studies from Scotland and Wales

Gerald Webber and Rebecca Davies

Scotland

'What you have to understand', a senior adviser to the Scottish National Party (SNP) told a group of University Secretaries in private, 'is that the party leadership distrusts the Scottish establishment . . . and that includes you'.

The press (*The Scotsman* at least), the police, the judiciary and the universities were, whether they realised it or not, unionist ramparts, culturally if not politically, and they were going to be reshaped by the new administration, one way or another. This was simply democracy in action, we were told. The question that we and our Principals (Vice-Chancellors) needed to ask ourselves was this: 'Who elected you?' In retrospect, it resonated strongly with other forms of modern-day populism, tilting at traditional elites.

In any event, the dogs were swiftly out of the traps once the SNP secured a majority in the May 2011 Holyrood elections. In June of that year the Scottish government established an independent panel to review higher education governance in Scotland. It was to be chaired by Professor Ferdinand von Prondzynski (colloquially referred to as 'Von Prond'), the newly arrived Principal of Robert Gordon University, who had assumed that role at the end of March 2011. He was to be supported in this work, some thought surprisingly, by government civil servants.

It was noted even at the time that the rationale for setting up the review was somewhat obscure. It was not entirely clear what the problems were that the review was intended to address, nor how any of the recommendations might improve teaching, research or operational efficiency. In the introduction to the final report there was reference to the 'democratic intellect' in Scotland, a swipe at the growth of 'managerialism' and a statement to the effect that 'university governance is not just a private matter', which of course it never had been. What flowed from the review was nevertheless quite simple in the end: a series of proposals designed to increase the perceived accountability of Scottish universities.

It was notable that, leaving aside the Chairman who had been hand-picked by the Minister, the involvement in the review group of experts from the universities themselves was limited. Although one independent member of a governing body was included in the membership of the review group, there were no places available for any Principal or Vice-Chancellor that might have been nominated by Universities Scotland (the representative body of Principals and Vice-Chancellors) nor for any of the Secretaries to any of the governing bodies who inevitably knew more than most about the operational reality of institutional governance in Scotland. There were however places for the trades unions (which the SNP had successfully courted, at least in part to weaken the Labour Party in Scotland), the Students Unions and an elected University Rector, the political journalist, Iain MacWhirter.

Those unfamiliar with the Scottish higher education system may be intrigued to note, in passing, that University Rectors are presently elected every three years by students (in one case by staff and students) and in principle, but not always in practice, they have chaired the governing bodies (University Courts) of most of the relevant institutions. However, only five Scottish universities have Rectors, namely the 'ancient' universities of Aberdeen, St Andrews, Edinburgh and Glasgow plus the University of Dundee, which was originally a part of St Andrews. Uniquely, the Rector at Dundee was never entitled to chair the Court.

The 2011 review was intended to be evidence-based but the bibliography to the report suggested that the evidence upon which they drew was at best limited in scale and scope. There were, of course, written submissions from various parties and face-to-face evidence sessions, to which one of the present authors (Webber) contributed. However, the extent to which the panel was able collectively to evaluate the evidence was unclear. It was reliably reported that members of the review panel found it very hard to meet as a group, and the report that eventually emerged was said to have involved a significant amount of last-minute 'horse-trading' over preferred solutions.

The final report was submitted to the Scottish Ministers on 16 January 2012 and made a series of recommendations which the Scottish government welcomed. The Minister declared shortly after publication that the government was minded to implement 'almost all' of it.

Many of the recommendations were innocuous. Others were not. In particular, the report recommended that:

- there should be a new 'statute' for Scottish universities – eventually taking shape as the Higher Education Governance (Scotland) Act 2016;
- the Chair of the governing body should be elected 'reflecting the democratic ideal of Scottish higher education' (recommended with one member dissenting), and once elected, remunerated;
- in addition to including two members nominated by the students' union and two elected staff members, governing bodies should include one member nominated by the academic trade union, and another by the support staff union;
- meetings of the governing body should be held in public but senior managers other than the Principal (Vice-Chancellor) should neither be members of the governing body, nor normally be in attendance, even though the meetings were intended to be open;

- the constitution of academic boards (Senates) should be prescribed in statute and limited to 120 members, the latter recommendation appearing quite bizarre to any institutions (who had much smaller academic bodies already) other than the ancient universities;
- the Scottish Funding Council (SFC) should commission the drafting of a new Code of Good Governance, despite the fact that there was already a UK Code (drawn up by the Committee of University Chairs) which had been adopted in 2004 and revised as recently as 2009; and
- a new definition of academic freedom should be included in the proposed Scottish statute even though an existing provision was already enshrined in law and broadly mirrored the UK provision.

It was difficult not to conclude that this was more about culture and identity than good governance. There was scant evidence of any serious problems with existing governance structures; the election of chairs and the inclusion of trades union nominees threatened to undermine the concept of the unitary board which was (and is) widely regarded as a central pillar of good governance; the executive branch of the governance framework would be significantly weakened, mainly it seemed as a curb on the ill-defined concept of 'managerialism'; and existing UK governance frameworks were to be supplanted by Scottish provisions regardless, or so it appeared, of their practical utility.

Certainly the debate over Scottish independence loomed large in the deliberations of the panel. The *Report of the Review of Higher Education Governance in Scotland* (Scottish Government, 2012) linked the two quite candidly:

> Over the next few years Scotland will discuss its constitutional future and how its politics and social institutions can best both represent and serve its people. The nation's universities should be at the centre of this discourse . . . recognising that their own role and how they conduct themselves has to come under objective scrutiny . . . No informed decision about the desirability of independence, or any other new constitutional settlement, can be made without including the future of the universities in the public debate. This approach underlies our recommendations.
>
> (Scottish Government, 2012, Section 7.2)

Who exactly those 'objective' scrutineers would be was a moot point.

In any event, there was a flurry of further activity in 2012 on two main fronts.

First, the Committee of Scottish Chairs reached an agreement with the SFC and the then Cabinet Secretary for Education and Lifelong Learning, Michael Russell MSP, to establish an independent group chaired by Lord Smith of Kelvin to draft a Scottish code of governance for universities which was published and adopted in 2013 (Committee of the Chairs of Scottish Higher Education Institutions, 2013). Whilst prompted by the 'Von Prond' report (Scottish Government, 2012), this was seen by many in the sector, at least in part, as being a pre-emptive defence against more direct intervention and an opportunity to persuade the government that there was little need for additional legislation. In that, it failed.

Second, 2012 was notable, at least in retrospect, for the introduction by the SFC of bilateral 'Outcome Agreements' with Scottish higher education institutions (HEIs), the first of which were negotiated for academic year 2012/13. As one wag noted at the time, they had little to do with outcomes and weren't really agreements. In fact, they provided the SFC (and by extension, though not directly, the Cabinet Secretary who issues the SFC with annual 'guidance') an additional means of control, albeit relatively benign and focussed on marginal change. In principle, Outcome Agreements were to be negotiated and to include proposed measures of success. However, as time passed, the measures metamorphosed into targets, and the Financial Memorandum, with which Scottish universities are required to comply if they wish to receive public funding, was amended to state baldly that 'the institution must deliver its Outcome Agreement with SFC' (Scottish Funding Council, 2014, Part 2 Para 4). It was a further erosion of university autonomy, presented of course, as an improvement in accountability, merely a part of our 'something-for-something' culture, the long-term impact of which is as yet unclear.

The screw was tightened further in 2013. The Post-16 Education (Scotland) Act, 2013 was primarily intended to pave the way for a series of mergers in the further education sector, required but not directly dictated by the Cabinet Secretary. Reform was in no way limited to universities at this time. The legislation did however contain one provision regarding the governance – 'good governance' of course – of higher education institutions. Section 2 of the Act stated that:

> The Scottish Ministers may . . . impose a condition that the [Scottish Funding] Council must, when making a payment to a higher education institution . . . require the institution to comply with any principles of governance which appear to the Council to constitute good practice in relation to higher education institutions.

It was a remarkably draconian form of words – 'must . . . require . . . comply . . . any principles . . . which appear to the Council'. It even breached the normal convention that Codes would be issued on a 'comply or explain' basis, eroding the distinction between guidance and regulation. It was a further wearing away of institutional autonomy, and however carefully this provision may have been implemented in the period since the legislation was enacted, it remains a potential instrument of control.

Universities might have hoped that the agreement of the Code in 2013 would be sufficient to deflect the government from further legislation. If so, the hope was misplaced. In November 2014, shortly after the referendum on independence had been narrowly defeated, the Scottish government returned to the subject and published a public consultation paper (Scottish Government, 2014).

It was one of Michael Russell's final acts as Cabinet Secretary, a last kick of the ball just when observers thought that the appetite for legislation might have been waning. The consultation covered six potential areas of change concerning: the Privy Council; academic freedom; the role of principals; the chairing of governing bodies; membership of governing bodies; and the composition of academic boards.

Much of it appeared at face value to be dry and technical, if not pointless: did changes to university statutes really need to be approved by a Scottish government committee instead of the Privy Council? Did it really matter if vice-chancellors were always referred to as principals and never as CEOs? In any event, it was no clearer than the 'Von Prond' report about which problems exactly the government was seeking to address, and although the document stated that the government's aim was 'not to increase Ministerial control . . . but to support our institutions to develop their own governance systems', the proposals were overwhelmingly prescriptive. As *Wonkhe*, a respected online publication concerned with politics and policy in higher education, put it at the time: 'the whole package looks like a one-way ticket to reduced autonomy, more standardisation and greater government control over higher education in Scotland' (*Wonkhe*, 2014). And so it proved.

The Higher Education Governance (Scotland) Bill was introduced in June 2015 and passed into law by the Scottish Parliament in March 2016. The Bill, as introduced, held few surprises but was notable for several omissions and one nasty shock.

Most of it was broadly as expected: Chairs were to be elected and remunerated; governing bodies would include TU nominees; academic boards would be reconstituted to ensure that at least 50 per cent of the members were elected and that the total number did not exceed 120 (still); higher education institutions were conveniently re-defined to exclude the Open University (which operates legally in England but with a significant presence in Scotland, Wales and Northern Ireland) to avoid a spat with Westminster; and there was a convoluted section on academic freedom. Missing was any reference to some of the original 'Von Prond' targets such as the Privy Council, Chancellors' Assessors, public meetings, and the exclusion of senior managers from governing body proceedings.

Shockingly, however, Section 8 of the Bill provided that 'Scottish Ministers may by regulation modify' both the categories of membership of governing bodies, and the number of persons appointed under each. After furious opposition both from the universities themselves and opposition MSPs, this section was eventually dropped. The government blamed sloppy drafting by the civil servants. Some suspected otherwise.

The Act that emerged from the process was a curious mix of prescriptive detail and procedural uncertainty which University Secretaries and others have been left to untangle. Chairs, who are now mysteriously referred to as 'senior lay members' even though the legislation makes reference to no other 'lay members', are to be elected by students, staff and members of the governing body. Student numbers will inevitably dominate, but there is no definition in the Act of a student, and in practice this can be complicated. Should a part-time, online, non-credit-bearing student in China have the same voting rights as a full-time on-campus undergraduate? Presumably so. But how and to what extent will that make governance more 'democratic'?

Similarly, elections are to be held only when there are two or more candidates that a committee of the governing body is satisfied meet such criteria as the governing body itself may agree, but in the event of there being only one such candidate, elections must be postponed, without any prescribed time limit, and the governing body is then permitted to select a chair from amongst its existing members. And so it goes on. There are convoluted rules regarding the respective roles of the (elected) chair and the (differently elected) rector in the ancient universities. Chairs are to be appointed by an electorate but may be removed by a majority of the governing body. Academic boards cannot be larger than 120 members, but there is no reference in the Act to the size of the governing body. All in all, it is a strange beast.

Indeed, the further revised Code of Good HE Governance (Committee of the Chairs of Scottish Higher Education Institutions, 2017) that was commissioned by the Committee of Scottish Chairs with the agreement of the SFC just three years after the first Scottish Code was published, has now become an essential companion-piece to the oddly framed legislation.

Looking back to the origin of these reforms in 2011, and their subsequent enactment over a period of some five years, it is hard to believe that history will judge these changes kindly. An ill-defined problem has been addressed by an ill-considered review resulting in an ill-drafted Act. Thank goodness universities have proven themselves to be so resilient and adaptive over the centuries. One can only hope that they remain so into the future.

The need for reform in Scotland was never strong, and seemed mainly to be driven by politics. The concept of the unitary board, which is central to good governance and is still required by the 2017 Code, will be put under enormous strain in practice as a result of having 'senior lay members' with an electoral base independent of the Court itself, and trades union nominees who cannot reasonably be expected to remain impartial, particularly when the stakes are high, and especially if their union is taking industrial action against the employer, i.e. the governing body on which they shall sit. The self-governing autonomy of universities, which elsewhere has been seen as the best guarantee of intellectual independence and competitive academic prowess, has in Scotland been persistently diminished by Ministers hungry for control.

The decision to enact a new, more distinctively 'Scottish' approach to academic freedom is another interesting example of the way in which even well-meaning but poorly considered reforms can have unintended and negative consequences. Academic freedom provisions had already been embedded in Scottish law via the Further and Higher Education (Scotland) Act 2005. This stipulated that 'a fundable body must have regard to the desirability of . . . ensuring the academic freedom of relevant persons' (S26) which was already weaker than the rest-of-UK provisions which required that governors 'shall take such steps as are reasonably practical to ensure that freedom of speech within the law is secured' (United Kingdom Parliament, 1986). Part 2 of the Higher Education (Scotland) Act 2016 weakened it further, presumably inadvertently. Universities have only to 'aim' to uphold academic freedom under the 2016 Act, and even then the rights of the individual are subjugated to the considered views of their institution:

> A post-16 education body must aim to – (a) uphold (so far as the body considers reasonable) the academic freedom of all relevant persons, and (b) ensure (so far as the body considers reasonable) that . . . [appointments and entitlements] . . . are not adversely affected by the exercise of academic freedom by any relevant person.
>
> (Scottish Parliament, 2016, Part 2 S23 (2) (1))

The road to hell is paved with good intentions.

Cross the border to the west: recent developments in governance in Welsh higher education – a tale of close and getting closer . . .

Devolution in Wales, as in Scotland, has not simply been a matter of 'copy and paste' from Westminster – and higher education governance has developed a distinctive Welsh flavour.

There's no need in Wales for a friendly (Labour) government adviser to meet with University Chief Operating Officers (COOs) and/or Secretaries and Registrars as a group as happened in Scotland to tell them that they weren't trusted. In Wales politicians and Ministers have the mobile numbers, direct email addresses and know the Chairs of governing bodies by first name (there may even be a WhatsApp group – but I think I may be inventing that) to get any messages out. The political landscape in Wales is also different. The outcome of the May 2016 elections means Wales has a Labour minority government – with an element of a coalition – in that the Cabinet Secretary for Education is the one and only Welsh Liberal Assembly Member, Kirsty Williams. To give but one example of just how 'close to you' the relationship is between politicians and any Welsh university, the First Minister (at the time of writing – a leadership election is underway) is an Alumnus, as are four cabinet members and the Llywydd (Speaker for the Welsh Assembly) of Aberystwyth.

Since the advent of Welsh devolution (1998) legislation has been used to cement the informal 'closeness' through the development of policy and processes, but notably without the granularity of the composition/appointment process for governing bodies as in Scotland. You have to read between the lines to reveal the subtle and nuanced 'Welsh' approach to governance that arises from the close connections between government, the funding body, the civil service and the university sector in Wales.

The Welsh government has been explicit and consistent since its inception on the role of the Welsh Government Sponsored Public Bodies (WGSBs): from the environmental regulator Natural Resources Wales to the Higher Education Funding Council for Wales (HEFCW) they are to ensure the delivery of Welsh government policy priorities – and that means all government priorities not just the 'theme subject' of the particular WGSB.

Back in 2009, at around the tenth anniversary of devolution, the role of the HEFCW was seen as a friendly body between government and the HEIs. In the Welsh Government (2009) 'Report on the Citizen-Centred Governance Review of the Higher Education Funding Council for Wales' the authors explained that during their considerations contributors raised an 'unprompted' issue – whether the HEFCW should continue to exist as a standalone organisation. This was included in the report as there was 'such a strong and unanimous view expressed by the higher education sector' that HEIs wanted a 'buffer' between them and government.

But a buffer won't ensure governmental policy priorities are at the forefront of university governing bodies' minds in agreeing university strategies and determining their delivery priorities, or in particular at this point in time, in their desire to 'merge'. The refrain from the then Education Minister Leighton Andrews in late 2010 was of a 'smaller and stronger' sector in Wales – and his unambiguous warning to HEIs was that they needed to 'adapt or die'. The HEFCW came out with a friendly 'buffer' version of the message saying that their 'expectation' was that the number of institutions should reduce from 11 to 'no more than 6' (BBC Wales News, 2010). A buffer can only expect, a regulator can require. The outcome was that the HEFCW's 'expectations' were not fully met – and now in 2018 instead of a reduction to six HEIs, there are eight in Wales.

One of the blockages to reaching the target of six was well reported in the media – Leighton Andrews as Minister went to the press in July 2012 to state that he 'noted the response of the Cardiff Metropolitan University Board to the planned merger of Newport and Glamorgan after it voted 13-1 in favour of staying independent' (BBC Wales News, 2012). The Minister followed this up with an announcement that there would be a statutory consultation on the merger of Cardiff Metropolitan – the rhetoric was clear – Cardiff Metropolitan was going to be required to merge. However this 'adapt or die' consultation was formally withdrawn by the Minister in November of that year, with the Cardiff Metropolitan University's Chair of Governors Barbara Wilding CBE QPM welcoming the decision:

> The University is pleased that the Welsh Government has decided to cancel with immediate effect the statutory consultation process involving the dissolution of Cardiff Metropolitan University which we believe was legally and financially flawed. The proposals put forward for the reconfiguration of the Higher Education sector in South-East Wales did not contain enough evidence to enable the Governors to take such a decision about any reconfiguration option.
>
> (Wales Online, 2012)

The message from the Chair of the Governors of Cardiff Metropolitan was clear, in Wales the power lay with the governors, and the Welsh government policy of merger was not enforceable. This is problematic if your WGSB is meant to ensure the delivery of policy priorities and it transpires that it can only expect delivery and not require it.

There is an interesting take on the failure to meet the target number of HEIs in the 2013 Policy Statement on Higher Education' published by the Welsh government (Welsh Government, 2013). The Policy Statement does not quite make it explicit that the target of six was not achieved. Instead the document states;

> Structural changes *driven* by successive Welsh Governments have resulted in a Welsh higher education sector that is stronger and more sustainable. In April this year, the former University of Glamorgan and University of Wales, Newport merged to become the new University of South Wales serving the whole of the south-east Wales region. The University of Wales: Trinity St David and Swansea Metropolitan University began operating as a single institution in 2012 and plans are now well advanced for those institutions formally to merge later in 2013. By the end of 2013, therefore, Wales will have a smaller number of stronger universities – institutions better placed to compete on the global stage and to contribute strongly to the economic, educational, cultural and social well-being of Wales.
>
> (Welsh Government, 2013, p. 4, authors' emphasis)

It's an interesting use of the word 'driven' – so the reduction in HEIs was 'driven' but not enforced by the Welsh government – but the Policy Statement draws a clear line in the sand to move away from the friendly 'buffer' expectations that the HEFCW could make. The document contains an interestingly large number of occasions when the words 'must' (27 times) and 'will' (56 times) are used – which infers that the places where these words are used are government requirements rather than expectations, for example (my emphases in italic):

- 'HEIs *must* continue to extend their offering outside their campuses to embed learning opportunities in communities and workplaces' (p. 17).
- 'HEIs in Wales *must* work with other education providers to improve the effectiveness of learner progression at all stages' (p. 19).
- 'HEIs *must* communicate the positive student experience and excellent learning and teaching that students can expect from studying at a Welsh university' (p. 20).

Considering the failure in 2012 of government to enforce a merger and overrule a governing body (which must have been fresh in the mind of the authors of the Policy Statement) it's interesting that the Policy Statement makes little explicit reference to institutional level governance. However, in their list of the fundamental challenges which face the higher education system (p. 32) they include:

[the] challenge of public accountability for the public money that is injected into the system, which in a climate of economic scarcity will sharpen, no matter how large a proportion of HE income comes from fees, and will result in stronger national governance and a requirement for better and more strategic institutional governance.

(Welsh Government, 2013, p. 32)

Note the reference to 'proportion of income coming from fees', and on p. 24 the clearest statement of all:

The Welsh Government will bring forward legislation to ensure that HEFCW has appropriate powers and duties in relation to quality assurance and regulation of the HE sector which take account of the new funding arrangements for higher education provision.

(Welsh Government, 2013, p. 24)

The line in the sand is now set with cement: there will be new powers for the HEFCW. The use, in the Policy Statement, of language which sounds like it must be enforceable, the recognition of the shifting fee landscape and the challenge of institutional governance to be 'more strategic' have been combined to create the impetus for change. In particular there is a significant move from having the HEFCW 'expect' delivery from HEIs to being able to require it. The power relationship has shifted – the annual funding 'cheque' issued by the 'buffer' body HEFCW was now replaced by each individual student paying student fees to individual institutions – a buffer who no longer signs the funding cheque could be perceived as significantly less relevant. So new legislation was consulted upon and drafted and the result was the Higher Education (Wales) Act 2015. This changed the relationship – the HEFCW was now defined as the regulator of the sector. The Act neatly defines the route to ensure that HEI governance, strategy and delivery would be required to take policy priorities into account. The HEFCW is no longer the buffer between HEIs and government who as a body 'expect' change, they are the regulator (admittedly with limited cash) who wants to, and will, regulate the sector in Wales.

So how has this translated into practice? The HEFCW now state clearly that its regulatory role is to

ensure that higher education (HE) institutions whose students can access public grants and loans meet Welsh Government priorities around fee levels, fair access, quality of education and financial management.

(HEFCW, 2015a)

But that statement seems a little 'buffery' and not too much like a body with teeth who regulate to ensure that wider policy priorities are delivered. Further exploration of the HEFCW's role regarding policy priorities makes direct reference to the 2013 Policy Statement – the HEFCW explains that it:

operate[s] in an overall policy environment set by the Welsh Government, with many of our priorities set out in the Welsh Government's Policy Statement on Higher Education.

(HEFCW, 2015a)

So the frequent use of 'must' and 'will' within the Policy Statement now take on a different flavour. The regulator points to them, and the regulator can require rather than simply expect. In operational terms the HEFCW receives an annual remit letter from the Welsh government outlining the priority work areas for the HEFCW for the following year, which are translated into the variety of submissions required from HEIs in Wales. The 2018 letter from the Cabinet Secretary for Education to HEFCW made direct reference to government priorities:

it is essential that the Council and sector maintains a focus on key Welsh Government priorities. I therefore welcome the Council's ongoing work to establish performance measures for the sector and look forward to the outcomes of this work.

(Cabinet Secretary for Education, 2018, p. 7)

The annual requirement for a Fee and Access Plan is one of the regulatory tools used by the HEFCW, and the guidance for the annual plan helps define, in this new regulatory environment, the role of governing bodies. It's made clear that the governing body has a particular responsibility for its institution's Fee and Access plans. The Fee and Access Plan application must be approved by the HEFCW in order for an institution wishing its full-time undergraduate and its postgraduate certificate in education courses for trainee teachers to be automatically designated for student support. With a HEFCW approved Fee and Access Plan, the institution will become a regulated institution permitted to charge up to the maximum fee limit, currently £9,000, and students studying courses at that institution will be able to receive student support. Therefore in this close, and regulatory, relationship, each governing body needs to be alive to the Welsh government priorities, and they will also need to be mindful in 2018/19 for their institution to be ready to respond on the performance measures for government priorities that will soon be required.

An interesting test for the relationship between government and the sector in Wales has been 'The Well-Being of Future Generations (Wales) Act 2015'.

The Act 2015 (WBFGA) gives a legally binding common purpose of seven well-being goals which apply to local authorities, public service boards, local health boards, HEFCW, most public bodies and the Welsh government. There has been debate about the inferred and fuzzy public sector perception of HEIs (particularly by politicians) which helpfully has been clarified under the Act – universities and colleges are not directly included. However this has not meant that HEIs are not contributing (or being required to contribute) – the HEFCW (the regulator) is bound by the Act and the HEFCW has stated that it:

will seek to contribute towards the delivery of the seven goals of the Act through implementation of the sustainable development principle and the actions that will be set out within our new corporate strategy and operational plan.

(HEFCW, 2015b)

Thus an Act, where HEIs are defined as not being *directly* included, will place requirements upon the sector to deliver against the WBFGA priorities as the regulator (the HEFCW) is bound by the Act – a very elegant solution for government.

The link between policy priorities and the governing body activity in a university can, and is being, regulated by the HEFCW – but nothing stays still, and on the horizon (but the sector is not precisely sure when) we know the regulatory landscape for post-compulsory education in Wales is changing. The Cabinet Secretary for Education, Kirsty Williams, announced in early 2017 that there would be a new authority to oversee skills and the higher and further education sectors in Wales. This body is being called 'strategic' and follows the acceptance of the recommendations of an independent review carried out by Professor Ellen Hazelkorn (Hazelkorn, 2016). If the new single regulator for the post-compulsory education sector is established to meet the Hazelkorn recommendations then this body will regulate the quality, funding, research, the needs of learners and 'the equal value of vocational and academic pathways' for all post-compulsory education in Wales, 'without boundaries'.

My (invented) WhatsApp group for the close and getting closer relationship between HEIs and politicians is now going to have to have a much wider membership base.

References

BBC Wales News (2010) Welsh universities 'to be cut by half by 2013'. www.bbc.co.uk/news/uk-wales-12057890 [Published 22 December 2010. Accessed 29 October 2018]

BBC Wales News (2012) Minister defends university merger of Cardiff Met, Newport and Glamorgan. www.bbc.co.uk/news/uk-wales-south-east-wales-18882493. [Published 18 July 2012. Accessed 29 October 2018]

Cabinet Secretary for Education (Wales) (2018) Annual remit letter. www.hefcw.ac.uk/documents/about_he_in_wales/WG_priorities_and_policies/2018-19%20Remit%20Letter.pdf. [Accessed 29 October 2018]

Committee of the Chairs of Scottish Higher Education Institutions (2013 and 2017). Scottish Code of Good Higher Education Governance, 2013 and 2017 editions. www.scottishuniversitygovernance.ac.uk/ [Accessed 22 October 2018]

Hazelkorn, E. (2016) Towards 2030: A framework for building a world-class post-compulsory education system for Wales. https://beta.gov.wales/sites/default/files/publications/2018-02/towards-2030-a-framework-for-building-a-world-class-post-compulsory-education-system-for-wales.pdf [Accessed 29 October 2018]

HEFCW (2015a) Welsh government priorities. www.hefcw.ac.uk/about_he_in_wales/welsh_govt_priorities_and_policies/welsh_govt_priorities.aspx [Accessed 29 October 2018]

HEFCW (2015b) The Well-Being of Future Generations (Wales) Act 2015. www.hefcw. ac.uk/about_he_in_wales/welsh_govt_priorities_and_policies/well_being_future_ generations_wales_act_2015.aspx [Accessed 29 October 2018]

Scottish Funding Council (2014) Financial memorandum. www.sfc.ac.uk/web/ FILES/Guidance_Governance/Financial_Memorandum_with_higher_educa tion_institutions_-_1_December_2014.pdf [Accessed 22 October 2018]

Scottish Government (2012) *Report of the Review of Higher Education Governance in Scotland.* www.gov.scot/Publications/2012/02/3646ISBN 978 1 78045 648 5, Web publication only [Accessed 22 October 2018]

Scottish Government (2014) *Consultation Paper on a Higher Education Governance Bill.* www.gov.scot/Publications/2014/11/2389ISBN: 9781784129101   [Accessed 22 October 2018]

Scottish Parliament (2005) Further and Higher Education (Scotland) Act. www.legislation. gov.uk/asp/2005/6/contents [Accessed 22 October 2018]

Scottish Parliament (2013) Post-16 Education (Scotland) Act 2013. www.legislation.gov. uk/asp/2013/12/contents [Accessed 22 October 2018]

Scottish Parliament (2015) Higher Education Governance (Scotland) Bill (June 2015). www.parliament.scot/parliamentarybusiness/Bills/90125.aspx [Accessed 22 October 2018]

Scottish Parliament (2016) Higher Education Governance (Scotland) Act (March 2016). www.legislation.gov.uk/asp/2016/15/contents/enacted   [Accessed   22   October 2018]

United Kingdom Parliament (1986) Education Act (No.2). www.legislation.gov.uk/ ukpga/1986/61/contents [Accessed 22 October 2018]

Wales Online (2012) Leighton Andrews scraps plans to dissolve Cardiff Metropolitan University. www.walesonline.co.uk/news/wales-news/leighton-andrews-scraps-plans-dissolve-2016212 [Published 6 November 2012. Accessed 29 October 2018]

Welsh Government (2009) Report on the Citizen-Centred Governance Review of the Higher Education Funding Council for Wales. www.hefcw.ac.uk/documents/council_ and_committees/council_papers_and_minutes/2010/10%2002%2002governance%20 review%20report%20annex.pdf [Accessed 29 October 2018]

Welsh Government (2013) Policy Statement on Higher Education. www.hefcw.ac.uk/ documents/publications/corporate_documents/Policy%20statement%20on%20 higher%20education%20English.pdf [Accessed 29 October 2018]

Wonkhe (2014) Governance goings-on north of the border. 9 December. https://wonkhe. com/blogs/governance-goings-on-north-of-the-border/ [Accessed 22 October 2018]

Chapter 7

Changing university governance in South Africa

David J. Hornsby and Ruksana Osman

Against the backdrop of the #FeesMustFall and #RhodesMustFall movements, South African universities are at an interesting crossroads. Questions persist regarding the role, relevance and place of South African institutions of higher education in the post-colonial and post-apartheid development project of the state – namely to reverse the socio-political, economic and educational injustices inflicted upon the majority of the population. What these two movements have uncovered is a deep-seated concern that universities are not doing enough to rectify structural inequalities that exist within South Africa and across the region. Some go as far as to say that universities are reinforcing power imbalances between racial groups and enabling structural racism and sexism to continue. This view seems to be supported, given that only 4 per cent of the total population of South Africa pursues university education and a majority of the professoriate across the 26 institutions continues to be dominated by whites and males; that the academy as a public entity has not sufficiently explored its relationships to the different publics it ought to be serving; and that its transformative impulses have not been as inclusive as they could be in so far as decolonised education has been pursued. Given these powerful claims and demands it is certainly possible and desirable to see why and how such narratives and public discourses hold weight. Of course there are a number of different ways one could approach responding to such a critique. For the sake of clarity and consistency with the book of which this chapter is a part, the focus will be on the changing governance modes of South African universities. As Professor Pumla Gqola recently noted in her TB Davie Lecture at the University of Cape Town, there is an internal power contestation taking place within South African universities that these protests have uncovered which are causing difficulties and discomfort, but are a necessary part of university environments (Gqola, 2018). It is our contention that by reconnecting to the idea of the social justice mission of the university, coupled or underpinned by a principled commitment to the knowledge project of the university and a commitment to transparent collegial governance, universities in South Africa can strengthen themselves as vibrant public institutions leading change and revitalisation of society more broadly.

In pursuing our analysis, we explore the conceptual underpinnings and structure of governance in South African universities since the emergence of democracy.

We recognise that the higher education sector in this country is unique in relation to other African states. South Africa is an outlier across the region in many respects – the number of institutions, the political and related infrastructure environment, the length of time which universities have been in existence, the types of institutions that exist, and their evolution over time. We start our analysis from 1994, when the apartheid system formally came to an end and a democratic South Africa emerged. Indeed, 1994 represented the first free and fair elections in South Africa where the black majority was permitted to vote, resulting in the election of a truly democratic and representative government. Thus, it seems appropriate to consider governance in South African universities from the moment when the formal system of oppression and exclusion ended, and a new sense of the developmental and transformative potential of higher education emerged. Further, the chapter considers university governance in light of the #RhodesMustFall and #FeesMustFall movements that have called for the decolonisation of university spaces, in addition to concerns over accessibility and support.

Higher education and the developmental project

Situating this chapter on university governance using a developmental lens is relevant as South Africa remains a developing country in many respects and its universities are considered an integral aspect of the aspirations to address issues pertaining to socio-economic development. Whilst South Africa is categorised as a 'middle income' country, the existence of extreme socio-economic inequality and poverty mean that there is still much to do to overcome the scourge of apartheid and a history of extractive colonialism.

The relationship between nation building and the university almost feels like a truism that needs little empirical verification. Particularly in Africa where Dillon (1963) explored the relationship between the university and nation-building, it is evident that higher education and development are considered part and parcel. Universities are spaces where ideas and knowledge are given space to emerge and are mobilised with the intent of improving society, posing questions about society and at the same time finding solutions to societal problems. In other words, public universities do not stand aside from society they inhabit: they are not removed from the politics of the contexts in which they exist and they are forced to think about how they respond to or represent the pressing politics of the state. Thus higher education institutions can no longer only be institutions of learning but also have to become 'learning institutions' that constantly evaluate and re-evaluate their relevance in the light of their interaction with and interdependence upon their surrounding social, economic and political environs (Bernstein and Osman, 2012).

Former Ghanaian President, Dr Kwame Nkrumah, believed deeply in the relationship between the university and development, noting that 'the whole future of Ghana depends to a very considerable extent on the success of our programme for higher education and research' (Dillon, 1963, p. 75).

The relationship between higher education and development is often framed as important to establishing and embedding of democratic traditions such as free enquiry and debate; inclusion and diversity; and political pluralism. Altbach (1992, p. 158) argues that:

> In newly industrializing countries, committed to the development of democratic institutions, universities are extraordinarily important. Universities provide the ideas that are necessary for democracy. They provide training for the future elites in an atmosphere of free inquiry and debate. They bring ideas to the wider society and often interpret trends from abroad . . . They are the training ground not only of the Establishment but also of the opposition . . . Nonetheless, academic institutions are of primary importance in building up democratic values and ideas.

But higher education also contributes to state development and transformation through acting as a site for technological and scientific innovation, research, enlightened and free social thinking, and a training site for the future workforce – spurring employment and economic growth (Altbach, 1992, p. 159).

There is also a clear link between university education, health, empowerment and economic development (Bloom *et al.*, 2005; OECD, 2008, p. 4). Bloom *et al.* (2005, p. 16) argue that tertiary education can lead to both private and public benefits for a country. Private benefits are seen in the rise in employment prospects, incomes and ability to invest and save money. This leads to improving productivity since university education is tied to overall better health and longer life expectancies. As for public benefits, higher education often results in higher earnings for individuals and tax revenue for the state. Further, university graduates tend to be capable of mobilising their knowledge and skills towards creating employment options and instilling a culture of entrepreneurialism (Bloom *et al.*, 2005, p. 16). According to Loots (2009) the links between education, socio-economic empowerment and poverty reduction have been clearly evident in developing Asian countries where population masses have been provided with excellence in education and training and it is these successes that have driven government initiatives within South Africa to look to universities as agents of socio-economic change and development (Bernstein and Osman, 2012). Bhengu *et al.* (2006, p. 849) note that:

> The recasting of higher education that is informed by different constituencies . . . state, labour market, civil society, professional practitioners and students . . . that is driven to ensure equality and quality . . . to balance economic imperatives and public good [while producing graduates of] quality and competence for the labour market and civil society, [are] conspicuous imperative[s].

Universities also play a role in changing social hierarchies, questioning entrenched power dynamics between groups and who holds social privilege and advantage in society. Marginson (2004, p. 178) argues:

that higher education institutions play a central role in the production and allocation of social status (social advantage, social position) in all societies. This struggle for status is a powerful motivating force for both students and institutions in higher education, i.e. in relation to both 'supply' and 'demand'. Like economic capital, with which it is not identical but is closely implicated, status is a social 'good' whose possession has fecund economic, political and cultural potentials for the possessor. Status in higher education thus functions in the manner of an individualisable commodity benefit, albeit one that can be possessed by whole institutions as well as single persons.

This matters in developing contexts as universities de facto provide opportunities for those from marginalised or impoverished backgrounds to traverse socio-economic positions, namely shifting from lower to middle and/or upper socio-economic classes. In this sense, higher education in developing contexts is meant to offer new opportunities to overcome historical and structural impediments to finding a better, more secure, life and to rectifying power imbalances that are inherent (Marginson, 2004).

So what does all this amount to in a chapter pertaining to university governance in South Africa? Simply put – the way universities are governed and how inclusive governance systems are pertain to the development project of a state. How ideas of democracy, technological innovation, entrepreneurship and social enquiry are embedded, reflected and practised within universities influences the potential for higher education to act as a catalyst for development and social change. For example, if universities in developing countries replicate colonial models, ideas and ways of thinking such as social hierarchies and what is valued, then it is reasonable to think that higher education systems in these spaces are not unlocking the full potential of society, rather they are reinforcing systems of oppression that prevent enlightenment and development from taking place.

In this sense, governance models in African universities matter to state development. In South Africa, given our multiracial heritage and imperatives for redress, equity and the need to serve the public good, how we govern ourselves is crucial not only towards economic ends but also social ends.

University governance in South Africa: past and present

To understand university governance in South Africa, it is relevant to first cover some of the history, principles and values underpinning the relationship of universities to the state and how these have progressed since 1994. Second, it is then important to understand how institutions are structured internally and consider how they reflect and take into account the imperatives placed on them, namely fostering development and societal transformation in South Africa.

Marginson and Considine's (2000, p. 7) approach to evaluating governance in Australian higher education is relevant when considering South African institutions.

Governance, they argue, encompasses 'internal relationships, external relationships, and the intersection between them. Institutions such as universities are doubly structured, by internal configurations of power, and by their intersection with outside interests. Governance occupies the pivotal position between the inner world (or worlds) of the university, and its larger environments'. Simply put, university governance involves a careful tension between internal university politics, broader national politics and interest groups.

Governance in South African universities is directly connected to the colonial past of the country. Thus institutions reflect structures and traditions derived from British and Dutch higher education sectors. Neave and Van Vught (1994) explain that early South African universities such as the South African College (now the University of Cape Town) and the University of the Cape of Good Hope (now the University of South Africa) were directly connected to the University of London and structured akin to Scottish institutions. Universities like the University of Stellenbosch derive their traditions and structure from Dutch institutions including being spaces where the primary mode of instruction is Afrikaans, a derivative of the Dutch language. With the emergence of apartheid, language and race became a defining feature of South African higher education and institutions were created with the intent of accommodating the separation of racial and linguistic communities.

Cooper and Subotzky (2001) note that higher education institutions during the period of 1959–1988 can be divided into sub-categories: English-medium universities originally reserved for white students, Afrikaans-medium universities originally reserved for white students, Technikons reserved for white students, Apartheid Homeland universities and Technikons located in rural spaces and reserved for African students, and universities and Technikons reserved for Coloured and Indian students. The legacy of these different institution types pervades even into modern-day South African higher education, where those universities that were traditionally 'white' continuing to be better resourced and capacitated. This has made the governance of higher education in a democratic, post-apartheid South Africa a particular challenge.

To address this the democratic government undertook a number of reforms of the sector which included merging and consolidating institutions from 36 to 24 (now 26) universities, closing the Technikons, establishing an arm's-length regulator called the Council for Higher Education, and changing the governance frameworks of these spaces. All this began with a process of reviewing the structure and function of South African higher education after the release of the National Commission on Higher Education (NCHE) report in 1996. This was followed by the White Paper and the Higher Education Act of 1997, and culminated in a National Plan for Higher Education in 2001 (NCHE, 1996; Department of Education, 1997; Republic of South Africa, 1997; Ministry of Education, 2001).

In the process of review, Hall et al. (2004, p. 94) identified four governance conditions that existed in South African universities: contested institutions (self-referential governance and poorly developed systems of delegation); management-focused institutions (inwardly focused systems of governance with well-developed capacity for administration and the delegation of authority); democratic institutions (broad governance participation and shallow systems of delegation); and democratic, well-managed institutions.

The initial response to this range of governance experience was to reconsider the structure and function of university governance across the sector, both within institutions and in relation to the state. Whilst a hierarchical structure for decision-making continued, attempts were made via legislation to foster greater inclusion across South Africa's disparate and differentiated universities and to foster a more democratic tone. Such interventions make sense given the history of the country and how a key facet of apartheid was exclusion. Thus the 1997 White Paper argued that transformation of governance in South African universities required:

a)   Increasing participation: that successful policy must overcome an historically determined pattern of fragmentation, inequality and inefficiency, by increasing access to higher education for disadvantaged groups, and developing new curricula and flexible models of learning and teaching.

b)   Responding to societal interests and needs: that, in order to meet the challenges of a globalising and technologically-oriented economy – and to simultaneously address the needs of a developing society – the higher education system and its institutions must be restructured to deliver the requisite research and knowledge, as well as produce high-level human resource capacity.

c)   Promoting co-operation and partnerships in governance: that the relationship between higher education, the state and civil society – and among institutions themselves – must be reconceptualised. More importantly, the governance arrangements and practices within institutions must reflect and strengthen the values and principles of South Africa's fledgling democracy and create an environment and culture that affirms diversity, protects individuals from racial discrimination and sexual harassment, promotes reconciliation and the respect for human life.

($1.12, 1997, p. 10)

In this moment, a new social contract was proposed between universities and the state called cooperative governance. This notion framed governance of universities as a key element in the reconstruction and development of a democratic and post-apartheid South Africa. This is best captured in the National Commission on Higher Education Report (1996, p. 199):

governance arrangements reflect values about the distribution and exercise of authority, responsibility and accountability. The Ministry is well aware that governance in higher education institutions continues to be characterised by struggles for control, lack of consensus and even conflict over differing interpretations of higher education transformation. Among employers, past students, parents, and other members of the wider community, many different views and expectations about higher education abound. Among those currently involved directly in the process of higher education – in particular, students, academic staff, administrative staff, service staff, and institutional managers – there are often competing views and priorities which give rise to tensions and sometimes to turmoil.

As such cooperative governance was meant to provide the impetus to set aside differences entrenched by apartheid and realise that universities in the new South Africa could help facilitate inclusion, transformation and development. Under the guise of cooperative governance reforms to university governance structures were proposed – namely the inclusion of students, support staff and civil society within decision-making bodies and the establishment of a new decision-making body called the Institutional Forum. The Forum was meant to supplement university councils and senates that previously formed the core of university governance structures.

Akin to other higher education contexts internationally, the council acts as the supreme governance body in universities. Councils are responsible for providing oversight of university management, ensure that principles of good governance are maintained, and act as the point of final appeal. In this sense, councils approve university budgets, monitor and evaluate the Vice-Chancellor as they execute their duties and ensure the mission of the institution is respected. Councils were reformed to comprise representatives of the academy, unions, students and the broader community, namely business and civil society. This was meant to foster the social contract of cooperative governance in a university's highest decision-making body.

The senate is the highest academic decision-making body of an institution and is comprised of academics. Decisions about curriculum and other academic matters get debated in this space, including the appointment of senior university leaders and managers. As it currently stands, university senates in South Africa are mainly comprised of full professors who hold an automatic right of membership upon appointment at this level. But these spaces also include a smattering of non-professorial rank academics, students and a nominal few support staff. Whilst this is meant to denote prestige and honour for the highest academic decision-making body, the reality given the composition of South African academia is that these spaces are heavily skewed in racial and gender terms towards whites and males. As such, it becomes hard to claim that they are spaces that represent or can effect transformation in the academic project in ways that cooperative governance intended.

Institutional forums are new structures stemming from this 1996–2001 reform period that have been set up to broaden participation in institutional governance. Forums are meant to act as the space where matters pertaining to the racial and gender transformation of institutions are debated and discussed. Whilst being a fully constituted decision-making body, like the senate, the forum acts in an advisory capacity to university councils, that then take final decisions.

The forum is meant to include all stakeholders from across the institution – support staff, unions, students, academics, university management and council members. Like university senates, the forum is also involved in the appointment of senior university leaders (Kulati, 2000, pp. 179–180). Whilst the intent has been for the forum to be a key decision-making body, in practice it has not lived up to this intention, often being overruled or considered corollary to the senate and council deliberations.

Such a governance structure and tradition persist to today, but Mthembu (2009, pp. 13–16) argues that the principle of cooperative governance has been slowly chipped away over time as government has sought to play a more supervisory role in university affairs. This type of shift resembles what has happened elsewhere in terms of government requirements for enrolment plans, financial audits, competitive benchmarking, teaching quality reviews and prudent fiscal management. Whilst there are examples of government stepping in to administer institutions in financial and organisational crisis, intervention in the daily functioning of universities is rare and the Department of Higher Education is restrained in its approach. In particular, the Council on Higher Education, which was set up to monitor and access quality through the Higher Education Qualifications Sub-Framework (HEQSF) continues to be the mediating body on matters of academic accreditation and programme development. Thus, it is our contention that cooperative governance has persisted into the present, although in a modified form.

The big question remains regarding how the governance of universities in South Africa will continue given recent events such as the #RhodesMustFall and #FeesMustFall movements that originated in South Africa. The #RhodesMustFall movement focused on decolonising how South African universities privileged individuals and ideas from abroad in the curriculum and on campuses. The key theme of this movement was to promote more black African thought in the curriculum and in campus spaces. The famous imperialist Cecil Rhodes came to symbolise the movement given the monuments to his philanthropy at the University of Cape Town and Rhodes University and has spread globally. The #FeesMustFall movement succeeded #RhodesMustFall and focused on issues of affordability, accessibility and privilege in South African universities. Both movements have posed challenges to the social contract adopted in the 1996–2001 period. Indeed, these recent events seem to reinforce the stark warning that Hall *et al.* (2004, p. 106) posed that modifying the structure of governance in universities, whilst helpful, does not necessarily resolve problematic governance cultures which can continue to exclude and marginalise key stakeholders in universities – namely students and workers.

And in many respects, the feelings of exclusion and concerns over learning culture embodied in these protests, particularly over the two most tumultuous and contested years of the movements – 2015 and 2016 – have emphasised that there is still work required within South African higher education. In particular, the notion of decolonisation has emerged as an important principle and objective of a set of protests that also focus on access to higher education and affordability. The question is, how will it influence university governance?

South African university governance: decolonisation and potential for reanimation

University governance in South Africa enjoys freedom from government intervention, but in exchange universities have had to tow the line around managed enrolment plans, full funding for particular degrees and programmes (usually STEM), diminishing funding for the humanities, accreditation of the quality of programmes, institutional audits, competitive benchmarking exercises, teaching quality reviews and so on. In short, performativity in exchange for academic freedom. That said, universities do maintain control over the governance models they employ and can enact changes to a certain extent.

Much has been written about all that needs to be decolonised, particularly since the #RhodesMustFall and #FeesMustFall movements have cast new attention not just on how inclusive universities are or should be in the domain of teaching and learning, but also in the domain of university governance (Badat, 2015; Hornsby, 2015). It appears that if the South African academy wishes to be responsive and relevant to wider societal needs, and if it wishes to emphasise its significance more broadly to country development and human flourishment, and to take into account the demands of decolonisation, it will need to reconsider its governance structures, that is structures that are inclusive and enabling. What staff members, unions and students take from such inclusive governance structures is complex and varied, but they advance their view of the university and how they see themselves in the university and the world. Such an inclusive approach may in fact change how students, workers and staff see others from different class and race backgrounds. Such new ways of seeing and being in the university in South Africa given our history of exclusion has a particular urgency and appeal.

The moment may be right to imbue contemporary governance processes with its social, political and cultural meanings again and for staff and students to imagine a new social order, one that is different and advances social cohesion. However, we need to be careful not to rationalise inclusion and decolonisation within an economic neo-liberal frame, where students are customers, universities are corporate organisations, or where the global knowledge imperative is the only priority. We recognise that since the demise of apartheid, government policy and practice has been more about cooperative governance, however recent events in higher education call for a reimagination once again. South Africa undertook such a reimagination post-1994 and now needs to do the same post #RhodesMustFall and #FeesMustFall protests.

As individuals interested in higher education, we are taking this opportunity to think anew about whether it is possible to reimagine and rethink the university in South Africa. As academics and participants in the university we are not controlled by power but in fact exercise differing levels of power. Such power can be used for inclusive practices like distributed leadership models that enable and encourage the sharing of ideas and input from staff and students and management, so that there is a shared ownership over governance within the university. Another way to advance inclusivity is to treat university governance and governance structures as a dynamic and living structure that needs new ideas and insights in membership (who is included in these structures), methods of governing (effective and efficient ways of laying a road map for the governance of the institution) and regular communications with others not in the structures, to reanimate them. Interestingly, block chain technologies and social networks may aid the adoption of flatter governance structures and using these technologies for effective, transparent and quick communications across a broad range of stakeholders with a vested interest in the university is something that could be explored. Here technology in fact may assist us in serving a new purpose and it may also have fundamental implications for inclusion and an inclusive society. In turn through inclusive governance structures we may reshape and show what good and accountable leadership in the academy can look like.

While the earlier government policies encouraged inter-institutional collaboration, this vis-à-vis governance also advances thinking and discussions about governance structures and in this way advances inclusivity in the sector. The power of thinking and sharing ideas in no small measure goes a long way in advancing inclusive governance structures in universities and changes the way in which students, staff members and management engage with each other and come together in support of a collective and shared intellectual and pedagogical project – which after all are the two main reasons why universities exist. Such collaboration offers many opportunities for thinking and acting in ways that are novel, creative and innovative. It is vital to educational contexts undergoing change as in South Africa. It helps navigate tensions and contradictions which always accompany such change and reform and opens up spaces for creative outcomes.

Such a vision for governance seeks to open the question of what constitutes collective governance in the university, particularly one that is located in the global south. What constitutes work in the university, and how do universities remain relevant and sensitive to the socio-political evolution of society? With renewed calls for transformation and decolonisation of the university, rethinking governance structures (alongside how we teach and what we teach) allows us to rethink how we interact and work with each other, New technologies cement and make efficient these news ways of communicating with each other.

Conclusion

Governance structures that are inclusive are not ones that remain unchanged, but where new and previously excluded stakeholders are brought on board. Whether the structure itself requires transformation or the methods used for consultation, discussion, transparent communication and clear agenda or priority setting – it is clear that South African universities are moving into a new phase of university governance, where decolonisation in addition to the principles embedded in cooperative governance will intersect and interact.

This will undoubtedly require identifying and eliminating exclusionary practices, policies and practices. Allan (2003) reminds us that inclusivity is an ethical project meaning that ethical leadership is a vital part of making university governance structures inclusive.

In the context of a decolonised university in South Africa, students will be one of the drivers of change. While they have always been part of university structures, greater effort from them to be leading the change will be essential and such leadership from students also calls for ethical leadership and dialogue. Dialogue like inclusion can mean different things to different people. In the context of rethinking university governance it cannot be through shallow conversations that lack in substance but which give the impression that consultation has happened, that ideas are shared and communicated. Dialogue will mean (and require) robust engagement, which can be contested, and through which we share and test ideas and in which we show a willingness to test the idea of others and have our own ideas tested, no matter how difficult. Unfortunately for too long we have had too much of the former and too little of the latter. If the university is to be responsive to the calls from #RhodesMustFall and #FeesMustFall, staff, students and management will have to engage in dialogue in a way that takes us all out of our comfort zones.

It is our contention that while the academy in South Africa has enjoyed considerable cooperation between the various stakeholders, that the events of 2015 provide for an opportunity to strengthen an already strong governance approach within universities. That inclusion in the way suggested above will allow for different thinkers within the academy and different ideas supported by new technologies can be brought together into a single but diverse and complex process and approach through which we can rethink governance and advance the social justice mission of the academy not just in South Africa but also globally.

References

Allan, J. (2003) Inclusion and exclusion in the university. In T. Booth, K. Nes and M. Stromstad (eds), *Developing inclusive teacher education* (pp. 130–145). London: Routledge.

Altbach, P.G. (1992) Higher education, democracy, and development: Implications for newly industrialized countries. *Interchange*, 23(1/2), pp. 143–163.

Badat, S. (2015) Deciphering the meanings, and explaining the South African higher education student protests of 2015–16. http://wiser.wits.ac.za/system/files/documents/Saleem%20Badat%20-%20Deciphering%20the%20Meanings,%20and%20Explaining%20the%20South%20African%20Higher%20Education%20Student%20Protests.pdf [Accessed 2 September 2018].

Bernstein, C. and Osman, R. (2012) Graduateness as a contested idea: Navigating expectations between higher education, employers and graduates. In M. Coetzee, J. Botha, N. Eccles, N. Holtzhausen and H. Nienaber (eds), *Developing student graduateness and employability: Issues, provocations, theory and practical guidelines* (pp. 45–63). Randburg: Knowres Publishing.

Bhengu, T., Cele, N. and Menon, K. (2006) Value for money and quality in higher education. *South African Journal of Higher Education*, 20(1), pp. 843–858.

Bloom, D., Canning, D. and Chan, K. (2005) *Higher education and development in Africa*. Washington, DC: World Bank. http://siteresources.worldbank.org/EDUCATION/

Resources/278200-1099079877269/547664-1099079956815/HigherEd_Econ_
Growth_Africa.pdf [Accessed 30 April 2013].

Cooper, D. and Subotzky, G. (2001) *The skewed revolution: Trends in South African higher education, 1988–1998.* Johannesburg: Bellville, Education Policy Unit, University of the Western Cape.

Department of Education (1997) A programme for the transformation of higher education. Education White Paper 3. Government Gazette No. 18207. Pretoria: Government Printers.

Dillon, W.S. (1963) Universities and nation-building in Africa. *The Journal of Modern African Studies,* 1(1), pp. 75–89.

Gqola, P. (2018) Between academic inheritance and the urgency of definitions. TB Davie Memorial Lecture 2018. University of Cape Town. www.news.uct.ac.za/article/-2018-08-16-retain-protect-and-defend-academic-freedom [Accessed 2 September 2018].

Hall, M., Symes, A. and Luescher, T.M. (2004) The culture of governance in South African public higher education. *Journal of Higher Education Policy and Management,* 26(1), pp. 91–107.

Hornsby, D.J. (2015) How South African universities are governed is the biggest challenge. *The Conversation,* 8 September. https://theconversation.com/how-south-african-universities-are-governed-is-the-biggest-challenge-47075 [Accessed 2 September 2018].

Kulati, T. (2000) Governance, leadership and institutional change in South African higher education: Grappling with instability. *Tertiary Education & Management,* 6(3), pp. 177–192.

Loots, A.G.J. (2009) Student involvement and retention in higher education: The case for academic peer mentoring programmes for first years. *Education as Change,* 13(1), pp. 211–235.

Marginson, S. (2004) Competition and markets in higher education: A 'glonacal' analysis. *Policy Futures in Education,* 2(2), pp. 175–244.

Marginson, S. and Considine, M. (2000) *The enterprise university: Power, governance and reinvention in Australia.* Cambridge: Cambridge University Press.

Ministry of Education (2001) *National plan for higher education.* Pretoria: Ministry of Education.

Mthembu, T. (2009) University governance and the knowledge economy: Reconditioning the engine of development. Development Planning Division Working Paper Series No.3, DBSA: Midrand.

National Commission on Higher Education (NCHE) (1996) *Report: A framework for transformation.* Pretoria: Human Sciences Research Council.

Neave, G. and van Vught, F. (1994) *Government and higher education relationships across three continents.* Oxford: Pergamon.

OECD (2008) Tertiary education for the knowledge society. www.oecd.org/dataoecd/20/4/40345176.pdf [Accessed 2 September 2018].

Republic of South Africa (1997) Higher Education Act No. 101 of 1997. Department of Higher Education. Gazette No. 18515, Notice 1655. Pretoria: Government Printers.

Chapter 8

Changing governance models in Australian universities

Gioconda Di Lorenzo and Julie Wells

Introduction

Over the past thirty years, Australian universities have been subject to a series of reforms, instigated and supported by both state and national governments, which have resulted in lasting changes to the way Australian universities are governed and managed. The reforms have contributed to a strengthening of corporate governance and changes to the composition of governing bodies, with a privileging of external-facing, commercial expertise and experience. With increasing acknowledgement of the importance of universities as drivers of economic development and as instruments for delivering policy outcomes, a culture of accountability and public scrutiny of institutional performance has also developed, alongside encouragement of universities to be more entrepreneurial, market-facing and innovative.

As Lacy *et al.* (2017) have noted, these reforms have also contributed to greater homogeneity among Australian universities, with funding and regulatory frameworks geared to support the model of a comprehensive university; rewarding research intensity, privileging the undergraduate degree, and applying common performance indicators across the sector. However, external pressures, including reduced government investment, the disruptive influences of technology and shifts in international markets, student demand and expectations, call for greater nimbleness in responding to changing operating environments. Competitive funding markets also encourage a greater diversity of mission and approach in the university sector. This has resulted in inevitable questions about the extent to which universities can diversify and respond strategically and quickly to these pressures, and whether existing governance structures are fit for this purpose.

This chapter will explore the history of Australian university governance reform and the drivers for change. It recognises that a critical element in achieving institutional diversity and responsiveness will be the capacity for universities to negotiate effectively with government around the tension between autonomy and state control in university governance structures, and advance solutions which support both autonomy and accountability.

Institutional autonomy and governance reforms, 1988–2018

Institutional autonomy – the capacity for an organisation to take decisions and act upon them, without interference from external agencies – has always been an important tenet for universities (Universities Australia, 2013). It is also a somewhat uneasy reference point for those concerned with university governance, going as it does to the relationships between the university and its key stakeholders and the role they play in decision-making.

Institutional autonomy is often depicted as necessary to the protection of academic freedom – the right and responsibility of academics to exercise independence in scholarship, inquiry and teaching, without interference, fear or favour (see for example Estermann, 2017; Gürüz, 2011; Yokoyama, 2007). Academic freedom is widely accepted as a key characteristic of a university and a prerequisite for academic life, and it is indeed a legal requirement in Australia. The Commonwealth Higher Education Support Act 2003 (Section 19–115) requires universities to have a policy 'that upholds free intellectual inquiry' (p. 51), as do the Threshold Standards of the Tertiary Education Quality and Standards Agency (TEQSA) (Commonwealth of Australia, 2015), Australia's national quality assurance and regulatory agency for higher education. The enabling legislation of most Australian universities also includes the promotion of critical and free enquiry and informed intellectual discourse in the objects of the university. However, an organisation established under law to meet a set of legislated objects and in receipt of significant amounts of taxpayers' money must also inevitably balance autonomy with a degree of accountability. This tension is at the heart of much debate about governance reform in Australia over the past thirty years (Christopher, 2014).

Australian universities have been described as 'independent institutions' with 'relatively high formal autonomy' (Baird, 2014, p. 146), largely because they have been established as institutions at law by State governments, empowered to manage their finances and operations and accredit their own courses.

However, in considering this proposition, it is important to understand the structural and jurisdictional context in which universities operate in Australia. There are forty-three universities in Australia, including forty public universities, two international universities and one private university (Australian Government, n.d.). Legislative responsibility for universities in Australia rests almost exclusively with State or Territory governments, and public universities are established by a State Act of Parliament. There are some exceptions. For example, the Australian National University is established under Commonwealth legislation. Private or semi-private universities in Australia are licensed to operate under a range of legislative arrangements – the Australian Catholic University is established under the Corporations Act, Bond University by an Act of the Queensland Parliament, and the University of Notre Dame is licensed by the State and recognised by the Commonwealth.

The State Acts regulate most aspects of university governance, including the powers, functions and composition of university governing bodies (primarily known as 'Councils' or 'Senates'[1]), the powers of the Chancellor and Vice-Chancellor, Council delegations, property, financial administration and audit provisions. Universities report annually on the fulfilment of these functions and other governance requirements via reports that are tabled in Parliament.

However, State and Territory governments do not fund universities. Funding support for higher education is provided mainly through the Commonwealth Government's Higher Education Support Act 2003 and associated legislative instruments. These include the Commonwealth Grant Scheme, which subsidises approximately 615,000 Commonwealth supported university places each year; the Higher Education Loan Programme (HELP) which provides $A6 billion annually in loans to students; and a range of grants for specific purposes including equity support, learning and teaching, research infrastructure and research training programmes. Total Commonwealth Government Grant support is $A11 billion or 38.6 per cent of universities' revenue. The fastest growing source of revenue for universities is student fees and charges at 26.5 per cent, and other revenue sources include: student fee help and deferred loans (17.5 per cent); State and local government financial assistance (2.2 per cent); upfront student contributions (1.7 per cent); investment revenue (3.2 per cent); consultancy and contracts (4 per cent); and other income including royalties, trademarks, licences and joint venues (6.3 per cent) (figures sourced from Australian Government Department of Education and Training, 2018, p. 3).

With both levels of government having a significant stake in Australian universities – whether it be in terms of regulatory power or direct investment – it is not surprising therefore that universities are subject to multiple forms of review and audit by both State and Commonwealth governments. As government funding declines, government measures to influence and regulate universities grow. TEQSA was established by the Commonwealth government in 2010, with powers of review that ultimately go to the self-accrediting status of universities. With more direct government intervention in recent years, Harman and Treadgold (2007) have suggested that the Australian case could be characterised as experiencing 'both detailed and direct steering' from both levels of government, and '"conditional" finance' (p. 16) which has on occasion been used not only to direct models and modes of governance but also to shape the outcomes and work of universities.

Following a period of expansion in the post-war era, enrolments in Australian universities were still increasing in the mid-1980s but 'growth had slowed . . . and Commonwealth Government funding was static' (Croucher *et al.*, 2013, p. 191). The historical model of Commonwealth government support for a small number of publicly funded universities in Australia was no longer viable. Increased global competition and pressure to expand the size and improve the effectiveness of the higher education system contributed to a chain of Commonwealth government reviews and reforms, which led ultimately to the adoption of more corporate models of governance in Australia.

Australian universities were not alone in having to respond to these challenges, but the rate and nature of the policy changes arguably resulted in tighter government regulation when compared to other jurisdictions such as the United Kingdom (Vidovich and Currie, 2011). In 1988, the Minister for Employment, Education and Training, John Dawkins, initiated a suite of radical and enduring reforms to Australia's higher education system. As Croucher *et al.* (2013) have observed, Dawkins 'remodelled higher education and how it was funded in only a few years' (p. 3). The reforms were comprehensive:

> He turned colleges into universities, free education into HECS,[2] elite education into mass education, local focuses into international outlooks, vice-chancellors into corporate leaders, teachers into teachers and researchers.
>
> (Croucher *et al.*, 2013, p. 1)

The White Paper he published that year made clear that 'the quest for quality and efficiency in an era of rapid change' (Australia. Department of Employment Education and Training, 1988, p. 101) would require governance reform. The White Paper touched on the need for: clearly defined roles and responsibilities of university governing bodies in relation to those of senior management; smaller-sized Councils (10–15 members); the overriding responsibility of Council members to act in 'the best interests of the institution'; and the expectation that governing bodies delegate clear responsibility and authority to Vice-Chancellors as Chief Executive Officers (Australia. Department of Employment Education and Training, 1988, pp. 101–103). Criticised widely for initiating measures which many saw as leading to a culture of corporate managerialism in universities, the reforms nonetheless set the tenor for more pointed recommendations on university governance and management in ensuing reviews.

Seven years later, the Hoare Report on Management in Higher Education made eighteen recommendations, focused on five areas of reform: higher education management: accountability; governance; strategic management; workplace reform; and finance and asset management. It called for greater strategic focus of university governing bodies; formal accountability of the Vice-Chancellor to the governing body; the need for regular self-review of governing bodies; a series of amendments to State enabling legislation to clarify the role and composition of governing bodies; and greater attention to the nature of appointments and membership of governing bodies (Higher Education Management Review Committee (Australia), 1995).

Dawkins and the authors of the Hoare Report positioned these changes as necessary if universities were to steer effectively the financial sustainability of their institutions in the face of a significant expansion in student numbers, a declining proportion of income from government, and a rapidly expanding international education industry. The subsequent criticism was that the focus on business-like management, cost effectiveness and cost reduction would lead to the '"commodification" of education, displacing academic distinctiveness in pursuit of corporate efficiency (Bok, 2003; Geiger, 2004)' (Trakman, 2008, pp. 69–70). Interestingly, the biggest single driver towards independent revenue generation and efficient financial management was the government's decision in 1994 no longer to fund staff salary increases, which meant universities were required to fund competitive salary increases from within existing budget envelopes.

The Dawkins reforms did not mandate changes to governance, but nonetheless set in motion several lasting changes. As Wells and Martin (2013) have argued, the reforms helped to assert the link between system governance and institutional governance and decision-making. The reforms led to stronger risk management, and more sophisticated business and strategic planning – aspects of governance which are integral to universities' capacity to set directions. The reforms also foreshadowed a period of greater Commonwealth government interest and influence in what is, in statutory terms, the responsibility of State governments in Australia: the composition and work of university governing bodies and the regulation of university governance.

In 1998, the final report of the government's Higher Education Financing and Policy Review Committee, chaired by Roderick West (the 'West Review'), observed that:

> Our current regulatory framework does not encourage or facilitate good management within universities. Outdated governance arrangements, which emphasise representation rather than experience and skills in the management of large enterprises, hinder many institutions in pursuing their objectives.
>
> (Higher Education Financing Policy Review Committee, 1998, p. 20)

A review of higher education commissioned by Federal Minister Brendan Nelson in 2002 drew similar conclusions. The review report, published in 2003, referred to the 'anachronistic governance arrangements' of universities and their large Councils, which were 'not conducive to sound decision-making' (Nelson, 2003, p. 15). Nelson (2003) argued that 'Universities are not businesses but nevertheless [they] manage multi-million-dollar budgets. As such they need to be run in a business-like fashion' (p. 15).

Exhortations alone would not effect further change. The cooperation of State and Territory governments was required to support it, unless the Commonwealth government could find a new lever. In 2003, after State and Territory governments declined an invitation by the Commonwealth to participate in the development of a set of national protocols for university governance, the Commonwealth government went ahead regardless. It developed protocols and made compliance a condition of increased Commonwealth funding for student places. The protocols largely reflected the recommendations of these previous reviews, prescribing a maximum size for university governing bodies (22) and a series of specific governance requirements in line with corporate sector standards. Faced with the prospect of losing growth funding to their universities, State and Territory governments amended the enabling legislation of public universities to reflect and enable compliance with the protocols, with all universities working towards compliance.

When the Commonwealth government changed in 2008 the funding conditions attached to Australia's 2004 National Governance Protocols were removed. The protocols themselves have remained, have undergone subsequent modest changes initiated by universities themselves, and are now deemed voluntary. However, by the time of the introduction of TEQSA, and with it the adoption of the Commonwealth government's Higher Education Standards Framework, many of the protocols were embedded in the threshold standards for university and higher education governance which now underpin TEQSA's accreditation and review processes. Through the TEQSA processes, universities are assessed on the effectiveness of governance processes at their institutions in meeting the thresholds for accreditation.

The twin reform imperatives of both the State and Commonwealth governments over the past thirty years – reducing the size of governing bodies, reshaping composition and mandating governance practice in line with corporate standards – have now largely been realised. The prescribed size of university governing bodies in all Australian states has declined since the early 1990s. The average membership numbers of university Councils 'saw a drop from 26.5 in 1990 to 21.4 in 2000' (Chan, 2018, p. 12), and decreased further by 2015 to 16.6 (Chan, 2018). The composition has also changed – while the principle of staff and student membership of governing bodies survives, they are no longer in all cases elected. Many are appointed by the governing body, along with a deliberate side-lining of the idea that staff and students are there to 'represent' constituencies. At the same time, the proportion of staff and student members of Australian university governing bodies has declined (see Chan, 2018).

Yet the focus on accountability and autonomy in discussions of Australian universities' governance and management continues. As government financing tightens, universities are under increasing pressure to demonstrate outcomes to both the public – for example through the Quality in Learning and Teaching (QILT) website established to present an expanding range of outcome data – and to government. In 2018, the Commonwealth government has mooted that future funding growth for student places will be dependent on a range of yet to be specified performance measures, most likely linked to measures of public value such as student success and graduate employment. The renewed focus of government on funding levers to shape institutional activity once again prompts inevitable questions about the extent to which universities can and should exercise control over their own future directions.

The pressure for greater accountability and transparency does not come solely from Commonwealth and State governments as universities grapple with the requirements of multiple jurisdictions and an expanded range of stakeholders. As public institutions operating in a variety of markets, some of them global, and with different forms of regulation, the autonomy of Australian universities is limited not just by the actions of government at home, but by the operations of extra-university laws, government controls on student fees and the regulatory environments of countries in which they operate.

The social compact which universities, as institutions established to serve the public good, rely upon to justify their claims to taxpayer support is also under pressure. The former United States Ambassador to Australia, Jeffery Bleich, made this point in his keynote address at the 2017 Universities Australia Conference. In the face of populist unrest, disruptive technologies, loss of confidence in governments, and changing demographic expectations, Bleich (2017) argued that it will be the role of educational institutions in the future to demonstrate their value and 'refocus on solutions that reboot our democracy and prepare our citizens for this new economy' (para. 125).

The autonomy of Australian universities has been preserved in the sense that the government rarely interferes directly in the affairs of individual institutions, nor their freedom to seek alternative sources of income. This is particularly important as Australian universities, challenged by disruptive market forces and constrained government funding, must be able to develop robust institutional strategies, diverse offerings, experimentation and innovation to survive (Davis, 2017). It is precisely this autonomy which will enable universities to 'refocus' on the solutions Bleich (2017) proposes. However, while universities can choose their own strategic direction, this is constrained by their reliance on declining public and student funding,[3] despite the capacity to generate funds from other sources, and the State's ongoing intervention in decision-making through regulation and funding levers (Baird, 2014). This includes the forms and practices of governance.

It is not surprising therefore that 'debates about the direction of policy for universities in Australia now mostly focus on the role of the state in balancing, distributing and checking power (Gayle, Tewarie and White 2003: 35)' (Baird, 2014, p. 149). As calls for accountability and transparency gather force, the question arises as to what models of governance and governance practice will most support universities in rising to this challenge, particularly as external pressures show no sign of diminishing. Shifts in student demand, technology, volatility in government policy and internationalisation all heighten the pressure on university governing bodies to deliver strong oversight of strategy, risk and management.

The corporate governance reforms in Australia have, in some respects, helped universities weather the increasingly fierce gaze of both government and the public. An example of how this can go wrong is in the United Kingdom, where the absence of a properly constituted remuneration committee and processes contributed to the furore in 2017 about the Vice-Chancellor's salary at the University of Bath (Weale, 2018; Halpin Partnership Ltd, 2018). After a freedom of information request by the University and College Union revealed that 95 per cent of university leaders in the UK were either members of their remuneration committee or entitled to attend meetings, critics suggested Vice-Chancellors were directly contributing to the setting of their own salaries and benefits.

Australia too has experienced recent debate about the escalating salaries of Vice-Chancellors. The majority of Australian universities run remuneration committees aligned with corporate standards and in Australia these discussions have not been linked to dysfunctional governance models, but rather to the rise of 'corporate universities', more intense global market competition for students and research funding, and thus more competitive Vice-Chancellor salaries and the need for universities to '"strategically differentiate" themselves' (Lyons and Hill, 2018, para. 18). The implication is that salary inequities divert resources from the academic mission, and 'constrain university research and education in the service of the public good' (Lyons and Hill, 2018, para. 21).

The debate about university executive salaries is but one example of public concern about the shifting mission of universities and their accountability to the taxpayer. At the heart of the debate are questions of control and autonomy. There is a clear need, therefore, to balance institutional accountability, transparency,[4] and a demonstrable focus on the public good, with a level of autonomy for universities to define and deliver with relative ease mission-specific and diverse institutional strategies. If that balance can be achieved, good corporate governance controls can minimise reputational or financial risks and support robust and transparent decision-making. Good corporate governance models should promote and protect academic distinctiveness, the 'service of the public good', and competitive institutional strategies.

Potential future directions for reform

The challenge lies in achieving this balance. The governance reforms over the last 30 years, the development of the National Governance Protocols in 2004, the 2011 Voluntary Code of Best Practice for the Governance of Australian Universities, and recent efforts to refresh the Voluntary Code, point to a broad recognition of the importance of good internal governance to ensuring universities in Australia remain sustainable, highly respected institutions able to compete in a global market. Some of the regulatory constraints, however, can provide unnecessary barriers to realising strategic ambitions and responding to changing conditions.

As Lacy et al. (2017) have noted, one effect of the Dawkins reforms was to introduce a high degree of homogeneity in the mission and strategies of Australian universities. Uniformity is partly a function of the Higher Education Threshold Standards, which require universities to be research active in at least three disciplines and to offer both breadth and depth in undergraduate education. It is also partly a function of the series of institutional mergers and transformations that created the Unified National System. Nineteen universities and seventy other higher education institutions were replaced by forty-three universities, all responding to common imperatives and with similar missions, goals and philosophies (Lacy et al., 2017).

However, the pressure for institutions to develop distinctive strategies relevant to their circumstances is rising. Volatility in government funding is increasing institutional reliance on international student revenue and the growth of partner-led research. The search for new markets, the pressure to diversify revenue sources and a shrinking pot of government funding all suggest that a 'one-size-fits-all' approach is not sustainable.

Nimbler regulatory frameworks enabling diverse strategies

By the late 2000s, the enabling legislation of Australian universities began to reflect, to varying degrees, the thinking which informed the recommendations of the Dawkins Report around more business-like Council structures, smaller governing bodies, the role of Vice-Chancellor as CEO, and the duties of Council members to act in the best interests of the university.

The internal legislation and regulatory frameworks of many Australian universities were perhaps less rapid to evolve in this developing landscape. The reasons for this are likely to be linked to institutional debates about the commodification of education mentioned earlier in the chapter (Trakman, 2008). While consequential amendments to university statutes and regulations most certainly followed, it was not until more recently that universities have contemplated wholesale changes to their internal legislation, with explicit objectives centred on enabling institutional strategy.

In 2015, for example, the University of Melbourne Council embarked on a 'once-in-a-generation' review of its statutes and regulations. The review examined the university's legislative needs from first principles. It addressed the challenges associated with Melbourne's existing regulatory framework including the need to reduce the volume of statutes requiring ministerial approval to promote university autonomy and agility. Melbourne was not the first to review its statutes and regulations within the State of Victoria. Other universities, such as Monash University, RMIT University and Swinburne University of Technology, reduced the red tape in their regulatory frameworks over several years.

In Melbourne's case, the review of its regulatory framework responded in part to a significant structural change, a re-organisation of the university's operating model, which was the impetus for the governance reforms. The review presented the opportunity for the university to clarify the powers of its Council, the relationship of the Council to management, and to the academic mission of the institution. Importantly, it raised the question of what was rightfully the concern of government, and therefore needing to be reflected in statute. It represented another shift away from the old model of university governing bodies enacting, through detailed statutes and regulations, 'the entire management' of universities. The review drew on corporate and academic governance models to ensure the university's Council could exercise the appropriate level of accountability and oversight over the university's multi-faceted financial and commercial activities without losing sight of its fundamental purpose as a 'body politic and corporate' promoting education, knowledge and the public good.

Importantly, the review recognised that governance structures should be supportive of institutional strategy, should be agile, should encourage better decision-making, and should be responsive to changing circumstances. As Harman and

Treadgold (2007) have stated, 'No aspect of governorship should impact negatively on the core business of universities' (p. 27).

Membership of governing bodies

By redefining their own internal legislation to reduce reliance on ministerial intervention, Australian universities have regained some autonomy, enabling them to respond more nimbly and strategically to commercial pressures. In many jurisdictions, however, enabling legislation precludes universities from managing entirely their own governance and financial affairs, with appropriate oversight from their governing bodies.

In defining their own strategies, university councils should ideally comprise members that collectively satisfy the skills and knowledge needed to deliver their strategies. Governments continue to have a direct influence over the membership of governing bodies, according to criteria that are not always clear or linked to a skills matrix. In only a small number of Australian universities – the Australian Catholic University, Bond University in Queensland, the University of Notre Dame in Western Australia, and all South Australian universities – the governing bodies appoint their own members. The South Australian case is particularly interesting because reforms in this State, enacted in 1997, have included public universities.

The benefits of council appointments are clear. Universities are multi-billion-dollar enterprises, requiring a sophisticated and expert governance team which understands the requirements of a global enterprise. Representative structures and requirements for finance expertise are outdated and may not get to the nub of what globally competitive universities require. There are clear opportunities for universities to enjoy increased autonomy and the capacity to be more responsive in achieving strategic goals by better aligning council skills with institutional strategy.

Universities in the State of Victoria have been advocating for some years for councils to appoint their own members, or at least exercise greater influence over the type of appointments government makes. In Victoria, councils comprise three official members – the Chancellor, the Vice-Chancellor and the President of the Academic Board – at least one elected staff and one elected student member, at least four council-appointed members and a least four government-appointed members. Victorian State governments have taken a variety of approaches to the latter category, ranging from constructive consultation with universities about prospective government appointments, to appointments made with little or no discussion.

It is not unreasonable for the State under whose legislation universities are created to seek some degree of oversight of or assurance around council membership. For example, much like the new process in the United Kingdom (Office for Students, 2018), Australian universities must demonstrate that members of their governing bodies are 'fit and proper persons' as part of the TEQSA Threshold

Standards (Commonwealth of Australia, 2015, p. 11). However, increased powers for university governing bodies to appoint their own members, according to an agreed skills matrix and with appointment processes subject to appropriate ministerial oversight, might facilitate greater organisational autonomy, council skills better aligned with strategic priorities, and faster processes for appointment. At the same time, the State would maintain the capacity to monitor risk in this regard.

Gaining control of commercial activities

State and Territory governments in Australia also continue to have a direct influence over university financial affairs. Public universities in Australia are creatures of legislation – they are statutory authorities. Governments are expected to take a targeted, risk-based approach to oversight of university activities, particularly their commercial activities, as university performance and reputation is invariably linked to community expectations and government accountability.

Most university Acts in Australia set the conditions for universities purchasing, selling or leasing land, borrowing money or entering into other financial arrangements in support of their operations. In Victoria, for example, ministerial approval is required for the sale and purchase of all 'Crown land'; for the lease of all 'Crown land' exceeding twenty-one years in duration; for the sale and purchase of all freehold land exceeding $A5 million in value; for the lease of all freehold land exceeding twenty-one years in duration; and for borrowing money. In the latter case, the time and effort associated with securing approval is amplified by the requirement for an agreement between both the Minister for Education and the Treasurer.

Delays caused by these requirements sometimes jeopardise opportunities that are time sensitive and undermine the financial performance of universities. Removing the requirement for ministerial approval would allow universities to respond to opportunities as they arise, but would leave other oversight mechanisms in place, such as the tabling of university annual reports in Parliament, routine audits conducted by the Victorian Auditor-General's Office, and the requirement to seek land valuations from the Valuer General Victoria.

In New South Wales (NSW), the State government has removed ministerial financial and property approvals to allow universities to manage their asset portfolios more efficiently. The NSW amendments were enacted as the Universities Legislation Amendment (Regulatory Reforms) Act 2014, and built on earlier legislation, the Universities Governing Bodies Act 2011. When the 2011 Act was introduced to the NSW Parliament, the then Minister for Education, Adrian Piccoli, made the point that NSW universities 'are both major public institutions of great strategic value to the State and very significant businesses and economic drivers for New South Wales' (Piccoli, 2014, p. 64). The 2011 and 2014 Acts affirmed the NSW government's 'commitment to university autonomy and independence, while also ensuring proper governance arrangements are in place' (Piccoli, 2014, p. 64). In many ways, the NSW position presents a sensible compromise.

A more mature relationship with government

Perhaps one of the more powerful arguments for reform is the need for a more mature relationship with government. University–government relationships in Australia are highly transactional. Universities are in fact contributors to the economy and society and in this sense share some common goals with government, which should inform a relationship based on partnership. In his speech to the National Press Club in August 2018, Professor Ian Jacobs, Chair of the Group of Eight Universities (Go8) in Australia, cited the findings of an independent report by London Economics commissioned by the Go8. The report revealed that the work of the Go8, Australia's eight 'sandstone' universities alone, delivered a return of over $A66 billion to the nation. Notwithstanding the financial contributions of universities to the nation, Professor Jacobs (2018) noted that universities 'serve Australian society in navigating the challenges and opportunities of our age' (para. 93).

The State hence has a strong interest in universities contributing to the State's labour market needs and economic development and carries both financial and reputational risk for the performance of universities. Moving towards a model which reduces the focus on transactional compliance requirements and focuses on strategic risks and broader public policy objectives presents the opportunity for government to develop a more strategic and productive relationship with universities. A new model, for example, could contain a strengthened strategic accountability framework that would apply to all higher education providers. It could be developed in consultation with the sector and the Commonwealth. Governance arrangements which balance government interests with institutional autonomy, and which reduce red tape, could support and reflect this.

Conclusion

Governance reforms in the Australian higher education sector, which have evolved over decades, have created a culture of accountability that has in many ways prepared Australian universities for the external pressures they face today. Good governance frameworks have enabled universities to withstand increasing demands from government and from the wider community, while promoting their public value and protecting their academic mission.

This chapter has argued, however, that the debate is shifting again to focus on accountability and autonomy. Challenged by disruptive market forces and constrained government funding, Australian universities must be able to respond nimbly to market forces, resist funding pressures and ultimately control their own futures, supported by governance structures that are equipped to achieve the appropriate balance of accountability and autonomy.

The challenge will lie in achieving this balance. First steps might include the removal of unnecessary barriers to realising strategic ambitions, nimbler internal regulatory frameworks, governing bodies which collectively comprise the skills and knowledge needed to deliver dynamic university strategies, and greater control of transactional commercial activities. Importantly, one of more powerful arguments for reform is the need for a more mature relationship with government, recognising the State's and indeed the broader society's strong interest in the success of universities.

Acknowledgements

We would like to acknowledge the helpful advice of Dr Gwilym Croucher, Heather Karmel, Louise Davidson and research support provided by Jennifer Steadman and Kate Alexander, University of Melbourne.

Notes

1 For consistency, governing bodies are referred to as 'Councils' in this chapter.
2 Higher Education Contribution Scheme (HECS) is the Australian form of income contingent loans and was introduced in 1989.
3 Australian government grants declined from 43.1 per cent in 2008 to 38.6 in 2016, and Australian government payments to students increased from 13.6 in 2008 to 17.5 per cent in 2016 (Australian Government Department of Education and Training, 2018, p. 3; Australian Government Department of Education Employment and Workplace Relations, 2009, p. 3).
4 The transparency argument goes beyond salaries and helps universities to make their case for autonomy. The government in Australia requires universities to publish data on websites such as the QILT Dataset and Website, and the Course Seeker website. Several universities internationally, such as the University of Edinburgh and the University of Manchester, are seeking to be more transparent in relation to performance and outcomes.

References

Australia. Department of Employment Education and Training (1988) *Higher education: A policy statement (Circulated by the Hon. J.S. Dawkins, MP, Minister for Employment, Education and Training)*. Canberra: Australian Government Publishing Service.

Australian Government (n.d.) Universities and higher education. Retrieved from www.stud yinaustralia.gov.au/english/australian-education/universities-and-higher-education

Australian Government Department of Education Employment and Workplace Relations (2009) Finance 2008: Financial reports of higher education providers. Retrieved from https://docs.education.gov.au/system/files/doc/other/finance2008.pdf

Australian Government Department of Education and Training (2018) Finance 2016: Financial reports of higher education providers. Retrieved from https://docs.educa tion.gov.au/system/files/doc/other/finance_2016.pdf

Baird, J. (2014) International, hierarchical and market influences on Australian university governance. In M. Shattock (Ed.), *International trends in university governance: Autonomy, self-government and the distribution of authority* (pp. 145–164). Oxford and New York: Routledge.

Bleich, J. (2017) Former ambassador Jeffrey Bleich speaks on Trump, disruptive technology, and the role of education in a changing economy. *The Conversation*. Retrieved from https://theconversation.com/former-ambassador-jeffrey-bleich-speaks-on-trump-disruptive-technology-and-the-role-of-education-in-a-changing-economy-73957

Chan, E. (2018) Legislative changes affecting the governance of Australian universities. Retrieved from www.ucc.edu.au/wp-content/uploads/2016/09/Legislative-changes-affecting-University-Governance-20180221.pdf

Christopher, J. (2014) Australian public universities: Are they practising a corporate approach to governance? *Studies in Higher Education, 39*(4), 560–573. doi:10.1080/03075079.2012.709499

Commonwealth of Australia (2015) Higher education standards framework (threshold standards) 2015. Retrieved from www.legislation.gov.au/Details/F2015L01639

Croucher, G., Marginson, S., Norton, A. and Wells, J. (Eds) (2013) *The Dawkins revolution: 25 years on.* Carlton: Melbourne University Publishing.

Davis, G. (2017) *The Australian idea of a university* (First ed.). Carlton: Melbourne University Publishing.

Estermann, T. (2017, 7 April). Why university autonomy matters more than ever. *University World News: The Global Window on Higher Education (Issue No. 454).* Retrieved from www.universityworldnews.com/article.php?story=20170404132356742

Gürüz, K. (2011) University autonomy and academic freedom: A historical perspective. *International Higher Education, 63*, 13–15. https://doi.org/10.6017/ihe.2011.63.8549

Halpin Partnership Ltd. (2018, May) The Halpin review: A review of council effectiveness at the University of Bath. Retrieved from www.bath.ac.uk/publications/the-halpin-review/attachments/halpin-review.pdf

Harman, K. and Treadgold, E. (2007) Changing patterns of governance for Australian universities. *Higher Education Research & Development, 26*(1), 13–29. doi:10.1080/07294360601166786

Higher Education Financing Policy Review Committee (1998) *Learning for life: Final report: Review of higher education financing and policy.* Canberra: Department of Employment Education Training and Youth Affairs.

Higher Education Management Review Committee (Australia) (1995) *Report of the committee of inquiry: Hoare report.* Canberra: Australian Government Publishing Service.

Higher Education Support Act 2003. Retrieved from www.legislation.gov.au/Details/C2018C00312

Jacobs, I. (2018, 14 August) National Press Club address: Ian Jacobs on universities, Australia's 'hidden' asset. *The Conversation.* Retrieved from https://theconversation.com/national-press-club-address-ian-jacobs-on-universities-australias-hidden-asset-101517

Lacy, W.B., Croucher, G., Brett, A. and Mueller, R. (2017, May) Australian universities at a crossroads: Insights from their leaders and implications for the future. Retrieved from https://melbourne-cshe.unimelb.edu.au/__data/assets/pdf_file/0005/2368895/Australian-Universities-at-a-Crossroads.pdf

Lyons, K. and Hill, R. (2018, 5 February) Vice-chancellors' salaries are just a symptom of what's wrong with universities. *The Conversation.* Retrieved from https://theconversation.com/vice-chancellors-salaries-are-just-a-symptom-of-whats-wrong-with-universities-90999

Nelson, B. (2003) *Our universities: Backing Australia's future.* Canberra: DEST.

Office for Students (2018) Regulatory advice 2: Registration of current providers for 2019–20. Retrieved from www.officeforstudents.org.uk/publications/regulatory-advice-2-registration-of-current-providers-for-2019-20/

Piccoli, A. (2014) Universities Legislation Amendment (Regulatory Reforms) Bill 2014. Retrieved from www.parliament.nsw.gov.au/bill/files/688/2R%20Universities.pdf

Trakman, L. (2008) Modelling university governance. *Higher Education Quarterly*, *62*(1–2), 63–83. doi:10.1111/j.1468-2273.2008.00384.x

Universities Australia (2013, 3 July) Legislation & governance. Retrieved from www. universitiesaustralia.edu.au/efficiency-and-governance/legislation-and-govern ance#.W9uPx0f3R-h

Vidovich, L. and Currie, J. (2011) Governance and trust in higher education. *Studies in Higher Education*, *36*(1), 43–56. doi:10.1080/03075070903469580

Weale, S. (2018, 16 February) Majority of university leaders involved in setting their own pay. *Guardian*. Retrieved from www.theguardian.com/education/2018/feb/15/ majority-of-university-leaders-involved-in-setting-their-own-pay

Wells, J. and Martin, L. (2013) Regulation. In G. Croucher, S. Marginson, A. Norton and J. Wells (Eds), *The Dawkins revolution: 25 years on* (pp. 191–209). Carlton: Melbourne University Press.

Yokoyama, K. (2007) Changing definitions of university autonomy: The cases of England and Japan. *Higher Education in Europe*, *32*(4), 399–409. doi:10.1080/ 03797720802066294

Chapter 9

Can there be a universal framework of good governance?

Nina Atwal, Mark Butler, Divia Mattoo and Michael Wood

Introduction

The governance of higher education globally is developing as a field of study. This reflects in part the growing internationalisation of education and research in the last decade and the emergence of comparative themes including the impact of cultural difference, the disputed value of segmented, comparative performance tables, changes in accountability regimes, and the legitimacy and authority of leaders and governance structures.

This chapter explores international models of governance and specifically whether any underlying principles guide and shape the governance of higher education institutions (HEIs) in their different policy, accountability, cultural and operating environments. Are there best practice approaches to governance which can be determined in respect of higher education irrespective of localised internal and external landscapes in an increasingly internationalised world?

In the UK, for example, there is an increasing political interest in managing higher education as a market, which encourages institutions to try to secure competitive advantage through increasing the effectiveness of governance in a rapidly changing operating environment. Governance is largely devolved to individual, self-directing, autonomous institutions with charitable status, working mainly within non-statutory codes and frameworks. Some of the dynamics within a devolved UK include state economic fluctuation and downturn; marketisation and the growth of mixed economy competition; the promotion of higher education as a business (or even a service industry); devolved regulation; demographic change; student consumerism; digital challenge and opportunity; and the growth of international partnerships and models of delivery. The role, shape and size of the governing bodies in the mixed economy of public and private provision, for-profit and not-for-profit, and the nature of accountability and legitimacy for decision-making are emerging issues within institutions confronting the realities of a very challenging and uncertain operating landscape. Thus, the changing landscape of accountability structures in the UK potentially creates an opportunity for the adoption of universal principles of good governance.

The set of dynamics described above are can be found across Europe, North America, Canada and the Australian diaspora, although there are distinct differences in terms of accountability and autonomy, which we address below. Governments almost everywhere have been rolling back the extent of direct state funding and intervention, encouraging market forces to flourish, and the consumer (what Marshall terms the 'autonomous chooser') to be king (Marshall, 1996). The increasing autonomy of HE systems and the encouragement of market forces signals an opportunity for institutions to incorporate good governance practices into their governance processes.

Accountability within HE systems can be defined in two ways. In broad terms, accountability refers to the returns to society for the investment made in maintaining universities, returns being quantified as cost/benefits or increase in efficiency to the economy, as well as more diffuse benefits to society (the current government focus in the English system on value for money to the student is apposite here). In a narrow sense, accountability refers to 'answerability to the superior (invariably funding) authority' (Gandhi, 2013) for implementation and achievement. Internationally, there has been a growing trend, or impetus, to increase the autonomy of public institutions by granting them greater independence and self-governance (Saint, 2009). To be truly successful in the modern age it has been observed that academic staff must be actively involved in university decision-making, which is especially the case in research-intensive institutions (Rosovosky, 2001).

The corollary to greater freedoms of course is more accountability with governments and education ministries around the world promoting more autonomy for public universities, so the demands for greater measurement of results and achievements have increased. Governing bodies are being charged more than ever before to be strategic and to monitor management's progress in achieving institutional goals, including greater accountability over the use of resources in whatever form. This has led to the predominance on many university boards of governors with financial planning, human resource management and legal expertise, often to the exclusion, or at least reduction, in individuals with knowledge of education, or civic and national government. Whilst the Good Governance Institute suggests that a governing body should not be overly large (the average in the UK is 19), a diverse range of skills and experience is essential (Good Governance Institute, 2017).

The direct state role in governance in Europe has diminished in recent years (De Boer et al., 2008) with a focus on leadership capabilities and capacity rather than the underlying principles of governance. But what is the picture elsewhere? What is the shape of governance around the world?

Here we examine three contrasting countries, India, China and South Africa, to illustrate the differences and similarities in governance structures and systems, and to highlight current levels of engagement with issues of governance, accountability and autonomy.

Case studies

India

India has one of the largest higher education systems in the world. Its governance is characterised by a high degree of complexity, central control and close regulation, with institutions (both public and private) enjoying limited autonomy. The 47 leading central (or union) universities are designated under the Central Universities Act, 2009, which regulates their purpose, powers and governance. The majority of the 330 state-controlled universities are of variable size, quality and mission. Typically, such institutions have an Executive Council and an Academic Council (or similar) both chaired by the Vice-Chancellor. Older universities have a Court (often several hundred strong) chaired by a Chancellor, mirroring older UK models of governance.

In 2012, the Indian government launched a five-year plan focused on a quest for excellence in teaching and research in order to improve the quality of the country's graduates and research outputs. However, improved quality has been compromised by 'rote learning, a shortage of qualified faculty, and out-dated curricula, leading to students [being] unprepared for employment' (University of Oxford, 2017). Other limiting factors have included poor English language skills, a lack of transferable skills and an inability to apply concepts in practical situations.

The perceived collapse of standards and worldwide competitiveness (as evidenced in international league tables) in India's higher education system is prompting government action, in the form of reform of the University Grants Commission and the All India Council for Technical Education (QS World, 2008).

Despite this, the bureaucracy surrounding HE is immense and the pace of change slow, with an extensive central administrative system of eight bureaus (and 100 autonomous bodies which sit beneath them) collectively constituting the Department of Higher Education. Furthermore, India is organised around 29 States and 7 Union territories, which have devolved responsibility for some 330 public universities (other than the central institutions above). Given the sheer scale of the sub-continent, it is not surprising that there is great local variation in the quality of governance, regulatory oversight, policy guidance and duplication with the centre.

In terms of quality assurance, there are three primary national bodies, the National Assessment and Accreditation Council (NAAC), the All India Council for Technical Education (AICTE) and the National Board of Accreditation (NBA), in addition to 13 profession-specific councils. The funding, regulatory and accreditation regime is therefore complex.

India is not being well-served by its university and tertiary education system (which includes some 18,000 colleges) in contributing effectively and strategically to meeting the economy's skilled workforce needs, particularly in knowledge management and digital technologies. The core governance problem for the sector centres on the separation of responsibility between national and state governments, as enshrined in India's founding Constitution. This brings with it a divergence in the quality and effectiveness of governance. For the sector to mature and serve the nation's economic revolution, the essential imbalance between accountability and autonomy at a national and state level must be resolved, with institutions being given greater self-determining powers. For many institutions, this may be an elongated process as their governance systems and mechanisms are at a low level of maturity, and governance is not accorded the prominence it requires.

China

The past two decades have seen a massive increase in educational capacity and quality in Chinese higher education which has created a mixed market economy, including student fees payments, private provision and international partnership arrangements, alongside the traditional state-directed institutions. Since 1998 the Higher Education Law of the People's Republic of China has led to greater flexibility for local and provincial governments and greater autonomy for HEI governance. Equally two projects, Project 211[1] and Project 985,[2] have opened up transnational education and the pursuit of a global standard university has brought about significant change in the sector.

At one level this situation has parallels with the UK and the Western dynamic, marking a shift to the 'massification' of higher education with market dynamics creating governance issues around quality, levels of autonomy and self-direction, student access and talent. The degree to which central government has actually released control and is allowing autonomy over key appointments and the shape of governance remains uncertain (Li and Yang, 2014). The notion of centralised decentralisation characterises institutional autonomy in China and in other undemocratic (and democratic) regimes alike.

In many ways, Chinese public universities do enjoy a great deal of autonomy over their own affairs: academic, strategic and financial. Their published research covers controversial areas such as the environment, pollution and health inequalities, which in such a tightly controlled state could be seen as challenging to the regime. Yet, the long-term plan to have leading Chinese institutions in the top 100 in the world requires a balance between freedom and control.

The accountability/autonomy dynamic in the case of China has been described as high and moderate, respectively (Saint, 2009). As a highly centralised and controlling state, even the most advanced and successful of institutions enjoy only a moderate level of autonomy. Accountability levels are high, but not in terms of wider stakeholder accountability per se, but largely due to the need to serve the state. Yet, this may be a distortion of what is happening in reality in what is a complex landscape.

Increasing autonomy has given rise to a corresponding increase in accountability, creating the paradox of centralised decentralisation, a phenomenon which is not limited to China and which has been observed in Western countries. Provincial governments within China have been accorded greater local autonomy and freedoms, leading to the development of joint governance arrangements between the centre and provinces. Significant levels of institutional autonomy extend to the design of the curriculum, including new course innovations; the appointment of faculty (senior academics being recruited from abroad to increase research capacity); financial control over the allocation of resources to meet specific strategic goals and objectives and student recruitment and retention targets. What is accepted and not challenged by institutions is that the state controls ideo-political education and the appointment of university presidents and party secretaries as a non-negotiable part of university governance (Saint, 2009). At the 19th National Congress of the Communist Party of China held in October 2017, the decision was taken to extend greater powers to party officials who sit on the over 2,000 joint venture trustee boards (i.e. those partnered with overseas universities) with regard to matters of academic freedom. This has significant implications for institutional governance since unanimous decision-making is the accepted norm on Chinese university boards (Feng, 2019).

Whilst this situation would be anathema to most other higher education systems in the world, China has developed its own concept of 'semi-independent' institutional autonomy distinct from the West, where a separation exists between the university and the state, and academic and organisational independence is respected as part of a robust governance and accountability framework.

It is certainly true, however, that individual institutional autonomy has been increasing since China embarked on the neo-liberal, market expansion of its higher education system over 40 years ago. Then, less than 2 per cent of 18-year-olds progressed to university; now, the figure is approaching 50 per cent and there are concerns that the HE revolution has gone too far in providing too many graduates (a familiar refrain is often heard in the UK in this regard).

But, there is evidence that the long-term strategy of the Chinese government has achieved a degree of international success, 'in the *Universitas 21 Ranking of National Higher Education Systems 2016*, China was the most improved country, having gained 12 places over four years to be ranked 30th out of 50 national systems' (University of Oxford, 2017). Additionally, the Chinese government has also forged ahead with plans to export its university model to Africa through a network of 46 Confucius Institutes (University of Oxford, 2017) and other training centres. This has led to South Africa including Mandarin Chinese in the national school curriculum.

South Africa

Southern Africa's (SA) public university system was a lynchpin of democratisation in 1994 and much was expected of it in terms of developing citizenship and addressing social inequalities (Higher Education South Africa, 2014).

Following substantial reforms in 2004, the system was remodelled and comprises three main types of institution: traditional; comprehensive; and technical

(27 in total), all of which enjoy a high degree of autonomy within an accountability framework that is consistent with Western institution structures. Coupled with these reforms was a desire to reposition SA universities on the world stage following the wilderness years of isolation.

In almost 25 years since independence, there is substantial evidence that SA universities have contributed greatly to the nation's democracy, social equity and its economic and social development (Shrivastava and Shrivastava, 2014). Yet, the system is showing signs of strain.

Student protests erupted in 2015 (and again in 2017 – the most significant since Apartheid) at the announcement that the government was to increase tuition fees by between 10 and 15 per cent (the parallel in the UK over the trebling of tuition fees prompted relatively muted protests in comparison). Many leading universities were forced to close in response to the severity of the student action. Whilst the government has established a fees commission to look into how fee increases could be introduced in a way that does not discriminate against poorer black students, the situation has echoes in other parts of the world.

Since 2001, SA has increased university funding by 70 per cent, but this is against a backdrop of record student enrolment. The challenge of sustaining such a mass HE system at the same time as an economic downturn has prompted a change in the government's fees policy.

On the continent of Africa, the focus for the work of both the Global Partnership for Education (GPE)[3] and the Association for the Development of Education in Africa (ADEA) are framed around the challenges for education itself, not its governance. The partnerships seeking to push forward collective capacity and impact in Africa, such as the Africa Centres of Excellence, Partnership for Skills in Applied Sciences, Engineering & Technology, the Pan African University, Harmonisation of African Higher Education Quality Assurance and Accreditation are fragile and their governance and sustainability unclear.

A major British Council study of the employability of African graduates found that 'employers across the region complain of a lack of basic, technical and transferable skills. Uneven and often poor-quality teaching, resulting from under-qualified staff, large class sizes, and out-dated teaching methods, are held responsible' (University of Oxford, 2017). These are vitally important matters, as we have discussed above in relation to India. Given the poor quality of educational provision across Africa, a sustainable framework could provide a progressive mechanism for essential improvements to governance in a global context.

Future governance challenges

The challenge is to devise accountability mechanisms which are not only arm's-length in terms of institutional autonomy, but which are also outcomes based. The drive for more outcomes-based accountability has been a process of evolution arising out of the changing relationship between government and universities, as institutions have been required to increase their focus on efficiency, value for money and globalisation (Huisman and Currie, 2004).

The essential dichotomy between accountability and autonomy is representative of the cultural and historical context in which all HEIs operates. It is also reflective of the nature of the relationship between the institution and the state, which can change from time to time.

Institutional autonomy can be categorised into substantive and procedural (Raza, 2009). Substantive autonomy covers the academic and research sphere, extending to curriculum design, research policy, quality and assurance mechanisms. Procedural autonomy, as the term implies, relates to professional and administrative frameworks and structures.

High accountability extends to institutions who are deemed to have well-developed, mature models of stakeholder engagement, internal and external. Analysis of a comparative study on accountability versus autonomy of HE institutions across the globe (Saint, 2009) finds that the UK shares moderate accountability with Ghana, Saudi Arabia, Brazil and Japan. This is not entirely unexpected; the UK HE system is still at a relatively low level when it comes to actively reaching out to stakeholders as a key lynchpin to effective governance. The representative governing body model can appear tokenistic and constrained in terms of both the student and staff voice, with little evidence of institutions reaching out to the wider stakeholder community in a way which will enhance good governance and wider public accountability.

Towards a universal framework

A comparative study will almost inevitably raise larger and broader questions. One conclusion we wish to explore further is concerned with whether any underlying principles of governance are shared beyond continental boundaries, even though the policy context, operating environment and constitutional and organisational structures are not. This shifted our focus to whether a set of guiding principles is necessary or even desirable.

We started with a clear sense of caution, principles are not bias-free. We wanted to ensure that in our work we avoided any perpetuation of a Western or imperial legacy model which sees an export of, or imposition of, culturally grounded values. In the international market for higher education these values are already visible. Models of internationalisation and partnership are driven by the 'Western' models of governance.

The offer of education which crosses cultural boundaries is inevitably challenging and challengeable. Campuses abroad can feel like they are about promotion a slice of the homeland (exact replicas in some cases) being made available to foreign settings, matching unshakeable standards of education not available in that country, a route for escape to work abroad. This argues strongly for a more explicit set of guiding principles for governance which directly address these types of lingering imperialist framing of offers.

This works in reverse too. The adoption of a set of universal principles could help provide a bedrock standard for benchmarking accurately across cultural and institutional boundaries in a way which increases the value and appreciation of the governance of higher education as a collective, international enterprise delivered to equivalent standards worldwide irrespective of the specific operating environments of countries or institutions. This could help nurture learning and exchange on a level playing-field basis.

So, what might a set of guiding principles look like? How could they be applied and sanctioned?

We wanted to identify a set of principles which potentially had wider applicability, were governance-specific, had been independently developed and verified as valid beyond organisational and cultural boundaries, and which, whilst they could be applied in higher education, had not been developed specifically for higher education.

A framework which will potentially ensure that governing bodies (in a global context) achieve high levels of accountability to their core stakeholder constituencies, is contained within the King IV Report on Corporate Governance (Institute of Directors of Southern Africa, 2016).

King IV comments and reflects on the changing context within which many public-sector organisations (including universities, state-directed or not) operate and how the external landscape impacts upon senior leadership and capacity. Key transformational issues are as diverse as inequalities, globalised trade (which can extend to the international student market), climate change, population growth, social and geopolitical tensions, digitalisation and scientific advancement.

According to King, organisations are being held accountable by a new demographic of (millennial[4]) stakeholders. These consumers (whether students, staff, business and research partners in an HE context) are now interested more than ever in the sustainability of organisations beyond the realm of the financial, extending to their social, civic and environmental impact and responsibility. It is this notion of wider accountability and sustainability that underlines the concept of Integrated Reporting, whose key principles are: financial, manufactured, human, intellectual, natural and social and relationship capital.

Public institutions, by virtue of their status (charitable in most cases), have an inherent higher duty of care to the primary beneficiaries or users of their services. It is important, therefore, that university governing bodies have robust ethical leadership facilitating good 'corporate citizenship' on the part of the institution, which embodies stakeholder inclusivity.

King asserts that the leadership strategy of the governing body should be informed by a number of principles which collectively form the basis of legitimate and effective governance outcomes: the 'cycle of good governance'. Taken as a broad framework, the 17 universal principles transcend national, political and cultural boundaries and could potentially act as an agent for nurturing the growth and maturity of good university governance practice.

The adoption of an international standard of governance, even if it is seen as desirable, would have potential implications and face a number of obstacles. One practical starting point however could simply come from the recognition of the value of an international benchmark in a changing, internationalised world, followed by the voluntary adoption of King IV and integrated reporting (the central principle of public accounting) by leading higher education providers in different countries. The King governance criteria could also form part of the assessment template for the international tables which hold such sway in the competitive international environment. This combination of relatively simple action would form a potentially powerful network which could, initially at least, avoid the bureaucracy of the formal statutory and regulatory bodies and their different administrative practices. Taking forward such an approach lies beyond the scope of this study but we suggest they are a suitable starting point for further action research, which could provide a foundation for greater international comparison of value.

Conclusion

This short, illustrative analysis suggests there are several themes which connect Western and non-Western higher education in an increasing international market, with shared ambition for global impact and recognition. The issues of changing regulation, increased levels of autonomy, a mixed economy approach to meet capacity and quality demands, growing movement to education as a business, greater attention to practical skills, economic and industrial impact, more overt performance and impact assessments and reform to core statutes and structures, are all shared. What is lacking is a shared model of good governance in which these issues are being assessed and addressed.

This situation provides an interesting contrast to the degree to which international standards have been developed in respect of aspects of academic governance and the protection of standards in scientific endeavour. The way academic governance and science is conducted is not a self-contained bubble. The effectiveness and integrity of academic activity interacts with the style of corporate governance and levels of managerialism which characterise the hosting organisations and partnerships. The degree to which this has not been the subject of active enquiry perhaps reflects a set of tropes about a battle between corporate and academic governance and creeping managerialism which has characterised the territory.

This chapter illustrates both the value and limitation of current international comparisons. There is a need for further research around several lines of enquiry. Is it possible to determine a set of guiding principles which would strengthen international exchange and consistency of governance of higher education standards? Would the specific operating environments of individual countries and territories prove more decisive than an overarching set of guiding principles? What is apparent and encouraging is that such core governance themes have resonance and potential value worldwide.

Notes

1 A policy focused on the top 100 universities.
2 A policy centered on developing the best 39 research-intensive institutions.
3 The Global Partnership for Education, founded in 2002, remains the only global fund solely dedicated to education in developing countries.
4 Young people born after 1981.

References

De Boer, H.F., Enders, J. and Schimank, U. (2008) Comparing Higher Education Governance Systems in Four European Countries. In N.C. Soguel and P. Jaccard (Eds), *Governance and Performance of Education Systems*. Dordrecht: Springer, pp. 35–54.

Feng, Emily (2019) Beijing Vies for Greater Control of Foreign Universities in China. *Financial Times*. [Accessed at www.ft.com/content/09ecaae2-ccd0-11e7-b781-794ce08b24dc]

Gandhi, M.M. (2013) Autonomy and Accountability in Higher Education: An Indian Perspective. *Journal of Research & Method in Education*, 3, Issue 5, pp. 33–37.

The Good Governance Institute (GGI) (2017) Benchmarking Research.

Higher Education South Africa (2014) Autonomy Lost: The Bureaucratisation of South African HE. *South African Journal of Higher Education*, 28, Issue 1, pp. 60–71.

Huisman, J. and Currie, J. (2004) Accountability in Higher Education: Bridge Over Troubled Water? *Higher Education*, 48, pp. 529–551.

Institute of Directors of Southern Africa (2016) The King IV Report on Corporate Governance for South Africa.

Li, M. and Yang, R. (2014) Governance Reforms in Higher Education: A Study of China. UNESCO. [Accessed at http://unesdoc.unesco.org/images/0023/002318/231858e.pdf]

Marshall, J.D. (1996) The Autonomous Chooser and 'Reforms' in Education. *Studies in Philosophy and Education*, 15, Issue 1–2, pp. 89–96.

QS World (2008) Will Education in India Ever Be 'World Class'? [Accessed at www.qs.com/world-class-education-system-in-india/]

Raza, R. (2009) Examining Autonomy and Accountability in Public and Private Tertiary Institutions. Human Development Network. World Bank. [Accessed at http://siteresources.worldbank.org/EXTHDOFFICE/Resources/5485726-1239047988859/RAZA_Autonomy_and_Accountability_Paper.pdf]

Rosovosky, H. (2001) Some Thoughts about University Governance. In W. Hirscht and L. Webber (Eds), *Governance in Tertiary Education: The University in Flux*. London: Economica, pp. 94–104.

Saint, W. (2009) Guiding Universities: Governance and Management Arrangements around the Globe. Human Development Network. World Bank. [Accessed at http://siteresources.worldbank.org/EXTHDOFFICE/Resources/5485726-1239047988859/University_Governance_and_Management.pdf]

Shrivastava, M. and Shrivastava, S. (2014) Political Economy of Higher Education: Comparing South Africa to Trends in the World. *Higher Education*, 67, Issue 6, pp. 809–822.

University of Oxford (2017) International Trends in Higher Education 2016–17. University of Oxford Strategy Office.

Part III

The English experiment

How current trends in UK corporate governance might influence future higher education governance and policy

Lorraine Young

Introduction: the corporate governance framework

In considering the potential influence of commercial and corporate governance on the governance of higher education institutions (HEIs), this chapter will focus on the governance arrangements of large, publicly quoted companies as the most relevant comparator group. They are governed by the UK Corporate Governance Code (the 'Code') issued from time to time by the Financial Reporting Council (FRC) (2018a). The most recent version of the Code was published in July 2018, accompanied by updated 'Guidance on Board Effectiveness' ('Guidance') (Financial Reporting Council, 2018b). These publications reflect recent developments in corporate governance in the commercial sector. This chapter will consider five key themes: culture, stakeholders, remuneration, viability and succession planning.

The Code

Background

The first governance code was issued by the Cadbury Committee (Committee on the Financial Aspects of Corporate Governance, 1992). It defined corporate governance as 'the system by which companies are directed and controlled'.

The early committees reviewing governance for the commercial sector were set up in response to corporate failures or poor practice. Despite all the subsequent developments, there are still high profile corporate failures and examples of poor governance practice in some businesses. No code alone will fix malpractice, which although widely publicised and damaging to the reputation of all businesses, is not so widespread. There are many well-run companies which bring employment and prosperity to communities in addition to the work done under their corporate responsibility programmes. Governance is always evolving, whether viewed from the perspective of each individual organisation on its own governance journey, or from the overarching perspective of the whole corporate and commercial sector.

The new Code

There have been regular reviews of what was originally called the 'Combined Code' and is now referred to as the UK Corporate Governance Code (Committee on Corporate Governance, 1998) since its first issue in 1998. The latest iteration has been produced following a thorough review of the previous version which for some time had been mostly 'added to'. It now contains 18 principles (labelled A to R) and 41 provisions. It comes into force for accounting periods beginning on or after 1 January 2019, so reporting against the new Code is expected to start in 2020.

In terms of the structure of the new Code, there has been a welcome initiative to remove much of the detail which is now well embedded into corporate governance from the Code itself into the updated Guidance. There is a renewed emphasis on applying the principles of the Code and fewer provisions with which to comply.

There is an increased emphasis on boards promoting the success of the company over the long term. The Code recognises that this can be a challenge for companies and their boards as there are demands from some investors for continual short-term performance increases, often with the expectation of perennially rising dividend payments. Companies will have to seek out investors who will support stewardship initiatives and be willing to stick around for the longer term.

The first principle of the 2018 version of the Code states:

> A successful company is led by an effective and entrepreneurial board, whose role is to promote the long-term sustainable success of the company, generating value for shareholders and contributing to wider society.
>
> (Financial Reporting Council, 2018a, p. 4)

Roles within corporate governance

It is important to understand the roles of the participants in the commercial governance realm:

Directors

Boards of directors are responsible for the governance of their companies. In the UK, the main model within the corporate environment is that of the unitary board, where directors share collective responsibility for oversight of the organisation. Directors are typically selected by the board itself through the nominations committee and there should be a transparent process for this.

Shareholders

Shareholders appoint the directors and the auditors. Although in practice they are asked to ratify appointments made by the board, they also have the power to remove directors and auditors. In some circumstances they may put forward a candidate for the board. They must satisfy themselves that an appropriate govern- ance structure is in place. They usually do this by engaging with the companies in which they invest (see below).

Stakeholders

There is a new emphasis on stakeholders other than shareholders and the wider benefits to society which companies should bring, rather than focusing purely on shareholder returns. This has developed in response to the loss of trust in busi- ness following not only the financial crisis of 2008 but also more recent corporate failures, such as BHS and Carillion.

How these participants interact is crucial in ensuring effective governance which works for everyone – but the system is not ideal. 'Enforcement' of the Code is carried out by shareholders who may indicate dissatisfaction by the way they vote at the AGM. They may withhold their vote, which is viewed as a warning of discontent and this may be followed up by a vote against if the company ignores the initial protest. A recent development to increase accountability has been the establishment of a 'dissent register' by the Investment Association. This will record all company resolutions proposed where more than 20 per cent of the votes cast were against the resolution. The new Code provides (provision 4) that if there is a shareholder vote of more than 20 per cent against a resolution recommended by the board, then the company should say what it will do to engage with sharehold- ers to understand why. An update on what the board has done in response to the feedback should be given within six months of the meeting, followed by a final summary in the next annual report – and the next AGM notice if appropriate.

A better outcome may be obtained if there is discussion (engagement) between the company and its shareholders before the meeting. If companies con- duct regular dialogue with their investors, then they stand a better chance of not presenting proposals which shareholders do not support. However, because of the number of listed companies and the limited resources of institutional inves- tors, this is not always practicable.

Although the FRC, as the regulator tasked with the guardianship of the Code does not have any powers of enforcement in relation to its implementation, it has indicated that it intends to escalate its monitoring of practice and reporting.

Reporting

A key part of governance for UK companies is reporting on how they apply the principles of the Code and comply with the provisions (or explain any non- compliance). For companies following the Code this will be primarily in the annual report, where there is a corporate governance report, reports by the audit and nominations committees as well as a separate remuneration report, which is gov- erned by regulations[1] as well as the Code. The reporting requirements have greatly increased since the Code's inception but present companies with an opportunity to explain to investors and other stakeholders how they approach governance. For companies listed on AIM (the Alternative Investment Market) there is a new requirement to put corporate governance disclosure onto their websites.

Culture

Introduction

Following the financial crisis in 2008 and various company misdemeanours since (for example the accounting scandal at Tesco and the emissions debacle at Volkswagen) trust in business hit an all time low. However, the 2018 Edelman Trust Barometer[2] results in the UK found trust in business at 43 per cent was higher than trust in government (36 per cent) – although it was still two points lower than the previous year. Major concerns were around executive pay, businesses not paying sufficient tax and dishonesty and a lack of transparency in business dealings. However, the credibility of CEOs and boards in the UK, according to the survey, was significantly up on the previous year.

The FRC undertook an exercise in 2016 (the 'Culture Coalition project') to explore corporate culture. Its report of observations 'Corporate Culture and the Role of Boards' (Financial Reporting Council, 2016a) was published in July 2016. It suggested a definition of corporate culture as 'A combination of the values, attitudes and behaviours manifested by a company in its operations and relations with its stakeholders'.

Sir Roger Carr's introduction to the City Values Forum and tomorrow's company publication which was released at the same time, says:

> Culture is about behaviour which reflects the values, beliefs and ethics of a business and ensures that it is understood that how a business makes money is as important as how much money it makes.
>
> For a company to be both economically successful and socially acceptable in the wider community, it must be performance-driven but values-led. The culture of an organisation which aims to strike this balance is created in the boardroom.
>
> (City Values Forum and tomorrow's company, 2016, p. 3)

The new Code and Guidance include more material relating to culture and values, and the board's role in this area.

Role of the board

Setting culture and values

Embedding the right organisational culture is easier said than done. The board has a role to play in determining the values and standards of an organisation as well as its purpose and strategy. The directors then need to lead by example and set the right tone from the top. Principle B in the new Code includes the following wording:

> Directors are expected to act in a manner consistent with their statutory duties, and to uphold the highest standards of integrity and support the chair in instilling the appropriate values, behaviours and culture in the boardroom and beyond.
>
> (Financial Reporting Council, 2018a, p. 4)

Implementation

Culture and values have to be embedded at every level of the organisation. The Guidance notes that the primary responsibility for setting an example to the company's workforce[3] lies with the chief executive, who also has to communicate the culture and values to those in the organisation. They should ensure that policies and practices throughout the organisation support the values and standards and communicate back to the board views from the workforce.

It is essential, therefore, that the board chooses the right chief executive who endorses the values and standards which the board believes the business should adopt. The individual will need to stand up for those values and standards against any pressure for short-term returns – wherever that comes from – and sometimes that might be from the board, albeit inadvertently. Care must be taken when setting performance measures and remuneration packages that these all encourage the desired culture. The board may need to act if members of the senior team fall short in their behaviour. This can be challenging if it happens with the chief executive and can have unfortunate consequences, as the board of Tesla discovered recently when Elon Musk made some controversial tweets about future funding for the business. Both he and the company paid fines of US$20m to settle with the USA Securities Exchange Commission (SEC) (although neither admitted or denied the SEC's allegations). Mr Musk has to step down as Chairman, a role he combined with that of CEO, and the board has to appoint two additional directors and set up a new committee of independent directors.

Assessment and monitoring

Provision 2 of the new Code states that:

> The board should assess and monitor culture. Where it is not satisfied that policy, practices or behaviour throughout the business are aligned with the company's purpose, values and strategy, it should seek assurance that management has taken corrective action.
>
> (Financial Reporting Council, 2018a)

The work of the Culture Coalition acknowledged that measuring corporate culture was not an easy task. The Guidance suggests indicators of both a healthy and unhealthy culture and ways to track the state of the culture in the organisation.

Higher education

Focus on culture and values in the corporate sector is recent. For many companies the new Code will provide the first impetus for them to consider this. In the HE sector, there are references in both the CUC Higher Education Code of Governance from 2014 ('the CUC Code') (revised June 2018) (Committee of University Chairs, 2018a) and the Scottish Code of Good Higher Education Governance (2017) ('the Scottish Code') (Committee of the Chairs of Scottish Higher Education Institutions, 2017) to governing body members demonstrating high standards of ethical behaviour, with the CUC Code referencing the 'Nolan Principles of Public Life' and the Scottish Code referring to the 'Nine Principles of Public Life in Scotland'. Element 2 of the CUC Code refers to the governing body gaining assurance that the policy framework in place is ethical as well as following legal and regulatory requirements and there is a similar reference in the Scottish Code. The Foreword to the Scottish Code also notes that governing bodies should guide the development of the HEI's ethics and values and demonstrate them by the way they act, referencing in particular their approach to equality and diversity and social responsibility.

Some HEIs have adopted Mission and Values Statements which may be communicated as part of the strategic priorities. The HEI's Student Charter is another example of how it can communicate its values and standards and demonstrate a commitment to them when dealing with the student body. The work on culture in the corporate sector may result in an increased focus on this area in HE as the pressure to drive up standards in all sectors continues. Governing bodies of HEIs will face their own challenges in embedding the desired culture throughout the institution.

Stakeholders

Introduction

Recently introduced legislation requires large companies[4] to report on how the directors have complied with section 172 of Companies Act 2006 (CA2006). This section (which itself has not changed and applies to directors of all companies registered at Companies House) sets out the key statutory duty of company directors and includes consideration of the impact of any board decision on the company's stakeholders. Stakeholders were considered in the work of the Culture Coalition referred to above and there is a great deal in the new Code about them. There was a political imperative in this area, particularly in relation to a company's workforce which has no doubt led to the new emphasis.

Company law considerations

The stakeholder issue is not a new one. When the company law review was underway which led to CA2006 there was much debate about to whom directors should owe their duty. In company law it remains that directors owe their legal duty to the company and not to other stakeholders. However, the corporate world has moved into an era of 'enlightened shareholder value' where directors must consider other stakeholders in decision-making. The section provides that the key duty for directors is to promote the success of the company for the benefit of its members as a whole. This was not considered to be materially different from the previous legislation, which referred to acting in the best interests of the company. However, there are additional sub-sections which require directors to consider other matters when making decisions:

- long-term consequences
- employees
- customers, suppliers and others
- community and environment
- business reputation
- acting fairly between members.

These factors are described as 'mandatory' and 'non-exclusive' – so directors must keep in mind any other issues and stakeholders not listed to the extent they are relevant.

Recent governance developments

The new Code contains several principles relating to stakeholders with the workforce getting particular attention – boards need to engage with the workforce by having one of the following:

- a director on the board from the workforce;
- a formal workforce advisory panel;
- a non-executive director (NED) designated to engage with the workforce on behalf of the board.

If the board chooses a different method it must explain what that is and why it is considered to be effective.

Stakeholders generally

In September 2017 ICSA, The Governance Institute and The Investment Association produced a joint publication called 'The Stakeholder Voice in Board Decision Making'[5] ('Stakeholder Guidance') (ICSA *et al.*, 2017). This looks at some of the practical aspects of stakeholder engagement. Many boards do consider stakeholders, for example looking at the results of employee surveys, customer feedback and the reaction of investors to results and other announcements. Social media is another important channel to monitor the stakeholder voice. Corporate responsibility reporting often overlaps a great deal with the areas mentioned in section 172. It does not feel as though there is a general lack of compliance.

The Stakeholder Guidance lists ten principles for boards in stakeholder engagement, including:

- Identifying and keeping under review who the key stakeholders are – and why.
- Identifying which stakeholders they need to engage with directly and which will be engaged with by the executive.
- Considering if they need a director with experience relevant to a stakeholder group when reviewing board composition and how stakeholder issues can be taken into account when recruiting, inducting and training directors.
- Ensuring decision-making processes give sufficient consideration to key stakeholders.
- Ensuring appropriate engagement with stakeholders is taking place.
- Reporting to shareholders on their stakeholder engagement and feedback to the stakeholder groups with which they have engaged.

Directors need to be advised of the outcome of any engagement and factor this into decision-making processes where relevant. The reporting and feedback loop complete the process. In many cases boards will not engage directly with stakeholders, however, meeting staff, customers and investors will be useful on occasion to moderate the feedback which comes via the executive team.

The workforce

As noted above, companies are given three choices in the new Code about how they might engage with the workforce.

There had been suggestions that all companies should have a member of the workforce on the board, however, the final version of the Code gives companies an element of choice. It is too early to say which option will prove most popular.

There are some difficulties with having a member of the workforce on the board. That person will have the same legal duties and responsibilities as all the other directors and have to be fully involved in all decisions relating to the company, not just those which impact workers. There could be issues around confidentiality. And the member will not be there just to represent the workforce as a constituency but will have to make decisions based on wider concerns. It will be difficult, if not impossible, to find one individual who can really represent the views of the whole workforce. Therefore, companies may prefer to use the option of a workforce panel as this will be able to gather views from more people.

Implementation

The new regulations and Code should not change practice too much. However, the new requirement for companies to report on stakeholder engagement may lead to a more formal approach.

Commercial organisations commonly use profitability as a measure of their success. This is often demonstrated by dividend payments to shareholders. Whether a greater focus on stakeholders will push companies into thinking in a longer term, more sustainable way remains to be seen – for example, will there be a different decision about whether the company should pay out the maximum dividend or reinvest in growth?

Even if stakeholder views are at odds with what the board wants to do and considers best for the company, greater engagement with stakeholders should improve relationships. The various groups may be able to gain a broader understanding of the issues facing the company and contribute to the debate. There is a need to improve trust and transparency and this could help.

Higher education

The governance codes for HEIs already require the involvement of stakeholders.

For example, the CUC Code states that the governing body should: 'be confident that the needs and interests of all stakeholders are adequately reflected in the strategic plan'. And in relation to academic governance: 'actively encourage student engagement in academic governance', 'receive regular reports from students' union or association officers and/or institution/student representation committees' and 'receive assurance that honest, accurate and timely information is provided to students, stakeholders and the public about all aspects of academic provision'. The Scottish Code has more – it provides (among other things) that the governing body should ensure it can consult with stakeholders' representative bodies, as well as the public and wider communities it serves. The HEI should hold an annual, public, stakeholder meeting, where the governing body gives an account of the HEI's performance and answers questions.

Most HEIs will have staff and student representatives on the governing body, so are already in the area which is currently uncharted territory for companies. Companies may be able to learn from the HE sector as the new provisions about the workforce are introduced. However, as with anything, there will be some HEIs which do this well and allow the staff and student representatives to add real value and others which will just see it as a 'box ticking' exercise. Companies will need to make sure they follow good practice, not bad.

Remuneration

Introduction

Senior executive remuneration is one of the most contentious and emotive issues for large, publicly quoted businesses and on which they receive much criticism. Remuneration has been in the headlines for years. Despite best practice guides, governance codes, remuneration codes and legislation there does not seem to have been much progress.

In broader governance discussions, investors and companies have expressed the opinion that there are other governance issues which are more important, but which get less attention from the media.

The current framework

Remuneration committees

These should consist of independent non-executive directors only and determine the remuneration policy for the company as well as the packages for the executive directors and senior management team. A fundamental principle is that no one should be involved in setting their own pay. Remuneration includes salaries, benefits, pensions and short and long-term incentives, including the performance targets set. The new Code and Guidance task the committee with reviewing workforce remuneration and related policies and to take these into account when setting pay for senior executives. The committee should explain to the workforce how its decisions reflect wider company pay policy and the board should monitor whether remuneration policies and practices support culture and strategy. The committee should consider the links between remuneration, strategy and long-term sustainable success. Simpler remuneration policies and structures are encouraged as is a greater use of discretion by the committee to ensure rewards are fair and not excessive. These all tie in and link to the other key governance themes.

Remuneration reporting

Reporting on remuneration was introduced for companies on the main London stockmarket by the Greenbury report (Report of a Study Group chaired by Sir Richard Greenbury, 1995) and Code, in the mid-1990s. The government has introduced regulations to necessitate more detailed disclosure, with the latest development requiring ratios of senior executive pay, compared to average worker pay, to be reported from 2020. These ratios have to be justified. The increased disclosure should allow investors to make informed voting decisions. However, there is a view that the information in company remuneration reports has simply ratcheted pay upwards, as senior executives can see what their peers receive.

Remuneration consultants

Large companies use remuneration consultants to help them devise pay structures and packages. The NEDs on the remuneration committee are unlikely to have the expertise themselves to do this.

A few issues arise from this.

Conflicts

Consultants would often work with the executive team to devise the pay structures and then present to the remuneration committee. They would also have to advise the committee if the proposals were appropriate. This led to inherent conflicts. Now there is a clear requirement that remuneration consultants should be instructed by and report to, the remuneration committee, not the executives.

This does not remove the issue that the executive team has still to be motivated and incentivised to deliver the company's goals and targets. The right remuneration is key to this and it will inevitably be challenging to strike the right balance.

Complexity

One of the criticisms about executive pay in recent years has been the complexity which has developed, particularly in relation to long-term incentives ('LTIPs'). When share option plans were first introduced, the executive gained if the share price rose between the grant and exercise of the option. This was unsophisticated, although it worked on a basic level. However, the share price could be affected by factors outside the company's control, such as macroeconomic and sector-specific issues.

It was not long before performance measures were introduced. This was accompanied by annual grants of awards. Executives are now sometimes accused of trying to manipulate the company's results to get a better return on their incentive awards. For example, share buybacks can affect earnings per share which is often a performance measure.

It is now the case that most people who read the complex disclosures in a company's annual report on an LTIP, will struggle to understand them – including the executives who have awards under the plan. At this point, the situation has gone too far. There are beginning to be calls from institutions to simplify such plans and as noted above, this is now reflected in the Guidance.

Accountability

The use of consultants does not remove accountability from the remuneration committee. NEDs will often have to rely on specialist advice but they also have to keep their wits about them and challenge when necessary. It is ultimately the directors who are accountable for the outcome of any decisions made. It will not be possible to hide behind the advice received.

A recent illustration of this was at the housebuilder, Persimmon. An LTIP had been introduced, with advice from consultants, to reward the executive team. Targets had been set. However, there was no cap on the maximum any award could reach. Between the introduction of the scheme and vesting of awards, the government's Help to Buy scheme was introduced. This resulted in the company making much bigger profits than was anticipated at the outset.

The payout due to the CEO under the LTIP was initially an eye watering £110m. In the end some was foregone but the final payment was still huge. Investors protested with a considerable vote against the remuneration report at the AGM – although they had also benefited from the significant returns. As a result of the flaw in the plan design, both the board chair and the chair of the remuneration committee of Persimmon resigned. The CEO has also now left the company.

Voting

Shareholders in companies on the main stockmarket now vote every three years on remuneration policy (which is a binding vote). The company must explain its remuneration policy, which, once approved by shareholders, must be followed. If the company wants to pay someone outside of the policy prior shareholder approval is required. This added hurdle seems to be bringing some improvement as companies have to think ahead about what they want to achieve with directors' pay.

The second vote is an annual one on the remuneration report. This is an advisory vote but may be used by shareholders to express dissatisfaction about a particular issue. For lower levels of support, companies have to take some action and engage with investors to address their issues and concerns, as noted in the introduction to this chapter.

Shareholders may also vote against individual directors if they are unhappy. So, in the area of pay, they would show their feelings by a vote against the remuneration committee chair, other members of the remuneration committee or the board chair. This is not often the first method that they use to express their views, but it is becoming more of a threat.

Latest developments

Section 5 of the new Code covers remuneration with three principles and 10 provisions. These give particular emphasis to the themes we have been exploring, culture (values and standards), viability (sustainability, longer term), stakeholders (both shareholders and the workforce). It also seeks to address some of the ongoing issues in this divisive area.

Higher education

There are many similarities between companies and HEIs in this area. There was much publicity over the controversial pay package for Professor Glynis Breakwell, Vice-Chancellor at Bath University and the handling of a Court[6] vote which attempted to censure the remuneration committee. The reaction was swift, with the CUC publishing a new Remuneration Code in June 2018 ('Remuneration Code') (Committee of University Chairs, 2018b) and the Office for Students issued an Accounts Direction on the reporting of senior pay in universities on its register. There is also continued government pressure for the HE sector to take action in this area.

The basic principles on remuneration in the HE sector are similar to those in companies, so that no one should be involved in setting their own pay. Although some media reports at the time of the Bath incident called for vice-chancellors to be barred from attending meetings of a remuneration committee this is not required by the Remuneration Code. It makes the point that when other senior staff pay is considered, it is essential for the Head of Institution to be present to provide information to the committee. However, they should not be a member of the committee, nor present when their own pay is under discussion. Membership should be made up primarily of lay members of the governing body with the addition of external expertise if needed.

The Scottish Code goes further:

> 80.   In addition, the remuneration committee is expected to seek the views of representatives of students and staff of the Institution, including representatives of recognised trade unions, in relation to the remuneration package of the Principal and the senior executive team. This requirement may be implemented in part through relevant members of the governing body serving as members of the remuneration committee or attending its meetings, or may be achieved through separate consultation with representatives of the student and staff communities. The relevant process should form part of the policies and processes approved by the whole governing body, as outlined above.
>
> (Committee of the Chairs of Scottish Higher Education
> Institutions, 2017, p. 24)

The suggestion that minutes of remuneration committee meetings should be made public is not practicable, because of the sensitivity of the personal information they could well contain. However, the Remuneration Code does provide that each institution must publish a readily accessible annual statement on remuneration, based on an annual report to its governing body and indicates what should be covered in the report.

Viability

Introduction

In the 2014 version of the Code a new requirement was introduced for companies to report on the future viability of the organisation. This is over and above the requirement for the board to consider whether it is appropriate to adopt the going concern basis of accounting. Boards will usually consider the cashflow forecast for at least the next 12 months to meet the going concern requirement.

The viability statement has proved to be a tricky area for boards, especially in determining what should be the appropriate period over which to consider the company's future prospects. Feedback from the FRC has been that there needs to be some improvement to reporting in this area. The Financial Reporting Lab (2018) has recently published an update to encourage better reporting by providing examples of good practice. Investors consider that reporting on business models, risk and viability is important but that such reporting should be more consistent and clearly linked throughout the annual report.

The new Code and related guidance

The main provision in the new Code concerning the viability statement reads:

> 31.   Taking account of the company's current position and principal risks, the board should explain in the annual report how it has assessed the prospects of the company, over what period it has done so and why it considers that period to be appropriate. The board should state whether it has a reasonable expectation that the company will be able to continue in operation and meet its liabilities as they fall due over the period of their assessment, drawing attention to any qualifications or assumptions as necessary.

The area of risk management and internal controls links into viability and the board must also explain how it manages the principal risks facing the business. Viability is a different concept to that of sustainability, which is broader and usually explained in a company's corporate responsibility reporting. Viability is to do with the sufficiency of liquidity and solvency. With the renewed emphasis on section 172 CA2006, there is plenty in the new Code and the Guidance on the need for the board to consider the long-term, sustainable success of the company.

The FRC Guidance on Risk Management, Internal Control and Related Financial and Business Reporting (Financial Reporting Council, 2014) from September 2014 ('the Risk Management Guidance') covers the viability statement. This guidance is also concerned with risk management and internal control processes, which are fundamental to safeguarding the future of an organisation, and as such, should be regularly considered by the board and (usually) the audit committee (if there is no separate risk committee).

The Risk Management Guidance clarifies that the board does not need to have absolute certainty when considering viability and it is accepted that the longer the period, the less certainty there will be. However, the board should have a 'reasonable expectation' that the company has a safe future and must be able to justify its statement. The timeframe is expected to be significantly longer than 12 months. Factors to be taken into account when deciding on an appropriate period include:

- stewardship responsibilities;
- previous statements (particularly when fundraising);
- the nature of the business and its stage of development;
- the company's investment and planning periods.

As well as considering the risks to the future viability of the company, boards must decide what can be done to mitigate those risks. The Guidance restates the four factors above, suggesting that basing the viability statement only on the company's medium-term business plan is not enough.

In promoting the long-term success of a company, boards also need to consider other aspects of sustainability, such as the impact of climate change. However, these are beyond the scope of this chapter.

Higher education

The concept of viability as explained in the Code, does not appear in the CUC Code. However, risk management and controls and sustainability are covered, for example:

> 3.3   It [the governing body] must rigorously assess all aspects of the institution's sustainability, in the broadest sense, using an appropriate range of mechanisms which include relevant key performance indicators (KPIs) not just for the financial sustainability of the institution but also for its impact on the environment.

The FSSG and CUC also issued a practice note on Institutional Sustainability (Financial Sustainability Strategy Group and Committee of University Chairs, 2017) in May 2017.

The Scottish Code has the following:

> 10.   The governing body must satisfy itself that the Institution's policies and actions are ethical and sustainable, taking into consideration their impact on the environment, on the wellbeing of its students and workforce, including health and safety issues and fair working practices, and on other communities, whether local or more distant.

So there is recognition in both sectors that risk management is essential and sustainability must be on the board's agenda. The HEFCE required governing bodies to publish ASSURE statements on sustainability. It is not yet clear if this will also be taken up by the OfS. The concept of viability, however, is an emerging one and this has not reached the HE sector yet. It remains to be seen if the regulators will consider it to be relevant, or whether they will be satisfied with the broader sustainability requirements.

Board composition and succession planning

Background

This has been a fairly recent area of focus by the FRC. In October 2015, it published a discussion paper (Financial Reporting Council, 2015) entitled 'UK

Board Succession Planning' which sought views on board succession for both executive directors and NEDs.

The paper considered the link between board succession planning and business strategy and culture, the role of the nomination committee, board evaluation and its contribution to board succession, identifying the internal and external pipeline for directors, ensuring diversity and the role of institutional investors. The discussion paper was followed by a feedback statement (Financial Reporting Council, 2016b) in May 2016.

Nominations committees

The areas noted above would normally be covered by the nominations committee, led by the Chair. There has been a suggestion that the nominations committee has been the poor relation compared to the audit and remuneration committees. However, the work of the nominations committee will often be carried out over the longer term and so be less visible.

'The Nomination Committee: Coming Out of the Shadows' (ICSA *et al.*, 2016) published by ICSA, The Governance Institute with EY, suggested nominations committees were being more strategic and not just meeting when a new director was needed. New areas of discussion include:

–   Linking strategy to future board changes – and looking several years out, not just to the next board appointment.
–   Evaluating board effectiveness and directors' performance.
–   Induction and continuing professional development for directors.
–   Overseeing the executive pipeline and talent development.

Diversity on boards

Diversity was first mentioned in the 2010 version of the Code in terms of gender and the 2014 version mentioned diversity in broader terms. The Davies report (Women on Boards, 2011; Women on Boards, KPMG and Cranfield University, 2015) set a target for women to make up 25 per cent of the boards of FTSE 100 companies by 2015. This was achieved, and a new target was then set of 33 per cent by 2020. In 2016 the Hampton-Alexander report (FTSE Women Leaders Sponsored by KPMG, 2016) focussed on increasing the number of women in senior positions below board level to improve the executive pipeline as many of the women on boards have non-executive directorship roles. To date, companies in the FTSE 100 are making better progress on diversity than those in the FTSE 250.

Sir John Parker (Parker, 2017) in his review (also published in 2016) looked at ethnic and cultural diversity. This is reflected in the Guidance which refers to a range of different aspects of diversity, including age, disability, ethnicity, education and social background as well as gender in relation to the executive pipeline, while Principle J of the new Code refers to promoting diversity of gender, social and ethnic backgrounds, cognitive and personal strengths.

There have been other initiatives too, with the well-publicised 30% Club encouraging leaders of FTSE100 companies to achieve a minimum of 30 per cent female representation on their boards. This target was achieved in September 2018 – but obviously needs to be maintained.

During the first round of gender pay gap reporting many organisations explained their pay gap was due to the lack of women in senior roles. Whether publishing details of the pay gap and having to explain it will prompt them to act to improve the gender imbalance at senior levels remains to be seen.

Board succession planning

One of the key risks to an organisation achieving its strategy is having the right people, yet many boards skate over the issue of succession planning, probably because it is not easy to deal with. If the chair can have open conversations with each board member about their ideal tenure and career plans this can greatly help succession planning. Boards will often plan to sequence changes of the key roles of Chair and CEO so that there can be an orderly succession. The nominations committee should consider emergency succession in case someone leaves unexpectedly, as well as the more measured medium-term planning.

In organisations where there is less choice about who the members of the board are, for example where certain constituencies have the right to elect a representative member, board composition and succession planning can provide even more of a challenge. However, it can be helpful in such circumstances to approach things from a different perspective. Carrying out a skills audit and strengths analysis of each member of the board team can be extremely valuable in encouraging useful contributions from all members.

Higher education

There is already an awareness of the benefits of diversity on governing bodies in HEIs.

The CUC Code states that 'there is evidence that board diversity promotes more constructive and challenging dialogue, which in turn can improve governance outcomes by helping to avoid "groupthink" and that as a result there is a strong business case for diversity alongside legal and moral expectation'. Both the CUC Code and Scottish Code provide that the governing body should set goals and policies for balance and diversity of its members and review its performance against these. The CUC practice note on the role of the nomination committee (Committee of University Chairs, 2017) states that 'The governing body must promote equality and diversity throughout the institution, including in relation to its own operation'.

There are suggestions in the CUC Code to help build a diverse pool of potential governors for the future, for example providing training for potential governors and inviting them to join sub-committees or board-related events to gain experience.

The Scottish Code provides that:

> 15 The governing body is expected to draw up and make public a register of the balance of skills, attributes and experience required in the membership of the governing body, to inform the recruitment of appointed lay members of the governing body as well as regular assessment of the balance of skills across the membership of the governing body.

This public accountability goes further than is required for either HEIs in England or the corporate sector.

Advance HE has launched a Board Diversification Project[7] which includes a Board Vacancies Portal[8] for roles in universities and colleges, supported by AdvanceHE, AHUA, the 30% Club and the CUC. Other elements of the initiative include the development of a Board Appointment Diversity Framework, workshops to support women in gaining a board appointment and a scoping study on the feasibility, effectiveness and practicalities of developing a Board Apprenticeship Scheme in the HE sector.

Conclusion

There are many areas in which corporate and HE governance are similar and sometimes overlap. However, due to the differences in organisational structure, purpose, stakeholders and so on there are also many variances. As the CUC updates its governance code for 2019 it will be interesting to see if it adopts any new initiatives from the corporate sector, such as addressing culture and values and a broader definition of viability in HEIs more specifically. As can be seen in this chapter, sharing good practice can work both ways and there are some areas (such as stakeholder engagement) where commercial organisations may be able to learn from HEIs.

Notes

1 The Large and Medium-sized Companies and Groups (Accounts and Reports) (Amendment) Regulations 2013.
2 www.edelman.co.uk/magazine/posts/edelman-trust-barometer-2018/
3 This is not a legally defined term, but one used in the Code and Guidance to refer to all of those who work for a company, whether formally employed or not.
4 As defined in Companies Act 2006.
5 This guidance will be reviewed in light of the publication of the new Code and may be revised if necessary to reflect the new requirements.
6 While the Council of an HEI is the overall governing body, some HEIs also have a Court which is mainly an advisory body of internal and external stakeholders of the HEI which can make representations to the Council.
7 www.lfhe.ac.uk/en/governance-new/board-diversification.cfm
8 www.universitychairs.ac.uk/vacancies/

References

City Values Forum and tomorrow's company (2016) 'Governing Culture, Risk & Opportunity: A Guide to Board Leadership in Purpose, Values and Culture' [Accessed at www.cityvaluesforum.org.uk/Tomorrows%20Company%20 Governing%20Culture%20vfl.pdf]

Committee of the Chairs of Scottish Higher Education Institutions (2017) 'Scottish Code of Good Higher Education Governance' (2017 Edition) [Accessed at http:// www.scottishuniversitygovernance.ac.uk/wp-content/uploads/2016/08/Scot-Code-Good-HE-Governance-A4.pdf]

Committee on Corporate Governance (1998) 'The Combined Code on Corporate Governance (the Combined Code)' [Accessed at www.frc.org.uk/ getattachment/53db5ec9-810b-4e22-9ca2-99b116c3bc49/Combined-Code-1998. pdf]

Committee on the Financial Aspects of Corporate Governance (1992) 'Report of the Committee on The Financial Aspects of Corporate Governance 1 December 1992', Gee and Co Ltd. [Accessed at www.icaew.com/-/media/corporate/files/ library/subjects/corporate-governance/financial-aspects-of-corporate-govern ance.ashx?la=en]

Committee of University Chairs (2017) 'Illustrative Practice Note 7: The Role of the Nominations Committee November 2017' [Accessed at www.universitychairs.ac.uk/ wp-content/uploads/2017/11/IPN7-Nominations-Committee.pdf]

Committee of University Chairs (2018a) 'The Higher Education Code of Governance' Revised June 2018 [Accessed at www.universitychairs.ac.uk/wp-content/ uploads/2018/06/HE-Code-of-Governance-Updated-2018.pdf]

Committee of University Chairs (2018b) 'The Higher Education Senior Staff Remuneration Code' June 2018 [Accessed at www.universitychairs.ac.uk/wp-con tent/uploads/2018/06/HE-Remuneration-Code.pdf]

Financial Reporting Council (2014) 'Guidance on Risk Management, Internal Control and Related Financial and Business Reporting' [Accessed at www.frc.org.uk/ getattachment/d672c107-b1fb-4051-84b0-f5b83a1b93f6/Guidance-on-Risk-Management-Internal-Control-and-Related-Reporting.pdf]

Financial Reporting Council (2015) 'UK Board Succession Planning: Discussion Paper October 2018' [Accessed at www.frc.org.uk/getattachment/5041c3b6-9a53-4fb2-ac15-d583e1406690/;.aspx]

Financial Reporting Council (2016a) 'Corporate Culture and the Role of Boards – Report of Observations July 2016' [Accessed at www.frc.org.uk/getattachment/3851b9c5-92d3-4695-aeb2-87c9052dc8c1/Corporate-Culture-and-the-Role-of-Boards-Report-of-Observations.pdf]

Financial Reporting Council (2016b) 'Feedback Statement: UK Board Succession Planning Discussion Paper – May 2016' [Accessed at www.frc.org.uk/getattachment/6c3ad8fe-c232-47c6-8169-5e93a5f1f4d5/Feedback-statement-on-Succession-Planning-Discussion-Paper-May-2016.pdf]

Financial Reporting Council (2018a) 'The UK Corporate Governance Code' [Accessed at www.frc.org.uk/getattachment/88bd8c45-50ea-4841-95b0-d2f4f48069a2/2018-UK-Corporate-Governance-Code-FINAL.PDF]

Financial Reporting Council (2018b) 'Guidance on Board Effectiveness' [Accessed at www. frc.org.uk/getattachment/61232f60-a338-471b-ba5a-bfed25219147/2018-Guidance-on-Board-Effectiveness-FINAL.PDF]

Financial Reporting Lab (2018) 'Business Model Reporting; Risk and Viability Reporting: Where are We Now?' Financial Reporting Council [Accessed at www.frc.org.uk/ getattachment/43c07348-e175-45c4-a6e0-49f7ecabdf36/Business-Models-Lab-Implementation-Study-2018.pdf]

Financial Sustainability Strategy Group and Committee of University Chairs (2017) 'Illustrative Practice Note 4: Institutional Sustainability May 2017' [Accessed at www. universitychairs.ac.uk/wp-content/uploads/2017/05/CUC_IPN4_Institutional_ Sustainability_May_2017.pdf]

FTSE Women Leaders Sponsored by KPMG (2016) 'Hampton-Alexander Review FTSE Women Leaders Improving Gender Balance in FTSE Leadership November 2016' [Accessed at //assets.publishing.service.gov.uk/government/uploads/system/ uploads/attachment_data/file/613085]

ICSA, The Governance Institute and EY (2016) 'The Nomination Committee: Coming Out of the Shadows May 2016' [Accessed at www.ey.com/Publication/vwLUAs sets/EY-ICSA-the-nomination-committee-coming-out-of-the-shadows/$FILE/ EY-ICSA-the-nomination-committee-coming-out-of-the-shadows.pdf]

ICSA, The Governance Institute and The Investment Association (2017) 'The Stakeholder Voice in Board Decision Making' [Accessed at www.icsa.org.uk/ assets/files/free-guidance-notes/the-stakeholder-voice-in-Board-Decision-Mak ing-09-2017.pdf]

Parker, J. (2017) 'A Report into the Ethnic Diversity of UK Boards: Final Report 12 October 2017', The Parker Review Committee in association with EY and Linklaters [Accessed at www.ey.com/Publication/vwLUAssets/The_Parker_Review/$FILE/ EY-Parker-Review-2017-FINAL%20REPORT.pdf]

Report of a Study Group chaired by Sir Richard Greenbury (1995) 'Directors' Remuneration' Gee and Co Ltd. 17 July 1995 [Accessed at www.ecgi.org/codes/ documents/greenbury.pdf]

Women on Boards (2011) [Accessed at assets.publishing.service.gov.uk/government/ uploads/system/uploads/attachment_data/file/31480/11-745-women-on-boards. pdf]

Women on Boards, KPMG and Cranfield University (2015) 'Improving the Gender Balance on British Boards: Women on Boards Davies Review Five Year Summary October 2015' [Accessed at assets.publishing.service.gov.uk/government/uploads/ system/uploads/attachment_data/file/482059/BIS-15-585-women-on-boards-davies-review-5-year-summary-october-2015.pdf]

Chapter 11

The legal framework for university governance in England

How to understand, comply and build on it

Smita Jamdar

To speak of a legal framework for university governance in England as if it was a single, coherent scheme is misleading. Governance in the sector reflects the ad hoc and piecemeal way the sector has developed and evolved. The legal requirements are therefore also diverse, occasionally incoherent and evolving. The aim of this chapter is to provide an overview of the relevant legal requirements, highlight some of the challenges these create, and the kinds of responses institutions are or should be considering.

Constitutional documents

Universities in England can take a number of different legal forms and the institution's constitutional documents will set out details of how governance should operate. Complying with these obligations is both a legal and a regulatory requirement, as well as a way of ensuring good governance more generally. The consequences of failing to comply vary depending on the type of constitution.

Take, for example, the constitutional powers of the institution, matters which are self-evidently important for university governors to understand and navigate, and which are also important for third parties who wish to contract with universities. Universities established by Royal Charter are regarded in law as having all the powers of a natural person, not just those set out in the charter. Therefore, a failure to follow the internal rules and regulations on governance cannot generally give rise to a complaint that the decision-making body has acted ultra vires (outside its powers), which would have the effect of rendering any decisions made unenforceable. However, a failure to follow the requirements of the constitutional documents can be pursued through a complaint to the University Visitor. A Visitor has untrammelled power to ensure appropriate redress on matters relating to the internal rules of a chartered corporation (but not individual staff and student disputes), including where necessary by quashing decisions that have been made, and hence it remains important to ensure that the appropriate governance processes are followed.

Other universities are statutory higher education corporations established under the Education Reform Act (1988) (ERA).[1] They have the powers set out in section 124 of the ERA and, unless they have secured Privy Council approval to amend it, the constitution (Instrument and Articles of Government) prescribed. An example of typical Instrument and Articles are those of Staffordshire University.[2] An example of an amended Instrument and Articles of Government is the University of West London.[3]

The consequence of being creatures of statute is that there is a risk that decisions made which stray beyond the powers set out in the ERA are deemed ultra vires and unenforceable. The primary powers of a statutory corporation are to deliver higher, further and in certain circumstances secondary education, and to carry out research. These powers are supplemented by a non-exhaustive list of subsidiary powers, to, for example, enter into contracts or acquire and dispose of property. There is however also a broad 'sweeping up' power to do anything that appears to the Board to be necessary or expedient for the purpose of or in connection with the exercise of the primary powers.

In practice, therefore, it is likely to be very difficult to attack any particular decision as being ultra vires provided that the Board can explain why it considered the decision 'necessary or expedient' for the purposes of delivering higher and further education. The remedy where a decision is considered to be ultra vires is an application for judicial review to quash the decision, putting statutory corporations in a different position to their chartered peers in terms of the possibility of court intervention.

The non-exhaustive list of example subsidiary powers has created problems in circumstances where being satisfied that the institution has the power to enter into a transaction is particularly important. In effect, the list became regarded as indicative and anything that did not fall squarely within the examples risked being regarded as of questionable legality. Anxiety around this issue has in the past affected, for example, the willingness of banks to enter into complex financial instruments with statutory corporations. This has led to the perception that statutory higher education corporations enjoy less constitutional freedom than their chartered peers. Whatever the strict legal position, the perception of ambiguity has been sufficient to persuade Parliament that a change in the law is required and under the Higher Education and Research Act (2017) (HERA),[4] the ERA will be amended to remove the non-exhaustive list of examples and thus put beyond doubt the broad constitutional powers of statutory corporations.

Some universities are constituted as companies limited by guarantee and some others as unincorporated associations. Those who have been designated to receive funding from the Higher Education Funding Council (HEFCE) under section 129 of the ERA[5] are required as part of the designation process to have an instrument and articles of government incorporated in their articles of association in a form approved by the Privy Council (see for example the Instrument and Articles of the University of Cumbria [a company limited by guarantee][6] and Bishop Grosseteste University [an unincorporated association]). Generally, the provisions of the articles of association of such university companies and unincorporated associations mirror the governance provisions the ERA specifies for higher education corporations.

The doctrine of ultra vires has no application to companies, at least in relation to the rights of third parties (Companies Act, 2006). Third parties are thus entitled to assume that a company has the power to do what whatever it has done, except in the case of charitable companies.[7] Many universities established as companies are charities and therefore this exemption is significant. This means that the acts of such a university may be struck down if they lay outside its powers, except in relation to third parties who do not know that they are dealing with a charity or (provided that they have paid full consideration) that the act is not permitted by the charity's constitution.

This means that in relation to the fundamental questions of what the university's powers are and what the consequences of failing to follow any constitutional constraints are, the governing bodies of different types of universities find themselves in different positions.

Another area of contention arising from a university's constitutional documentation can be the respective roles of the different bodies that together make up the governance of the institution, sometimes not helped by the rather opaque drafting of charters in the past. As an example, take the description of the, or the respective roles of the, Council and the Senate[8] in the University of Warwick's Charter. This states that:

12.

There shall be a Council of the University (in this Our Charter called 'the Council') which, subject to the provisions of this Our Charter and of the Statutes, shall be the executive governing body of the University and shall jointly with the Senate appoint a Chancellor and shall have the custody and use of the Common Seal and shall be responsible for the management and administration of the revenue and property of the University and, *subject to the powers of the Senate* as provided in this Our Charter and the Statutes, shall have general control over the conduct of the affairs of the University and shall have all such other powers and duties as may be conferred upon it by the Statutes.

13.

There shall be a Senate of the University (in this Our Charter called 'the Senate') which shall, *subject to the powers of the Council* as provided in this Our Charter and the Statutes, be responsible for the academic work of the University, both in teaching and in research, and for the regulation and superintendence of the education and discipline of the students of the University.

(Italics added for emphasis)

The powers of the two bodies are thus stated to be 'subject to each other' and in controversial areas such as faculty restructurings or departmental closure, questions may arise as to whether the Senate can in effect veto proposals. It is submitted that it cannot: Council as the 'executive governing body' must have the final say, although it must diligently and demonstrably take into account Senate's views. Nevertheless, there have been a number of recent reports of petitions being lodged with University Visitors challenging, for example, decisions about the restructuring of departments or faculties, on the basis that the delicate balance of decision-making required under the Charter and Statutes has not been achieved.[9]

Chartered universities may have other bodies such as Warwick's Assembly, the Court (Stakeholder's Forum) at City University London[10] or the Court at Lancaster University.[11] These tend not to be decision-making bodies, but rather bodies that permit a wider range of university stakeholders (e.g. alumni, the staff of the university and/or local employers and authorities) a mechanism to discuss and debate matters relating to the university. Despite their lack of formal decision-making powers, such bodies can be influential: at the University of Bath, for example, the decision of the Court to call for the resignation of the Vice Chancellor over concerns about the level of her remuneration, was widely reported, putting pressure on the University Council to take action.[12]

Higher education corporations and companies have less ambiguity in the roles of the Board and the Academic Board, at least as articulated in the Instrument and Articles of Government. The Board is unequivocally responsible for the determination of the educational character and mission of the university and oversight of its activities. The Vice-Chancellor is responsible for making proposals to the Board about the educational character and mission of the university. The Academic Board discharges its responsibilities subject to the responsibilities of the Board and the Vice-Chancellor.

As these examples demonstrate, the governance implications of university constitutional documents can be complex and subtle, creating challenges for governing bodies particularly when seeking to implement major changes or innovations or embark on new strategies.

Charity law

Many universities are charities, whether exempt or registered, and their governing bodies are also charity trustees and subject to the duties imposed as a matter of charity law as set out in the Charity Commission's 'The essential trustee' (2018). In summary, members of university governing bodies have the following obligations as charity trustees:

- To ensure the university operates within its charitable objects for the public benefit.
- To ensure the university complies with the law/regulatory framework.
- To act at all times in the charity's best interests.
- To ensure that they engage in collective decision-making and critical challenge.

- To avoid conflicts of interest or conflicts of loyalty and to register other interests they may have.
- Not to receive any benefit from the university unless they are properly authorised to do so.
- To manage the resources of the university effectively and efficiently and to manage risk appropriately.
- To act with reasonable skill and care.

The charitable objects of chartered universities and universities constituted as companies are set out in their constitutional documents. The University of Manchester's Charter,[13] for example, describes its objects as follows: 'to advance education, knowledge and wisdom by research, scholarship, learning and teaching, for the benefit of individuals and society at large'. As an example of a company limited by guarantee, London South Bank University's objects are described in its Articles of Association[14] as being to:

> conduct a university for the public benefit for the advancement of education, promotion of research and dissemination of knowledge, to provide full time and part time courses of education at all levels; and to provide facilities to promote these objects and provide associated support and welfare for students.

However, the constitutions of statutory higher education corporations do not contain their objects. Instead, these are found in the ERA (see above).

The governing body's duty is to ensure that these objects are pursued for the public benefit. This means that there must be a beneficial outcome (or at least, any detriment or harm caused by the university's activities must be outweighed by the benefit it offers). The benefit must accrue to the public or a sufficient section of the public, and any private benefit accruing to an individual or organisation must be merely incidental to that wider public benefit. The poor, or persons of modest means, must not be excluded from access to the benefit purely because of an inability to pay.

Most of a university's activities will self-evidently satisfy the requirements of public benefit. However, it is a question university governing bodies may need to revisit regularly, particularly in relation to decisions around scholarships and bursaries, and also in relation to activities designed to benefit individual donors or industrial or commercial partners.

Many universities are 'exempt' charities and thus not generally subject to direct regulation by the Charity Commission. On 1 June 2010, the Higher Education Funding Council for England (HEFCE) became the principal regulator for most universities, with an express duty to promote compliance with charity law. This meant that for the first time, universities that were exempt charities were scrutinised for their compliance with charity law and in particular to articulate the public benefit their activities delivered. Prior to the coming into force of the Charities

Act (2006), the advancement of education was presumed to be for the public benefit. The Act removed that presumption, and hence the need for universities to set out expressly how their activities are delivered for the public benefit.[15] With the dissolution of the HEFCE on 1 April 2018, the principal regulator role for universities in England transferred to the Office for Students (OfS).[16]

An example of how the obligation to comply with charity law can affect the governance of a university is the question of whether members of governing bodies should be paid for acting in the role. The general expectation is that it is a voluntary and unpaid role. However, there is an ongoing debate as to whether this remains appropriate given the greater responsibilities on and expected time commitment from members of governing bodies, and also the need to attract a more diverse governing body. Payment of non-executive directors is common in the private sector and also some parts of the public sector, such as the National Health Service.

Payment of university governing bodies either needs to be included in the governing instruments of the university (see for example paragraph 5 of the University of Salford's Charter[17]) or specifically authorised by the Charity Commission. The Commission will only authorise payment if it is satisfied that there is a significant advantage to the charity in so doing. This might be because the university is struggling to recruit appropriately qualified candidates, or because there is a particularly high time demand given the circumstances the institution finds itself in. Further, payment tends only to be considered appropriate for those members who discharge specific roles such as the chair of the governing body or chairs of committees. Universities seeking to pay members of the governing bodies will be expected to keep remuneration within reasonable amounts, to ensure that any conflicts of interest are managed, and that the performance of the individuals is kept under active review to ensure remuneration remains justified.

Company law

Members of governing bodies of universities who are also company directors must also comply with all relevant obligations under company law. The following duties are particularly relevant (all references are to the Companies Act 2006[18]):

- to act within the powers of the company (s171);
- to promote the success of the company (s172);
- to exercise independent judgement (s173);
- to exercise reasonable care, skill and judgement (s174);
- to avoid conflicts of interest (s175);
- not to accept benefits from third parties (s176);
- to declare interests in proposed transactions or arrangements (s177).

Members of university governing bodies who are also company directors need to be particularly aware of the risks of insolvency and the provisions relating to wrongful and fraudulent trading.[19] If a university were to be unable to pay its debts as and when they fall due, the university governing body could become personally liable if it continued to incur liabilities. These provisions do not apply to chartered universities or statutory corporations (or unincorporated associations, but in those cases, the university governing body is personally, jointly and severally responsible for the liabilities of the university in any event). Continuing to operate whilst insolvent could also be a breach of duty as a charity trustee and/or result in personal liability. Whether or not the duty has been breached will depend on whether, for example, the governing body acted reasonably and in reasonable reliance on assurances given by the executive and/or the institution's financial advisors. Directors' and officers' insurance policies are usually also provided by institutions for the benefit of their governors in such circumstances. However, the presence of clear differences in the risk of personal liability for governors in different types of institution may mean that they would not act similarly when faced with financial instability and volatility.

Regulation

Regulation of institutions in the higher education sector in England has, historically, been fragmented and piecemeal, developing ad hoc as the sector moved from a small number of (largely) publicly funded institutions to a large and comparatively diverse sector incorporating many 'alternative' providers.

The HERA sought to address this to create a single regulatory framework for all providers, irrespective of their legal form, source of funding or history.

The HERA created a new regulator, the Office for Students, and a new statutory register of higher education providers. This new framework will come fully into force in August 2019, and the period 1 August 2018–2019 is a transitional year from the old system administered by the HEFCE.

In setting up and administering the register, the OfS is to have regard to a number of different factors, namely the need to:

- protect institutional autonomy;
- promote quality and choice for students;
- encourage competition between providers whilst also having regard to the benefits of collaboration;
- promote value for money;
- promote equality of access and participation;
- use its resources efficiently and effectively; and
- to observe the principles of best regulatory practice by behaving in a proportionate and consistent way and intervening only where necessary.

Any provider wishing to allow their students to draw down tuition fee or maintenance support, recruit international students, award degrees, or continue to call themselves a university or university college must be on the register. This creates a common Regulatory Framework (Office for Students, 2018a) for a sector which, as has been demonstrated, comprises institutions the governance of which is subject to a variety of legal requirements. The risks of failing to comply with the regulatory framework are serious for institutions, financially, reputationally and in terms of being able to continue to operate.

Being on the register entails complying with a range of general registration conditions, ranging from the quality and standards of the education on offer, the wider student experience, compliance with consumer protection law, student protection in the event of provider closure or insolvency, the effectiveness of management and governance, financial sustainability, public interest governance principles and the facilitation of student electoral registration. The OfS has the power to impose specific conditions of registration where particular risks are identified at individual providers. These conditions are generally published, although the OfS reserves the right not to publish if it considers it inappropriate to do so, and an area of emerging interest is the extent to which the publication of conditions which reflect the regulator's specific assessment of the risks posed by a particular institution may affect future recruitment and therefore the viability of that institution.

Failing to comply with conditions of registration can result in a number of OfS interventions, from enhanced monitoring and specific conditions of registration through to the imposition of sanctions. The sanctions that will be available to the OfS are fines, suspension of registration or deregistration.

The maximum fine the OfS will in due course be able to impose is 2 per cent of teaching income or £500,000, at the time of publication, whichever is the greater.

If the OfS suspends a provider's registration, it will specify what aspects of the registration are being suspended, for example, access to student support or recruitment of international students. Deregistration means loss of all rights as a registered provider. The HERA enables university title to be removed from providers who are not on the register.

The risks for institutions arising out of the regulatory framework are thus not to be underestimated. It remains to be seen whether the main model of governance in the sector (volunteers attending sporadic meetings and heavily dependent on the information about institutional performance and risk they receive from management teams) is able to perform the regulatory role expected of it. The regulatory framework is not prescriptive as to the model of governance registered providers must adopt and therefore offers the opportunity to adopt new models of governance, provided they comply with the broad precepts of the governance and management registration conditions.

There are two specific conditions that relate to governance and management. One is a requirement for all providers to have in place adequate and effective management and governance arrangements to operate in accordance with its governing documents, deliver the applicable public interest governance principles (see below), provide the higher education courses advertised and to comply with all the conditions of registration (Condition E2). The requirement that the institution's governing instruments (i.e. its constitutional documents) must uphold the public interest governance principles makes up the second directly relevant condition (Condition E1). These principles thus introduce a common set of expectations for the governance of registered providers, although some are already enshrined in universities. The biggest practical change is therefore likely to be for 'alternative providers', whose constitutions have not to date been as constrained by these common expectations. The term 'alternative providers' has evolved to deal with those providers (usually new entrants into the higher education sector) who were not established as universities and whose constitutions fall outside the categories above. Expanding this group of providers has been seen by the government as key to its aspiration to create a functioning market in higher education in England.

The public interest principles are:

- To ensure academic freedom within the law for academic staff to test received wisdom and put forward new ideas and unpopular or controversial opinions, without risking their jobs or privileges.
- To operate openly, honestly, accountably and with integrity, demonstrating values appropriate to be recognised as an English higher education provider.
- To ensure students have opportunities to engage with the governance of the institution, allowing a range of perspectives to have influence.
- To receive and test assurances that academic governance is effective through explicit protocols with the senate or academic board.
- To operate comprehensive corporate risk management and control measures.
- To ensure adequate and effective arrangements to provide transparency about value for money for all students and the taxpayer.
- To take such steps as a reasonably practicable to ensure freedom of speech within the law within the provider.
- To ensure that the size, composition, diversity, skills mix and terms of office of the governing body are appropriate given the nature, scale and complexity of the provider.
- To ensure that members of the governing body, those with senior management roles and individuals exercising significant influence over the provider are fit and proper persons.
- Where the provider receives grants from the OfS or research funding from United Kingdom Research and Innovation (the body set up by HERA to superintend research at universities) to have at least one if not more independent governors and to have appropriate arrangements to ensure regularity, propriety and value for money in the use of those grants and funds.

Taken together these principles are instructive as to how governance may need to change to comply with the new regulatory framework. For example, the expectation of student engagement in the governance of the institution is likely to go beyond the constitutional requirement to have one or two student governors and the need to permit a range of perspectives to have influence may mean going beyond the students' union. How will governing bodies ensure that a wide number of students can engage with them? In terms of the need for explicit protocols with the Senate or the Academic Board to ensure oversight of academic governance, these may help to address some of the ambiguities and areas of contention around the roles of these bodies. The duty to ensure value for money is not new but is extended beyond its traditional definition of efficient use of public funds (through, for example, tightly controlled and effective procurement) to transparency about the value for money for all students. This may shift focus to questions such as how much tuition a student receives and whether graduate outcomes represent a good return on investment for individual students. Survey work carried out by the OfS has shown that this is a growing concern for students, who are keen to see where and how their fees are spent (Office for Students, 2018b). This is creating pressure on the near universal practice in the sector to use tuition fees to cross-subsidise other courses and activities, such as research, outreach activities and civic engagement.

The duty to ensure freedom of speech within the law 'within the provider' reflects but is not entirely the same as the duty imposed on universities and colleges (but not alternative providers) under section 43 of the Education (No 2) Act (1986), which was limited to members, students, employees and visiting speakers. It is fair to say that there has been a significant amount of controversy about, though not necessarily much evidence of, restrictions on free speech on campuses (see for example the report of the inquiry into freedom of speech in universities by the Joint Committee on Human Rights Report of Inquiry intro Freedom of Speech in Universities (2018)). It is not clear how the new regulatory dimension to the duty will affect its operation in practice, as the OfS has made it clear that it does not intend to investigate specific complaints that the duty has been breached, but it will undoubtedly mean that arrangements for ensuring free speech will be higher up the agenda for governors.

This may turn out to be one of the most significant implications of the new regulatory framework for university governance: it offers a direct route for the OfS and through it the government in the form of the Secretary of State to force matters onto the agenda of the governing bodies of theoretically autonomous bodies. Although the OfS must have due regard to the need to protect institutional autonomy as part of its general duties under section 2 of the HERA, it is only one of a range of matters to which it must have due regard. The OfS must also have regard to guidance issued to it by the Secretary of State, who in turn when issuing guidance must also have regard to the need to protect autonomy. The only matters that such guidance must not relate to are matters of pure academic judgement such as the content or courses or how they are taught and assessed. The net effect of these provisions is that where the Secretary of State considers that a matter is of such public importance that it warrants guidance to the OfS, the fact that it may stray into areas which are traditionally considered within the scope of institutional autonomy is not a bar to such guidance being given.

Codes of corporate governance

Under the regulatory framework, one measure of the effectiveness of management and governance at an institution is the extent to which it complies with recognised codes of corporate governance. The Higher Education Code of Governance, which is the most commonly used code in the higher education sector, is maintained by the Committee of University Chairs (2018). However, the regulatory framework is not prescriptive and, in future, registered providers are free to follow any other recognised code of governance (or indeed none, if they can demonstrate that they meet the expectations of the regulatory framework in some other way). This could lead to a further departure from a uniform set of expectations for university governors if significant numbers of providers begin to adopt other codes or demonstrate compliance in some other way.

Under the Higher Education Code, governing bodies are:

- Collectively accountable for institutional activities, taking all final decisions on matters of fundamental concern. This entails having oversight of all institutional activities, establishing an appropriate scheme of delegation, and ensuring that there is due diligence in the making of institutionally significant decisions.
- Responsible for protecting the university's reputation by ensuring there is a framework of regulations, policies and procedures which ensure legal and regulatory compliance and ethical standards, and checking that these are consistently applied. In particular members of governing bodies must be able to demonstrate it operates free of conflicts of interest or undue pressure from any particular interest group.
- Expected to ensure the university's sustainability by working with the executive to set the institutional mission and strategy and measures for risk management. This entails agreeing the institutional strategy, budget and key performance indicators and regularly monitoring the university's performance against those.
- Expected to receive assurance that academic governance is effective by working with the Senate/Academic Board. The governing body should, through reports and monitoring KPIs, be satisfied that there is an effective academic strategy in which students are actively engaged.
- Required to work with the Executive to ensure effective control and due diligence for any significant external activities, particularly significant partnerships, subsidiary companies and donations.
- Under a duty to promote equality and diversity throughout the institution, including in relation to its own operation, by setting equality objectives and then monitoring performance against those objectives.

–   Obliged to ensure that governance structures and processes are fit for purpose by periodically reviewing and benchmarking them against recognised standards of good practice. Governing bodies must establish a Nominations Committee to advise on new members and how to maintain an appropriate skills balance on the board.

On the face of it, these are appropriate and suitably broad expectations and the absence of significant institutional failure in the sector could be taken as evidence that governance is operating effectively and in line with the Code. However, a number of recent controversies could be seen as cause to question how effectively the Code is operating. For example, public disquiet over Vice-Chancellor and senior executive pay (Hymas, 2018) may call into question the extent to which the framework of policies and procedures relating to remuneration (and compliance in particular with ethical standards) has been sufficient to safeguard institutional reputation. Similarly, given concerns about grade inflation,[20] unconditional offers (Adams, 2018) and value for money for students (Office for Students, 2018b), to what extent have governing bodies sought assurances about the effectiveness of academic governance? Given ongoing evidence of a BAME achievement gap among both staff and students (Buckley-Irvine, 2017) are governing bodies properly discharging their duty to promote equality and diversity throughout the institution?

The new regulatory framework offers for the first time a route to police compliance with the provisions of the Code, and it is likely that governing bodies will face greater challenge from the OfS to tackle these perceived problems in higher education than they have been used to experiencing from the HEFCE, which had far more limited regulatory levers at its disposal.

Common issues faced by governing bodies

In view of the legal and regulatory frameworks described above, a growing problem in English universities is how to identify and to respect the difference between governance and management, in terms of identifying the correct balance between too much intervention in day-to-day operations and too little critical challenge to executive management. The governor role is clearly intended to be a non-executive one, yet a board that has a majority of non-executives is simultaneously the principal seat of responsibility for, say, compliance with a very broad regulatory framework. Some of the tests applied under the regulatory framework are the same both for members of the governing body and the executive. See for example the fit and proper persons test which applies equally to members of the governing body and to those fulfilling senior management responsibilities. It is therefore unsurprising to see an increasingly blurred line between management and governance, and a greater likelihood that members of governing bodies, especially chairs, risk discharging increasingly executive roles.

Concern that university boards had struggled to establish appropriate links between the governance of academic activities and broader corporate governance meant that governing bodies were required, as part of HEFCE's quality assessment process, to provide annual assurances covering the student academic experience, student outcomes, and the standard of awards (HEFCE, 2016). There was thus recognition of a risk that the established system of university governance had been ineffective in guaranteeing assurance of a core activity, namely teaching and learning. As stated above, ongoing sector-wide controversies regarding academic issues such as grade inflation, unconditional offers and graduate outcomes suggest that work still needs to be done on governance in these areas.

Oversight of external partnerships and activities, particularly international activities, is becoming increasingly important. As universities diversify their income streams through such activities, the risks of financial failure, reputational damage and undue external influence over the institution increase and need to be managed. The report by Lord Woolf into the LSE's connections with Libya (Woolf Inquiry, 2011) was a powerful example of how both the immediate and the cumulative risks of such external activities can elude a governing body, with significant consequences for the institution. The report considered a range of interactions LSE had with the Libyan government, from having a member of the Gaddafi family as a postgraduate student, to a donation from a foundation connected to Colonel Gaddafi, to a range of contracts and other engagements with the Libyan government. Cumulatively, these had exposed the LSE to a great deal of adverse public comment and criticism.[21] Lord Woolf recommended that governance at LSE needed reform of both the structures that enabled it to identify and oversee risk, and also a way to embed a culture that was capable of recognising ethical and reputational concerns. Although the Woolf report was written eight years ago, its lessons and recommendations remain important for university governance today.

Another lesson that derives from a high-profile governance failure from some years ago is the importance of governing bodies satisfying themselves that they have access to sufficient, accurate and timely information about what is going on at an institution to discharge the duties set out above. This became an express condition of funding after London Metropolitan University faced a substantial claw-back of funding from the HEFCE for incorrect student completion returns.[22] Subsequently the entire governing body resigned. The governing body was not provided with correct data, but a HEFCE investigation also criticised it for not being sufficiently diligent in scrutinising the data and identifying data that was fairly obviously questionable and/or incomplete. The entire governing body resigned as a result. It remains an ongoing challenge for many governing bodies to strike the correct balance between not enough and too much information.

Many institutions report difficulties in ensuring a sufficiently diverse governing body to reflect the general population or even the institutional population. The time commitment, combined with the fact that these are unpaid positions, is considered to limit the pool of people available to serve on governing bodies.

Some universities have in response amended their governing documents to pay members of governing bodies, particularly those in key roles such as the Chair, as discussed above. Yet this identification of the Chair as being a special position on the board brings other challenges. A paid Chair can begin to see him- or herself as having more of an executive role and inadvertently create a conflict of interest. Other governors can feel that their contribution is less valued. This can lead to those other governors feeling disengaged, thus narrowing the diversity of views that are brought to bear in the board's decision-making, undermining the purpose of having a large and diverse board.

Finally, the concentration of legal and regulatory responsibilities on the governing body can conflict with the wider democratic and collegiate nature of universities as self-governing communities of scholars. This was a tension identified as far back as 1985, with the Jarrett Report on Efficiency Studies in Universities (CVCP, 1985) although at that stage the concern was that governing bodies were exercising insufficient power and were subservient to Senates, which had become excessively powerful. The pendulum may now have swung too far, certainly as far as academic staff are concerned, as discussed above. A variant of this concern can be seen in concerns about excessive managerialism in universities (Shepherd, 2017), where the executive and administration is seen as having too much power. These perceived imbalances and democratic deficits are problematic, as they can leave staff and indeed students feeling alienated and excluded from matters relating to the direction and operation of the institution of which they are a vital part. This in turn can make implementing major strategic change more difficult as there is an innate lack of trust amongst the key stakeholders.

Improving university governance

As described above, the context in which university governance must operate is evolving. Not only is the sector becoming more regulated, but this is at a time when risks to institutions are increasing amid volatile student recruitment and threats to university funding (Hall, 2018). The role of the governing body in steering institutions through choppy waters has never been more important. Equally, institutions have never had as much flexibility to determine the model of governance that best suits their individual circumstances and priorities. Institutions should take the opportunities presented by the new Regulatory Framework to consider the suitability of the current arrangements against the aims and aspirations of the institution to agree on the best model and role of governance for the future. How will the Board deliver the necessary focus on accountability? How will it ensure governors are sufficiently engaged and add value? The starting point for such considerations is often an effectiveness review, as to which see Chapter 15.

Having identified what role the governing body is expected to play, there are a number of steps institutions are or could be considering to ensure the governing body is well equipped to discharge that role.

The first is to consider modernising and revising their constitutional documents. It is very hard to deliver effective governance when the constitutional framework is archaic and arcane. The governance framework should reflect what an institution wants its governing body to do (including ensuring it can discharge its legal and regulatory responsibilities) and how that fits with the roles of the other key parts of the institution's broader governance, namely the executive and the senate.

This modernisation could consider whether there is an actual or perceived deficit in engagement between the governing body and the wider university community. When a governing body has to make decisions such as closing campuses or departments or advocate mergers or invest in a campus overseas, it is important that the people affected by those decisions know and trust the decision-makers, otherwise there will inevitably be even greater hostility than the substance of the decision might ordinarily merit. Institutions should consider what could be done to improve the visibility of the governing body among staff and students, and to allow these groups to highlight their concerns and issues to the governing body. This will also enable the governing body to identify regulatory risks arising from these concerns before external regulators become involved.

Institutions already recruit governors to a specific skills matrix, and this should be routinely reviewed to ensure it remains the right mix of skills. However, institutions also need to consider what induction and training they offer governors to ensure that they can fulfil their duties diligently and proactively. Even though governors are (normally) unpaid, that does not mean that there should not be appropriate investment in their personal development in the role.

Beyond modifications to how the existing governing body operates and is supported, institutions may want to consider changes to the size of the governing body. There has already been a trend towards smaller boards, and the CUC Higher Education Code of Governance recommends a board of between 12 and 25 members. The regulatory framework merely requires the governance arrangements to be adequate for the nature, size and complexity of the provider. There is therefore considerable scope for individual institutions to review and modify the size and composition of the governing body to ensure that it reflects the needs of that individual institution. For some that might be to deliver additional effective routes for scrutiny and challenge for staff and students than solely through the appointment of one or two staff and student governors. For others it might be about introducing a smaller board with more co-opted and advisory members. The key is to identify what the governing body is for (beyond its legal and regulatory compliance functions) and develop a board structure the size and composition of which is right for the role and duties it is expected to perform.

Institutions may consider that the root of some of the governance challenges they are experiencing is the constraints imposed by their corporate form or their charitable status. Corporate forms can be changed, in that chartered bodies and statutory corporations could dissolve and transfer their property, assets and liabilities to a company limited by guarantee specially created for that purpose. Of itself, however, this would not necessarily achieve any greater improvement in the quality of governance that could be delivered through a deep and broad review and refresh of governance in the existing corporate form.

An alternative to changing corporate form is to create a group structure so that different strands of institutional activity are settled in different group companies, particularly those which are higher risk or non-core. An example of such a group is the Coventry University Group.[23] The Group has separate companies focused on separate activities, including a very successful 'university college' model delivering flexible and low-cost provision, under the supervision of their own boards, pursuing a common strategy and vision articulated and overseen by the University Board of Governors. The creation of a group in principle enables bespoke and focused governance of specific activities. However, it still requires the group parent, the institution, to be responsible for the activities of the group and to that extent may simply compound rather than alleviate the difficulties facing governors, especially if any underlying issues about the effectiveness of governance are not addressed.

Conclusion

The legal framework for university governance is complex and fragmented, while the regulatory framework fixes members of governing bodies with responsibility for compliance with wide-ranging registration conditions. This calls into question whether long-standing models and approaches to governance remain appropriate. Effective governance can take institutions beyond mere compliance to the development of an organisation where all stakeholders, internal and external, are aligned to a distinctive institutional strategy and values. There is much that could be modernised and improved about university governance without radical change to institutional forms, but this requires careful consideration and investment of time and resources in supporting and developing governors, to deliver governance that is fit for the future.

Notes

1　Education Reform Act 1988, section 121.
2　www.staffs.ac.uk/assets/instrument_articles_by the government_tcm44-43303.pdf
3　www.uwl.ac.uk/sites/default/files/Departments/About-us/Web/PDF/UWL%20 Instrument%202015.pdf and www.uwl.ac.uk/sites/default/files/Departments/ About-us/Web/PDF/Articles%20of%20Government_2015.pdf
4　Schedule 8 paragraph 6 HERA 2017, which amends paragraph 124 of the ERA.
5　Education Reform Act 1988, section 29, Designation of Institutions.
6　www.cumbria.ac.uk/media/university-of-cumbria-website/content-assets/public/ vco/documents/legal/20.-Revised-Articles-of-Association-Feb16-final.pdf
7　Companies Act 2006, sections 39 and 42.
8　www2.warwick.ac.uk/services/gov/calendar/section2/charterstatutes/
9　www.leeds.ac.uk/forstaff/news/article/983/petition_to_the_visitor_list_of_corre spondence; https://www.ft.com/content/2f4bcdf0-0a96-11e8-839d-41ca06376bf2

10 www.city.ac.uk/__data/assets/pdf_file/0018/331092/City_Supplemental_
    Charter_2016.pdf
11 www.lancaster.ac.uk/users/gap/GAP2007/Charter-Statutes-Ordinances.pdf
12 www.bbc.co.uk/news/uk-england-bristol-42708001
13 http://documents.manchester.ac.uk/display.aspx?DocID=16239
14 www.lsbu.ac.uk/__data/assets/pdf_file/0003/36858/articles-of-association.pdf
15 This requirement is now contained in s 4 Charities Act 2011.
16 www.officeforstudents.org.uk/media/1449/ofs2018_23.pdf
17 www.salford.ac.uk/__data/assets/pdf_file/0009/1258947/Charter.pdf
18 www.legislation.gov.uk/ukpga/2006/46/contents
19 Sections 213 and sections 214 of the Insolvency Act.
20 www.bbc.co.uk/news/uk-45935193
21 hwww.bbc.co.uk/news/education-15966132
22 https://webarchive.nationalarchives.gov.uk/20180319143151/http://www.hefce.
    ac.uk/news/newsarchive/2009/HEFCEs,dealings,with,London,Metropolitan,
    University/.
23 www.coventry.ac.uk/the-university/about-coventry-university/coventry-university-
    group-explained/

References

Adams, R. (2018) 'Rise in unconditional offers prompts call for university admis-
    sions overhaul', *Guardian*, 26 July [Retrieved from www.theguardian.com/educa
    tion/2018/jul/26/rise-in-unconditional-offers-prompts-call-for-university-admissions-
    overhaul]
Buckley-Irvine, N. (2017) 'Universities' shame: unpicking the black attain-
    ment gap', *Wonkhe*, 10 August [Retrieved from https://wonkhe.com/blogs/
    analysis-universities-shame-black-attainment-gap/]
Charities Act (2006) [Retrieved from www.legislation.gov.uk/ukpga/2006/50/
    contents]
Charities Act (2011) [Retrieved from www.legislation.gov.uk/ukpga/2011/25/
    contents]
Charity Commission for England and Wales (2018) 'The essential trustee: what
    you need to know, what you need to do' [Retrieved from https://assets.pub
    lishing.service.gov.uk/government/uploads/system/uploads/attachment_data/
    file/734288/CC3_may18.pdf]
Committee of University Chairs (2018) 'Higher education code of governance'
    [Retrieved from www.universitychairs.ac.uk/wp-content/uploads/2015/02/
    Code-Final.pdf.]
Companies Act (2006) [Retrieved from www.legislation.gov.uk/ukpga/2006/46/
    contents]
CVCP (1985) 'Report of the Steering Committee for Efficiency Studies in Higher Education
    (the Jarratt Report) Committee of Vice-Chancellors and Principals, London' [Retrieved
    from www.educationengland.org.uk/documents/jarratt1985/index.html]
Education (No2) Act (1986) [Retrieved from www.legislation.gov.uk/ukpga/1986/61]
Education Reform Act (1988) [Retrieved from www.legislation.gov.uk/ukpga/1988/
    40/pdfs/ukpga_19880040_en.pdf]

Hall, R. (2018) 'What's driving decisions in universities?', *Guardian*, 1 February [Retrieved from www.theguardian.com/higher-education-network/2018/feb/01/whats-driving-decisions-in-universities]

HEFCE (2016) 'Revised operating method for quality assessment' [Retrieved from https://webarchive.nationalarchives.gov.uk/20180319114124/http://www.hefce.ac.uk/pubs/year/2016/201603/]

Higher Education and Research Act (2017) [Retrieved from www.legislation.gov.uk/ukpga/2017/29/schedule/8/enacted]

Hymas, C. (2018) 'Vice chancellor salary study demolishes claims pay rises performance based', *Daily Telegraph*, 6 June [Retrieved from www.telegraph.co.uk/news/2018/06/06/vice-chancellor-salary-study-demolishes-claims-pay-rises-based/]

Insolvency Act 1986 [Retrieved from www.legislation.gov.uk/ukpga/1986/45/contents]

Joint Committee on Human Rights Report of Inquiry intro Freedom of Speech in Universities (2018) [Retrieved from https://publications.parliament.uk/pa/jt201719/jtselect/jtrights/589/58902.htm]

Office for Students (2018a) 'Regulatory framework' [Retrieved from www.officeforstudents.org.uk/publications/securing-student-success-regulatory-framework-for-higher-education-in-england/]

Office for Students (2018b) 'New research shines spotlight on student perceptions of value for money' [Retrieved from www.officeforstudents.org.uk/news-blog-and-events/press-and-media/new-research-shines-spotlight-on-student-perceptions-of-value-for-money/]

Shepherd, S. (2017) 'There's a gulf between academics and university management and its growing', *Guardian*, 27 July [Retrieved from www.theguardian.com/higher-education-network/2017/jul/27/theres-a-gulf-between-academics-and-university-management-and-its-growing]

Woolf Inquiry, The (2011) 'An enquiry into the LSE's links with Libya and lessons to be learned' [Retrieved from www.lse.ac.uk/News/News-Assets/PDFs/The-Woolf-Inquiry-Report-An-inquiry-into-LSEs-links-with-Libya-and-lessons-to-be-learned-London-School-of-Economics-and-Political-Sciences.pdf]

Chapter 12

The development and purpose of corporate governance codes

John Rushforth

Introduction

Between them, the UK Higher Education and Research Act 2017 and the Office for Students' Regulatory Framework consists of over 300 pages of text. The Higher Education Governance Code produced by the Committee of University Chairs (CUC)[1] has 30 pages. To some extent that simple comparison explains why in recent years voluntary codes have been increasingly employed across the globe in the hope of avoiding government intervention.

Higher education (HE) has a history of developing its own guidance on governance to pre-empt government interference. The origins of the current United Kingdom (UK) HE Governance Code probably lies in the Committee of Vice-Chancellors and Principals (CVCP) Report of the Steering Committee for Efficiency Studies in Universities in 1985. The Report focused on improving the management of institutions and made references to governance, for example:

> It is evident that over the past three decades the influence of Councils within universities has weakened. We believe that Councils now need to play a much more active role . . . the key areas in which this is necessary are those of academic and financial planning.
>
> (Committee of Vice-Chancellors and Principals, 1985, p. 24)

Taggart (2004) argues that one of the then CVCP's purposes in establishing the committee was to distance the universities from the efficiency studies in train across Whitehall under the Prime Minister's Adviser on Efficiency, Sir Robin Ibbs of ICI (see also Scott, 1995).

The production of reports and guidance in order to avoid government intervention is a recurring theme when we look at the development of the Code itself. Shattock (2004) argues that this began when, after a series of governance scandals in the post-1992 sector (Huddersfield, Portsmouth and Glasgow Caledonian Universities and Southampton and Swansea Institutes) the Committee of University Chairmen (CUC), under the threat of government action, issued advice on university governance and subsequently created a Guide on Governance aimed at governing body members (CUC, 1995, 1998, 2000, 2004 and 2009).

The CUC guidance was regularly reviewed and updated in the light of a changing context, with the latest review initiated late in 2012. Again, there was an element of reacting and attempting to forestall events. On the one hand, the loss by London Metropolitan of its licence to recruit international students had brought home to many governing bodies their responsibilities in monitoring key risks, the publication of the Government White Paper 'Students at the Heart of the System' in 2011 made it clear that increased competition via encouragement to alternative providers to join the sector was to be encouraged, and the shift in funding away from HEFCE grants to fees paid by students supported by loans generated an expectation that there would be some form of legislation on higher education in the next parliament. Whilst many accepted the benefits of competition, there was anxiety that a doctrinaire market-led approach, that accepted the possibility and even desirability of the market failure of an HE institution, represented a reputational risk to the sector. Similarly, whilst many in the sector could see the need for legislation to enable HEFCE to regulate all of the providers in the sector, there was as also anxiety that as legislation passed through parliament this might involve some intervention in respect of governance – an anxiety that was exacerbated by events in Scotland where the Scottish government also initiated a separate review of university governance, chaired by Professor Ferdinand von Prondzynski, Principal of Robert Gordon University, which reported early in 2012. His Report proposed that the Chairs of Court (the governing body of a Scottish university) should be subject to an election process by a constituency of staff and students and potentially wider stakeholders. There were also prescriptive recommendations about the remuneration of senior management and the role, composition and appointment of governing bodies, for example that there should be union-nominated as well as elected staff members.

The other driver for change in respect of the 2012 review of the Code was a definite feeling amongst Chairs and secretaries that its current version was not fit for purpose, since it conflated principles, policies and practice. As a result, the Code was unwieldy, at over 200 pages long, and governing bodies found it difficult to demonstrate that they were compliant with it, particularly since they were required to assure the funding bodies that they were. There were also seen to be some significant omissions, for example in respect of governing body responsibilities for ethics and diversity.

The main reason that CUC was willing in the first place to develop, review and maintain this Code of Governance, was clearly articulated by HEFCE in its 2013 Accounts Direction:

> Adopting the CUC Code of Practice, with the principles of the code adapted as appropriate to each HEI's character, is an important factor in enabling HEFCE to rely on self-regulation within HEIs and hence minimise the accountability burden.

(HEFCE CL25/2013)

However, the CUC saw other benefits, namely that the production of a revised version of the Code was a way to illustrate the high-quality governance practices already in evidence within the sector; to set the bar for good governance in the HE sector for both traditional HEIs and others wishing to enter the market; and to support members of governing bodies in their role.

In undertaking the review to produce these wider benefits, the CUC sought to defend institutional autonomy, a key tenet underpinning its work more generally.

THE CUC Executive was clear that it wanted a Code that was principle-based with some examples of practice: a concise document with an increased emphasis on:

- governors' relationship with academic governance;
- equality and diversity;
- ethics and sustainability;
- the risks of international activity.

However, writing in detail about good practices and processes was, in part, what had made the previous version unwieldy – so early on the decision was taken to develop separate guidance notes on process and practice – as Illustrative Practice Notes. The language used is important – with the intention that 'Illustrative' was designed to signal a proactive approach that was interesting and would encourage consideration, adaptation and adoption rather than the more usual 'good practice' – with its implication that there was a standard, one-size-fits-all prescriptive statement of what institutions should do.

The CUC is not a regulatory body, and it was clear that the Code would be voluntary, but the desire was for it to be sufficiently flexible, for it to be useable by all providers of higher education.

So, what are the key components of a code and why is a code preferable to direct intervention by regulators? A voluntary code can offer three distinct elements versus a mandatory approach to regulating HE – useful ideas, acceptance and flexibility.

Useful ideas

If developed appropriately a sector-owned voluntary code can set out helpful suggestions on practice. The key here is not the simple writing and publication of the code, but rather the process of developing it. The current CUC HE Governance Code (2014) took nearly two years to produce with a number of different phases:

- an initial research phase where practice in other sectors and countries was reviewed;
- an analysis of other codes, for example the UK Corporate Governance Code;
- preparation and iteration of a number of drafts with a steering group consisting of representatives of different stakeholders (UUK,[2] AHUA,[3] the Funding Councils, etc);

- a public consultation with the whole sector, supported by presentations at various conferences and workshops – a consultation that showed that although there was recognition that the draft was an improvement on the old Code, there was significant disquiet about a perceived level of prescription inherent in the consultation draft and an anxiety that the Code did not help clarify the distinction between the management and governance of the institution;
- in the light of these misgivings, the CUC agreed to the formation of a technical advisory group, which supported a complete redrafting of the document;
- further consultation with stakeholders;
- final redrafting after a plenary discussion involving over 100 Chairs of governing bodies.

These phases and the wide engagement they supported gave good opportunities to discuss and explore different ways of doing things and to test the language within the Code to make sure that the meaning was clear, without being prescriptive.

Acceptance

The consultation demonstrated just how important of the type of language used was. What generated the most disquiet in the consultation draft Code was the perception by many that there was an excessive use of phrases like 'that institutions should . . .' or 'Governing bodies must . . .'. Although the draft Code made it clear that compliance was voluntary, the anxiety was that governing bodies, with a majority of lay members, would overreact and seek compliance with all such statements.

In the revised draft, this was dealt with, first, by editing out wherever possible words like 'must' and 'should', second, by clearly setting out that 'must' was something that was either required by law or regulation (and not something being imposed by the Code), 'should' as something where there was a strong consensus that this was a good idea or a practical approach to an issue (but voluntary) and everything else was expressed as 'might' or 'could consider' to show it was illustrative.

Exception was also taken to phrases like 'the Council must ensure . . .'. This was interpreted as encouraging governing bodies to cross the executive/non-executive boundary. That concern was dealt with in the main by changing wording to 'The Council will need to get assurance that . . .'.

As a result of this engagement and responsiveness in drafting, the resulting Code was widely accepted and implemented. In a sector where autonomy is so important, this acceptance was a major positive aspect of the Code. This is further strengthened by the 'apply or explain' principle – given the diverse nature of the sector where each institution has a distinct institutional profile and represents a unique blend of history and legacy, managerial temperament, values, governance habits, and current needs and imperatives there will inevitably be instances where not all aspects of any code can apply to all institutions. Accordingly, CUC right from the start of the review insisted that the Code be on an 'apply or explain' basis. This not only gives institutions the ability to adopt practices which suit their context and history, it also prompts a constructive dialogue between management and the governing body, as well as with the institution more widely, and with the regulator. This is clearly preferable to onerous monitoring regimes imposed by regulators or complex processes to 'get around' the requirements of the Code adopted by institutions.

Engagement through the work of the Steering Group, meant that acceptance by the regulator was always likely. This in turn meant the development of the Code was taken seriously and that institutions could see the benefit of committing resources to participate in the dialogue that generated the final product. It was then open to the regulator to use the Code in the way that they deemed most appropriate, for example HEFCE required HEIs to include in their annual financial statements a statement on internal control (corporate governance) and commended the Code as good practice.

The Office for Students (OfS) has a similar requirement within its 2018 Accounts Direction:

> A provider must include a 'statement of corporate governance' in its financial statements. The statement of corporate governance must set out a description of the provider's corporate governance arrangements and a statement of the responsibilities of the governing body.

However, OfS regulations makes no reference to the Code of Governance and OfS has made it clear that it does not endorse the Code as the only one for the sector and that an institution may adopt any Code or none as long as it meets the public interest principles relevant to its category of registration (although it does make repeated references to the other CUC Code, the Higher Education Senior Staff Remuneration Code (2018)).

If acceptance is to be achieved, then the development of the Code has to consider a range of other influences and requirements. Examples include:

- charity law and regulations;
- the requirements of the various funders;
- the accounts directions of the various regulators;
- the Statement of Recommended Practice for Further and Higher Education (SORP2015);
- relevant company law;
- equality law and associated duties;
- Freedom of Information and Data Protection legislation;
- procurement law.

Increasingly other duties and responsibilities have been placed on governing bodies, for example

- Counter-Terrorism and Security Act 2015;
- any changes in legislation on health and safety;
- requirements in respect of quality assurance;
- requirements in respect of long-term sustainability of the institution.

Some of these additional requirements can arise quite quickly and here the flexibility of a sector-owned voluntary code based approach can be particularly helpful. So, for example, the additional duties placed on governing bodies to deliver external opinion on quality assurance could be quickly accommodated.

Flexibility

An OECD study in 2010 (OECD, 2010) considered 12 different sets of higher education governance codes and guidance across a range of countries. Such governance codes and guidance notes are popular (compared to legislation or other government intervention) because they are flexible instruments that rely on sector mechanisms and expertise for their development, implementation, enforcement and subsequent evolution. In contrast to the more rigid and prescriptive nature of mandatory legislation and regulation, the Code not only accommodates – but in fact expects – some degree of non-compliance with its provisions. Moreover, codes can be amended to reflect changing needs and circumstances much more quickly than legislation can.

Yet, deciding where to draw the boundary between voluntary codes and mandatory law is not as straightforward as it may appear. This is due to, among other things, the contrasting approaches of different jurisdictions on similar issues. For instance, the current Scottish HE governance Code reflects Scottish legislation which requires Chairs of governing bodies to be elected by a broad constituency including staff and students. Such divergence of approach extends to other areas, such as remuneration committees, academic quality and sustainability.

So, why have corporate governance codes worked comparatively well in the UK up to the current point? Self-regulatory instruments are widely used in the UK capital market, covering matters from corporate governance to takeovers to dealings among market participants. Within both the government and the private sector, there is a general preference for economic activities to be governed, where feasible, through industry-based tools rather than statutory and regulatory instruments. Several elements have contributed to their success, namely:

- a tradition of self-regulation and consensus on the utility of a code;
- clearly defined standards;
- availability of information regarding code compliance;
- an interested and supportive regulator;
- a supportive legal framework.

In higher education, the emphasis on autonomy and self-regulation, the support of a regulator, and the consensual way codes have been developed are the keys to their success.

It also helps that a large proportion of lay members of governing bodies in the UK come from the private sector, where the use of voluntary governance codes is well established.

For a governance code to be effective, the standards and behaviours expected of institutions, governors and management must be clearly defined. However, in higher education, these need to be flexible enough to enable adaptation to individual circumstances which vary widely. This flexibility is provided by encompassing not only written guidance but also useful practices that others in the same community can consider. The Code is supplemented by Illustrative Practice Notes – these focus on how individual institutions have chosen to implement the principles set out in the Code. The availability of best illustrative examples is important because it signals sector support for a particular practice and shows how compliance can be achieved in reality as well as circumstances under which deviation from the Code would be justified.

In developing the CUC Code, the core dynamic was one of trying to maintain a balance between conflicting needs of the different stakeholders. On the one hand the regulators will be looking for precision, clarity and consistency – this arises out of their need for each institution to be treated fairly, to have an instrument that can be applied in a straightforward manner and be capable of application easily, sometimes by their staff who may not be expert in the operation of an institution. That can conflict with the institutional need for flexibility to support different and changing needs and ultimately a code that is sufficiently nuanced to support the diversity of the sector.

However, there are other perspectives as well – typically large, well established institutions look for focused and relatively short statements of principle, rather than explanatory text and examples. Whereas the priority from newer and smaller institutions can be exactly the opposite – a strong appetite for clear guidance and definitive examples and a suggested template, which other institutions would see as prescriptive. This in part reflects the dynamic within such institutions where senior managers may have to work with governing body lay members, who are not expert in higher education, who generally are risk-averse and accordingly want to be reassured that they are complying with every element of the Code.

The different backgrounds of governors can have an impact, again with some with less experience of HE, perhaps being more used to more regulated, centrally directed sectors – like the NHS or local government – who expect codes to be directive and instructive of institutions – as against those that understand the need to adapt to the differing contexts and priorities of institutions, with the goal of protecting autonomy always in sight.

Different regulators will also have different perspectives. This is certainly the case with the regulators in the devolved nations of the UK. They have a much closer relationship with their smaller set of institutions than their English counterparts and have a capacity and an expectation to be much more closely engaged with individual institutions – whereas the English approach of necessity had to be a broader approach that looked at the needs of groups of institutions rather than individual ones.

So those charged with the development of codes need to manage the processes to resolve these tensions – and the best way is to adopt an open process that is heavily consultative, so that the various different players understand the perspectives of others. This suggests a public consultation that looks at specific questions, then can generate the discussion and the data that can support consensus building. It requires regulators to be clear as to what their 'red lines' are and what is negotiable and what is not, and it needs institutions to be clear about the relative risks of state intervention and to understand the benefits of adopting and implementing a code.

It is not just regulators that influence the development of codes. The recent experience of the UK sector in respect of senior staff remuneration has seen that one of the drivers for developing a Senior Staff Remuneration Code (in effect a Code of Governance for Remuneration Committees) was a significant and heavily negative public discourse on the remuneration of senior staff, which in turn started to affect perceptions of the quality of governance generally in institutions and their overall reputation and standing. The development of a code accepted by the sector gave the opportunity to institutions, ministers and regulators to say that something was being done collectively to recognise and tackle the perceived problem. The approach adopted – drawing upon good practice and evidence from other sectors – provided evidence to the public of positive action.

Future perspectives

Governance does not stand still. Whilst many of the values of good governance endure – trust, transparency, honesty, integrity, etc. – the rapidly changing context in which universities operate means that some of the approaches and structures must be susceptible to evolution. In the UK, the most fundamental evolutionary leap has been the passing of the Higher Education and Research Act in 2017. This changes the very nature of regulation in England. This replaced what was perceived as a benign buffer body (HEFCE) between the government and institutions, whose principal regulatory instrument was the control of public funding, and whose remit was the promotion of excellence within all aspects of HE, with a market-based regulator. The OfS as that regulator is charged with enforcing minimum standards, supporting new entrants to the market, and with a primary focus on the needs and support of students. Its remit does not extend to the overall well-being of the higher education sector.

The new regulator has a clear remit to support government to encourage innovation both in the types of institution and types of provision through encouragement of a market dynamic which is seen as the best way to encourage quality and diversity.

This significant shift takes place at the time when the HE Governance Code is due for review. It is already clear that the contextual dynamic for its review and production will be different – whereas in the past HEFCE has coordinated the different regulatory responses (both interfacing with the devolved administrations and other regulators) – the OfS does not see that as its role. HEFCE was clear that it wanted an HE Governance Code that it could endorse across all the institutions it funded. The OfS has a clear view that a revised HE Governance Code developed by CUC will be a code that it will recognise but not one it will endorse as a preferred code. It does not want innovation to be inhibited and will want to leave open the possibility that other codes of governance – like the UK Corporate Governance Code 2018 might be adopted by some institutions – to enable other and new participants to come into the sector. The sector has always been diverse but with the direction of policy being to enable a much wider range of corporate forms to operate. This includes those that operate for profit, those that are in effect small family businesses, as well as those that are subsidiaries of major corporations or of possibly professional associations.

Whilst this may, at the present time, be generating uncertainty within the established sector – it does offer the possibility of some interesting new approaches – so, for example, work is underway to see if the principles of the co-operative movement, for example, could be applied to an HE provider, whether greater community engagement could be accommodated, and the extent to which the balance of power might be shifted more towards students and away from governing bodies in their current form.

This new intellectual dynamic in thinking about models of governance, coupled with the very different approach to regulation adopted currently in the devolved administrations in the UK, means it remains to be seen whether in the future there will be a single HE governance code covering the UK as a whole or whether over time what is generated is a more minimalist set of values – with different parts of the sector using different codes. How different such a values-led code will be from the OfS's mandatory public interest principles currently promoted by it, remains to be seen.

At the same time governance is evolving in other sectors with greater emphasis on:

- the board's role in monitoring and assessing culture;
- mechanisms for gathering the views of the workforce;
- reporting on how stakeholder interest has influenced the board's decision-making;
- succession planning and board member contribution.

Examples exist in the charities sector – where Atkinson (2017) picks out the greater emphasis on values and behaviours and greater demands on diversity and transparency, in health where Kershaw explains that evolving patterns of care means that governance in integrated care is developing fast and there is more to be done, and in central government where the 2017 'Corporate Governance in

Central Government Departments', published by Treasury, emphasised the need for departmental boards to have an increasing focus on performance, risk management, talent and the challenge and scrutiny of major projects.

The strong connections between UK HE and other sectors, mean inevitably that these issues will be considered and debated as they evolve, and those debates will shape and influence future iterations of codes of governance and the requirements of regulators.

Notes

1 The CUC is the representative body for the Chairs of UK universities. It provides a peer-support network for Chairs in leading both their governing bodies and more broadly. It seeks to promote high standards in university governance.
2 Universities UK (UUK) is the successor to the Committee of University Vice-Chancellors and Principals, with the key aim of supporting its members to achieve their aims and objectives (www.universitiesuk.ac.uk).
3 The Association of University Heads of Administration (AHUA) is the representative body of senior university managers in the UK and Ireland. It represents the collective views of members on key issues and policies to the higher education (HE) sector, government and other stakeholders. It also brings together members to exchange information, share knowledge and experience (https://ahua.ac.uk).

References

Atkinson, S. (2017) The Changing Face of the Governance Code [Retrieved from https://charitycommission.blog.gov.uk/2017/02/02/the-changing-face-of-the-governance-code/]

Committee of Vice-Chancellors and Principals (1985) Report of the Steering Committee for Efficiency Studies in Universities [Retrieved from www.educationengland.org.uk/documents/jarratt1985/index.html]

CUC (1995) Guide for Members of Higher Education Governing Bodies in England, Wales and Northern Ireland.

CUC (1998) Guide for Members of Higher Education Governing Bodies in England, Wales and Northern Ireland.

CUC (2000) Guide for Members of Higher Education Governing Bodies in England, Wales and Northern Ireland.

CUC (2004) Guide for Members of Higher Education Governing Bodies in England, Wales and Northern Ireland.

CUC (2009) Guide for Members of Higher Education Governing Bodies in the UK [Retrieved from www.dera.ioe.ac.uk/4503/2/01_20.pdf]

CUC (2014) The Higher Education Code of Governance [Retrieved from www.universitychairs.ac.uk/wp-content/uploads/2015/02/Code-Final.pdf]

CUC (2018) The Higher Education Senior Staff Remuneration Code [Retrieved from www.universitychairs.ac.uk/wp-content/uploads/2018/06/HE-Remuneration-Code.pdf]

Higher Education Funding Council for England (2014) Para 7 HEFCE's Accounts Direction to Higher Education Institutions for 2013–14 Financial Statements

[Retrieved   from   http://webarchive.nationalarchives.gov.uk/20180322111401/ http://www.hefce.ac.uk/pubs/year/2013/CL,252013/]

Higher Education and Research Act (2017) [Retrieved from www.legislation.gov.uk/ ukpga/2017/29/contents/enacted]

HM Treasury (2017) Corporate Governance in Central Government Departments: Code of Good Practice [Retrieved from www.gov.uk/government/publications/ corporate-governance-code-for-central-government-departments-2017]

OECD (2010) Governance and Quality Guidelines in Higher Education [Retrieved from www.oecd.org/education/imhe/46064461.pdf]

Scott, W. Richard (1995) *Institutions and Organizations.* Thousand Oaks: Sage.

Shattock, M. (2004) The Lambert Code: Can We Define Best Practice? *Higher Education Quarterly,* Volume 58, No. 4, pp. 229–242.

Students at the Heart of the System (2011) [Retrieved from https://assets.publish ing.service.gov.uk/government/uploads/system/uploads/attachment_data/ file/31384/11-944-higher-education-students-at-heart-of-system.pdf]

Taggart, G.J. (2004) A Critical Review of the Role of the English Funding Body for Higher Education in the relationship Between the State and Higher Education in the Period 1945–2003. A dissertation submitted to the University of Bristol in accordance with the requirements of the degree of Doctor of Education in the Graduate School of Education, Faculty of Social Sciences and Law.

von Prondzynski, F. (2012) Report of the Review of Higher Education Governance in Scotland [Retrieved from www2.gov.scot/Publications/2012/02/3646/downloads#res386780]

Chapter 13

Regulating higher education markets

The English policy experiment as a case study

David Palfreyman

This chapter considers the economics of higher education (HE) and how a given economic model drives the governance and management of higher education institutions (HEIs), treating them as businesses – as well as exploring the concept of the student-consumer and his/her legal relationship with the provider HEI (the university–student contract to educate as a Business–Consumer (B2C) contract covered by consumer protection law). The consequences of the marketisation of HE are examined, how the potential negative consequences might be mitigated while seeing how the benefits for the student-consumer come through to them as individual beneficiaries. It does so only for England as a case study where over almost 20 years the funding of undergraduate degrees for English citizens has been shifted pretty well entirely (there is still a modest state subsidy for Science, Technology, Engineering and Mathematics (STEM) subjects) from the taxpayer/government to the student/family – universities as once a free public good with no tuition fees (since the early 1960s) now operate in a (quasi-)market (tuition fees for undergraduates having been introduced initially at £1,000 pa, then increased to £3,000 and next by 2012 to £9,000, and are £9,250 as at 2018/19). (The term '(quasi-)market' is used since the politicians' hope for a market based on price competition by way of HEIs charging differing fees has not happened – see Willetts (2017) as the architect of the 2012 £9,000 fees jump.)

The English state thus retreats from the direct financing of modern mass HE (but provides a progressive loans system for funding these tuition fees which involves significant indirect subsidy in that eventually a sizeable proportion of the student loans debt will have to be written off as not fully repaid by a majority of graduates). This is a global trend towards cost-sharing between taxpayer and the student-family as the burden of paying for mass HE is shifted (Heller and Callender, 2013) – although England has moved to an outlier position on the free-HE/fees spectrum. It arises since, arguably, the state, any state, every state eventually faces a harsh choice in trying to finance mass HE where 40–60 per cent of young people enter HE – the state can settle for an under-resourced and over-crowded mediocre HE system or it can tackle the difficult politics of introducing tuition fees as bringing an end to the era of HE as a free public good that became the norm in most OECD countries as part of the post-war welfare state political consensus (on common themes and issues comparatively and globally across HE systems see Palfreyman and Temple (2017), who explore the shifting historical idea and ideal of the 'university' since its creation in medieval Europe: Bologna, Paris, Oxford, Cambridge, and so on).

The UK (and hence England) 'massified' HE – somewhat belatedly – from the mid-1980s: until then participation had crept up to c15 per cent from less than 10 per cent in the 1960s; and when tuition fees were first introduced by 2000 the unit of resource (as the funding per undergraduate per annum) had declined by almost half as the government sought expansion without a proportionate funding increase. This process of discovering that well-funded mass HE is unaffordable for the taxpayer will be seen especially where there are (as is usually the case) significantly more politically important calls on the state's coffers (say: schooling, health services, pensions and social care for an ageing population). Some nations try to avoid the fierce fees furore (where the middle classes as the socio-economic group disproportionately favoured by 'free' HE are robustly vociferous in trying to defend their welfare state perk) by relying on an expansion of for-profit private commercial HE supply to meet demand – and then often witnessing the contraction of this provision if the nation's demographic profile leads to a reduced cohort of young folk 'going to uni' (Palfreyman *et al.*, 2018).

If tuition fees are (re-)introduced at anything more than a nominal annual amount, the paying student-customer (and his/her supportive family) become consumerist minded – it is one thing to tolerate a shoddy but free 'public good' service but another to do so while stumping up a significant level of tuition fee (for English citizens at English HEIs, as already noted, currently at £9,250 pa of a typically three-year undergraduate degree course – but with some courses at four years) and incurring a heavy 30-year burden of graduate debt (approaching £50k counting fees loans and living-cost loans – perhaps £100k when interest is added!). Given that government has as a matter of public policy created this HE (quasi-)market, does it then have a duty to introduce measures to ensure its regulation in the interests of the student-consumer? (See Palfreyman and Tapper (2014) for discussion of the need for and the rise of 'the regulated market in higher education'.) The political response from the Conservative government has been the passing of the Higher Education and Research Act 2017 (HERA17) that establishes the Office for Students (OfS) as the new regulator of HE providers (HEPs – aka 'universities'). The OfS has clear obligations and also relevant regulatory powers under HERA17 – all as discussed in detail below – to ensure the student receives value-for-money (VfM) as an informed and empowered consumer of HE as a service (teaching and examining/assessment) delivered by the university as (in the blunt language of the Consumer Rights Act 2015 – CRA15) a 'trader' (ss 1 & 2, CRA15) under the Higher Education Provider–Student (HEP-S) contract (Farrington and Palfreyman, 2012, chapter 12 on 'The Student-HEI Contract'; Palfreyman and Tapper, 2014, chapter 6 on 'The Student as Consumer: Legal Framework and Practical Reality').

This chapter also considers the impact on HEI/HEP governance and management of the necessity to ensure compliance with the 'conditions' set by the OfS for its registration of a HE provider, especially given the strong sanctions that the OfS can impose upon its HEPs under HERA17. The question of the balance of authority within the governance triangle – the lay-dominated Council/ Board as the sovereign body at the apex, the academics-dominated Senate at one corner, the CEO/Vice-Chancellor (VC) and his/her senior management team (SMT) in the other – will be an issue, together with the organisational culture of the entity (Scott, 2018; Shattock, 2006, 2010, chapter 6, 2014). Time will tell in terms of both the regulatory style of the OfS – likely to be 'modern' (Hodges and Steinholtz, 2017) – and also whether the HEPs 'get it' in that the word 'for' in Office for Students signals a change in culture from the days of the government financing of HE (the benign buffer of the UGC from 1919 having been replaced by the UFC and then by HEFCE, the latter having to reluctantly assume an increasingly regulatory role). [Here the author of this chapter must declare an interest as a Member of the Board of HEFCE 2017/18 and currently of the Board of the OfS – nothing written in this chapter should be taken as OfS policy, other than where below OfS public domain documentation is quoted.]

This chapter takes as its starting point in considering the economics of HE the insightful economic analysis of the HE industry set out by Martin (2011). The essence of our concern is the economic transaction between the student and the HEI/HEP that occurs within a legal framework where the undergraduate degree is sold by the university (as a business) to the student-consumer. It is thus, as already noted above, delivered under a B2C contract-to-educate duly governed by consumer law within the wider context of contract law (in England, CRA15; Barry *et al.*, 2016). Its key components are both the provision of teaching (backed up by adequate learning-support services) and also the process of assessment/examining; and these activities are to be supplied 'with reasonable care and skill' (s49, CRA15), as well as being 'performed within a reasonable time' (s52, CRA15). And the student gets two new legal rights under CRA15 – the right 'to require repeat performance' where the 'trader' has failed to deliver the service 'to the extent necessary to complete its performance in conformity with the contract' (s55, CRA15): and to get this repeat performance 'within a reasonable time and without significant inconvenience'.

The second important new consumer protection right is the right 'to a price reduction' of 'an appropriate amount' where the trader is unable or unwilling to deliver repeat performance 'within a reasonable time and without significant inconvenience to the consumer' (s56, CRA15) – and any such refund 'must be given without undue delay' and without the trader imposing 'any fee on the consumer in respect of the refund'. Both these new rights may well soon be tested as to their precise application to HE in the context of the 2018 strike action by academics that led to the cancellation of teaching – and, where such lost teaching was not later provided by way of 'repeat performance', the issue will be whether the student is entitled to 'a price reduction' and, if so, what will be 'an appropriate amount' as a proportion of the £9,250 tuition fee (or similarly of the relevant fee for, say, a postgraduate taught-degree where teaching was also cancelled). The HEI concerned in a test case – or the HEIs in the event of 'class' litigation – may well seek to invoke a force majeure clause, and the Court will have to determine whether such industrial action is a matter of force majeure and, even if it is something beyond the control of the HEI, whether any such term within the university–student contract is caught under s62 CRA15 which requires 'contract terms and notices to be fair' – was it 'transparent and prominent' in being properly brought to the attention of the student when entering the contract and is it 'expressed in clear and intelligible language' (s64, CRA15)?

Moreover, the calculation of 'appropriate' will be complex: if the lost teaching was over three weeks of a supposed 30-week teaching year, is it simply to be 10 per cent of £9,250? Or 10 per cent of the direct cost of undergraduate teaching (say, £5–6k of the £9,250 that actually reaches the chalk-face?). HEIs are usually very coy about releasing information on how fees are spent, despite Which? and the Minister for Universities having called for them to do so. Or is the refund to be only the actual cost of delivering the specific lost lectures/seminars, which may have been sourced cheaply from hourly-paid casual/adjunct part-time staff?! Or, as for many degree course where the undergraduate teaching is compressed into the first two terms, is the calculation of the 'appropriate amount' to be based on three weeks missing from 20 weeks? What if the HEI offers to deliver 'repeat performance' during the next academic year? Would that be within 'a reasonable time' and might it, however, involve 'significant inconvenience' to the student? If it offers 'a price reduction' will it manage to do so 'without undue delay'? And just what does s56(5) CRA15 mean in the context of the Student Loans Company paying the tuition fee direct to the HEI in the case of almost all UK citizens at English HEPs? (That wording is: 'The trader must give the refund using the same means of payment as the consumer used to pay for the service, unless the consumer expressly agrees otherwise.') Yet, without clarity on these aspects of the application of consumer law to the University–Student contract, the students' consumer protection rights remain murky and HEIs as businesses are uncertain as to their contractual liability in the event of their breach of the *HEP-S* contracts.

Before exploring the specifics of HERA17 and the duties/powers of the OfS, it is worth noting that there is no credible rational basis for determining the ratio of public/social to private benefit arising from HE and hence no sophisticated policy mechanism nor any convenient algorithm for deciding on the exact proportions of the cost of undergraduate teaching to be borne by the state through subsidies to universities as opposed to being carried by the student paying tuition fees. It is simply a matter of 'the politics of higher education' at any one time in any one nation and how the relative claims of HE are compared to other areas of public expenditure in the context of austerity for public spending. McMahon (2009) makes an (the only?) attempt to allocate such private and public benefits – concluding that the fees:subsidy balance should be roughly 50:50 to reflect the estimated split of public and private benefits (but, since the private investment is taken also to include the opportunity cost to the student of employment income foregone while in HE, the current level of tuition fees in most US states and certainly in England breaches McMahon's suggested c50 per cent private input).

This process of change in the financing of HE through the introduction of and steady increasing of undergraduate tuition fees for a nation's citizens gives rise to the creation of a new and usually controversial market in the 'sale' of undergraduate education to 'home' students (the English outlier example has not only been swift in moving from no fees in 1999 to £9,250 now but, as already noted, also has reached a high fees figure: although in-state undergraduate tuition fees at, say, Berkeley are similar at c$15k). Yet this is simply the creation of another market just like the one already long-operated enthusiastically and lucratively by the HE industry since the 1980s in selling undergraduate degree courses to international students paying very high tuition fees, and also like the one by way of the sales from an extra and very profitable product-line more recently created through an explosion of postgraduate taught courses (notably in business schools). As this marketisation (based on the charging of tuition fees) of the core undergraduate activity of universities develops, 'the provider state' becomes 'the regulatory state' and now, arguably, incurs a clear new moral if not an actual legal duty in terms of ensuring effective consumer protection for undergraduate students paying for what will probably be their third largest item of life-long expenditure after the buying of a house/flat and after the long-term commitment to a pension scheme (Palfreyman and Tapper, 2014). The state, rightly, wishes to encourage an effective market in undergraduate education but, as indeed for most markets, needs to offer some sort of regulation to protect against market failure (Grauwe, 2016) – just as it has created (the hoped-for) market competition in the first place to protect against producer-capture of monolithic, moribund, incumbent, traditional HE providers.

How, then, does the regulatory state fulfil this moral and political duty of care to 16/17-year-olds in receipt of marketing hype from universities and then as undergraduates of 18/19 to 21/22 purchasing degree courses? The HE industry is extreme in having a relationship with its customers stretching from marketing to them as 16/17-year-olds, often then waiting a year while the customer is on a gap-year, and then delivering the three/four-year degree course – potentially six or seven years during which marketing promises in year one may need to be honoured operationally in year seven; and this lengthy B2C relationship is additionally complicated by the student not just being a passive recipient of the HE service in that, as with gym membership, some effort on the part of the consumer is needed to get any desired result! The regulatory mechanisms over recent decades have been reliant on a voluntary and costly quality and standards bureaucracy involving over the years an avalanche of acronyms and a cascade of aborted agencies as differing levels of intervention are experimented with in terms of trusting (or not) the HE industry to play fair by the student, whether once fully funded by a generous taxpayer or now paying £9,250 pa tuition fees. This pyramid of staff within 'the quality industry' – the 'teaching and learning' experts, the 'teaching quality' monitors, the 'student experience' pundits – seem largely everywhere to have failed to prevent a perceived secular decline in the quantum and quality of undergraduate teaching in relation to exactly what happens at the chalk-face, in the lecture theatre and in the seminar room on a daily basis (Land and Gordon, 2013; and, for a scathing critique of the failure of accreditation as a quality assurance mechanism in US HE, see Phillips and Kinser, 2018): it is no longer, if ever it was, fit-for-purpose and requires radical overhaul if intrusive external regulation is to be avoided in an attempt to provide the student with a much-needed improved 'consumer information and protection'. Left to the vested interest, producer-oriented, rent-seeking English HE industry, however, there is a risk that the newly invented Teaching Excellence Framework (TEF) will become just another forgotten acronym and failed agency, the same tired quality-assessment and quality-enhancement ideas being recycled and yet again failing to tackle the baked-in problem of the university–student transaction (although, that said, there are some indications that even HEIs hugely successful in the much longer established sister REF (Research Excellence Framework, as previously the Research Assessment Exercise) are embarrassed to receive a Bronze TEF Award and may be seeking belatedly to correct the long neglect of undergraduate teaching so as to maximise research productivity).

The innate problem, as analysed by Martin (2011), is that undergraduate HE is an extreme example of 'an experience good' for these reasons: the (typically young and hence arguably vulnerable) student-purchaser is seriously underinformed because of significant 'information asymmetry' in consumer knowledge about HE; he/she tends, therefore, to rely on high-price/fees hopefully signalling high quality (the Chivas Regal effect: and why all English HEIs charge the maximum allowed annual fee of £9,250 for any and every undergraduate degree course); the university is tempted to engage in 'quality cheating' to protect its reputation, having no incentive because of severe unaddressed agency problems in the governance and management of universities to facilitate the student-consumer being better informed; the good is expensive and is purchased only once, and there is limited scope to transfer from one university to another if the student feels a wrong purchase-decision has been made; and the purchaser often is unable to assess the value of the degree until some years after purchase. A state of affairs not helped by there being pockets of both weak governance and also of poor management across the HE sector, as well as systemic sector-wide governance failings that show as, for example, the egregious over-payment of some CEO-VCs, the unexplained grade-inflation in degree results (notably tracking the shift to £9,000 fees in 2012), the startling rise in unconditional offers for admission (ditto), and the increased number of students regarding their undergraduate teaching experience as poor value-for-money (ditto): all wicked issues that, sadly, the HE industry, through its trade body the UUK, shows no signs of being capable of addressing via some sort of pre-emptive self-regulation and timely self-imposed best practice standards. External robust and rigorous regulation seems to be the only way forward if the student-consumer is to be protected in the funding system that has been created with its competitive and cash incentives.

And a key starting point, whether it might ever emerge from imaginative and anticipatory enlightened self-regulation or has to be imposed by a combination of the relevant regulatory agencies (notably the OfS but also the Competition and Markets Authority (CMA) along with the Advertising Standards Agency (ASA) and perhaps with the involvement of the Consumers Association (CA) as 'Which?'), is to oblige HEP governing bodies to take direct responsibility for teaching quality (see further discussion below) – and, crucially, for there also to be the adoption of an industry-wide standardised university–student contract-to-educate that meets the requirement of CRA15. Most universities do not have an explicit detailed contract and hence the student-consumer is spending c£30k without the sort of contract that would be normal for, say, the buying of a new or used car, an expensive holiday, a home extension – and now even the pensions industry has begun to get its act together under pressure from sharpened financial services regulation. A specimen or model agreement/contract was offered in Farrington and Palfreyman (2012, pp. 443–447) – but, of course, has been utterly ignored by the HE industry! Such a contract could be easily and speedily finalised by the UUK as the trade body in consultation with key interested parties such as the NUS and 'Which?' before being recognised by the OfS and the CMA in the way that other bodies (e.g. the used-car dealers) have over recent decades moved to standard contracts duly registered with the CMA's predecessor, the Office for Fair Trading (which will have vetted the contract for unfair terms, etc.). Some of the few student–university contracts until recently in use were egregiously one-sided and contained many of the unfair terms long-outlawed by the OFT (Farrington and Palfreyman, 2012, pp. 400–420, and especially paras 12.112/113) but, following a CMA warning-shot to the HE industry in 2015, have, hopefully, fallen out of use.

This standard (and clear, fair) contract, it is proposed, would incorporate as legally enforceable terms the representations made by the university to the appli-cant/student-consumer via a data table/template that the applicant could usefully use as comparative information – thereby beginning to overcome the information asymmetry problem referred to above. Under consumer protection law, the provision by the trader of material pieces of information to the potential consumer that are then reasonably relied upon by the consumer in reaching his/her decision to make the purchase of a service from that supplier become terms of the contract and the supplier is in breach if the service is not delivered in accordance with that specific information (s50, CRA15). Similarly, the failure to provide material information may be a misleading omission on the part of the trader if it should have realised the information would have been a key factor in the consumer deciding on the B2C transaction. This shift to a contractual approach for ensuring quality will, of course, be firmly resisted by universities – as, they will typically assert, damaging some supposed precious relationship between university and student based on the medieval concept of membership within the studium generale or on the basis that students are (in the trendy recent term) 'co-producers' of their academic progress so that, supposedly, the university can shift the burden of failure to the consumer where it neglects adequately to resource teaching.

It is suggested that in the age of mass HE amounting to tertiary education (TE) providing skills and competencies vocation degrees such a line of thinking is anachronistic, as if mass HE simply meant more Oxbridge liberal arts HE. Putting to one side the squeals from the groves of academe about wicked neoliberal plots to impose the marketisation, commodification and commercialisation of the ivory tower and its relegation from the lofty acropolis to the grubby agora (Brown, 2013; Busch, 2017; Collini, 2012), the real reason for resistance is that universities are only too well aware that they lack effective quality-control mechanisms because their middle-management is weak at departmental level whatever they may have at the top of the managerial hierarchy by way of Pro Vice-Chancellors (PVCs) pontificating on teaching quality and churning out policy papers for presentation to visiting quality-audit teams (and cynically 'gaming' these audit and assessment processes). Paradoxically, the shift here suggested, while appearing to increase pressure on the chalk-face academic, may, in fact, be welcomed by rank-and-file university lecturers as requiring remote corporatist management to properly resource undergraduate teaching in order to deliver over three to four years the package of teaching and assessment promised in the marketing and enshrined in the contract-to-educate.

The information in any such data template will very largely be about the quantum of teaching rather than focusing on its quality – such a template, in a very tentative and draft form in need of much refinement, is set out in OxCHEPS Occasional Paper No. 60 (July 2016) to be found at oxcheps@new.ox.ac.uk. This focus on the measurable quantum rather than the elusive quality of undergraduate teaching is partly because the teaching process is a black-box in terms of assessing quality, universities almost everywhere also are resisting all attempts to explore the concept of value-added. And it is partly because universities possess a unique Get-Out-Of-Gaol-Free card in being able to invoke 'academic judgement' when challenged on the alleged poor quality of teaching and the Court in all legal jurisdictions offers this legal immunity by not second-guessing the proper exercise of such academic judgement (Farrington and Palfreyman, 2012, pp. 360–366; Palfreyman and Tapper, 2014, p. 123; Palfreyman and Temple, 2017, pp. 115–117). The same concept of judicial deference to the proper exercise of expert academic judgement prevents under the Higher Education Act 2004 the OIA taking up a student complaint concerning academic judgement.

Every other professional group has lost such privileged protection over the last few decades (Davies, 2014), and it is debateable whether the UK Supreme Court would strike down this judicial convention in the modern context of: students funding their own HE and increasingly paying high tuition fees to for-profit 'private' commercial HE providers; modern mass HE being in effect vocational tertiary education; and the traditional 'public' university anyway now behaving in a thoroughly business-like way (Davies, 2014, at para 3.03: 'the continuation of academic immunity in the face of increasing consumerisation of the student-university relationship remains problematical'). Given, however, this continued but arguably anachronistic legal immunity, it is far easier for the aggrieved student to show contractual breach and invoke consumer protection law where promises or representations have been made about concrete issues, about quantum rather than quality – for example, that there will be delivered X contact hours per week, there will be required Y hours of assessed work per term/semester, such work will be marked and feedback provided within Z days, seminar sizes will not exceed XX students.

It is thus asserted that, if the student had contractual certainty over these key aspects of the quantum of teaching and assessment (as delivered by appropriately qualified, trained and managed academic staff), then much of the student dissatisfaction over seeming poor value-for-money of undergraduate education would be addressed – and, indirectly, the quality of undergraduate teaching and learning would be monitored and improved in that universities would have less opportunity to hide the reality of their egregious neglect of the resourcing of teaching while strategically diverting resources to the pursuit of the cash and kudos of research and/or to funding other non-teaching activities such as building glitzy new buildings and presiding over 'administrative bloat'. The enforcement of these contractual terms will be in the first instance by the university being required (it is suggested) by the OfS to gather and make available the template data, and then have a robust internal complaints process: failing that, by the individual student as now taking a complaint to the OIA (and/or to Trading Standards as for dodgy used-car dealers!). In addition, where there is a generalised complaint from a group or cohort of students concerning a degree course, there should be a procedure for it to be investigated by the OfS. The OfS will (it is proposed) also exercise a random audit check on the accuracy of data being inserted into the course template by universities, and will require that HEP Councils and Boards of Governors/Directors take steps to ensure the data populating the template is independently audited and that they, as the governors/directors, sign-off on the accuracy of the data just as they do the audited accounts.

And to be clear, sovereign power as well as responsibility lies formally and de jure with these lay-dominated Councils/Boards, albeit that in some HEIs a stronger sense of collegial or shared-governance applies in that, de facto, the Senate as the academic body, as the professoriate or faculty, is deferred to by Council on purely academic matters. See Tapper and Palfreyman (2010, 2011) on Oxford for the purest form of collegial self-governance by the academic guild for 800 years: where the donnish lunatics really are in charge of the medieval asylum! Within the governance triangle referred to above the Council/Board really is in charge – despite a usual (mis-)interpretation of university constitutions, especially in relation to the older chartered entities that are not the ex-polytechnics as statutory corporations, to the effect that the Senate has the final say over purely academic matters. The governors were very explicitly in control when the 1900s civics were created (at the University of Birmingham the professors, as the hired-help in gowns, were simply refused access to the grand Council Chamber for meetings of the Senate!), but by the 1960s the high water-mark of 'donnish dominion' was reached (Halsey, 1992; Moodie and Eustace, 1974) – and it has been in decline along with a matching trend for the reassertion of lay-power ever since the 1980s, reinforced more recently by the charity trusteeship role of the Council Members being increasingly stressed along with the such individuals carrying unlimited personal financial liability for any loss incurred by the university in the event of reckless mismanagement. Indeed, in the last years of HEFCE the Council/Boards were in fact being asked to sign off on key academic issues – the quality of teaching and the maintenance of degree standards – just as they did the annual accounts (but it is unclear how they would have known what they were signing-off in absence of an external audit function as with the accounts).

This then is unashamedly a consumerist approach to quality issues in HE undergraduate teaching, and is promoted because the bureaucratic quality-audit/assessment approach conveniently favoured by the HE industry has signally failed to deliver. Thus, it might be hoped that England can avoid the further decline of HE seen in the careful analysis of US HE set out in Arum and Roksa (2011). And also, hopefully, reverse the emerging corrosive cynical mutuality of a cosy convenient conspiracy between academe and student by way of a contract of disengagement (the former gets on with research while neglecting teaching and the latter gets the degree credential with less effort in terms of work set and exams passed) – as identified way back in mass US HE by Riesman (1958 and 1980/1998), when considering the dumbing-down of and grade-inflation within degree courses:

> Even the most shoddy, cut-rate, and cut-throat degrees are not necessarily frauds on the student consumer. They may, in fact, be examples of collusion between academic vendor and student buyer to secure a credential at some monetary cost but almost no cost in time and effort.
>
> (1980, at p. 116 in the 1998 edition)

But it is conceded that the chance of all the above coming to pass in the teeth of concerted opposition from the vested interest and complacent HE sector is not high! The OfS may well yet need to be bold and robust, so, finally, a brief review of the duties and powers given to it by HERA17 as well as of its early-days proposed use of registration 'conditions'.

HERA17 begins (s1) by establishing 'a body corporate called the Office for Students' which (s2) 'must have regard to', inter alia, the following: 'the need to protect the institutional autonomy of English higher education providers'; 'the need to promote quality, and greater choice and opportunities for students in the provision of higher education by English higher education providers'; 'the need to encourage competition' among such HEPs 'where that competition is in the interests of students and employers'; and 'the need to promote value for money in the provision of higher education'. But 'institutional autonomy' is very firmly protected (all English HEIs are private corporations, mainly as non-profit charities; they are not in any way, as in many countries, public bodies owned and directly controlled by the state (Farrington and Palfreyman, 2012, chapter 3 on the legal status of universities; Palfreyman and Temple, 2017, pp. 50–53 on the public–private divide in HE)). It is defined (s8) to mean 'the freedom of English higher education providers within the law to conduct their day to day management in an effective and competent way' with total control over the content of courses, the appointment of academics/faculty, and the selection of students; and in addition individual academics have 'freedom within the law' both 'to question and test received wisdom' and also 'to put forward new ideas and controversial or unpopular opinions' all 'without placing themselves in jeopardy of losing their jobs or privileges they may have at the providers' (Farrington and Palfreyman, 2012, chapter 13 on academic freedom and institutional autonomy; Palfreyman and Temple, 2017, pp. 103–110 on academic freedom and academic tenure).

The OfS is to set up a 'register' (s3) of HEPs, and in doing so can stipulate 'registration conditions' to be met by HEPs, some of which are mandatory and some variable in that they will assist it as 'proportionate to the OfS's assessment of the regulatory risk posed by the institution' (s7) – and notably the OfS can set a condition that a HEP will have 'a student protection plan which has the OfS's approval' (s13) so that in the event of institutional insolvency or campus/course closure the interests of students as consumers can, hopefully, be better protected (although in the absence of an explicit standardised *HEP-S* contract as discussed above and any binding case-law establishing levels of compensation due for its breach by the 'trader', it will be hard to concoct or assess the robustness of any such SPP). The OfS can also require HEPs to be governed in compliance with 'a public interest condition' (s13) that sets out (s14) the principles applicable to ensure good governance – including the protection of individual academic freedom as above. The OfS is given 'power to impose monetary penalties' upon its HEPs that fail to comply (s15), to suspend a HEP's registration (s16), and ultimately to de-register a HEP (s18); while it must also make arrangements for 'assessing the quality of, and standards applied to, higher education' (s23), including the 'rating' of such (s25 – the TEF), as well as being concerned with the HEP having 'an access and participation plan' (s29). The sanction powers of the OfS are, of course, subject to specified appeal mechanisms to a Tribunal/Court and, as with any public body (as was the case with HEFCE), OfS decision-making is subject to judicial review in the High Court (Farrington and Palfreyman, 2012, on judicial review at pp. 421–442).

The concept of academic freedom and the OfS's 'duty to protect [institutional] academic freedom' pops up, again, in s36 with the same repeated definition as in s8. The OfS has 'authorisation' to grant new degree-awarding powers (DAPs) to a HEP (s42) – and to take them away (s44) or (under s45) to take them away where they have been awarded under an Act of Parliament (to the statutory corporation universities) or by Royal Charter (to the chartered corporation universities): the OfS could, in effect, close down (subject to appeal and/or judicial review), say, the University of Cambridge! Similarly the OfS controls the use of the word 'university' in the title of an entity (s56). It has 'powers of entry and search' (s61) and, for all of this activity and these services, the OfS can 'charge fees' to its HEPs (ss 67, 70, 71 – and, under s73, recover its costs where it is sanctioning a HEP); while also fulfilling a 'duty to monitor and report on financial sustainability' of these HEPs (s68) and carrying out 'studies for improving economy, efficiency and effectiveness' in their management (s69). The OfS is required to spell out its 'regulatory framework' (s75), and it is subject to the 'Secretary of State's power to give directions' to it (s77) – but he/she is obliged in giving any such directions to 'have regard to the need to protect the institutional autonomy' of HEPs (as again defined as in s8 and s36). The Act then ensures that HEFCE 'ceases to exist' (s81) and also OFFA (s82) before going on to create the UKRI to cover the research side of the HE industry.

And so the OfS has duly issued its 'regulatory framework' as required to do under s75 of HERA17, entitled 'Securing student success' (February 2018, OfS 2018.01). It intends to be 'a world-leading regulator' of 'a world-leading higher education sector', while 'working for positive outcomes in the student interest' – 'promoting social mobility [and] inspiring teaching, and contributing to economic growth'. Also 'prospective students' will get better information for making 'informed choices'. The OfS 'bold, student-focussed, risk-based approach' to regulation is set out; and the various obligations upon it under HERA are unpacked, as well as its HERA powers/sanctions being explained. The Register is introduced, along with the 'conditions' for registration and for remaining registered – and there is discussion of the OfS's process to grant DAPs and how it intends to control use of the word 'university'. The conditions take up pp. 86–148, covering, inter alia: Condition A1 re the 'Access and participation plan'; Conditions B1-5 re 'Quality and standards'; B6 re the TEF; C1 re 'Guidance on consumer protection law' (the HEP must get its own and apply it!); C2 on a 'Student complaints scheme'; C3 on a 'Student protection plan'; D on 'Financial viability and sustainability'; E1/2/3 on 'Public interest governance' and aspects of 'Accountability'; the Fs re transparency and information flows; G1 on charging tuition fees and G3 re OfS fees. Annexes spell out the 'public interest governance principles', and give more information on the procedure for seeking DAPs.

Closely following the OfS has issued its 'Strategy 2018 to 2021' (April 2018, OfS 2018.19) – it stresses that is indeed the Office FOR Students, aiming at their getting 'a high quality academic experience' and at ensuring 'their interests are protected while they study or in the event of provider, campus or course closure'; and the OfS will also ensure that 'their qualifications hold their value over time' and that they 'receive value for money'. It will be 'uncompromising in intervening to prevent poor quality provision, behaviour or performance that damages students' or public interests'. Similarly the OfS has issued a 'Business plan 2018–19' (OfS 2018.18) which, inter alia, hopes to 'address known barriers to entry' by new HEPs into the HE industry ('identify and remove barriers to competition' and 'facilitate new and alternative forms of provision'), as well as both intending to refine the SPP concept ready for any 'market exit' by HEPs and also hoping to 'develop approach to student contracts' (which might, presumably, include considering the case as set out above for a standardised *HEP-S* contract?). In line with being expected by the Secretary of State to tackle HE's wicked issues as listed above, the OfS plan includes 'develop approaches to ensure the reliability of degree standards' and 'develop OfS approach to value for money for students' – and 'promote restraint and accountability in senior staff remuneration' (as perhaps its most ambitious challenge!). Finally, OfS 2018.26 (June 2018) provides 'Regulatory advice' re 'preparing and publishing financial statements' – and requires 'disclosures about senior staff pay' along with 'a justification for the total remuneration package for the head of the provider' and also detailed explanations of any 'severance payments' (the media furore of 2017/18 has not been just about the overall high salaries of some VCs but also the massive level of 'compensation' a few have received for retiring early). The 'advice' covers in addition 'corporate governance' and the need for 'a statement of the responsibilities of the governing body'.

In conclusion, it is hoped that this chapter has explained the shift to a (quasi-) market in English HE that, notably in terms of the introduction and then ratcheting up of undergraduate tuition fees, has created the student-consumer whose interests government, via HERA17 and the establishment of the OfS, is now seeking to protect against HEPs acting as businesses inevitably do in unregulated markets – the economics of HE and the economic model of the university engendering such producer-oriented practices as in any other area of economic activity. Hence the provider state, having retreated from direct funding of HE, becomes the regulatory state that establishes an agency, the OfS, with a brief to tackle the HE industry's wicked issues which it appears unable to even acknowledge let alone address by self-regulation. Only time will tell if the OfS – via its use of the regulatory conditions as part of the powers given to it under HERA17 – can get HEP Councils and Boards (and their lay-member majority memberships) to fully engage with such issues as excessive remuneration for some VCs and senior management teams, consistency of teaching delivery, grade and degree inflation, the marketing-hype of and dubious recruitment practices to courses, the student/graduate's concern that HE seems poor VfM, the need for a standardised HEP-S contract that helps engender the informed HE applicant and the empowered student-consumer. In an ideal world the HE industry via its trade-body as the UUK and its Committee of University Chairs (CUC) will respond openly (even proactively) to a concerted effort of all linked agencies (not just the OfS but also the CMA, ASA and CA/Which?) as well as key stakeholders such as the NUS (and perhaps most powerful of all, Mumsnet, as the next cohort of 18–21-year-olds reach HE . . .).

Meanwhile, of course the politics of HE may change suddenly and dramatically – the pendulum between government provision or market provision may swing: although Grauwe (2016) argues that 'a mixture will always be required'

(p. xiii); see on markets also Palfreyman and Tapper (2014, chapters 4 and 5). The Augar Review of the £9,250 tuition fee may propose a reduction, perhaps to achieve a long-needed shift of priority from HE towards neglected and under-funded FE (Further Education) and even take the nation towards a more strategic concept of (HE + FE =) TE delivery. There may be a change of government and a return to free public good HE so that the English experiment with HE tuition fees over almost 20 years will fade into history as a policy blip along with memories of 'a body corporate called the Office for Students' as created by a repealed Higher Education and Research Act.

References

Arum, R. and Roksa, J. (2011) *Academically Adrift: Limited Learning on College Campuses.* The University of Chicago Press: Chicago.

Barry, D., Jenkins, E., Sumnall, C., Douglas-Jones, B. and Lloyd, D. (2016) *Blackstone's Guide to the Consumer Rights Act 2015.* Oxford University Press: Oxford.

Brown, R. (2013) *Everything for Sale? The Marketisation of UK Higher Education.* SRHE/Routledge: Abingdon.

Busch, L. (2017) *Knowledge for Sale: The Neoliberal Takeover of Higher Education.* The MIT Press: Cambridge (MA).

Collini, S. (2012) *What are Universities For?* Penguin: London.

Davies, M. (2014) *The Law of Professional Immunity.* Oxford University Press: Oxford.

Farrington, D. and Palfreyman, D. (2012) *The Law of Higher Education.* Oxford University Press: Oxford.

Grauwe, P. de (2016) *The Limits of the Market: The Pendulum between Government and Market.* Oxford University Press: Oxford.

Halsey, A.H. (1992) *Decline of Donnish Dominion: The British Academic Profession in the Twentieth Century.* Oxford University Press: Oxford.

Heller, D.E. and Callender, C. (Eds) (2013) *Student Financing of Higher Education: A Comparative Perspective.* Routledge: Abingdon.

Hodges, C. and Steinholtz, R. (2017) *Ethical Business Practice and Regulation: A Behavioural and Values-Based Approach to Compliance and Enforcement.* Hart Publishing: Oxford.

Land, R. and Gordon, G. (2013) *Enhancing Quality in Higher Education: International Perspectives.* Routledge: Abingdon.

Martin, R.E. (2011) *The College Cost Disease: Higher Cost and Lower Quality.* Edward Elgar: Cheltenham.

McMahon, W.W. (2009) *Higher Learning, Greater Good: The Private and Social Benefits of Higher Education.* The Johns Hopkins University Press: Baltimore.

Moodie, G.C. and Eustace, R. (1974) *Power and Authority in British Universities.* George Allen & Unwin: London.

Palfreyman, D. and Tapper, T. (2014) *Reshaping the University: The Rise of the Regulated Market in Higher Education.* Oxford University Press: Oxford.

Palfreyman, D. and Temple, P. (2017) *Universities and Colleges: A Very Short Introduction.* Oxford University Press: Oxford.

Palfreyman, D., Tapper, T. and Thomas, S. (Eds) (2018) *Towards the Private Funding of Higher Education: Ideological and Political Struggles.* Routledge: Abingdon.

Phillips, S.D. and Kinser, K. (2018) *Accreditation on the Edge: Challenging Quality Assurance in Higher Education*. The Johns Hopkins University Press: Baltimore.

Riesman, D. (1958) *Constraint and Variety in American Education*. Doubleday Anchor Books: New York.

Riesman, D. (1980, reissued 1998) *On Higher Education: The Academic Enterprise in an Era of Rising Student Consumerism*. Transaction Publishers: New Brunswick.

Scott, R.A. (2018) *How University Boards Work*. The Johns Hopkins University Press: Baltimore.

Shattock, M. (2006) *Managing Good Governance in Higher Education*. Open University Press: Maidenhead.

Shattock, M. (2010) *Managing Successful Universities*. SRHE & Open University Press: Maidenhead.

Shattock, M. (Ed.) (2014) *International Trends in University Governance: Autonomy, Self-Government and the Distribution of Authority*. Routledge: Abingdon.

Tapper, T. and Palfreyman, D. (2010) *The Collegial Tradition in the Age of Mass Higher Education*. Springer: Dordrecht.

Tapper, T. and Palfreyman, D. (2011) *Oxford, the Collegiate University: Conflict, Consensus and Continuity*. Springer: Dordrecht.

Willetts, D. (2017) *A University Education*. Oxford University Press: Oxford.

Part IV

Elements of governance

Public good(s), public benefit and the public interest

A critical examination of three public purposes of English universities

Adam Dawkins

Introduction

A critical examination of three public purposes of English higher education (HE) forms the focus of this chapter. National differences abound in the definitions and characteristics of public universities and colleges as set by the relevant governments and/or states. Locating the discussion in this chapter in the context of England will be underpinned by the Office for Students (OfS) taxonomy of 'approved' and 'approved fee cap' institutions from the Securing Student Success: Regulatory Framework for Higher Education in England (2018), and those elements of the system to which registered providers have access, namely student support funding for tuition fees and loans across both approved categories, and publicly funded teaching and research grants for the vast majority of mainstream providers registered under the approved fee cap category.

The first of the three purposes identified is the 'public good' role of universities which, historically, refers to those values intrinsic to an institution's founding mission enshrined in its governing instruments, namely the pursuit and advancement of knowledge through education and enquiry. It will be argued that any definition of the public good contribution of universities, and stakeholder expectations of this, has shifted as part of changing regulatory and funding conditions. The second purpose is the 'public benefit' inherent in most 'public' universities' powers or 'objects', in the currency of charity legislation. The public benefit concept is located in the Charities Act 2006 in England and Wales, and relates to the intended outcomes for beneficiaries of a university performing its charitable purposes. The third purpose is the 'public interest', as an obligation or duty to general public accountability for a HE provider's performance and value, which it will be argued here, is deployed through tests such as the Freedom of Information Act (FoIA) 2000, principally to satisfy government and media and self-selecting scrutineers' priorities for the societal contribution of universities.

It will be argued as the focus of this chapter that whilst several commentators have traced the evolution of the public good as contributed by universities (Calhoun, 2006; Nixon, 2011; Marginson, 2011), its examination and interaction with the other two public purposes has not been undertaken. The starting point for a discussion is that the three public purposes elude shared understanding.

Whilst the public interest and public benefit each has a statutory basis, the two terms do not have definitions in law. A symptom of this is an insufficient understanding and assessment of the three purposes on both an individual and collective bases, risking incoherence across policy formulation, regulatory development and local institutional interpretation and delivery. An intended outcome of this chapter in examining the three purposes is a potential to support more effective policy development and institutional engagement, given a moral and civic obligation on university executive management teams and governing body actors to exemplify the public good, and their legal obligations to uphold the public interest and deliver public benefit. The author contends that a critical examination of these purposes might extend an understanding of universities' role in government and third sector policy-making, and a wider public consciousness, and their place as anchor institutions contributing to host community stability and economic growth in times of volatility and downturn (Goddard and Kempton, 2016).

A paradox which presents itself is the increasing 'publication' (i.e. rendering of the public status and place) of universities in political, regulatory and media discourses at a juncture where the 'neo-liberal' university (Olssen and Peters, 2007; Collini, 2012; Rustin, 2017) is potentially at its height as 'providers' adopt the traits of corporate entities through their governance and leadership structures and business models. The adoption of corporate characteristics by higher education institutions (HEIs) which are regarded as principally public bodies in many stakeholders' perceptions is largely driven by market pressures and the regulatory apparatus within which they are required to operate in order to be registered and recognised, and feature a reduced reliance on public funding of the sector and as a consequence, a parallel escalation in financial growth and revenue generation and diversification beyond tuition fee income, and the centralised control and standardisation of performance management frameworks for 'academic' activities. An intensification of the public scrutiny of providers is evident in the stances and responses of various governmental and societal actors. To illustrate, provisions enacted by the Higher Education and Research Act 2017 for the OfS to assume intervention powers over providers, will be implemented by the OfS Regulatory Framework through the 'formal sanctions' (2018, p. 53) of monetary penalties through to deregistration for breaches of the registration conditions. Robust ministerial commentary and mainstream and education-specific media and taxpayer scrutiny is signalled by criticism of the sector or specific institutions in relation to vice-chancellor remuneration, academic staff gender and racial pay and progression disparities and socio-economic and racial iniquities in undergraduate admissions to elite universities. The existence of greater accountability of universities to public opinion is arguably marked by a parallel diminution of societal deference to universities, along with other national 'public' institutions such as the BBC and museums (Kogan and Hanney, 2000). Simultaneously we are arguably witnessing further exhibiting of what Sennett (1976) terms the 'public problem', as the degraded status of public life, whereby any former value placed by the state and citizens on the sociability and richness of exchange in the public sphere is reduced to 'a matter of formal obligation' (p. 3). These perspectives resonate with the view posited throughout this chapter that the three public purposes for English HE risk being figured and measured in perfunctory and transactional terms as 'functions' of a market regulated environment, rather than a broader set of constructive and beneficial outcomes of universities' educational and civic purposes.

Ideological influences on the public function of universities

Ideological drivers for the shift in the public perception of (and the public status of) universities across successive government policy merits discussion, including the New Public Management (NPM) inaugurated by the Conservative governments of the 1980s administration and which can be traced through to New Labour administrations. NPM sought to increase effectiveness and value for money across public services, with universities not exempt from a reforming regime (Deem *et al.*, 2007) importing the 'rhetoric and practices of business efficiency' (Bargh *et al.*, 1996, p. 8) into HE. The Steering Committee on Efficiency Studies in Higher Education (the 'Jarratt Report') (1985) embodies the tenets of NPM, by recommending reduced authority for what were perceived as dominant and unwieldy senates (to focus solely on academic standards and policy), the development of strategic and resource-savvy councils and chief executive style vice-chancellors. This shift in the culture and configuration of university governance, whilst at best gradually instituted (even now), formed a precursor to a neo-liberal emphasis on the market as part of a system of 'academic capitalism' (Slaughter and Leslie, 1999) or 'knowledge capitalism' (Burton-Jones, 2001).

The majority of 'insider' (i.e. academic staff) commentators on a neo-liberal agenda for HE, trace its detrimental influence on the public ethos and identity of universities, through the 'ascendancy of industrial over democratic and old humanist conceptions of what education should be' (Rustin, 2017, p. 160). The damaging impact of accountability, audit and performance management regimes on academic staff agency, through the measurement and surveillance of academic quality and standards or research performance, are voiced in these perspectives (Shore and Wright, 1999; Morley, 2003). Henkel (2005) charts a decline in a 'communitarian' ideal (which connotes a common good ethos of academic staff) and a breakdown of disciplinary and departmental entities which had characterised academic identities and communities prior to the major policy reform of the 1980s, 1990s and into the new millennium. It is unclear, however, whether the principal intention or outcome of academic staff autonomy is to support a wider public good, or is self-serving for scholarly actors and communities. More recently, Collini (2012) argues that a market-led model of HE threatens the intrinsic values of learning and scholarship and that there is minimal evidence of significant benefits for graduates, research quality or enterprise growth. Commentators adopting the above perspectives seldom acknowledge the positive outcomes of a shift from a collegial to a corporate culture in HE, whether in the form of universities' improved ability to build knowledge and human capital, the innovative capacity of the private or public sector organisations through learning, research and enterprise, or the maximised contribution a more centralised institutional approach to research might make in responding to global challenges (Pusser *et al.*, 2012), such as identified in the Department for Business, Energy and Industrial Strategy's UK Industrial Strategy (2018). In contrast, this chapter adopts a stance which eschews arbitrary and absolutist critiques of the state, the market, or neo-liberal or (new) managerialist institutional governance and leadership structures. However, the author acknowledges the ubiquity of a state-regulated market for HE (Palfreyman and Tapper, 2014) and argues that the public purposes feed into, and are reshaped through, regulatory and policy discourses upholding government priorities for how universities can more effectively engage with and help society. These dynamics will be traced later in the policy discourses section of this chapter.

The public(s) of the university

The 'public', as a prefix to the 'good', 'benefit' and 'interest' contributions of universities, raises questions around which constituencies comprise those public(s) (Calhoun, 2006). The public ranges from direct beneficiaries of HE as will be discussed in the section on public benefit, to wider populations with an interest or societal stake in universities. A non-exhaustive set of publics includes:

- students as applicants, learners, consumers of education and support and advice services;
- parents and other sponsors;
- alumni as ambassadors, mentors and employers of students, and donors;
- current academic and professional support staff;
- future graduate employers;
- research, innovation and knowledge exchange and enterprise partners;
- placement providers for students and staff;
- government and non-departmental government bodies such as the OfS and Research England;
- sector bodies and other co-regulators;
- policy-makers;
- taxpayers.

Insufficient scope exists here to examine the application and adaptation of corporate governance theories to key institutional actors in the university sector (Massy, 2010). However, application of stakeholder theories of the company (Freeman, 1984) to universities provides a lens through which to view the range of 'publics' to which universities should have regard. In turn, legitimacy theory (Dowling and Pfeffer, 1975) lends itself to examining the multiple publics of the university, in its focus on organisations' strategies to secure societal legitimacy by displaying behaviours and performing actions which are 'desirable, proper or appropriate within some socially constructed systems of norms, values and beliefs' (Suchman, 1995, p. 574). Shedding light on the public purposes of universities provides a potential means for universities to better understand their engendering of multiple stakeholders' trust, confidence and forms of support. As expected of private sector companies, universities' achievements need not be solely altruistic given the pressures of operating in a competitive marketplace to recruit and retain high-calibre students and staff. The evolving nature of the public good will now be examined.

Public and private good(s)

The contribution of universities to the public good is not a recent notion, seen in Lockean conceptions of education's pivotal role in the peace and safety of peoples, or the Humboldtian ideal of a holistic university education, straddling arts and sciences disciplines and embracing research to create active and informed citizens, bringing benefits to wider society. A public good mission is compatible with private origins or objectives, as illustrated by the philanthropic industrialists, instrumental in the founding and funding of many nineteenth-century redbrick and civic HEIs in England with aim of providing working class and mercantile access to education, which 'until the introduction of the post-1945 welfare state, private contributions towards English institutions of higher education were both generous and essential' (Pellew, 2012, p. 203). In more recent history, the public good role of universities is charted in government policy, starting with the Robbins Report (the report of the Committee on Higher Education) (1963) recommending the expansion of access to universities for young people' and the associated 'general social ends' (p. 22) to be 'served' by HE, and 'the transmission of a common culture and common standards of citizenship'. The Report aspires to universities entering into a compact with another social institution – the family – to create a 'background of culture and social habit on which a healthy society depends' (p. 28).

Policy discourses around the public good

Following a move from an elite to a mass HE system, the framing of the public good purposes of universities shifts under a New Labour, neo-liberal model for HE. Policy of this period positions universities as anchor institutions in civil society, whilst simultaneously requiring them to operate as 'hybrid organizations' (Menard, 2004) spanning public, private and third sector spheres, as quasi-corporate bodies (Olssen and Peters, 2007) operating in a regional, national and global marketplace. The National Committee of Enquiry into Higher Education (the 'Dearing Report') (1997) echoes the Robbins ambition for universities to harness national moral and spiritual well-being, as social agents inculcating and transmitting citizenship and culture in a 'learning society'. However, this is not treated as an end in itself, as its purpose is to advance 'the economic wellbeing of the nation, localities and individuals' and, under this new compact, 'be account-able to students and society' (para 1.4, p. 8). This neo-liberal focus on individu-alism and enterprise is inscribed in the Dearing Report and, alongside its claims for HE's role in national economic advancement, the 'public good' purpose of universities is secondary as a result of its privileging of 'private economic gains for which students become investors in their own stock of human capital' (Williams, 2014, p. 624). The casting of the student as an economic actor engaging more rationally and tactically in their HE experience, upheld the recommendation in the report that undergraduates should contribute to the cost of their own tuition fees. Leathwood and O'Connell (2003) capture the contradiction between the New Labour 'dominant discourse of widening participation' (p. 597) in HE and the introduction of student tuition fees and the potential barriers for working-class applicants' access this inaugurated.

Subsequent major HE policy reform comprise barely distinguishable ministe-rial forewords making the case for the public contribution of universities, but which serve as prefaces to an imperative to drive economic competitiveness. This is evident in the then Department for Business, Innovation and Skills (BIS) HE White Paper (2016), which echoes the Robbins rhetoric of universities' social transformation role with the principal purpose of driving competition, student choice and economic growth. It constitutes a policy embodiment of the shift from a subservient (but deferent) status for universities 'serving' the public good, to commodified bodies 'among the most valuable national assets, underpinning both a strong economy and a flourishing society'.

This window into the placement of public good discourses in HE policy, and their interweaving with market orientations, marks a change in government and societal expectations of universities, and the articulation of a new narrative about what 'excellence' and 'value' means. Nixon (2011) regards this shift as a sign of the 'public in retreat' in the HE sector, and the loss of 'something intrinsically good and worthwhile about higher education regardless of its extrinsic goods and costs' (preface, p. 2). This perspective presents a neo-liberal narrative around the 'hollowing out' of state championing and subsidisation of public institutions (Rhodes, 1994), including universities. Other critics observe universities mov-ing from operating in 'The Public Good' to a commoditised and instrumental function to produce 'public goods' (Marginson, 2011; Watson, 2013, p. 28). In current terms, such 'products' include the Teaching Excellence Framework (TEF) measures on attainment volumes for 'good honours' degrees and 'highly-skilled' graduate employment. Universities' capacity to generate commercially oriented, employable graduates is becoming a mainstream expectation of govern-ment and consumers, with cohorts of graduates entering professions serving the public interest as a diminishing sub-set of this. A challenging question remains around whether, and how, the public good purpose for HE is best protected when globalisation is driving the 'private goods' of a university education (St. John, 2005), which economic theory informs us would mean that choice and access to the social and economic capital derived from a university education is rivalrous, and therefore not universally accessible despite the rhetoric of 'competition equals choice' in a system characterised by reputation, consumerism and the corollary of cost to the student as direct beneficiaries of that education. However, it can be argued that any dual role for HE to deliver, or as a minimum, contribute to, public and private goods is not incompatible, and regarding them as such is built on a neo-classical economics fallacy which neglects a positive co-existence between 'private economic enrichment' for graduates and local and global public goods (Marginson, 2007). McMahon (2009) provides examples of the private benefits of a university education, namely better health outcomes and financial prospects and management after graduation and across the life course, which also contribute to a wider social good.

In the sphere of research, ongoing debates about research impact and the future shape for the Research Excellence Framework (REF) 2021, provide parallel examples of the complex and, for the most part, constructive co-operation of public and private goods, despite many critics remaining fundamentally opposed to any performance-based mechanism to measure in the short term, quantify and allocate an economic and social value to the impact of research. The potential positive outcomes of an endeavour to identify the impact of research, to improve its reach and help focus finite university financial resources, staff, infrastructure and materials (whether funded through public or private sources) where these could yield the most benefit to society, health, the environment, the economy. A collective good aspect of research influencing and helping inform public policy to improve the lives of society at large, co-exists with the impact of research on healthcare interventions, for example, which transform the outcomes of individual citizens, which may be the produce of decades of research or an intervention. In turn, the private goods and benefits of institutional reward, recognition and promotion, and wider recognition for academic staff who prosper in an institutional environment valuing research impact should not be overlooked. Alongside this, the REF 2021 consultation on the Draft Guidance on Submissions (2018) recommendation to build critical mass by linking the number of impact case studies submitted to the volume of full-time equivalent (FTE) REF returned staff, is intended to embed and extend unit-level and institutional research cultures attuned to research impact, and seek to maximise a contribution to the public good.

The relative nature of the public good role of universities (Calhoun, 2006) is evident in the variant values placed on it by governments and societies, stemming back to national psyches or political legacies, and how this is regulated and enacted. As an illustration, free tuition fees in publicly-funded universities and state university colleges in Norway reflects the esteem in which tertiary education is regarded as a wider social good, contributing to 'human purposefulness in creating a society of active citizens rather than passive subjects' (Nixon, 2011, p. 115). Another Northern European example is the Swedish Act on Amendment of the Higher Education Act 2013, which requires universities to promote sustainable development for a sound and healthy environment for current and future generations, social welfare and justice, gender equality and a promotion of understanding of other countries. The apex of the public good potential of universities is evident in post-Apartheid South Africa where this is regarded as an obligation, pivotal to the redressing of entrenched racial and social injustices. The Higher Education Act 101 of 1997 legislates for each public university to establish an 'institutional forum' to play an influential role in advising council, senate and student representative councils on race and gender equality, and holding university councils and senior management to account in ensuring that tolerance, respect and fundamental human rights are upheld. It is unclear whether this statutory requirement to build diversity and equity safeguards into universities' governance and leadership structures is fully effective in bringing about positive change within universities and society in South Africa. However, it represents a more transparent and targeted inclusivity intervention than the general obligations of the public sector equality duty in the Equality Act 2010 in the UK, as applied to universities and other bodies under the somewhat ambiguous banner of 'public authorities'.

The benefits of public benefit?

Delivery of the public benefit applies to those universities (the majority) which are 'exempt' charities, where direct registration with, and reporting to, the Charity Commission in England and Wales is dispensed with, and the minority of universities as directly registered charities. 'Public benefit' is not defined in the Charities Act 2011, beyond a 'public benefit requirement' (s4 (1)). Whilst Lord Hodgson regarded introduction of the requirement as a lever to explicitly 'encourage charities to consider how they deliver the public benefit' (in Walker and Blake, 2016, p. 15), its definition or delivery is not well-understood, despite Charity Commission guidance on its measurement and assessment. There is broad, if not full consensus, that the 2011 Acts (and its 2006 predecessor) removed the presumption that public benefit was automatically delivered by virtue of undertaking their core functions, including universities, who are required to demonstrate how their stated charitable purposes operate for the public benefit.

The most obvious of the 12 charitable purposes delivered by universities, disclosed by default in universities' public benefit reporting structures, is the 'advancement of education', which under s3(1)(b) of the Act, extends beyond the formal transmission of knowledge to include 'an individual's intellectual, physical, emotional and spiritual capabilities' (Charity Commission, 2008, p. 13). The frame of beneficiaries is arguably honed for universities in the context of widening participation, access and tuition fees, which is statutorily defensible for safeguarding universities' charitable status given that the 'public(s)' benefiting from charitable activities can be restricted to a sub-section of the public, which in the case of universities is predominantly its student beneficiaries.

However, the complex histories, missions and activities of universities as social institutions mean that they support a much wider range of charitable purposes, which the Higher Education Funding Council for England (HEFCE) (the predecessor funding council and regulator to the OfS) termed 'secondary' but which rather than subordinate activities, have a potentially powerful and positive influence and impact, such as the 'advancement of health and the saving of lives', the 'advancement of religion' for a sub-set of universities with ecclesiastical origins (which could be re-imagined to refer to the promotion of inter-faith dialogue), through to the advancement of amateur sport for students, staff and the community and the 'advancement of the arts, culture, heritage or science' through public lecture programmes and university theatres, galleries and museums. The increasing re-alignment, and in some cases re-branding of, universities' research agendas and activities to respond to global societal themes or 'Grand Challenges' (e.g. UCL, Exeter, Bath, Surrey) may be driven by government policy priorities for research impact and maximising access to external research funding. However, it also serves to underscore and advance the contribution of university research to the wider suite of charitable purposes in relation to health, life-saving, the relief of poverty, justice and human rights.

In turn, a signal of the perfunctory and transactional basis on which public purposes are being treated and enacted in universities in a market-regulated context, is evident in public benefit reporting requirements through HEFCE and, since 2018, the OfS as 'principal regulator' of exempt charity universities, in place to demonstrate accountability for the public funding received by universities and tax exemptions enjoyed by virtue of this status. The reporting requirements include the production and sign-off by university councils or boards of governors as the trustee bodies, of a public benefit statement located in the annual report and financial statements.

The extent to which the public benefit statements provide substantial commitment and evidence of delivering positive outcomes for students and graduates as the principal beneficiary populations of universities is difficult to measure. Most universities' public benefit statements, in a context of evidencing access and participation plans, devote attention to the financial quantum of bursaries and scholarships expenditure, and widening access initiatives to support students from less advantaged backgrounds, with scant attention paid to the wider transformative value of education for individuals, and how a university education contributes to wider social goods. The public benefit statement's retrospective and confirmatory compliance with charity law is often regarded as 'an afterthought of strategic and financial reporting' (Dawkins, 2017, p. 23), with minimal evidence that the narratives are comprehensively reviewed by university governing bodies as trustee boards charged with their annual sign-off. Going forward, the continued relevance of a narrow statutory application of the public benefit for universities requires examination. One area of focus might be the requirement that the detriment or harm resulting from a charitable purpose activity must not outweigh its benefits, which may become increasingly challenging for university trustee boards to demonstrate in a context of rising student debt and whether a return on their investment is realised post-graduation, in terms of study progression or graduate level employment. However, the capacity of university trustee boards to engage in such balancing exercises is predicated on a well-developed understanding of their universities' status as charities and their stewardship duties as trustees. There is limited evidence to indicate that the trustee aspects of university governorship are well understood by the role-holders or senior management teams. This is unsurprising given that the charitable status of universities, and the trustee role of governing body members is at best implicit in effectiveness frameworks to evaluate university governance arrangements, such as the 'enablers of effective governance' and the measures under the 'commitment to organisational vision, culture and values' enabler developed for the HE sector by the Leadership Foundation for Higher Education (LFHE)[1] (2009).[2]

Con(testing) the public interest

This chapter concurs with Birkland's diagnosis that the 'public interest' is at best heterogeneous and is shaped by diverse interest groups involved in policy-forming, from government, mission groups, trades or students' unions through to 'unofficial actors' including the media (2015, p. 134). For the HE sector, the public interest is 'fuzzy enough to be co-opted by other sides of the argument' (Rammell, 2016, p. 8), namely those who consider that universities appropriately uphold it, and critics who do not. An Economic and Social Research Council (ESRC) project sought to advance an understanding of the public interest as a 'troubled idea' for courts and many areas of 'civil service business' (Anthony et al., 2011). Whilst universities were outside the project scope, universities are caught in a range of public interest tests to be undertaken in being a part of the public administration landscape, in being incorporated as either a chartered body, by an Act of Parliament, a Higher Education Corporation (HEC) or a guarantee company. However, the statutory bases of the public interest are sporadic (and undefined) across a range of legislation as these apply to universities, from the FoIA, through to the public sector equality duty, public interest disclosure (whistleblowing) and employment or procurement legislation as applied to public contracting authorities. Alongside this, many governing bodies and senior management teams commit to upholding the Seven Principles of Public Life (1995) as developed and periodically reviewed by the Committee on Standards in Public Life, and an augmentation of accountabilities witnessed through the OfS 'public interest' governance conditions, including the requirement to assess key governance and leadership actors as 'fit and proper' persons to hold office.

Continuing the theme presented at the start of this chapter that the public purposes of the universities is constituted on an increasingly transactional basis in a market regulated environment, it is argued that there is reduced expectation for universities to act in the public interest by performing responsible and socially desirable actions, to act instead as a public 'interest'. The prepositional shift from 'in' to 'as' may be subtle, but the latter positioning marks universities out as assets in which media, government, funders and student beneficiaries, recast as consumers, expect to have a stake.

The status of universities as public bodies

Examining the public dimensions and status of universities is made more complex when read in conjunction with an unclear statutory definition of the public interest, and: (1) debates around the public dimensions of universities' corporate structures; and (2) their principal sources of public/private revenue. Addressing the legal form of universities first, the majority of UK pre-1992 HEIs were incorporated by, or have subsequently been granted, a Royal Charter by the Privy Council, a condition of which is to act in the public interest. The extent to which this historical requirement has heightened the accountability of the chartered corporation universities is questionable, with universities' ability to attract public funding as the principal reason they adhere to public policies (King, 2004). Also, in English law the majority of universities are private institutions, whether their legal structure is as a chartered corporation, a 1988 statutory Higher Education Corporation (HEC) (most of which gained university title in 1992) or a private limited company (Farrington and Palfreyman, 2012). Wider (i.e. non HE-specific) legislation has tended to overlook this position, and relied on universities' receipt of public funds as the basis for justifying their status as public authorities (Palfreyman and Tapper, 2014). The reduced reliance of universities on public funding plays out in debates around the status of Student Loans Company (SLC) support. To illustrate, the government's recent sale of the 2002–6 repayment segment of the student loan book is presented as a value for money exercise for taxpayers through Treasury de-risking for government of long-run loan liabilities associated with partial or non-repayment of loans by graduate borrowers, and subsidised interest rates (Institute for Fiscal Studies, Crawford and Jin, 2014). The irony this presents is that the ostensible promotion of the public interest of the taxpayer through the recouping of Exchequer funds, entails a dilution of the public status of student funding support through private company acquisition of the loan book.

Universities, Freedom of Information and the public interest

Universities deemed public authorities undertake specific judgments through their obligations under the FoIA 2000, applying a public interest test to assess whether to withhold information requested under FoIA, or confirm or deny whether the information is held. Increasingly, accusations have been levied against universities by the media or recognised sector trades unions, for example, of over-reliance on exemptions to disclosure based on flimsy commercial sensitivity arguments. Despite the transparency benefits of FoI, the accountability burden in responding to FoIA requests and whether this represents value for money in the use of university resources (itself a topic of public interest) has been surfaced.[3] In turn, the extent to which information released by universities (and other public authorities) consistently represents the broader public interest is questioned, and that it more regularly reflects a more restricted set of preoccupations and priorities of journalists, researchers or trade unions requestors with specific interests to reinforce or repudiate.

Office for Students (OfS): public interest governance conditions

This section concludes by focusing on the OfS 'public interest' governance principles, which form a condition of registration for approved providers. The conditions represent a codification of requirements with varying degrees of statutory, regulatory or policy precedent. This comprises pre-existing statutory duties around academic freedom and freedom of speech being exercised in universities, formal accountability activities such as risk management, value for money, student engagement, academic governance and the size, composition, diversity, skills mix, and the terms of office and fitness and properness of governing body members and, in the case of the last area, also senior managers. The extent to which these conditions uphold the requirement under HERA 2017 that the OfS operates a 'transparent, accountable, proportionate and consistent' (2(1)g) regulatory regime, or safeguards the institutional autonomy staunchly fought for in the Lords Amendments to the Bill, is doubtful. The OfS conditions exemplify the 'evaluative state' (Neave and van Vught, 1991) espousing remote governmental control of the sector and increased institutional autonomy, whilst intending to 'cleave to central steering' (p. 250) and control.

The interplay between the three public purposes

Freedom of speech

The statutory obligation on universities to enact freedom of speech illustrates the complex interplay between the three public purposes. As stated in the section above, freedom of speech is a public interest governance condition, and the capacity for free, frank and sometimes controversial exchange and debate on campus is also a wider public good, which in turn may provide, or be at odds with, a university's public good, or benefit roles where 'controversial' speakers are permitted (or denied) a platform on campus. The environment in which freedom of speech is enacted is now more complex than when enacted in the Education Act (No. 2) 1986. This includes the interaction of freedom of speech with other legal duties placed on universities by virtue of their public status and standing, including the Equality Act 2010 and the public sector equality duty which applies to universities, and the prevent duty as derived from s26 of the Counter-Terrorism and Security Act 2015, which requires 'scheduled bodies', including universities, to have regard to the need to prevent their students and staff from being drawn into terrorism. The prevent duty requires sensitive judgements and risk assessments around academic freedom of staff and the broader freedom of speech of speakers on (and off) campus, often in relation to students' unions, guilds and associations (and their recognised societies), as predominantly independent, registered charitable entities with democratic and decision-making mechanisms (which may mirror and require escalation up to host university policies), and duty to deliver their charitable purposes for the public benefit of their student members. Reporting in May 2018, the UK Parliament's Joint Committee on Freedom of Speech in Universities, did not uphold allegations of widespread risk aversion of senior management teams on campus which had the effect of suppressing freedom of speech on campus. However, the report concluded that the ability to balance freedom of speech with the related statutory considerations was a challenge for decision-makers.

The 2016 EU referendum

The 2016 referendum on the UK's continued position in the EU provides a case study of the complex and sometimes contradictory relationships between the public good, public benefit and public interest purposes. In relation to this first of these is universities' public good role in providing robust and evidence-based information, opinion and a platform to help inform public opinion on the implications of leaving the EU, drawing on academics in the fields of constitutional and EU law, economics or politics. In turn, many universities hosted and organised debates in the lead-up to the referendum. However, the public good contribution of universities in helping to move forward the debate was arguably weakened, partly as an outcome of their own inward-looking focus on how exiting the EU would affect their own student and staff recruitment from the EU and internationally, the implications for what this meant for EU student loan support, staff visas and European research funding and collaboration. These preoccupations on the implications of EU exit are located in the domain of several OfS public interest governance conditions as discussed earlier, particularly in relation to academic freedom and freedom of speech, with many academics and university heads speaking out in a personal capacity to benefits for their institutions and the sector of the UK remaining within the EU, whilst encouraging staff and student to exercise their vote irrespective of their position.

Specific public interest implications, drawing on FoIA requirements as discussed earlier in the chapter, were played out in Conservative MP and self-proclaimed Eurosceptic Chris Heaton-Harris's 2017 FoIA request that universities disclose the names of professors involved in the teaching of European affairs in relation to Brexit, and access copies of syllabuses and lecture materials for the topic. The request was condemned in part of the sector, on the grounds that it was a rebuttal of academic freedom and institutional autonomy to curricula, and implied a bias in favour of remaining in the EU. Despite these condemnations, the incident invites a wider reflection on what Carl (2017) recently coined 'lackademia' to describe the minority of right-wing perspectives amongst university staff. The extent to which the political make-up of staff populations represents the wider public good or public interest is questionable, given that it does not reflect the more balanced party political affiliations of the general populace. The majority of universities in England maintained a neutral stance in the lead-up to the EU referendum in the context of freedom of speech and institutional impartiality, and instead relied on representative bodies such as Universities UK (UUK) to deliver the message to government and beyond on the benefits for HE of the UK remaining within the EU. However, a minority of the governing bodies of universities, including Northumbria and Kent, adopted a formal, 'corporate' published position on the EU referendum on behalf of the institution in favour of the UK remaining in the EU, directly linked to their status as charitable bodies, based on evidence that doing so would protect and further their institutions' charitable objects to deliver teaching, learning, research collaboration and funding and promote staff and student diversity for the public benefit

Futures for managing the public purposes of universities

The commentators cited in this chapter who chart an onslaught of the hollowing out of the public purposes of universities, are contradicted by national and international examples of (and wider exemplars for) the re-imagining and re-invigoration of the public good, benefit and interest contributions of universities, which appear to work within, rather than in resistance to, market-regulatory frameworks. To illustrate, a changing policy and funding landscape for research and innovation presents new opportunities to configure the public good, and wider conceptions of the public interest and the public benefit. The UK's 2017 Industrial Strategy signals government support for university–industry–civil society collaborations to address Grand Challenges, including Clean Growth and the Ageing Society, as which could realise major long-term public goods and benefits. Prior to this, many world-leading research centres and clusters have well-developed infrastructures to help deliver and govern impact, such as Newcastle University's Public Engagement Committee for its Institute of Genetic Medicine. Sustainable examples of universities adopting a coherent and multi-faculty platforms and focal points include Queen Mary, University of London's (QMUL) Centre for Public Engagement.[4]

An alternative example which merits discussion is the Jubilee Centre for Character and Values in the School of Education at the University of Birmingham, with its stated mission to advance research and practice into virtues and values as integral to the flourishing and development of humanity. The Centre has been influential in public policy domains, including character education in school curricula and the place of virtue, ethics and gratitude informing the development of a range of professional codes of practices. Arguably, intellectually rigorous teaching and learning of this type on the fundamental aspects of virtues and character pushes the boundaries of the contributions universities could make to the public good and well-being outcomes, with the potential for deep and far-reaching social benefits beyond the public good domains of education, and civic contributions.

Avoiding short-termism in demonstrating outcomes and impact should be a consideration of university senior management in the direct and indirect investment of financial resources in public good and engagement activities. Alongside this, the importance of institutions, government and other funders giving credence to the valuable but often unrecognised or ring-fenced roles of universities in an 'informal knowledge economy' should not be understated, including the role of staff and students and alumni in volunteering and social entrepreneurship activities (Hancock *et al.*, 2014, p. 118). The potential for these activities includes enriching teaching, research, enterprise and wider public outreach and engagement and creating bottom-up, meaningful public goods in practice.

An international model for the institutional embedding of public good delivery, for which there are no institutional comparators in English HE, include the Johnathan M. Tisch College of Civic Life at Tufts University in Massachusetts. Dating back to 1954, the philanthropic donations of the eponymous alumnus and trustee of Tisch have helped propel and extend the mission of the College to offer both learning opportunities and extra-curricular programmes for all students including community service, volunteering and funds research and a thriving research programme including the Centre for Information and Research on Civic Learning and Engagement (CIRCLE) in areas including youth democracy and voting.

A system-wide example of the institutional integration of public good and interest governance in Spain's university system is the requirement under the University Reform Law (1983) to convene a *consejo social* (social council) as an organ linking each public university to its social milieu, as a government commitment for universities to act as a 'public service relating to national and regional interests' (Llorent-Vaquero, 2016, p. 13). Whilst the size and composition of social councils vary,[5] common membership include governing board members, teachers, students, administrative staff and municipality external representatives. One part of their remit is to commission studies of university and society relations and award prizes to students and alumni, a diluted equivalent of which is seen in the remit of the (now largely defunct) courts of some English pre-1992 universities. However, *consejo sociales* also oversee the approval of university annual budgets and accounts, strategic planning and academic staff policy, with a greater public-facing orientation and obligation than the councils and boards of English universities in performing similar duties.

In UK HE, institutions' widespread acknowledgement of performance in the key university league tables is evident, as tools influencing reputation, on and offshore student and staff recruitment, research and wider funding and partnering opportunities in a globally competitive environment (King, 2009). However, HEIs are not uncritical participants in such ranking regimes, and are alert to the risks, and short-term possibilities of, performing well in, and 'gaming', league table performance at the expense of sustainable and meaningful outcomes. The footprint of public good and social good activities is not wholly absent component of the rankings machinery, and is evident in the People and Planet University table in the UK, which despite relatively low visibility as a ranking tool, has been a lever for improvements in some HEIs' environmental performance and wider sustainability and social responsibility endeavours. Until public-engagement and social responsibility measures feature in the national and global league tables, including the QS World University Rankings, the strategic importance placed on, and the associated investment in, the public purposes agenda by institutions' governing bodies and executive teams will likely remain limited in a context of competing resource priorities. The subsidiary QS Stars Rating System includes a Social Responsibility measure comprising social obligations, local community investment and environmental components. The majority of the top 200 institutions QS World University Rankings (with exceptions such as RMIT in Melbourne, or Dalhousie in Canada) do not participate in this measure, and it therefore represents a missed opportunity for globally leading universities to positively influence change across HE systems.

Conclusion

The chapter has endeavoured to critically examine three public purposes for English HEIs and the complex and changing societal, statutory and regulatory sources from which each purpose stems, and the consequential troubled and fragmented relationships each one has in relation to universities and each other. The extent to which these factors shape the interpretation and enactment of each sector at sector and institutional level, reveals a fragmented landscape where an overarching and coherent approach to the public purpose of universities is absent, which if in existence might engender greater confidence in the HE sector, and merit the major and continuous contributions to public life which universities make to their communities and society more widely on a daily basis. The chapter concludes by offering up alternative and unifying terminologies for the public good, public benefit and public interest purpose of the HE sector in England. A single conception of the public contribution of universities could be to refer to universities' 'public responsibility' role. This presents an alternative articulation to accommodate the three public purposes, which renders in more neutral terms any moral mission or value judgement applied to universities operating as public 'good', and replaces the inadequate attempts to make universities accountable under public benefit and in the public benefit, with a focus on trust and confidence that universities will seek to do their best by a range of beneficiaries and stakeholders. Any single statutory or regulatory enactment of a public responsibility duty, and associated dismantling and streamlining of the current apparatus examined in this chapter, is not proposed. Instead, the solution may be that the most effective way for universities' public purposes to thrive in a marketised and highly regulated environment is to focus less on the transactional aspects of demonstrating and defending how they operate for the public good, benefit and in its interest, and attend to their contribution as enablers and facilitators of societies' engagement in these purposes through their core purposes of knowledge creation through research and innovation, knowledge dissemination through teaching and civic engagement. Universities' 'public civility' purpose rises to the fore with this facilitative role in mind, to reflect a wider obligation on universities to create the conditions of a free and more just society built on common civility, facts, evidence and allowing controversial and challenging issues to be debated, in a spirit of 'robust civility'[6] (Garton Ash, 2016) as a precondition of free speech. The potential of universities as sites where discourse is created, consumed, communicated and contested through teaching, research, enterprise and freedom of speech, is arguably the most fundamental purpose at what appears to be a critical juncture of public life and civil society.

Notes

1 LFHE became part of the new body Advance HE in March 2018.
2 The Higher Education Leadership and Management Survey (HELMs) of governors' views of their institutions, leadership and governance (Greatbatch, 2014) found that 49 per cent of respondents' motivations for becoming a governor was to contribute to society. The status of universities as a charity and motivations to become a university trustee does not feature in the survey feedback.
3 The November 2015 HE Green Paper, Fulfilling Our Potential: Teaching Excellence, Social Mobility and Student Choice, cites an estimated cost of HEIs administering FoI requests in excess of £10m annually.
4 QMUL was awarded the Engage Watermark Gold Accreditation from the National Co-ordinating Centre for Public Engagement.
5 For example, the *consejo social* comprises six members at the Autonomous University of Madrid, and 31 members at the Universidad de Salamanca.
6 The Chair of the OfS, Sir Michael Barber, quotes the phrase as a key condition for the sector, in his Foreword to the OfS Regulatory Framework.

References

Anthony, G., Morison, J. and Doukas, D. (2011) Public Interest in UK Courts. Project funded by the Economic and Social Research Council (ESRC). [Accessed on 4 May 2018 at www.publicinterest.info/]

Bargh, C., Scott, P. and Smith, D. (1996) *Governing Universities: Changing the Culture?* SRHE and Open University Press: Buckingham, UK.

Birkland, T.A. (2015) *An Introduction to the Policy Process: Theories, Concepts, and Models of Public Policy Making* (3rd edition). M.E. Sharpe: New York and London.

Burton-Jones, A. (2001) *Knowledge Capitalism: Business, Work, and Learning in the New Economy.* Oxford University Press: Oxford.

Calhoun, C. (2006) The University and the Public Good. *Thesis Eleven*, Volume 84, Issue 1, pp. 7–43.

Carl, N. (2017). Lackademia: Why do Academics Lean Left? Adam Smith Institute. [Accessed on 3 July 2018 at www.adamsmith.org/research/lackademia-why-do-academics-lean-left]

Charities Act 2011. [Accessed on 8 July 2018 at www.legislation.gov.uk/ukpga/2011/25/contents]

The Charity Commission for England and Wales (2008) The Advancement of Education for the Public Benefit. [Accessed on 8 July 2018 at https://assets.publishing.service. gov.uk/government/uploads/system/uploads/attachment_data/file/358536/the-advancement-of-education-for-the-public-benefit.pdf]

Collini, S. (2012) *What are Universities?* Penguin Books: London.

Committee on Higher Education (The Robbins Report) (1963) [Accessed on 6 June 2018 at www.educationengland.org.uk/documents/robbins/robbins1963.html]

The Committee of Vice-Chancellors and Principals (CVCP). Jarratt, A. (1985) The Steering Committee for Efficiency Studies in Universities.

Crawford, C. and Jin, W. (2014) Payback Time? Student Debt and Loan Repayments: What Will the 2012 Reforms Mean for Graduates. Institute of Fiscal Studies. [Accessed on 20 July 2018 at www.ifs.org.uk/comms/r93.pdf]

Dawkins, A. (2017) *Trustee Responsibilities in Higher Education: A Guide for Governors*. Leadership Foundation for Higher Education: London.

Deem, R., Hillyard, S. and Reed, M. (2007) *Knowledge, Higher Education, and the New Managerialism: The Changing Management of UK Universities*. Oxford: Oxford University Press.

Department for Business, Energy and Industrial Strategy (2018) Industrial Strategy. [Accessed on 8 July 2018 at www.gov.uk/government/policies/industrial-strategy]

Department for Business, Innovation and Skills (2015) Fulfilling Our Potential: Teaching Excellence, Social Mobility and Student Choice. [Accessed on 8 July 2018 at https://assets.publishing.service.gov.uk/government/uploads/system/uploads/attachment_data/file/474227/BIS-15-623-fulfilling-our-potential-teaching-excellence-social-mobility-and-student-choice.pdf]

Dowling, J. and Pfeffer, J. (1975) Organizational Legitimacy: Social Values and Organizational Behaviour. *Pacific Social Review*, Volume 18, Issue 1, pp. 122–136.

Farrington, D. and Palfreyman, D. (2012) *The Law of Higher Education* (2nd edition). Oxford University Press: Oxford.

Freeman, E.R. (1984) *Strategic Management: A Stakeholder Approach*. Pitman Publishing Imprint: London.

Garton Ash, T. (2016) *Free Speech: Ten Principles for a Connected World*. Atlantic Books: London.

Goddard, J. and Kempton, L. (2016) The Civic University: Universities in Leadership and Management of Place. [Accessed on 3 July 2018 at www.ncl.ac.uk/media/wwwnclacuk/curds/files/university-leadership.pdf]

Greatbatch, D. (2014) Governors' Views of their Institutions, Leadership and Governance. Higher Education Leadership and Management Survey (HELMs). Leadership Foundation for Higher Education (LFHE). [Accessed on 3 July 2018 at www.lfhe.ac.uk/download.cfm/docid/B48920C1-205C-45F4-A105D5A816F54D80]

Hancock, S., Hughes, G. and Walsh, E. (2014) Universities and the Informal Knowledge Economy. In *Universities in the Knowledge Economy: Higher Education Organisation and Global Change*. Ed. P. Temple. Routledge: Oxon, pp. 118–136.

Henkel, M. (2005) Academic Identity and Autonomy in a Changing Policy Environment. *Higher Education*, Volume 49, Issue 1–2, pp. 155–176.

Higher Education Act 101 of 1997. [Accessed on 3 July 2018 at www.che.ac.za/sites/default/files/publications/act101.PDF]

Higher Education and Research Act 2017. [Accessed on 3 July 2018 at www.legislation.gov.uk/ukpga/2017/29/contents/enacted/data.htm]

Jonathan M. Tisch College of Civic Life. [Accessed on 3 July 2018 at https://tischcollege.tufts.edu/]

The Jubilee Centre for Character and Virtues, University of Birmingham. [Accessed on 20 October 2018 at www.jubileecentre.ac.uk].

King, R. (2004) *The University in the Global Age*. Palgrave Macmillan: Basingstoke.

King, R. (2009) *Governing Universities Globally: Organizations, Regulation and Rankings.* Edward Elgar: Cheltenham and Northampton.

Kogan, M. and Hanney, S. (2000) Reforming Higher Education. *Higher Education,* Volume 40, Issue 4, pp. 491–494.

The Leadership Foundation for Higher Education (LFHE) and The Committee of University Chairs (CUC). Schofield, A. (January 2009). *What is an Effective and High Performing Governing Body in UK Higher Education?* [Accessed on 3 July 2018 at www.lfhe.ac.uk/en/governance-new/index.cfm]

Leathwood, C. and O'Connell, P. (2003) 'It's a Struggle': The Construction of the 'New' Student in Higher Education. *Journal of Education Policy,* Volume 18, Issue 6, pp. 597–615.

Llorent-Vaquero, M. (2016) Student Participation in the Governing Bodies of Spanish Universities. *Asian Social Science,* Volume 12, Issue 8, p. 11.

McMahon, W.W. (2009) *Higher Learning, Greater Good: The Private and Social Benefits of Higher Education.* Johns Hopkins University Press: Baltimore.

Marginson, S. (2007) The Public/Private Divide in Higher Education: A Global Revision. *Higher Education,* Volume 53, Issue 3, pp. 307–333.

Marginson, S. (2011) Higher Education and Public Good. *Higher Education Quarterly,* Volume 65, Issue 4, pp. 411–433.

Massy, W. (2010) Managerial and Political Strategies for Managing Accountability. In *Accountability in Higher Education: Global Perspectives on Trust and Power.* Ed. B. Stensaker and L. Harvey. Routledge: London and New York, pp. 221–224.

Menard, C. (2004) The Economics of Hybrid Organizations. *Journal of Institutional and Theoretical Economics,* Volume 160, pp. 345–376.

Morley, L. (2003) *Quality and Power in Higher Education.* SRHE and Open University Press: Buckingham.

The National Committee of Enquiry into Higher Education (NCIHE). Dearing, R. (1997) Higher Education in the Learning Society. [Accessed on 3 June 2018 at www.leeds.ac.uk/educol/ncihe/]

Neave, G. and van Vught, F.A. (1991) *Prometheus Bound: The Changing Relationship Between Government and Higher Education in Western Europe.* Pergamon Press: Oxford.

Nixon, J. (2011) *Higher Education and the Public Good: Imagining the University.* Continuum International Publishing Group: London and New York.

Office for Students (OfS) (2018) Securing Student Success: Regulatory Framework for Higher Education in England. [Accessed on 2 July 2018 at www.officeforstudents. org.uk/publications/securing-student-success-regulatory-framework-for-higher-edu cation-in-england/]

Olssen, M. and Peters, M.A. (2007) Neoliberalism, Higher Education and the Knowledge Economy: From the Free Market to Knowledge Capitalism. *Journal of Education Policy,* Volume 20, Issue 3, pp. 313–345.

Palfreyman, D. and Tapper, T. (2014) *Reshaping the University: The Rise of the Regulated Market in Higher Education.* Oxford University Press: Oxford.

Pellew, J. (2012) A Metropolitan University Fit for Empire: The Role of Private Benefaction in the Early History of the London School of Economics and Political Science and Imperial College of Science and Technology, 1895–1930. *History of Universities,* Volume 26, Issue 1, pp. 202–245.

Pusser, B., Kempner, K., Marginson, S. and Ordorika, I. (Eds) (2012) *Universities and the Public Sphere: Knowledge Creation and State Building in the Era of Globalisation.* Routledge: New York and Oxon.

Queen Mary, University of London. Public Engagement at Queen Mary. [Accessed on 8 July 2018 at www.qmul.ac.uk/publicengagement/]

Rammell, B. (2016) Protecting the Public Interest in Higher Education. Higher Education Policy Institute, Occasional Paper 15. [Accessed on 4 May 2018 at www.hepi.ac.uk/wp-content/uploads/2016/10/Hepi_Protecting-the-Public-Interest-in-Higher-Education-WEB.pdf]

Rhodes, R.A.W. (1994) The Hollowing Out of the State: The Changing Nature of the Public Service in Britain. *The Political Quarterly*, Volume 65, Issue 2, pp. 138–151.

Rustin, M. (2017) The Neoliberal University and Its Alternatives. *Soundings: A Journal of Politics and Culture*. Project Muse [Accessed on 3 July 2018 at https://muse.jhu.edu/article/627933]

Sennett, R. (1976) *The Fall of Public Man*. Penguin Books: London.

Shore, C. and Wright, S. (1999) Audit Culture and Anthropology: Neo-Liberalism in British Higher Education. *Journal of the Royal Anthropological Institute*, Volume 5, Issue 4, pp. 557–575.

Slaughter, S. and Leslie, L. (1999) *Academic Capitalism: Politics, Policies and the Entrepreneurial University*. Johns Hopkins University Press: Baltimore.

St. John, E.P. (2005) Academic Capitalism and the New Economy: Markets, State, and Higher Education. *Contemporary Sociology: A Journal of Reviews*, Volume 34, Issue 5, pp. 506–507.

Suchman, M.C. (1995) Managing Legitimacy: Strategic and Institutional Approaches. *The Academy of Management Review*, Volume 20, Issue 3, pp. 571 –610.

The Swedish Higher Education Act 2013. [Accessed on 8 July 2018 at www.uhr.se/en/start/laws-and-regulations/Laws-and-regulations/The-Swedish-Higher-Education-Act/]

Walker, A.F. and Blake, J. (Eds) (2016) *The Charities Acts Handbooks: A Practical Guide*. Jordan Publishing Limited: Bristol.

Watson, David (2013) *The Question of Conscience in Higher Education: Higher Education and Personal Responsibility*. Institute of Education Press: London.

Williams, J. (2014) A Critical Exploration of Changing Definitions of Public Good in Relation to Higher Education. *Studies in Higher Education*, Volume 41, Issue 4, pp. 619–630.

Chapter 15

Effectiveness and effectiveness reviews

Andy Shenstone

Introduction

Commissioning a review of institutional governance arrangements is intended to enable the governing body to secure assurance (both for itself and external stakeholders) that the institution's governance structures and processes are fit for purpose against accepted principles and standards.

This chapter considers how institutions ensure that they maximise the benefit to be had from such a review process and examines five key facets:

- The rationale – why review.
- The brief – ensuring that institutional context and priorities shapes the requirement and specification for the review.
- The review process – emphasising the importance of a mixed modes approach that triangulates key sources of evidence and effective external comparisons in securing a rounded insight into salient issues.
- The capabilities and credentials of the review team – aligning your priorities for the review with the experience and skills of the reviewers.
- Embedding a commitment to continuous improvement – applying the insights from independent review into future practice.

Rationale

Why review?

Higher education institutions committed to critical self-reflection and the principles of continuous improvement embrace the opportunity to periodically evaluate their performance.

> Governing bodies need to adopt an approach of continuous improvement to governance, in order to enhance their own effectiveness and provide an example to institutions about the importance of review and evaluation.
> (Committee for University Chairs, 2018a, p. 26)

In England the higher education code of governance also explicitly encourages a degree of externality in the review process. Beyond that it is left to the governing body, and in practice this should mean the Chair (taking advice as necessary from the clerk/secretary), to determine what approach to adopt.

> Governing bodies must conduct a regular, full and robust review of their effectiveness and that of their committees . . . Many governing bodies find an external perspective in this process useful, whether provided by specialist consultants or peer support from other governing bodies.
>
> (Committee for University Chairs, 2018a, p. 26)

Guidance for the UK charity sector is equally clear:

> The board reviews its own performance and that of individual trustees, including the chair. This happens every year, with an external evaluation every three years. Such evaluation typically considers the board's balance of skills, experience and knowledge, its diversity in the widest sense, how the board works together and other factors relevant to its effectiveness.
>
> (Charity Governance Code Steering Group, 2017, Principle 5.82)

An effectiveness review is an important means through which a governing body may engage in proportionate, timely and purposeful self-reflection. The involvement of a third party, whether as part of an institutional panel or as an independent reviewer, should be additive – in terms of skills, experience and objectivity.

> Many thanks for this report. I was delighted to read it, because it both mirrors back to the board their concerns and priorities, and frames them in a way that sees the wider sector and will help us ensure the appropriate benchmarking of our governance. We can work with the entire report as it stands and are grateful also for the practical suggestions as well as the recommendations.
>
> (Vice-Chancellor, writing to an independent reviewer, 2018)

A critical dimension is stakeholder and wider public confidence in the integrity of HE governance. In the UK this clearly includes government and regulatory bodies such as the Office for Students (OfS) in England and the funding bodies in the other home nations. While it is not, in England, an explicit condition of registration with the OfS, there is a requirement for self-assessment against public interest principles.

> Your self-assessment of how your governing documents uphold the public interest governance principles and the extent to which your management and governance arrangements are adequate and effective.
>
> (Office for Students, 2018b, section 4, p. 19)

Self-assessment can be accomplished by stating the institution follows the CUC Code of HE Governance (which requires reviews of the governing body's effectiveness to be carried out every four years).

> If you follow a code of governance you can also use this as evidence (of the effectiveness of management and governance) by describing: the name, date and version of any governance code you follow how long you have used the code . . . outcomes of the most recent effectiveness review of the governing body and any of its committees.
>
> (Office for Students, 2018c, Annex G)

There are other codes (e.g. the UK Corporate Code) that a HE provider may choose to use that are equally valid that also mandate periodic evaluation.

> There should be a formal and rigorous annual evaluation of the performance of the board, its committees, the chair and individual directors. The chair should consider having a regular externally facilitated board evaluation.
>
> (Financial Reporting Council, 2018, 1, p. 9)

While an effectiveness review is not strictly a condition of registration, it is possible that the OfS may correlate a HE provider's governance effectiveness with evidence that they had carried out an effectiveness review. It is also conceivable that the OfS might either reject the provider's application to become registered, or place as a condition of registration that the provider carries out an effectiveness review within a given timeframe.

Public interest in and discourse regarding what constitutes good governance has touched many sectors in recent years. For HE this was especially acute during 2017/18 on the question of Vice-Chancellor (VC) pay which demonstrated how events within individual HE providers have the potential to materially impact the wider sector. It led directly both to extensive press coverage and active intervention from government.

> More robust leadership is needed to address senior pay, the Universities Minister Jo Johnson told representatives from the country's leading higher education institutions at a meeting today. The Minister called on universities to deliver greater transparency and independence of remuneration committees, stricter oversight of severance pay, and the publication of the pay ratio of top to median salaries of all staff.
>
> (Department for Education, 2017)

In response the sector published revised guidance on this important topic (Committee for University Chairs, 2018b). Individually the institutions involved also commissioned their own independent governance reviews, at least one of which has been published (Halpin Partnership, 2018). At the time of writing press interest remains acute.

> The most comprehensive study into university vice-chancellors' pay has demolished their claims that their huge rises are based on performance. It is much rather a benchmarking behaviour where those universities with below average pay increase their VC pay quicker than those with average pay.
>
> (*Telegraph* online, 6 June 2018)

While the UK's HE sector generally enjoys a reputation for good governance, the issues raised regarding the handling of VCs' pay shows that this cannot be taken for granted and the dangers of complacency. Such high-profile cases illustrate how both real and perceived failings in governance can be seized upon by those whose response maybe an inclination to introduce further levers of control/accountability upon the sector. At the very least such issues serve to undermine the public trust in the HE system. At worst they could lead to disproportionate regulatory structures that would undermine institutional autonomy, a cornerstone of the UK's HE system.

The purpose of an effectiveness review is not just therefore an exercise in providing assurance to the governing body and its stakeholders within the institution. Governing bodies must recognise that such reviews also offer an important opportunity for a provider to demonstrate to external stakeholders that institutional governance is both effective and subject to regular and proportionate scrutiny.

It is also important to emphasise that the value of governance effectiveness reviews is promoted in many other sectors other than HE. In the UK examples include the Charity Governance Code, the UK Corporate Governance Code (both previously cited) and the Code for Sports Governance (UK Sport, 2017).

The brief

> 'Would you tell me, please, which way I ought to go from here?'
> 'That depends a good deal on where you want to get to,' said the Cat.
> 'I don't much care where—' said Alice.
> 'Then it doesn't matter which way you go,' said the Cat.
> '—so long as I get SOMEWHERE,' Alice added as an explanation.
> 'Oh, you're sure to do that,' said the Cat, 'if you only walk long enough'.
>
> (Carroll, 2015)

The assessment of what constitutes an effective governing body or otherwise in HE is complex and sometimes contentious. Views range from those who think recent changes to HE governance have been unduly influenced by thinking on governance in other sectors and threaten traditional benefits of collegiality, through to those who believe that governing bodies do not provide sufficient challenge to executive teams. It follows that assessing the effectiveness of individual HE governing bodies can be challenging as widely differing views may be involved about what a governing body should be and what therefore constitutes good governance.

HE (especially that which is publicly funded) can tend to be reflective in character – sometimes to a fault, where a tendency to over analyse can constrain necessary action and impede positive momentum. Conversely the sector jealously (and rightly) guards institutional autonomy. Somewhat ironically this has sometimes led to less attention being given to developing practice outwith HE than might be expected from a sector devoted to the acquisition and transmission of knowledge.

To agree the brief and hence the purpose and focus of an effectiveness review merits careful reflection and quite often demands a degree of iteration. This may involve consideration of some or all of the following variables:

- The character and nature of the institution and the underlying maturity of existing governance arrangements, e.g. is the institution about to seek to secure Taught Degree Awarding Powers, or has it enjoyed the status of being an awarding body for many decades?
- The extent to which the Board has an agreed model of governance it wishes to deploy.
- The timing of the review – has it been triggered by a specific event or is it taking place as part of an ongoing process of evaluation?
- Whether the review is to build on a previous exercise (and any recommendations arising) or represents the first time the institution has invited such scrutiny.
- If there are specific issues the governing body would like the review to examine, e.g. the effectiveness of processes and policies designed to promote diversity within the governing body.
- When the review is to take place and how this will align with the governance cycle of the institution.
- Whether there are particular external/policy/environmental factors that must be considered, e.g. changing regulatory requirements.
- How members of the governing body, the secretariat and the executive are to be involved, both in agreeing the terms of reference and thereafter as stakeholders and consultees.

All of these factors will influence the 'flavour' of the review – added to which the UK HE sector is very diverse. In practice this means that any one provider's governing body effectiveness review will both likely be different to that of their peers as well as varying from their own past reviews. Moreover, individual governing bodies must consider and decide what type of body they aspire to be and will judge their own effectiveness through reviews in this light.

What is essential is that institutional context and priorities shape the requirement and specification for the review. Consider this example of 'generic' terms of reference (synthesised from multiple sources) for a third-party led review:

To conduct an independent review that examines the overall effectiveness of institutional governance including the role of and interaction between the Board of Governors, Secretariat, Executive and the wider university and specific issues as detailed in the body of this specification.

The review should be forward looking, formative and be aligned with and contribute to the long-term ambitions of the University. It should draw upon examples and evidence of effective practice from within and beyond UK HE including other leading universities. Overall the review should provide:

- A developmental focus. The emphasis will be upon how the institution can improve governance effectiveness.
- A contextual focus. The review will be fully contextualised and not 'off the shelf'. The report will be fully aligned with the vision, the strategic plan and the core goals of the institution.

Specific areas the review must address include:

- The structure, and composition of the Board, including its skills and diversity base, and size;
- The working relationship between the Chair, Vice Chancellor and Board Secretary;
- Governance processes, including the content of the board agenda, the timeliness, quality and user friendliness of the reports and information provided to board members and the quality of the board discussions and deliberations;
- The recruitment, appointment, and induction processes for members;
- The operation and membership of the key Committees and their relationship with the Board and the balance of business;
- The nature and effectiveness of the Board's involvement in the strategic planning process for the University, and the role of the Board in reviewing and monitoring the performance of the institution against its Strategic Plan;
- The role of the Board in the management of key risks and opportunities for the University;
- The approach being taken to secure assurance on academic matters.

The above synthesis places an emphasis on the review not simply being focused upon the governing body itself. A review brief that embraces a holistic (i.e. a whole systems approach) recognises the critical interdependencies between the key governance actors – and especially the triumvirate of Chair, Vice Chancellor/ Executive and Secretary to the Board.

This is turn points to the need to adopt a process for the review that can unpack and explore all the key facets of governance effectiveness; the enablers, relationships and outcomes.

The process

Just as form follows function so should the process of any review suit the priorities expressed in the brief. Hence, effectiveness reviews can range from facilitated workshops to a full-blown data-driven comparative exercise. Whatever approach is adopted it is important to have a process that is fit for purpose and which enjoys the confidence and support of stakeholders.

To be effective a review requires evidence, and to be of value this evidence needs to be credible. A mixed modes approach that triangulates key sources of evidence and effective external comparisons is key to securing a rounded insight into salient issues. Sources can be documentary in nature as well as informed by interviews and workshops. These methods lend themselves to an exploration of policy and process. However, it is through direct observation, especially of board-room behaviour, that a review can secure insights of real value.

A typical approach may comprise:

- Establishing a Steering Group to meet regularly to specify the detailed terms of reference and oversee the process.
- Detailed planning of the review, initiation meeting and review of all paperwork.
- Deployment of a survey for Board members and key staff, analysis and benchmarking of results against other institution. In addition to Board members, key consultees should normally include the Executive, and relevant bodies such as the Senate/Academic Board, and staff and student communities (and possibly key external partners).
- Conducting interviews and observation of Board meetings and key sub-committees.
- Preparation and delivery of a workshop with members of the Board to consider emerging findings.
- Analysis, review team internal challenge, drafting of the report and submission.
- The review team meeting with the university Steering Group to review the draft report, finalise outputs and present as required.

In 2017 the Leadership Foundation for Higher Education (now Advance HE following merger in March 2018) updated the UK sector's Framework for Supporting Governing Body Effectiveness Reviews in HE (LFHE, 2017). It is the only such published framework specifically designed for evaluating the effectiveness of governance in UK HE.

The Framework sets out the key factors for consideration of effectiveness, based on three inter-related elements:

- Enablers that provide the foundations for effective governance and the building blocks on which governance rests.

- Working relationships which encompass the relationship between the governing body chair, the head of the organisation and the secretary to the governing body and the wider aspects of boardroom behaviour.
- Outcomes and impact to evidence governance effectiveness and a governing body's added value.

Without the enablers a governing body cannot be effective, these are the fundamental processes that establish the conditions for effectiveness. The key question is whether and how they are used. Poorly presented papers, an excessive reliance on tabling key information on the day thus precluding effective orientation with key issues, unclear minutes, an agenda that gives inadequate time for considering the key issues are examples of the sort of basic issues that should not arise in a well governed institution.

Working relationships encompass the critical nature of the relationship between the governing body chair, the head of the organisation and the secretary to the governing body. These three roles anchor institutional governance though the importance of working relationships extend to how each and every member of the governing body engages and makes use of their position. Boardroom behaviours can be readily evaluated by reference both to the degree of individual participation (from well prepared, engaged and actively contributing through generally absent and or silent) and to the form of engagement (from constructively challenging through to overly passive/disengaged).

My own experience is that when things 'go wrong' in governance they often do so because of the people and the associated behaviours and especially a breakdown of trust. Low levels of trust in turn generate poor and/or guarded communication and a lack of openness and candour which is crucial to effective working relationships. This may arise as a result of inter-personal friction following a series of challenging events. It can also be present as a consequence of an institution's underlying leadership and management culture.

Unfortunately, failures of governance continue to occur in organisations (across many sectors, not just HE) where the processes of governance are well developed and meet existing sectoral codes. It is crucial that effectiveness is considered in terms of both 'what boards do' but also 'how boards work' and the value that they provide. This speaks to the third element of the Framework; Outcomes. Some may be relatively generic and uncontentious (e.g. financial sustainability). Others will be specific to an institution's context (e.g. the successful implementation of a major capital project or an overseas campus).

Defining and measuring the 'added value' of a governing body is a challenge and identifying causality is difficult. However, for many HE providers with well-established and embedded governance processes, considering what governing bodies do and how they do it is more relevant for consideration during effectiveness reviews than simply looking in detail at whether the enablers of effective governance are in place.

My own reflections on the some of the most regularly cited contemporary issues causing difficulties include:

- Arriving at an agreed approach to the executive/non-executive boundary. Chairpersons with a career experience in sectors other than HE can if they are not careful lean towards adopting the executive chair persona expected and required of the private sector. This is not the model in HE (or indeed the wider charitable sector). At the same time the executive need to provide enough information for the governing body to perform its assurance role (without second-guessing management decision-making) and shape the overall strategy.
- The escalating demands on governors who are volunteers giving freely of their time. The increasing amount (of sometimes quite technical) information to be processed together the greater emphasis being placed upon the role and responsibilities of the governing body (for example by the OfS) is for some in the sector calling into question the basic model of unpaid voluntary membership of HE governing bodies. This can be especially acute for the Chair for whom the commitment can be very significant indeed.
- Ensuring all members of the governing body are equally and equitably sighted on the key issues. The risk of a small core of Board members unduly influencing engagement with key issues has arisen in some providers and must be guarded against. It risks group think, encourages a closed culture and diminishes trust. Fundamentally it undermines good governance.

The review team

How the review is delivered will vary depending upon the brief for the review. This in turn will influence decisions regarding the review team. Different approaches include:

- The appointment following competitive tender of a wholly independent review team or consultancy firm specialising in such work. This has the advantage of resilience, capacity to conclude the review relatively rapidly, and the benefit of review team members being able to challenge each other's thinking as well as access to a range of expertise.
- Contracting an individual advisor with suitable experience. This can be less costly than employing a team though reliance upon one individual can present risks. However, their depth of applied expertise (especially if a recently former governance professional) can be of great value.
- Securing the input of a governance professional from another provider, perhaps on a reciprocal basis whereby each provider reviews the others governance arrangement and shares lessons learned and insights arising. This requires a high level of trust and may take time to undertake given the day-to-day commitments of the senior staff involved but at the same time offers a distinctive approach to sharing learning and practice.

– Establishing a sub-committee of the Board chaired by the senior non-executive director/deputy chair with stakeholder representation and one or more independent members. This can be a very cost-effective solution, though the role of the independents as advisors rather than the leaders of the review process will likely constrain its objectivity.

There is a natural tendency to require reviewers to have in depth experience and expertise of the HE sector. Certainly, it is difficult to conceive of a review process that could add value without a good working knowledge of the HE sector's regulatory environment for example, or the governance implications arising out of the different legal forms universities can take. There is also clearly value in being able to access expertise that can offer insight into how different providers are taking similar issues.

However, learning and insight can also be usefully derived from taking on board practice from elsewhere, for example, the wider charities sector and in the practical guidance offered by (in the UK) the Charities Commission. HE sometimes thinks of itself as being 'too different' from other sectors for insight to be derived from the experience and solutions adopted by others. However, the fundamentals of good governance are universal and bear no loyalty to one sector over another. Reviews conducted by teams that have access to expertise may well be able to more value than those whose experience is limited only to HE.

Commitment to continuous improvement

> She generally gave herself very good advice, (though she very seldom followed it).
> (Carroll, 2015)

A commitment to continuous improvement means acting upon the insights from review and applying these in order to improve future practice. It also means a commitment to regular review.

> Reviews must be conducted at least every four years with, as a minimum, an annual summary of progress towards achieving any outstanding actions arising from the last effectiveness reviews.
> (Committee for University Chairs, 2018a, section 2, p. 27)

Governing bodies need to embrace continuous improvement to governance both to enhance their own effectiveness and provide an example to institutions about the importance of review and evaluation.

> Acting on the outcomes of effectiveness reviews is as important as undertaking them, and it is desirable that outcomes and associated actions are reported widely, including in the corporate governance statements.
> (Committee for University Chairs, 2018a, section 2, p. 27)

Alongside any major review that may take place every few years, providers should also embed processes for annual reflection:

> on the performance of the institution as a whole in . . . and the contribution of the governing body . . . the extent to which it and its committees have met their terms of reference . . . Benchmarking . . . against other comparable HEIs, and relevant institutions outside the HE sector.
> (Committee for University Chairs, 2018a, section 2, p. 28)

It is notable that the UK HE sector has introduced a range of measures in recent years to strengthen HE governance and support governing bodies in improving their effectiveness. Aside from the guidance on setting senior pay these include:

- Clarification of the roles and responsibilities of governing bodies following publication of the CUC Code of Practice (2014 and further revised in 2018) and in Scotland the Code of Good Higher Education Governance (revised in 2017; Committee of Scottish Chairs, 2017).
- The creation of a broad range of development and training resources designed to support continuous improvement. Notably the launch, in 2014 (with the close support of the Committee of University Chairs) of the sector-wide Governance Development Programme by Advance HE (formerly the Leadership Foundation for Higher Education; Advance HE, 2018) and the associated publication of a wide range of resources including 'Getting to Grips Guides', a governance new alert service and briefing notes on topical issues.
- Specific governance requirements expressed by the UK funding bodies (and in England now the OfS) as set out in their accountability/funding memoranda, e.g. the public interest governance principles that now apply to all registered providers in England set out by the OfS.

Personal experience from having supervised over 20 external governance reviews in the period 2015–2018 indicates that governance within 'publicly-funded' higher education institutions in the UK is generally effective and well developed – and that recommendations arising from independent reviews are generally implemented. Notable trends within individual institutions include:

- The decision by some governing bodies to reduce their size to improve effectiveness.
- Increasing diversity in the membership of governing bodies to reduce the risk of 'group think' and improve effectiveness – though this is an area where there remains much more to be done.
- An increased emphasis on the governing body's role in the assurance of academic quality.
- Governing bodies paying increased attention to the organisation's financial sustainability and strategic direction.

- Strengthening of the student voice.
- An increased commitment to regular critical review and self-assessment.
- A greater commitment to overall transparency.
- More regular, structured and informative governor appraisal.

All these elements point towards an increasingly deep-rooted commitment to continuous improvement within institutions and the networks and agencies that support sector governance – all the more necessary given the turbulence and challenges facing UK HE and the increased prominence this has given to the importance of effective institutional governance.

References

Advance HE (2018) Governor Development Programme 2018/19. www.lfhe.ac.uk/en/research-resources/publications-hub/index.cfm/GDP2018-19 [Accessed 1 January 2015].

Carroll, Lewis (1865) *Alice's Adventures in Wonderland*. London: Macmillan and Co.

Carroll, Lewis (2015) *Alice Through the Looking Glass*. London: Pan Macmillan.

The Charity Governance Code Steering Group (2017) Charity Governance Code. www.charitygovernancecode.org/en [Accessed 9 October 2018].

Committee of Scottish Chairs (2017) The Scottish Code of Good HE Governance. www.scottishuniversitygovernance.ac.uk/2017-code/ [Accessed 9 October 2018].

Committee for University Chairs (2018a) Higher Education Code of Governance. www.universitychairs.ac.uk/wp-content/uploads/2018/06/HE-Code-of-Governance-Updated-2018.pdf [Accessed 9 October 2018].

Committee for University Chairs (2018b) HE Senior Staff Remuneration Code. www.universitychairs.ac.uk/higher-education-remuneration-code-2/ [Accessed 9 October 2018].

Department for Education (2017) News Story, 'Universities Minister Calls for Stronger Oversight of Senior Pay'. www.gov.uk/government/news/universities-minister-calls-for-stronger-oversight-of-senior-pay.

Financial Reporting Council (2018) UK Corporate Governance Code 2018. www.frc.org.uk/getattachment/88bd8c45-50ea-4841-95b0-d2f4f48069a2/2018-UK-Corporate-Governance-Code-FINAL.pdf [Accessed 9 October 2018].

Halpin Partnership (2018) The Halpin Review, an Independent Review of Council Effectiveness at the University of Bath. www.bath.ac.uk/publications/the-halpin-review/ [Accessed 9 October 2018].

Leadership Foundation for Higher Education (2017) A Framework for Supporting Governing Body Effectiveness Reviews in Higher Education. www.lfhe.ac.uk/en/governance-new/governing-body-effectiveness/index.cfm [Accessed 9 October 2018].

Office for Students (2018a) Public Interest Governance Principles. www.officeforstudents.org.uk/advice-and-guidance/regulation/public-interest-governance-principles/ [Accessed 1 January 2015].

Office for Students (2018b) Regulatory Advice 3: Registration of New Providers for 2019–20 Guidance for Providers about the Application Process Reference OfS 2018.05. www.officeforstudents.org.uk/media/1100/ofs2018_05.pdf [Accessed 9 October 2018].

Office for Students (2018c) Regulatory Advice 2: Registration of New Providers for 2019–20. :www.officeforstudents.org.uk/media/1094/ofs2018_04.pdf [Accessed 9 October 2018].

Telegraph online (6 June 2018) Vice Chancellor Salary Study Demolishes their Claims that Pay Rises are Based on Performance. www.telegraph.co.uk/news/2018/06/06/vice-chancellor-salary-study-demolishes-claims-pay-rises-based/ [Accessed 1 January 2015].

UK Government website (2017) Universities Minister Calls for Stronger Oversight of Senior Pay. www.gov.uk/government/news/universities-minister-calls-for-stronger-oversight-of-senior-pay [Accessed 9 October 2018].

UK Sport (2017) Code for Sports Governance. www.uksport.gov.uk/resources/governance-code [Accessed 9 October 2018].

Chapter 16

Assurance of academic standards and quality by and beyond the academy

John Rushforth

Introduction

The Universities and Colleges Admissions Service (UCAS) sets out a widely held view as to the high quality of United Kingdom higher education (HE) – its website states:[1]

> The UK is one of the world's most popular destinations to study higher education, with more than 500,000 international students enrolling each year.
>
> – One of the world's leading destinations for international students, second only to the USA.
> – UK universities are among the best in the world, and consistently perform well in world rankings.
> – They also have a reputation for world-class research.
> – UK higher education degrees and qualifications are recognised by employers and academics worldwide.

Despite this success, UK HE is facing fundamental changes with government legislation (the Higher Education and Research Act, 2017) that sees the answer to driving up quality in the encouragement of market behaviour, treating students as consumers, introducing new mechanisms to inform students as purchasers in that market and setting up a new regulator to impose a burden on governing bodies to externally report on quality.

The impact of this, the instrumentalising of the measurement and evidencing of proxies for quality, remains to be seen and only time will tell if any of this actually improves teaching quality.

At the same time, the higher education sector continues to attract a high level of media attention, not all of which is positive. For example, there are articles questioning the fact that the proportion of first- and upper second-class degrees being awarded has been on the rise (Press Association, 2017; Radcliffe and Shaw, 2015). This grade inflation is now reported as being challenged by the regulator (Turner, 2018).

Other media stories reflect the concerns from the schools sector on the growth of unconditional offers (Adams, 2018), students' perceptions of poor value for money delivered by their courses (HEPI, 2018) and ministers warnings against running low-quality 'threadbare' courses.[2]

The debate on quality is further complicated by ministers' belief that by providing students with what they believe is information about quality (through the TEF[3]) and outcomes (via a new metric based on graduate salary data from the Longitudinal Educational Outcomes (Department for Education, 2018), quality will be improved through market competition mechanisms. Whether those beliefs are well founded or not, managing institutional reputation has never been more important. That in turn means quality management, both enhancement and assurance, face a significant challenge, both institutionally and sector-wide.

Prime responsibility for quality rests with the institutions themselves, but in the UK, this is supplemented by external organisations, such as the OfS, QAA and professional bodies.

Within institutions

UK Higher Education Institutions (HEIs) have a diverse range of missions. This richness is an important part of the UK HE sector. It follows that while for all UK HEIs a high-quality student experience underpinned by effective quality assurance and enhancement arrangements is key, for some HEIs academic governance may also cover research and/or knowledge transfer activities. Whatever the mission of the HEI, it is the case that the quality of its academic activities is critical to the institution's overall sustainability. Therefore, for any UK HEI, its governing body, working with the wider institutional community, needs to satisfy itself that the institution's academic governance and quality assurance is operating effectively. As the CUC (2017) puts it:

> Effective academic governance is at the heart of the governance of UK Higher Education (HE). It is separate from (but related to) corporate governance for which the governing body is unambiguously responsible.
>
> (CUC, 2017, paragraph 1)

Advance HE[4] (2014) makes it clear in its advice on academic governance that:

> Having separate bodies responsible for academic and corporate governance means that normally for public higher educational institutions there is a binary structure of governance, with one body (e.g. the senate or academic board) being responsible for academic matters and a separate body (e.g. the governing body) being responsible for resources.
>
> (Advance HE, 2014, paragraph 4)

Traditionally, in many HEIs the governing body may have had relatively little engagement with academic governance, beyond routine receipt of minutes from bodies such as the senate or academic board. In practice, of course, academic decisions impact corporate governance and vice versa – decisions about academic practice can have resource implications and resource decisions will affect the learning environment. This means that how the academic decision-making body and governing body interact is important for effective institutional governance. Also, as times change and the external environment for HE becomes much more competitive, student expectations change and there is an increasing public interest in HEIs, it is inevitable that governing bodies will need to become more aware of the activities undertaken within their institution's academic governance framework. That need, however, does not mean that there should be any change in ensuring that the competence for assessing or ensuring academic standards continues to properly sit with the senate or academic board and not with the governing body.

In the UK a post-1992 university or modern university is a former polytechnic or central institution in the United Kingdom that was given university status through the Further and Higher Education Act 1992, or an institution that has been granted university status since 1992 without receiving a royal charter. They were created with broadly similar articles of government, which gave governing bodies an explicit responsibility for 'determining educational character'. There is no such a reference in the charter or statutes of those institutions created by Royal Charter. In practice, these provisions have not been central to considerations of academic governance within institutions, since often the education character of the institution has not been explicitly defined and is not something that is specifically discussed. However, there will be discussion on the mission and nature of the institution , when say a new VC is to be recruited or a major overhaul of the institutional strategy is commissioned. In some instances, in the pre-1992 universities it isn't always clear within charters and statutes where precise ultimate responsibility for academic matters resides, but in practical terms, within the UK it is seen as area where the governing body, the senate/academic board and the executive have to work together.

It is not reasonable for the governing body to be expected to understand all the complexities of academic governance. The language, the acronyms, the labyrinthian committee structures all make it a challenge for the average lay member, who usually does not have an academic background. However, governing body members do not have to manage all the nuances and subtleties. The role of the governing body is not to run academic governance but to be assured. The role here is similar to the role it needs to play with respect to other areas of assurance (although perhaps more complex). Governors have tended to concentrate on strategy, finance, audit, HR and get their assurance from regular reports, often using Key Performance Indicators (KPIs) and risk registers. The equivalent response then is to rely on annual reports on academic quality and standards; to consider agreed academic KPIs relating to education, student experience, research and knowledge exchange. This is then supplemented by effective risk management (in this case academic risk), with the senate/academic board providing academic assurance as appropriate.

The CUC (2017) is clear that:

> the underlying principles of sound academic governance are based upon collegiality, and it follows that the governing body must understand and respect the role, as defined within charters, statutes or articles, of the senate/academic board and other bodies involved in academic governance.
>
> (CUC, 2017, p. 1, paragraph 2)

Governing bodies will need assurance that academic governance is effective and risks (such as those involving partnerships and collaboration, recruitment, progression and retention, data provision, quality assurance, academic standards and research ethics and integrity) are being effectively managed.

The main deliberative body responsible for academic governance is the senate (in pre-1992 universities) or the academic board (in post-1992 HEIs), in both cases usually supported by a committee structure and, in some instances, faculty (or school) boards. Originally in the pre-1992 universities, senates tended to be large bodies, and although now typically much smaller there are still some universities with senates with a hundred or more members. They can be an important 'safety valve' when contentious issues arise. The size of academic boards has generally tended to be much smaller (usually less than 30).

In England, the senate/academic board is typically chaired by the head of the institution (as chief academic officer) and specific responsibilities normally include:

- awarding of degrees;
- approval of the content of the curriculum and new programmes;
- oversight of quality assurance and enhancement arrangements;
- upholding academic standards and the student learning experience;
- approving procedures for the award of qualifications;
- the appointment of internal and external examiners;
- policies and procedures on examinations;
- criteria for admission of students;
- student discipline.

It may also have a role in matters concerning academic strategy.

In practice, many of these regulatory issues may be dealt with in delegated committees (with various levels of delegated authority), and where authority is so delegated, the senate/academic board receives reports so that it can execute its oversight role. Preliminary drafting, evaluation and consultation on key academic policies and strategies may be undertaken by sub-committees of the senate/academic board. It is now established practice for student representatives to be members or in attendance at both the senate/academic board and many of its sub-committees.

Beyond these functions there may be considerable variation in the powers of senates/academic boards and these are typically defined in governing instruments. Quite often the head of institution reports to the governing body on the operation of the senate/academic board. Each HEI works out the best way for its governing body and senate/academic board to work together. However, expectations of governing body engagement in this area are increasing: governing bodies are now required to provide formal assurances on the quality, standards and enhancement of their institution's provision on an annual basis to the Office for Students as a new regulator and so are re-visiting what they receive from their senates/academic boards.

In addition, there is, of course, an academic line management function usually involving a senior member of the executive team (a deputy or pro vice-chancellor) and deans of faculty (or similar senior academic roles).

External elements

Externality has a long history in respect of quality assurance in HE. The external examiner system has its origins in the employment of examiners from Oxbridge by the University of Durham in 1832. The more recent position of external quality assurance is summarised by Unistats[5] on its website as follows:[6]

> in England and Northern Ireland, the core mechanism for assessing quality has been the Annual Provider Review process . . . The Annual Provider Review drew on existing data and information (such as National Student Survey data) and uses indicators and metrics to form its judgement . . . For recent entrants to the sector, the Quality Assurance Agency (QAA) carried out a Quality Review Visit on behalf of HEFCE or DfENI.
>
> For alternative providers in England, quality was assessed through an external quality assurance review carried out by the QAA.
>
> . . . in Scotland quality is assessed through an Enhancement-led Institutional Review carried out by QAA Scotland as part of the Quality Enhancement Framework.
>
> . . . in Wales quality is assessed through an external quality assurance review as part of the Quality Assessment Framework for Wales. The most recent QAA review acts as the external review for Welsh institutions.

The HEFCE's Quality Assessment model had moved towards a more outcomes-based process, but this sat awkwardly beside a similar exercise driven by the DfE: the TEF. Both collect similar data in different ways and are interconnected at many points

These mechanisms were supplemented by individual subject reviews carried out by various accreditation and professional bodies and publication of various data sets – most notably the National Student Survey (NSS).

Even though the existence of external (and for that matter and internal) quality assurance is widely accepted nowadays, the debate continues in many universities where scholars still accuse quality assurance of being both a bureaucratic burden and an illegitimate interference that exists in order to 'regulate and discipline academics' (Lucas, 2014). The QAA approach prior to the advent of the OfS has been criticised for taking a 'one size fits all approach' and, in England, not having sufficient emphasis on quality enhancement. The changing context in England may well change the standard approach, with a greater emphasis on risk-based approaches, but it is unlikely that much will be done to shift the emphasis to enhancement.

A changing context

The OfS became the regulator for higher education in England on 1 April 2018, in line with the Higher Education and Research Act 2017.

The OfS has the following regulatory objectives:

– that all students, from all backgrounds, and with the ability and desire to undertake higher education, receive a high-quality academic experience, with their interests protected while they study (or in the event a provider, campus or course closes);
– that all students can progress into employment or further study, and their qualifications hold value over time.

It expects providers to:

– maintain the quality of academic experience they offer to students;
– ensure the qualification they gain is reliable, has been rigorously assessed, and is comparable to similar qualifications offered by other institutions.

The OfS states that it is a risk-based regulator and that its assessment and monitoring activities are targeted at providers who represent a higher risk to students and their outcomes. Through ongoing monitoring, it believes that it will be able to identify those organisations who are not providing the academic experience and the reliable standards students should expect.

The OfS (2018a) will monitor that a provider meets its conditions of registration, as follows:

Condition B1: The provider must deliver well-designed courses that provide a high-quality academic experience for all students and enable a student's achievement to be reliably assessed.

Condition B2: The provider must provide all students, from admission through to completion, with the support that they need to succeed in and benefit from higher education.

Condition B3: The provider must deliver successful outcomes for all its students, which are recognised and valued by employers and/or enable further study.

Condition B4: The provider must ensure that qualifications awarded to students hold their value at the point of qualification and over time, in line with sector recognised standards.

Condition B5: The provider must deliver courses that meet the academic standards as they are described in the Framework for Higher Education Qualification (FHEQ) at Level 4 or higher.

(Office for Students, 2018a, p. 87)

The regulatory framework sets out these conditions, the behaviours that are expected from a provider, and behaviours that would indicate a provider is not continuing to meet these conditions.

Whilst there is nothing radically challenging in these requirements, the language used is different to that used by the HEFCE (its predecessor) – with a much greater emphasis on transparency, demonstrating compliance, consistency and evidence. The risk is that this type of language will generate a compliant, more risk-averse culture – which in turn would limit and constrain innovation and development.

The Act required the appointment of an organisation to carry out quality and standards assessment functions to support the OfS regulatory process. The QAA was designated by the Secretary of State for Education, also with effect from 1 April 2018. The QAA has now agreed with the OfS that it will:

- design and deliver a quality and standards review method for assessing whether a higher education provider satisfies initial conditions of registration;
- design and deliver a method to review higher education providers in relation to actual or suspected breaches of registration conditions;
- design and deliver a quality and standards review method as part of the Foss's approach to random sampling;
- provide advice to the OfS about applicants for new degree awarding powers and full degree awarding powers.

When the government on behalf of the OfS (2017) consulted on proposals for the new regulatory framework it made it clear it was prepared to reshape the current system:

the OfS will not undertake routine reassessment of providers, either along the lines of Annual Provider Review or of annual redesignation. Instead its approach will use data and intelligence to identify where further scrutiny is needed to combat the risks outlined above.

(Government consultation on behalf of the Office for Students, 2017, p. 39, paragraph 37)

The ending of the Annual Provider Reviews (APR) represents both an opportunity and a challenge to some institutions. In removing these reviews, it is possible that the burden of accountability will be reduced. However, some governing bodies relied on externally mandated quality reviews to give them assurance that their quality arrangements were fit for purpose. It will be interesting to see whether governing bodies have an appetite to commission their own quality reviews on an ongoing basis.

The OfS is indicating that it will have an interest in sector standards, such as degree classifications. These standards fall under the autonomy of degree awarding bodies to set, so engagement here has the potential to cause significant debate. There is also the prospect of the OfS looking to alternative methods of assessment, such as Grade Point Average (GPA), to inform its work on sector-recognised standards.

Quality enhancement is missing from the whole regulatory framework. By moving to an almost entirely metric-based system with baseline lead indicators, as reported by WonkHE,[7] the government consultation on the Office for Students (OfS) made it clear it would only be interested in those who dipped below baseline, rather than those who dipped below excellence. Instead, it argued that the competitive market would provide the enhancement incentivisation required to ensure improvement, as follows:

> Once meeting a high minimum standard, the OfS will leave autonomous institutions to flourish on their own terms and will instead shape the market by supporting effective demand (in particular, through effective provision of information).
>
> (Department for Education, 2017, paragraph 63)

This is different to the Welsh and Scottish regulatory systems, so it's hard to imagine how quality assurance can remain UK-wide (see Chapter 6). Now that the QAA is the designated quality body, it will have to deliver in a way which is dramatically different from the quality assurance it originally developed. As a UK-wide organisation, it will have a task ahead of it to keep this increasingly fragmented sector together.

What does seem likely, however, is that data both internally and externally developed will be an increasing feature of the system

Use of data

For over ten years, data has been published on students' perceptions of quality, in the National Student Survey (NSS), a national survey of final-year undergraduate students. It operates across the UK, though not all institutions in Scotland participate. It is managed by an independent market research agency and covers final-year students, both full- and part-time, and asks students a series of questions about their perceptions of different aspects of their experience at their HEI. The survey results are then published at institutional level on the Unistats website, linked to UCAS.

Cleary high quality teaching is an important factor in student satisfaction; and the power of student choice alone is enough to ensure that a university which does not deliver its key product (effective teaching) to its consumer base (students) has not got a sustainable future. How effective NSS data is in driving quality directly is of course debatable since it is not a direct measure but one of perception. Nevertheless, in part because of its impact on institutional positioning within the nationally published league tables, changes in NSS scores (both at subject and institutional level) can be a matter for intense debate and scrutiny or celebration and increased marketing, depending on whether the score has gone up or gone down. If nothing else, the impact of NSS has been to change the nature and focus of debate on teaching quality in institutions.

Longitudinal Education Outcomes (LEO) data is a newer data set which shows how much UK graduates of different courses at different universities are earning now, either one, three or five years since graduating. It does this by linking up tax, benefits and student loans data.

However, as Morris (2017) says, it's just as important to state at the outset what LEO and the NSS are not. They do not help us identify the universities with the best or most effective teaching, nor are they a measure of the 'value added' by a university degree.

LEO isn't even a predictor of how much students at any university or on any course will earn in the future. Human beings are complex. We are much more than our qualifications, and research has shown that there are many factors that affect graduate outcomes. The biggest factor, according to Belfield and van der Erve (2018), is family background. Gender, race and socio-economic background are also major contributors – and come into effect as early as one year after graduation.

A key concern echoed in the recent Select Committee is the issue of place. The Industrial Strategy encourages universities and their graduates to be 'builders of place' to redress economic imbalances: providers which support local economies by encouraging graduates to stay in their local areas, or recruit students from nearby who are likely to remain at home post-study. Yet where graduates work has a huge impact on what they earn. There are concerns that an undue focus on LEO will disproportionally advantage the London-based institutions, for example, at the expense of the regions.

Another concern with any simplistic use of LEO to measure success means that social value is excluded. In effect, such an approach suggests that the education of economists and accountants is more valuable than that of nurses and teachers.

Internally generated data has probably always been used to support quality assurance – with emphasis on retention rates and student success. Within institutions, what is changing is the accessibility of hundreds of thousands of data points every day that institutions collect from online assessments, learning management systems and massive open online courses. Learning analytics is growing because of the access to all this data. All this data is useless unless institutions can unlock its potential. Universities, for example, might want to analyse data to detect patterns in student enrolment to improve a programme's success. When students drop out of a programme, when does it occur? If it's after a particular course, what changes could be made to improve student retention?

Universities might also want to analyse the gaps within a student's background. If a student drops out of a course, is it because they're missing a level of preparation necessary to succeed? If they are missing a historical qualification or course, the university might consider designing a one-credit refresher or piece of content to help them succeed.

The OfS Data Strategy (Office for Students, 2018b) is clear that the OfS will want to make better use of data in its monitoring of students, with its aspiration to be able to use lead indicators based on real time data to pick up issues before they become problems:

> At this stage, we are still scoping many of our detailed data uses. In order to take timely regulatory actions we will need data in close to real time. We recognise that the timing of data collection affects provider burden.
>
> (Office for Students, 2018b, p. 10, paragraph 52)

This might include some elements of learning analytics, or at least some of the data sets within learning management systems.

TEF

The TEF is an assessment exercise introduced by the government in England with the objective of determining the excellence of universities and colleges at teaching and ensuring students get good outcomes in terms of graduate-level employment or further study. It is designed for universities and colleges in England, but those in Scotland, Wales and Northern Ireland are also able to choose to participate. There are systems in place to help ensure that all UK colleges and universities meet national quality standards. The TEF looks at what they are doing above and beyond these standards, and awards them:

- Gold for delivering consistently outstanding teaching, learning and outcomes for its students. It is of the highest quality found in the UK.
- Silver for delivering high quality teaching, learning and outcomes for its students. It consistently exceeds rigorous national quality requirements for UK higher education.
- Bronze for delivering teaching, learning and outcomes for its students that meet rigorous national quality requirements for UK higher education.

There is also an award of provisional for a university or college that meets the rigorous UK quality requirements, and takes part in the TEF, but does not yet have enough data to be fully assessed

Institutions in the TEF are assessed to see if they have performed significantly well or badly (in a statistical sense) compared with a benchmark value in each of the six core metrics (teaching on my course, assessment and feedback, academic support, non-continuation, graduate employment or further study, and highly skilled employment or further study). However, the use of data within TEF itself is subject to change, since this year the weighting given to three of the metrics – those from the NSS – was halved when assessors made a first decision about whether a university was gold, silver or bronze.

The use of data within TEF is contested, particularly the use of benchmarked data which has the result that an institution with higher raw scores can produce a lower grade than another with a lower absolute score because they are compared to a different benchmark group. With some marketing communications suggesting that the TEF scores are absolute measures of success, this can confuse students.

Some go further, such as Shah (2018), arguing that TEF only uses what is measured rather than what should be measured, and that if TEF was an assessment of excellence, a more expensive burdensome scheme would be needed, which included unannounced observation of classes.

The OfS is supporting the pilot exercise to test a subject-level TEF. The two-year pilot tests two models of the subject-level TEF: one in which a university will be rated 'gold', 'silver' or 'bronze' overall, with the subject-level score differing only where metrics are significantly different, and another in which individual subject-level ratings feed into the overall assessment.

The expectation is that all higher education providers will participate in subject-level TEF in 2019–20.

Although originally participation in institutional level TEF was voluntary, the new regulatory framework makes TEF entry a condition for all approved providers over a certain size on the new register. TEF has three ratings and, although the gold/silver/bronze award mechanism was intended to reassure the outside world that everyone was still a winner, Custer (2017) reports that a survey of 3,300 international students by Hobsons reveals confusion among international students about the controversial scheme and a real lack of understanding.

Of the students who claimed to know about the scheme, a quarter think a bronze award means teaching quality is 'unsatisfactory' and half thought results were based on random inspections of lectures and classes from the Department of Education.

In a highly competitive international recruitment market, this perception of bronze as unsatisfactory is a real problem. TEF is still in its infancy though, and it is difficult to predict how long will it endure, but with a government that believes that higher education is a form of market, it's unlikely that a public 'quality rating system' won't be kept in some form.

Many in the sector would be quite happy for it to disappear without trace but, as the recent announcement about subject-level TEF demonstrates, the government is pressing ahead with the next phase of its development. What is more likely, is that the sector will continue to develop it and seek to improve it. The key will be the extent to which it influences behaviour and whether there is definite incentive. If TEF doesn't influence market behaviour, then the likelihood is that it will gradually disappear. The TEF is subject to statutory review in 2018, and the OfS will take the outcomes of this review into account as it considers the future scope and shape of the TEF.

The availability and impact of these various datasets means that increasing amounts of information on academic assurance is coming to governing bodies. As for other areas, the governing body needs to receive enough information to give assurance about the robustness of academic governance. This is being provided in several ways, for example:

- regular reports from the senate/academic board – some institutions ask for a formal annual opinion on the effectiveness (or otherwise) of the management of academic quality and standards to be sent to the governing body by the senate/academic board;
- relevant reports from the executive, that include the advice of the senate/academic board, to the governing body meeting;
- regular discussion of academic KPIs or key academic risks, sometimes within the context of regular risk management reporting;
- receiving an annual report on academic activities;
- reviews of academic governance and/or the effectiveness of the senate/academic board.

So far as information about the achievement of the academic strategy is concerned, many governing bodies will incorporate reviewing it within their overall performance monitoring arrangements, and CUC guidance has identified a number of possible academic KPIs, including: the character of the student population; evidence of academic distinctiveness; position in peer group and league tables; contribution of strategic academic relationships; and the integration of academic and strategic planning.

In many HEIs, reports on such KPIs are presented to governing bodies through devices such as a balanced score card or a traffic lights system to monitor progress.

The external examiner system

Originally, the external examiner was an additional marker, but the role was extended to include responsibilities for the moderation of marks, endorsing the judgements of internal examiners, and confirming the awards made to students. This role has largely been sustained over time with modest adjustments to cope with change, including greatly expanded numbers and different types of degree programme. The OfS expects institutions to make scrupulous use of external examiners including in the moderation of assessment tasks and student assessed work. Institutions will need to demonstrate they have given full and serious consideration to the comments and recommendations contained in external examiners' reports and provided external examiners with a considered and timely response to their comments and recommendations.

The actual activities undertaken by external examiners tend to include contributions to the setting of examination papers, marking or judging the standard of internal examiners' marking, and participating in examination board meetings held for the purpose of determining the award of degrees. They may also be asked, or choose, to comment on curricula. At postgraduate level external examiners are involved in examining doctoral theses and masters dissertations.

There are regular calls for overhaul or abandonment of the external examiner system, for example the HEFCE (2015) review, 'A Review of External Examining Arrangements across the UK', that called for greater professionalisation, including enhanced training, an independent appointments process and consideration of equitable and appropriate remuneration. The most recent comments have been on the back of further growth in the award of first-class degrees, for example those of Nick Hillman, Head of the Higher Education Policy Institute, as quoted on the BBC website in July 2017:

> There are people who think the system isn't as robust as it might be, it can all be a bit cosy – you ask someone you know to be an external examiner.
>
> (BBC, 2017)

But there is no real evidence to suggest that this actually happens in any significant way. External examining in the UK as it stands now still looks like an extremely efficient and light-touch system, but it also serves as something of a firewall against attacks on academic standards as well as a means of defending institutional autonomy, hence the continued widespread support for it within universities.

However, externally determined judgements of quality through expert assessment is not the only way that perceptions quality can be reported on. Research from Griffiths et al. (2018) indicates that universities and colleges that are rated highly on Facebook and other online review sites tend to do better in more formal measures of learning. The findings mirror work of Griffiths and Leaver (2017) in the healthcare sector, which also found social media ratings were predictors of a healthcare provider's Care Quality Commission assessment outcomes.

Griffiths et al.'s research finds that, in general, online feedback about UK universities and colleges is positive. Universities and colleges were assigned a star rating out of five based on the combined social media ratings. The average score over all 210,000 online reviews is high at 4.18 stars. This positive rating aligns with the generally high scores given for overall student satisfaction in the National Student Survey over the course of recent years.

A similar trend is found with the outcomes of the TEF. The average star ratings online were generally highest for providers with a gold TEF award, followed by silver-rated providers, and lowest for bronze.

Conclusion/the future

The increased importance of reputation, the more accessible, innovative and changing sources of data and assessment (however flawed they might be), and increased expectation of students and governments , all mean that governing bodies will have to shift their focus away from a preoccupation with finance and construction projects towards a much greater engagement with the core business of universities, namely their teaching and research, together with a much greater understanding of the work of the senate/academic board.

The other, perhaps more fundamental, change institutions face is the shift from a context with a regulator with a remit for excellence and process, to one charged with maintaining a minimum standard, reflecting the belief within government that the best means of raising quality in HE lies in promoting competition, as institutions respond to the choices of the well-informed student consumer. The question is whether the sector will reject the limited vision of student as mere consumer and insist that the key to maintaining and improving quality is supporting the professional urge to do better, stimulated and informed by peer processes and an investment in development (of people, systems and environment).

What this in turn means is that there will be more time spent on discussing academic matters at governing bodies, a much greater need for specific HE experiences on governing bodies, possibly more universities commissioning more regular external reviews of academic governance and the oversight of quality enhancement activities.

Notes

1 www.ucas.com/undergraduate/applying-university/international-and-eu-students/studying-uk
2 www.bbc.co.uk/news/education-44399444
3 TEF is the Teaching Excellence Framework, an assessment exercise introduced by the government in England with the objective of determining the excellence of universities. See www.officeforstudents.org.uk/advice-and-guidance/teaching/what-is-the-tef/
4 Advance HE is a sector owned body that, amongst other things, provides information and expert advice on all aspects of HE governance and management. See www.advance-he.ac.uk/about-us
5 Unistats is the official site that allows a search for and comparison of data and information on university and college courses from across the UK.
6 https://m.unistats.ac.uk/find-out-more/quality-and-standards
7 https://wonkhe.com/blogs/whats-happening-to-quality/

References

Adams, R. (2018) 'Rise in Unconditional Offers Prompts Call for University Admissions Overhaul', *Guardian*, 26 July 2018 [Retrieved from www.theguardian.com/education/2018/jul/26/rise-in-unconditional-offers-prompts-call-for-university-admissions-overhaul]

Advance HE (2014) 'Governor Briefing Note 4 Academic Governance and Quality' [Retrieved from www.lfhe.ac.uk/en/governance-new/governance-briefing-notes/governance-briefing-note-04.cfm]

BBC (2017) 'University First-Class Degrees Soaring' [Retrieved from www.bbc.co.uk/news/education-40654933]

Belfield, C. and van der Erve, L. (2018) 'What Determines Graduates' Earnings?' Institute for Fiscal Studies [Retrieved from www.ifs.org.uk/publications/13058]

CUC (2017) 'Illustrative Practice Note 3 Academic Governance' paragraph 2 [Retrieved from www.universitychairs.ac.uk/wp-content/uploads/2017/01/CUC-IPN3-Academic-Governance-Jan-17.pdf]

Custer, S. (2017) 'Survey Reveals Most International Students Confused by UK's TEF' [Retrieved from https://thepienews.com/news/hobsons-survey-reveals-most-international-students-confused-by-uk-tef/]

Department for Education (2017) 'Securing Student Success: Risk-Based Regulation for Teaching Excellence, Social Mobility and Informed Choice in Higher Education: Government Consultation on Behalf of the Office for Students' [Retrieved from https://consult.education.gov.uk/higher-education/higher-education-regulatory-framework/supporting_documents/HE%20reg%20framework%20condoc%20FINAL%2018%20October%20FINAL%20FINAL.pdf]

Department for Education (2018) 'Graduate Outcomes (LEO): Subject by Provider, 2015 to 2016' [Retrieved from https://assets.publishing.service.gov.uk/government/uploads/system/uploads/attachment_data/file/718167/210618_main_text.pdf]

Government consultation on behalf of the Office for Students (2017) 'Securing Student Success: Risk-Based Regulation for Teaching Excellence, Social Mobility and Informed Choice in Higher Education' [Retrieved from https://consult.education.gov.uk/higher-education/higher-education-regulatory-framework/supporting_documents/HE%20reg%20framework%20condoc%20FINAL%2018%20October%20FINAL%20FINAL.pdf]

Griffiths, A. and Leaver, M.P. (2017) 'Wisdom of Patients: Predicting the Quality of Care using Aggregated Patient Feedback', *British Medical Journal Quality and Safety* [Retrieved from https://qualitysafety.bmj.com/content/27/2/110.info]

Griffiths, A., Leaver, M.P. and King, R. (2018) 'The Wisdom of Students: Monitoring Quality through Student Reviews' [Retrieved from www.qaa.ac.uk/docs/qaa/about-us/the-wisdom-of-students-monitoring-quality-through-student-reviews.pdf?sfvrsn=4ac9ff81_2]

HEPI (2018) 'Higher Education Policy Institute Student Academic Experience Survey 2018' [Retrieved from www.hepi.ac.uk/wp-content/uploads/2018/06/STRICTLY-EMBARGOED-UNTIL-THURSDAY-7-JUNE-2018-Student-Academic-Experience-Survey-report-2018.pdf]

Higher Education Funding Council for England (2015) 'A Review of External Examining Arrangements across the UK' [Retrieved from https://webarchive.nationalarchives.gov.uk/20180322111229/http://www.hefce.ac.uk/pubs/rereports/year/2015/externalexam/]

Higher Education and Research Act (2017) [Retrieved from www.legislation.gov.uk/ukpga/2017/29/contents/enacted]

Lucas, L. (2014). 'Academic Resistance to Quality Assurance Processes in Higher Education in the UK', *Policy and Society*, 33 (3), pp. 215–224.

Morris, D. (2017) 'A Beginner's Guide to Longitudinal Education Outcomes (LEO) data', WonkHE Policy Watch [Retrieved from https://wonkhe.com/blogs/a-beginners-guide-to-longitudinal-education-outcomes-leo-data/]

Office for Students (2018a) 'Securing Student Success: Regulatory Framework for Higher Education in England' [Retrieved from www.officeforstudents.org.uk/publications/securing-student-success-regulatory-framework-for-higher-education-in-england/]

Office for Students (2018b) 'Office for Students Data Strategy 2018 to 2021' [Retrieved from www.officeforstudents.org.uk/media/83cf5ba5-e2ea-4787-a83b-44e048ddaf3c/ofs2018_50.pdf]

Press Association (2017) 'Number of UK Degree Students Receiving Firsts Soars', *Guardian* [Retrieved from www.theguardian.com/education/2017/jul/20/uk-universities-awarding-more-firsts-students]

Radcliffe, R. and Shaw, C. (2015) 'Academics Under Pressure to Bump Up Student Grades', *Guardian* [Retrieved from www.theguardian.com/higher-education-network/2015/may/18/academics-under-pressure-to-bump-up-student-grades-guardian-survey-shows]

Shah, H. (2018) 'Awarding University Subjects Gold Medals is Deeply Flawed', *Guardian* [Retrieved from www.theguardian.com/higher-education-network/2018/jun/01/awarding-university-subjects-gold-medals-is-deeply-flawed]

Turner, C. (2018) 'Universities Warned to Curb "Spiraling" Grade Inflation', *Telegraph* [Retrieved from www.telegraph.co.uk/education/2018/12/19/universities-warned-curb-spiralling-grade-inflation/]

Chapter 17

Performance and risk

The light and shade of trust and accountability

Tony Strike

Introduction

The governing body of an institution will usually want or be required to use or agree a monitoring framework to assess institutional performance and risk. It can be argued that provision of summative information on performance and risk to the governing board increases trust in the executive or in the academy, which in turn allows them greater autonomy. This logic operates at national and institutional levels. It is equally possible, though, to argue that: 'The notion of trust . . . is . . . the antithesis of accountability. If two parties totally trust each other, there is in principle no need to establish an accountability scheme' (Stensaker and Harvey, 2011, p. 11). This balancing act requires governing bodies to consider carefully what they want to see, why and for what purpose. Governing bodies are not homogenous, but made up of opinionated individuals, and different members may have different experience, interests and levels of trust and want different things, so the body corporate will need to balance that out to determine what they see.

Accountability, trust and autonomy

The pressure to manage and account for performance may come from outside the institution because as the OECD (2017) explains: 'Ultimately, there is increasing pressure to demonstrate that the significant public and private investment on higher education pays back, economically, socially, and culturally' (p. 25). Equally, governing or supervisory boards may be constitutionally charged to monitor institutional performance or want to do so in pursuing their own or others' strategic goals. As Alexander (2000) put it:

> The accountability movement currently inundating many OECD nations is premised on the perception that traditional measures of institutional performance and effectiveness such as peer review and market choice are not sufficient indicators of institutional value.
>
> (p. 414)

The motivation may also come from within the institution – in a context of increasing competition, expectations and volatility these forces each drive the steering body to desire to know if the institution is responding and performing.

In either case it is legitimate to examine the influence governance structures, processes, culture and attitudes have on institutional performance and whether governors can add value (Sarrico, 2010). It is also worth considering what performance and risk mean in the context of a higher education institution – that is performance and risk from whose perspective; the institution itself, the students, teaching and research staff, corporate and strategic partners, government and regulators or society. It is not difficult to agree with Burke (2005, p. 23) that accountability is about finding a good balance between conflicting demands and expectations and that higher education institutions should 'serve all while submitting to none of these imperatives' (Stensaker and Harvey, 2011, p. 11).

The diversity between higher education systems means the environment for performance monitoring differs between countries and institutions. The main factors where this diversity seems to be significant to the board's role in assessing performance were identified by the CUC (2008) as:

- the size of boards;
- the involvement of governors in strategy;
- the place of KPIs (Key Performance Indicators) in institutional governance;
- the separation of roles;
- the relationship between the board, its committees, the executive, and the officers who produce the KPIs.

If governing bodies have a responsibility for the long-term sustainability and strategic direction of institutions they have to be involved to some extent in performance and risk. The question, as mentioned above, is to what extent they should seek to be involved. The justification, if justification is required, for the involvement of the governing board in assessing performance and risk, rather than treating this as an executive or academic matter, is often to provide proper accountability. Or as Bovens (2006) put it: Accountability is 'merely used as an ideograph, as a rhetorical tool [used] to convey an image of good governance . . . [and] has become an icon for good governance both in the public and the private sector' (p. 7).

In many higher education institutions, the Secretary or Clerk will have a role in ensuring that information is presented to the board in such a way as to enable them to assess institutional performance and risk in an agreed and manageable way. This means the Secretary, working with the governing body and the executive, can help both conclude what is required.

In some countries, the board must not only assess institutional performance and risk but must do so in a way that means it can subsequently demonstrate to a third party (government, regulator or auditor) how it met this responsibility. For example, in Denmark from 2003 it became compulsory for university governing boards to enter into development or performance contracts with the Ministry of Science, Technology and Innovation. These contracts were used as a tool to hold the university leadership to account for the performance of the institution (Wright and Ørberg, 2009, p. 80) so the elected academic leader became accountable not to their electorate but to the governing board and they to the state. Similarly, some US public universities and colleges have seen the application of performance contracts, which include targeted goals and so-called charter colleges and universities remain accountable to the state through performance contracts, which define state expectations (McLendon and Hearn, 2009, p. 168). In the UK the Office of Students and Research England through a new regulatory regime (and excellence frameworks for assessing research, teaching and knowledge exchange) have increased the pressure on governing boards to ensure performance as defined by others. This raises questions whether governors are stewards or agents, on whose behalf they are acting and to whom they are accountable.

Differentiating board-level and executive reporting

The Leadership Foundation for Higher Education (LFHE, 2012) described a helpful device for board reporting which takes the focus off the underlying data and instead presents performance assessments 'at a glance' as follows:

> The development of such KPIs and the involvement of the governing body raises a number of interesting challenges for the clerk, including the amount of detail provided to boards and the extent to which often highly specialised information can be presented in a succinct and helpful way to board members. To do this, a number of HEIs are using approaches such as the balanced score card, often coupled with so-called 'traffic light' systems whereby coloured indicators are regularly provided in board papers to enable members to see at a glance how specific indicators show performance.
>
> (p. 62)

This is helpful in my experience as it is likely that the high-level KPIs sought by governors will be a summative assessment of a number of different underlying factors or measures, some or all of which may be qualitative rather than quantitative. This requires members of the executive contextualising and commenting on their assessments, which in turn makes the KPIs more accessible to governors and lifts the discussion above particular data, definitions and validity to help them make informed judgements.

The executive board will similarly want information about the performance of the institution primarily in their case to manage, control and improve operations or to inform plans or resource allocations. This means they are likely to want more detailed, timely and regular information and insight than the governing body needs or wants, to inform executive actions and decisions in real time. This introduces the notion of a PI pyramid – the front-line manager or academic leader needs the detail and in a timely way and at each step up the hierarchy, the detail is summarised and the data is time-lagged to an increasing extent. PIs can be about detailed operational performance management and support and be nested within the KPIs, which are linked to long-term strategic planning.

The governing body is not involved in data collection, nor is it taking a detailed operational view. It does, however, need assurances about data quality and that the detail is being collected and managed – and occasionally may wish to do a deep dive into a narrow area. The performance information wanted by governors is more likely to be selective, high-level, summative, retrospective, benchmarked in some way against comparators or targets and derived to allow the executive to be held to account for outcomes. This separation of roles and the constructive 'oversight and challenge' by governors is fundamental to the successful operation of performance monitoring rather than performance management. This means the KPIs for the board should be designed for it, adapted to the level of monitoring it requires, and it should not receive second-hand executive reports designed with different purposes in mind. Equally, it should not get reports that only it gets and no one else is interested in. There should be some relationship between these different levels of monitoring, so the governing body and executive are focused on similar priorities and goals, but appropriate to each audience.

Officers who are not members of the university executive will often do the work required to support the production of the high-level KPIs for the governors. Planning teams may provide data, benchmarks and trend information, for example, and the secretariat may work with the executive and governors on how performance is to be judged or reported so the governors are enabled to ask relevant questions. This may involve work with the governors on what they want to see, to enable appropriate selectivity to match their priorities, to highlight matters by exception or enhance areas of institutional distinctiveness.

Key performance indicators

KPIs (key performance indicators) give an overview of changing institutional performance through time often closely linked to a strategic plan or goals.

Cave *et al.* (1988) are more specific in their definition, saying:

> PIs differ from simple indicators in that they imply a point of reference, for example a standard, an objective, an assessment, or a comparator, and are therefore relative rather than absolute in character. Although a simple indicator is the more neutral of the two, it may become a PI if a value judgement is involved.
>
> (p. 22)

Institutions in higher education are not short of underlying data or choices in creating performance indicators. Indeed, the multiple goals of complex organisations like higher education providers combined with rich data means the problem is more likely to be one of selectivity and validity in the necessary choices to be made. As Wilsdon (2018) put it:

In the past decade, there has been an explosion in the range and reach of metrics and league tables to benchmark institutional performance, research qualities and impacts, teaching and learning outcomes. Yet some of the most precious qualities and contributions of higher education resist simple quantification.

(p. 247)

The Quebec guidelines suggest both qualitative and quantitative indicators (IGOPP, 2007, p. 18) to help solve this problem. Indicators can also be used to benchmark the institution against selected comparator institutions (to assist with identifying variances) or with an aspirational group whose performance levels are sought as a goal (to assist with identifying gaps).

It seems important to draw indicators that express the uniqueness of the institution, its values, history, strategy and distinctiveness. It has been argued that institutions with similar purposes and facing similar pressures will adapt in a way that leads inevitably to homogenisation (DiMaggio and Powell, 1983). If this is believed, then:

[A]nother way of comparing universities nationally and internationally is to use nationally available standardised quantitative measures of performance as adopted by third parties e.g. government, regulatory bodies, league table compilers.

(Strike and Labbe, 2016, p. 125)

However, Strike and Labbe conclude by asserting that the strategic plans of institutions demonstrate different narratives, providing information about institutional character, priorities and choice-making which suggests each institution should look beyond standardised, imposed, externalised performance indicators and (re-)discover or assert their differences or diversity in how they measure their own success. You would have to imagine a league table where each higher education provider set its own targets in line with its character and mission and values rather than have third parties imposing theirs. Submitting to external regulation or rankings can encourage institutional isomorphism, suffocating choice.

Hazelkorn (2015) adds that lack of sufficient thought in adopting national or international rankings as institutional goals causes a loss of institutional autonomy, surrendering control to the complier of the rank:

In many countries, governments and institutions have pursued the world-class university designation without sufficient consideration of the implications – making plans into the future based effectively on a moving methodological target. To me, such actions constitute an abdication of national sovereignty and/or institutional autonomy.

(p. xvii)

Risk indicators

KPIs can be used as the quantifiable underpinning for judgement and oversight of the successful delivery of a strategic plan and as such they have a clear link to the management of the risks associated with the delivery of the plan.

Risk management involves:

- deciding the institutional risk appetite;
- identifying risks;
- assessing their inherent likelihood and impact;
- prioritising those risks;
- allocating risks to owners;
- developing and deploying mitigating actions so the residual risk is reduced;
- deciding whether to take further action, or to avoid, share or accept the remaining unmitigated risk.

Some of the discussion above on KPIs can be applied to the governance of risk – the need for a pyramid of risks with increasing levels of focus as one goes up the pyramid and a need to balance requirements of external regulators and those of the institution. Most institutions have a risk management process, which helps governors to monitor a small number of high-level strategic risks. The executive board may also have a larger risk register, which is a more comprehensive catalogue of operational risks. As Lam (2006) put it: 'The old adage "what gets measured gets managed" holds true in risk management.'

Risks can be identified 'top-down' and 'bottom-up' and then assessed for impact and likelihood and thus prioritised and allocated to owners to be managed and monitored. However, for risk management to be a value-adding, active exercise rather than a passive bureaucratic burden the focus should be as much on the action taken by risk owners to mitigate the inherent risks identified as on identifying and recording risks and allocating them to an owner. Moreover, where the residual risk after mitigating action is still assessed as high the executive board and the governing board have an active role to play in either driving further mitigating actions, accepting or choosing to avoid the risks identified.

While meeting or exceeding external governmental, regulatory and legal requirements can be a necessary condition for good governance it is important not to let the regulatory requirements direct the institution. Risk management is about the risk of not achieving strategic goals and the management and mitigation of those strategic risks, not simply about (non-)compliance or (mis-)conduct. Compliance with regulatory and legal requirements are a necessary condition for, but not a measure of, success. Indeed, it may be sensible to separate out strategic and regulatory or compliance risks to avoid this confusion.

Another confusion can come about if risk is perceived only as negative and as such only to be avoided. Pursuing opportunities involves positive risk taking. Birch *et al.* (2018) say:

> Risk management does not always focus on threats or negative occurrences; it can also be used to think about the degree of acceptable (or even expected) risk to maximise opportunities, by identifying actions that would enhance the positive outcomes of a situation or project, or harness existing organisational strengths (often termed opportunity management).
>
> (p. 148)

In the UK the CUC (2014) asserts a particular role for the governing body in this process, stating:

> Governing bodies need to assure themselves of the following:
>
> – There is a proactive and effective process for identifying potential risks,
> – Key areas of risk have not been overlooked,
> – A detailed and objective assessment and evaluation of the identified risks, their impact and likelihood has been undertaken,
> – There is a clear process for selecting the most 'critical' risks, and that these are then given appropriate attention,
> – Actions to mitigate the risks have been identified and have been implemented,
> – The risks are understood and managed at all relevant levels in the organisation.

Combining risk and performance reporting

KPIs are likely to have a close relationship to the high-level strategic risks. This may not be an exact one-to-one relationship, but governors would expect a clear framework which brings the two processes close together. KPIs express whether and to what degree the institution is meeting or progressing towards its strategic goals. The risk register expresses the risks inherent to the achievement of those same goals, and what is being done, by whom, to mitigate those risks. KPIs and Key Risk Indicators (KRIs) are sides of the same coin and are often implicitly linked and complementary. Risk and performance metrics after all relate to the same strategic objectives.

However, the Chartered Institute for Management Accountants (CIMA, 2011) calls for care to be taken when considering combining risk and performance information into a single management tool. Because not only the periodicity of reporting may need to be different but because self-evidently KPIs show changing performance trends and KRIs show whether running the institution is becoming more or less risky. It says (CIMA, 2011, p. 4) that: 'The same element can be interpreted in different ways if a risk perspective or a performance perspective is embraced.' For example, if the goal is to ski down a slope quickly and reach the bottom safely, the KPI may be the speed of descent while the KRI will be to minimise or eliminate falls. The balance between the two will produce an accepted risk appetite for a target speed. Joint reporting could either enhance or inhibit both, while they remain obviously linked. In a higher education context this complex complementarity exists between many of the potential variables, such as student numbers and the student experience, student quality on entry and continuation rates and so on.

Utility and function

If a nation state wants innovation and skills, research funders want results, graduating students want employability and ultimately to get good jobs, cities want to attract businesses and growth and so on then is it the job of the university to respond and be measured on the success of its chosen response. The approaches to performance and risk management described here are and sound utilitarian, arguably trying to reduce higher education to inputs and outputs, each measured or weighed. They are features of the new public management in higher education. Some may say that 'Unfortunately, university leaders who are unable to define and demonstrate educational objectives and achievements in utilitarian terms will have limited success in meeting the new demands placed on higher education' (Alexander, 2000, p. 427). Others may argue that the idea of higher education as a protected community of independent thinkers, engaging in intellectual pursuits not for any external purpose, but pursuing knowledge for its own sake, should be protected from measurement and assessment. Certainly most measures used in higher education are imperfect proxies for the outputs actually sought. Also, the mechanisms that deliver performance are not always well understood – so setting a target to reduce, say, differential outcomes based on ethnicity or to increase the number of students employed in graduate jobs and so on, sets targets where the causes may be out of the control of the institution. The friction caused between proper academic criticality of the processes of accountability and the processes themselves is positive in that through the heat of debate, examination and review the tools themselves will become more valid and thus improve through time. In the UK the Research Assessment Framework has matured through time and is broadly accepted as a reasonable proxy measure of research quality. By contrast the Teaching Excellence and Outcomes Framework is new, politically derived and yet to evolve.

Conclusion

This chapter has examined the role of performance and risk indicators as tools for supervision by governing bodies or improvement through accountability and whether these are prerequisites for good governance, however defined. The need to balance trust and autonomy with transparency and accountability between the governing and executive boards requires reflection on what information is sought, at what level and in what detail, and its use or purposes, so the governing board can add value. The role of external third party actors, whether state actors or league table compilers, in affecting the behaviour of governing boards towards their executives and the academy requires consideration to determine who is the steering mind and what is the institutional strategy and to whom accountability is owed. The relationship between performance and risk, how they differ, and how they are complementary will help to determine when and how each is reported. Finally, for governors to consider who defines what 'performance' is, in whose eyes, and whose 'risks' are being managed. Governors reflecting on whose behalf they are acting can illuminate this. Contextualised, critical reflexivity will help governing bodies to decide what role they have to play, what choices they have, their duties and responsibilities, and how they can support and hold the executive to account to deliver the institutions objectives on their own behalf or on behalf of legitimate others including students and taxpayers.

References

Alexander, F. King (2000) 'The Changing Face of Accountability: Monitoring and Assessing Institutional Performance in Higher Education', *The Journal of Higher Education*, Vol. 71/4, pp. 411–431.

Birch, R., Pye, R., McDonald, C. and Baker, J. (2018) 'Risk Management'. In Strike, T. (Ed.) *Higher Educational Strategy and Planning: A Professional Guide*. London: Routledge.

Bovens, M. (2006) 'Analysing and Assessing Public Accountability: A Conceptual Framework' (European Governance Papers [EUROGOV] No. C-06-01) [Retrieved 8 August 2018 from www.connex-net work.org/eurogov/pdf/eg p-connex-C-06-01.pdf]

Burke, J. (Ed.) (2005) *Achieving Accountability in Higher Education: Balancing Public, Academic and Market Demands*. San Francisco: Jossey-Bass.

Cave, M., Hanney, S., Kogan, M. and Trevett, G. (1988) *The Use of Performance Indicators in Higher Education: A Critical Analysis of Developing Practice*. London: Jessica Kingsley.

CIMA (2011) 'Integrating Risk and Performance in Management Reporting', Chartered Institute of Management Accountants, April 2011 [Retrieved 8 August 2018 from www.cimaglobal.com/Documents/Thought_leadership_docs/6307_R269_Integrating%20 risk_FINAL.pdf]

CUC (2008) 'CUC Report on the Implementation of Key Performance Indicators: Case Study Experience' Committee of University Chairs, June 2008 [Retrieved 31 July 2018 from www.universitychairs.ac.uk/wp-content/uploads/2016/07/CUC_report_on_ KPIs_case_studies_2008.pdf]

CUC (2014) 'Governors' Briefing Notes 08. Risk Management' [Retrieved 8 August 2018 from file:///C:/Users/admin.DESKTOP-QH82J5L/Downloads/08_gb_risk_ management_4web.pdf]

DiMaggio, P.J. and Powell, W.W. (1983) 'The Iron Cage Revisited: Institutional Isomorphism and Collective Rationality in Organizational Fields', *American Sociological Review*, Vol. 48, pp. 147–160.

Hazelkorn, E. (2015) *Rankings and the Reshaping of Higher Education: The Battle for World-Class Excellence* (2nd ed.). Basingstoke: Palgrave Macmillan.

IGOPP (2007) 'Report of the Working Group on University Governance', Institut sur la gouvernance d'organisations privées et publiques, Montréal.

Lam, J. (2006) 'Emerging Best Practices in Developing Key Risk Indicators and ERM Reporting', James Lam & Associates, Inc. [Retrieved 8 August 2018 from ftp://service.boulder.ibm.com/software/data/sw-library/cognos/pdfs/whitepapers/wp_best_pract_in_dev_key_risk_indicators_erm_rep.pdf]

LFHE (2012) 'A Guide for New Clerks and Secretaries of Governing Bodies of Higher Education Institutions in the UK', Leadership Foundation for Higher Education, November 2012, version 2 [Retrieved 31 July 2018 from file:///C:/Users/admin.DESKTOP-QH82J5L/Downloads/guide_for_new_clerks_-_nov_2012.pdf]

McLendon, M.K. and Hearn, J.C. (2009) 'Viewing Recent US Governance Reform Whole: "Decentralisation" in a Distinctive Context'. In *International Perspectives on the Governance of Higher Education: Alternative Frameworks for Coordination*. Abingdon: Routledge.

OECD (2017) 'Benchmarking Higher Education System Performance: Conceptual Framework and Data', Enhancing Higher Education System Performance, OECD Paris. [Retrieved 31 July 2018 from www.oecd.org/education/skills-beyond-school/Benchmarking%20Report.pdf]

Sarrico, C.S. (2010) 'On Performance in Higher Education: Towards Performance Governance?', *Tertiary Education and Management*, Vol. 16/2, pp. 145–158.

Stensaker, B. and Harvey, L. (eds) (2011) *Accountability in Higher Education: Global Perspectives on Trust and Power*. New York: Routledge.

Strike, T. and Labbe, J. (2016) 'Exploding the Myth: Literary Analysis of Universities' Strategic Plans'. In *Positioning Higher Education Institutions: From Here to There*. Edited by Pritchard, R.M.O., Pausits, A. and Williams, J. Rotterdam: Sense Publishers.

Wilsdon, J. (2018) 'Responsible Metrics'. In *Higher Education Strategy and Planning: A Professional Guide*. Edited by Strike, T. London: Routledge.

Wright, S. and Ørberg, J.W. (2009) 'Prometheus (on the) Rebound? Freedom and the Danish Steering System'. In *International Perspectives on the Governance of Higher Education: Alternative Frameworks for Coordination*. Abingdon: Routledge.

Index

Aberdeen, University of 101
academic board *see* Senate
academic freedom 53, 56, 62, 66, 70,
  81, 102, 105–106, 121, 126, 141,
  181, 212, 230–231
academic governance 43, 55, 133,
  148, 161, 181–184, 193, 230,
  253–255, 263
academic quality 10, 55, 196, 221, 249,
  254, 263
accountability 28, 38, 43–44, 140–141,
  145–147, 163, 268–269
Accreditation Organisation of the
  Netherlands and Flanders 89
Advertising Standards Agency 208
agenda setting 14, 41, 43, 122, 182,
  244, 246
All India Council for Technical
  Education 142
Alternative Investment Market 156
American Association of University
  Professors 70
American Council on Education 70
Annual Provider Review 256, 258
apply or explain 103, 194–195
articles 174, 176, 177, 254, 255
Association for the Development of
  Education in Africa 145
Association of Australian University
  Secretaries 32
Association of Governing Boards 70
Association of Heads of University
  Administration 32
Association of Universities in the
  Netherlands 88
audit committees 44, 166
Australia 32, 116, 125–137
Australian Catholic University 126, 134

autonomy 4, 14–15, 26, 40, 53, 82–85,
  87, 103–104, 126, 131, 146,
  197, 268

Bath, University of 131, 164, 176
benefits realisation 21, 51, 115–116,
  141, 159, 177–179, 226–228, 232
Birmingham, University of 210, 232
bicameral, structure 29, 61, 72, 73
board composition 160, 167, 169
Bologna process 82, 90, 203
Bond University in Queensland
  126, 134
Brazil 146
Brexit 17, 231
British Council 145
bureaucracy 3, 28, 38, 56, 90, 97, 142,
  148, 206, 211, 257, 273

Cadbury, report 27, 153
Cambridge, University of 48, 56,
  203, 213
Canada 61–64, 72–74, 76, 141, 234
Cardiff Metropolitan, University 108
Chair, governing body 9, 15, 29,
  37–38, 104–105, 186, 192,
  240–241, 247
Chancellor 73, 104, 127, 134,
  142, 175
Charity: law 175–178, 195, 211;
  purposes 226–227, 240
Chartered Institute for Management
  Accountants 274
China 17–18, 143–144
City University London 176
clerk *see* Secretary
collegiality 242, 255
Combined Code 154

Committee for University Chairs 12
Companies Act 2006 158, 175, 178
Common Seal 175
competition 11, 14, 20, 51, 53, 70, 77,
    127, 132, 179, 192, 202, 211,
    224, 253
Competition and Markets
    Authority 208
comply or explain 55, 103, 194
conflict of interest 33, 39, 42, 52, 65,
    71, 73, 163, 178, 183, 186
Consumer Rights Act 2015 203
cooperative governance 118–120
Corporate Governance Code, UK 34,
    153–154, 193, 199, 242
Court, of the University 28, 101, 105,
    142, 164, 176, 192, 233
Coventry University Group 188
Cumbria, University of 174
curricula 5, 68, 70, 77, 81, 86, 118,
    120, 142, 146, 231, 255, 264

Davies, report 168
Dawkins, report 128–129, 132–133
Deans 29, 40, 73, 91–94, 256
Dearing, report 223, 224
democracy 4, 56, 84, 86, 94, 100, 105,
    113–115, 118, 144–145, 186,
    221, 230
delegation 27, 39, 41, 118, 127, 183
deputy and pro-vice chancellors
    31, 209
devolution 44, 106, 107
diversity 4, 192, 193, 226; of provision
    91; of the sector 74, 125, 197, 198,
    269, 272; on governing bodies 168,
    230, 240, 243–244, 249; student
    66–67, 232
Durham, University of 256
Dutch Association of Universities 90

Economic and Social Research
    Council 228
Edinburgh, University of 137
Education Reform Act 1988 31, 173
effectiveness reviews 41, 186, 239–251
efficiency 90, 100, 118, 128, 141, 186,
    191, 213, 221
ethics 42, 156, 158, 192,
    122–123, 232
European Association for Quality
    Assurance in Higher Education 90

European Union 11, 18, 26, 82
external examiners 263

financial reporting 21, 166; Council 34,
    153, 157
Financial Sustainability Strategy
    Group 167
fit and proper 42, 134, 181, 184, 228
freedom of information 131, 229; Act
    195, 219, 229
freedom of speech 56, 68, 106,
    181–182, 230–231

Ghana 114, 146
Glasgow Caledonian 191
Glasgow, University of 101
Global Partnership for Education 145
going concern 165
grade point average 259
Greenbury, report 162
Group of Eight Universities 136

Higher Education and Research Act 11,
    49, 51, 92, 174, 191, 198, 203, 215,
    220, 252, 257
Higher Education Funding Council for
    England 49–51, 167, 174, 178, 184,
    192, 198–199, 211, 256
Higher Education Funding Council for
    Wales 15, 107
Huddersfield, University of 191
Humboldtian, model 26, 84, 233

India 17, 18, 117, 142–143, 145
induction 42, 168, 187, 224
Institute of Chartered Secretaries and
    Administrators 159, 168
integrated reporting 147, 148

Japan 18, 26, 146
Jarrett, Report 186, 191

key performance indicator(s) 43, 167,
    183, 254, 269, 271–272
key risk indicator 274
King IV, report 6, 147–148

legal advice 33, 42
Lancaster University 176
Leadership Foundation for Higher
    Education 228, 245, 249, 270
league tables 4, 142, 233, 260, 263, 272

London Metropolitan University
    185, 192
London School of Economics 185
London South Bank University 177
longitudinal education outcomes 260

Manchester, University of 137, 177
massive open online courses 19, 260
Melbourne, University of 133
mergers 77, 103, 132, 187
Mexico 61, 74–76
minutes 3, 30, 40, 41, 43, 165,
    246, 254
Monash University 133

National Assessment and Accreditation
    Council 142
National Audit Office 13
National Autonomous University of
    Mexico 74
National Board of Accreditation 142
National Commission on Higher
    Education 117, 118
National Student Survey 256,
    259, 264
Napoleonic, model of 26
Netherlands 81–98
New Public Management 87, 221, 275,
Nolan, principles 6, 158
nominations committees 42, 155, 168
Notre Dame, University of 126, 134

Office for Fair Access 51
Office for Fair Trading 53, 208
Office for Students, the 12, 50, 53, 134,
    178–179, 191, 195, 204, 211,
    213, 230
Office of the Independent Adjudicator 51
Organisation for Economic
    Co-operation and Development 5,
    18, 26, 33, 196, 203, 268
Oxford, University of 48, 56, 142,
    203, 210

performance agreements: Netherlands
    88, 90, 94; Scottish Outcome
    Agreements 103
Portsmouth, University of 191
President 10, 26, 28–29, 37, 94, 104,
    128, 134, 144, 176, 221, 244
Prondzynski, Professor Ferdinand von
    100, 102, 104, 192

QS World University Rankings 234
quality assurance 75, 89–90, 109, 126,
    142, 145, 196, 207, 253, 255–257
Quality Assurance Agency 51, 256
Queen Mary, University of London 232

rankings 233, 234, 252, 272
remuneration: codes 198; committees
    162; of executives 132, 161, 184; of
    governors 21, 186, 247; of vice-
    chancellors 131, 214, 241;
    reporting 162
reputation 10, 22, 72, 95, 132, 135,
    153, 159, 183–185, 192, 207, 225,
    233, 242, 253, 265
research 29, 49, 51–52, 54, 63, 65,
    82–83, 125, 177, 211, 225, 232–233
Research Excellence Framework 15,
    207, 225
risk management 43, 129, 166–167,
    181, 230, 263, 273; register 254
RMIT University 133, 234
Robbins, report 50, 223, 224
Robert Gordon University 100, 192
Royal Charter 173, 212, 229, 254

Salford, University of 178
Saudi Arabia 146
Scotland 15, 100–106, 158, 192, 249,
    256, 259, 261
Scottish Code 158, 170
Scottish Funding Council 102, 103
Scottish National Party 100
Secretary: university 30–34, 75, 84, 104,
    106, 240, 244, 246; characteristics
    35–40; role 40–44; status 34–35;
    triumvirate 37, 39,
    244, 246
Senate 29, 40, 73, 84, 119, 175, 183,
    210, 221, 255, 263
senior pay see remuneration
shareholders 63, 88, 154–155, 160–
    161, 164
social responsibility 158, 233–234
South Africa 67, 113–123, 141,
    144–145, 226
Staffordshire University 174
stakeholders 4, 6, 23, 44, 72, 77, 88,
    94, 120, 122, 155, 158–161, 192,
    220, 222
standing orders 35
Student Loans Company 205, 229

Students: access 51, 54, 67–69, 76, 117, 145; as customers/consumers 12, 51–52, 61, 63, 70, 77, 121, 205–206, 252; experience 29, 92, 117, 257, 259; information for 77, 82, 213, 253; international mobility 18; 89–90, 180; outcomes 227, 257, 260–262, 275; participation 22, 233; value for money 17, 50–51, 182, 184, 207; voice 21, 71, 73, 77, 86, 93, 101, 119, 181, 186, 250
Students' Union 101, 161, 182, 228, 230
Student Protection Plan 55, 212, 213
succession planning 42, 65, 153, 167–169, 199
Swinburne University of Technology 133

Teaching Excellence Framework 15, 207, 224
terms of reference 41, 49, 243, 245, 249
Tertiary Education Quality and Standards Agency 126

transparency 13, 21, 28, 39, 43–44, 54, 64, 73, 82, 130, 132, 156, 161, 181, 198, 229, 258
tuition fees 145, 182, 202, 205–206, 213, 219, 224
Tufts, University 233

ultra vires 39, 173–175
United Kingdom Research and Innovation 181
United Nations Educational, Scientific and Cultural Organization 26
United States 18, 40, 61–72, 84, 131
Universities UK 52, 54, 231
University Government Reorganisation Act 84

Vice-Chancellor see President
Visitor, university 173, 176
voting 41, 71, 73, 105, 162, 164, 233

Warwick, University of 175, 176
Well-being of Future Generations (Wales) Act 110
West London, University of 174
Woolf, Lord 185